8/68

QD
181
S1
P7

D0874101

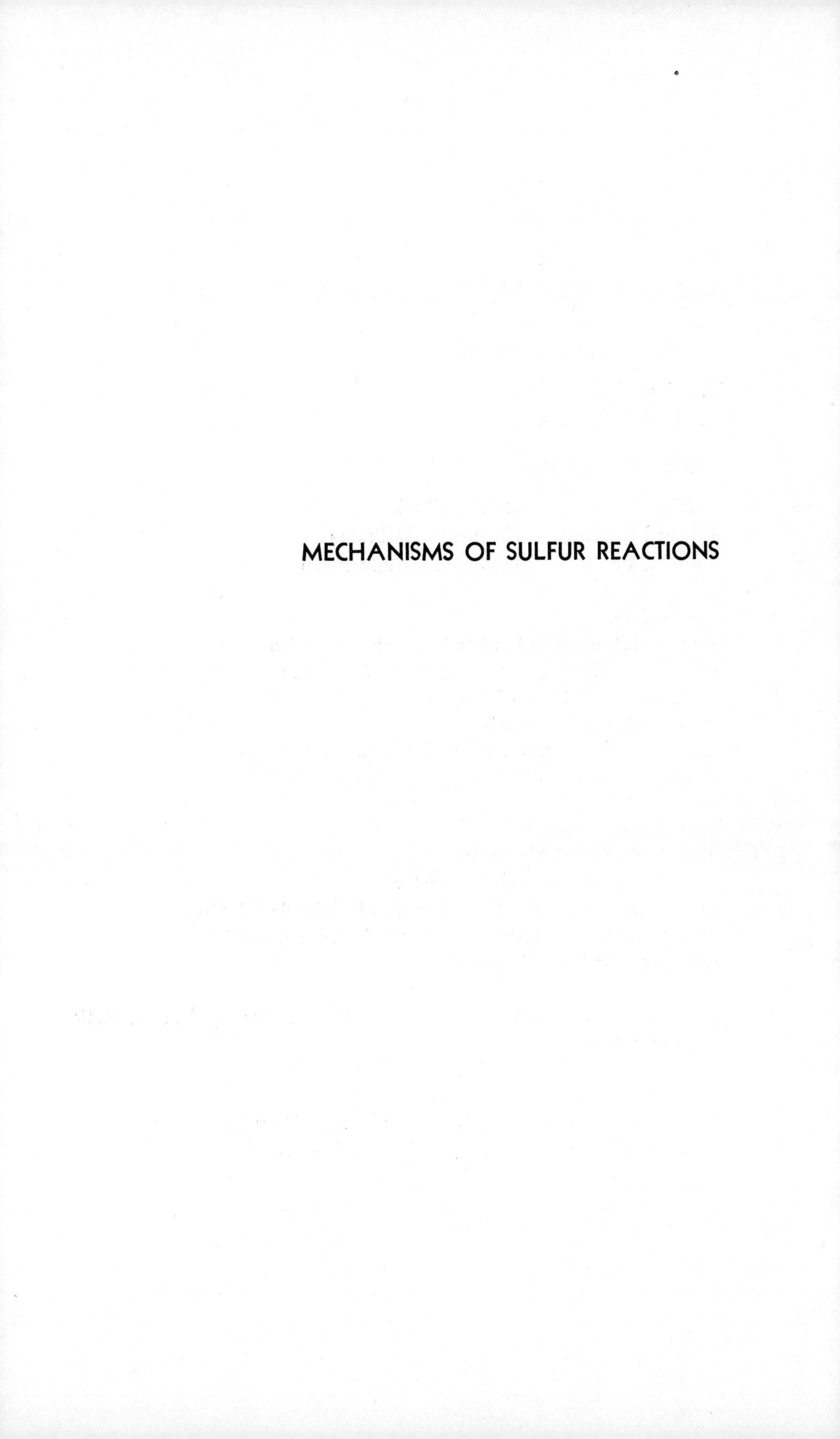

MECHANISMS OF SULFUR REACTIONS

McGRAW-HILL SERIES IN ADVANCED CHEMISTRY

SENIOR ADVISORY BOARD

W. Conard Fernelius
Louis P. Hammett

EDITORIAL BOARD

David N. Hume   Gilbert Stork
Edward L. King   Harold H. Williams
John A. Pople   Dudley R. Herschbach

BAIR Introduction to Chemical Instrumentation
BENSON The Foundations of Chemical Kinetics
DAVIDSON Statistical Mechanics
DEAN Flame Photometry
DJERASSI Optical Rotatory Dispersion
ELIEL Stereochemistry of Carbon Compounds
FITTS Nonequilibrium Thermodynamics
HELFFERICH Ion Exchange
HILL Statistical Mechanics
HINE Physical Organic Chemistry
KASHA AND OPPENHEIMER Theory of Molecular Excitons
KIRKWOOD AND OPPENHEIM Chemical Thermodynamics
LAITINEN Chemical Analysis
LEWIS AND RANDALL Thermodynamics
POPLE, SCHNEIDER, AND BERNSTEIN High-resolution Nuclear Magnetic Resonance
PRYOR Mechanisms of Sulfur Reactions
ROBERTS Nuclear Magnetic Resonance
ROSSOTTI AND ROSSOTTI The Determination of Stability Constants
WIBERG Laboratory Technique in Organic Chemistry

MECHANISMS OF SULFUR REACTIONS

WILLIAM A. PRYOR

Assistant Professor of Chemistry, Purdue University

McGRAW-HILL BOOK COMPANY, INC. 1962

New York San Francisco Toronto London

MECHANISMS OF SULFUR REACTIONS

Copyright © 1962 by the McGraw-Hill Book Company, Inc. Printed in the United States of America. All rights reserved. This book, or parts thereof, may not be reproduced in any form without permission of the publishers. *Library of Congress Catalog Card Number* 61-17344

50900

THE MAPLE PRESS COMPANY, YORK, PA.

To
M.
and to
m.t.l.

D. HIDEN RAMSEY LIBRARY
ASHEVILLE-BILTMORE COLLEGE
ASHEVILLE, NORTH CAROLINA

Bring fire that I may burn sulfur, the divine curer of ills.

Homer, "The Odyssey," 850 B.C.

Burning sulfur will keep out enchantments—yea, and drive away foul fiends.

Pliny, " Historia Naturalis," 23 A.D.

PREFACE

The purpose of this book is to provide a framework of mechanisms upon which some of the reactions of sulfur and sulfur compounds can be organized and more easily understood. Since the reactions of sulfur have been studied less than the analogous reactions of oxygen, gaps exist in the framework, and these have sometimes been filled by speculation. It is hoped, nonetheless, that this outline will provide useful working hypotheses for current research.

Many of my friends and colleagues helped during the preparation of this volume, and it is a pleasure to acknowledge their aid. The manuscript was originally written as a brief review article on sulfur as an oxidant. I am greatly indebted to Drs. L. L. Ferstandig and I. E. Levine, of the California Research Corporation, for their support and encouragement in beginning that review. During the 1960–1961 academic year at Purdue University, the review was entirely rewritten and expanded to the present text. The ideas presented here were frequently tested on members of the Chemistry Department at Purdue, and their comments and insights have been uniformly helpful.

The original review article was read by many friends, including Dr. William G. Toland, who made several suggestions which increased its coverage; Dr. S. J. Lapporte, who edited the entire text; and Alan E. Straus and Dr. P. S. Magee. The final text was edited by Profs. Cheves Walling and Robert E. Davis and by Dr. Leonard E. Miller, each of whom offered many helpful and valuable suggestions toward making the text clearer, more accurate, and more readable. I am grateful also to the following students at Purdue who helped with the tedious task of checking galley proof: T. L. Pickering, E. P. Pultinas, P. K. Platt, Sara Anne Millard, and H. Weiner.

To the management of the California Research Corporation go my special thanks; they encouraged me in preparation of the original review, and they have generously supported the clerical help necessary for preparing the final manuscript. Finally, I am indebted to Mrs. Harry Frazier, who checked the reference numbering and assembled the author index.

William A. Pryor

CONTENTS

1

INTRODUCTION

1-1. Introduction

Sulfur is one of the few elements which are found in the free state; it was therefore known and used by our earliest ancestors. It was burned in religious ceremonies as early as 2000 BC, and its acrid odor and bluish flame were felt to be mystic and purifying. (Ulysses employed it, according to Homer, when he returned to Greece, to fumigate the apartment—it also helped dispatch his wife's suitors.) The Egyptians were using sulfur dioxide as a bleach and sulfur compounds as dyes as early as 1600 BC.

The alchemists had the notion that sulfur was part of phlogiston and therefore present in all matter. Even Davy thought that sulfur was a combining form of oxygen. Lavoisier, during his dramatic experiments on combustion, showed that sulfur was an element and opened the door to a rational approach to its chemistry.

Sulfur burns in air to form sulfur dioxide. However, in 1740, the English chemist Joshua Ward found that saltpeter oxidizes sulfur to sulfur trioxide; he thus invented a route to sulfuric acid. The modern technology of sulfur dates from that discovery, since the major use of sulfur is in the manufacture of sulfuric acid. The "lead chamber" process for sulfuric acid, in which nitrogen dioxide is used to oxidize sulfur dioxide to sulfur trioxide, is a descendant of Ward's original discovery.

Sulfur was found in America as a contaminator of petroleum from Louisiana wells as early as 1867, but these deep-lying deposits could not be mined by conventional techniques. In 1900, despite the scepticism of his contemporaries, Herman Frasch demonstrated the practicability of pumping molten sulfur from these deposits in a stream of hot air and steam. The Louisiana mines yield sulfur free of arsenic, tellurium, and selenium, and with low organic content; with modern improvements, the Frasch process now provides some of the world's purest sulfur.

Sulfur is thus a readily available element—the world production in 1960 was 18 million long tons—and it is employed in industrial applications of tremendous value. Despite this, no organizing scheme of sulfur reactions has yet appeared. Many sulfur reactions still have unexplored mechanisms; furthermore, correlating the reactions of sulfur is made even more difficult by its many allotropic forms. However, current research is revealing principles common to many sulfur reactions. It seems worthwhile, therefore, to review present knowledge and to attempt to organize the better-known reactions of sulfur into their mechanistic types.

In some of the reactions discussed, elemental sulfur is the reactant, and in some it is used in the form of a polysulfide. Usually, but not always, the sulfur or polysulfide acts as an oxidant. Related, nonoxidation reactions are also discussed here, e.g., the addition of thiols to olefins. Also, some reactions are considered in which part of the substrate molecule is oxidized and part is reduced; for example, the conversion of acetophenone to phenylacetamide, Eq. (1-1), and of *p*-nitrotoluene to *p*-aminobenzaldehyde, Eq. (1-2).

$$C_6H_5-\overset{\overset{\displaystyle O}{\|}}{C}-CH_3 \xrightarrow[H_2O,\ 180°C]{(NH_4)_2S_x} C_6H_5-CH_2-\overset{\overset{\displaystyle O}{\|}}{C}-NH_2 \tag{1-1}$$

$$p\text{-}NO_2-C_6H_4-CH_3 \xrightarrow[\text{Aqueous ethanol, 80°C}]{Na_2S_4} p\text{-}NH_2-C_6H_4-\overset{\overset{\displaystyle O}{\|}}{C}-H \tag{1-2}$$

Sulfur frequently shows this ability to oxidize one site in a molecule and to reduce another; in fact, this often makes sulfur the unique reactant for a desired transformation in synthetic organic chemistry. Studies of largely technological interest are not discussed. In particular, the vast technology of rubber and of vulcanization is not reviewed, except for special studies with clear-cut theoretical conclusions.

1-2. Nomenclature

Elemental sulfur occurs in a variety of molecular forms, some of which have more than one crystalline modification. Over the years, these allotropic forms have been labeled with a Greek letter code designating the method of preparation (Table 1-1). The identification of the molecular and crystalline forms which these code names represent is not yet complete, but the more important have been reasonably well characterized. Several of the Greek letters represent the same species prepared by two different methods. The unraveling of this unsatisfactory tangle in nomenclature obviously must await the molecular and crystalline identification of all the forms.

Table 1-1
Sulfur allotropes (765, 928, 1098)

Greek symbol	Notes	References
α	Ordinary sulfur; rhombic S_8 crystals; stable to 95.5° C, where it slowly converts to β; mp 112.8° C; soluble in CS_2	4, 6, 286, 290, 1133
β	Monoclinic crystals, stable from 95.5° C to its mp, 118.7° C; soluble in CS_2; probably S_8	334, 546, 751, 856
γ	"Muthmann sulfur"; monoclinic with different crystal form from β; converts to α or β with E_a of 20 to 26 kcal; probably S_8	177, 334, 532, 785, 928
λ	The sulfur which precipitates from CS_2 at −79° C. Liquid sulfur at 120 to 160° C, where it is predominantly S_8, is also called λ	1098
π	The sulfur which is soluble in CS_2 at −79° C; it is unstable and is converted first to μ, then to λ. Sometimes identified as S_4 and sometimes as S_8	765, 933, 1098
μ	Prepared by chilling liquid sulfur; insoluble in CS_2; converts to either α or β, whichever is stable at that temperature; usually called amorphous, but is probably crystalline	334*a*, 765, 783, 855, 857, 858, 999, 1098
ν	"Plastic" sulfur prepared by chilling liquid sulfur; rubbery	288, 479, 507, 1098
ϕ	Fibrous sulfur; stretched ν; consists of two modifications, one soluble and one insoluble in CS_2; polymeric; probably helical but the nature of the helix is unknown	287, 291, 334*a*, 857, 873, 874, 892
ψ	Polymeric sulfur recrystallized from CS_2 until nearly white	
ω	Nonoriented polymeric sulfur	289
ϵ, ρ, φ	Rhombohedral, trigonal; S_6	335

Table 1-2 identifies the important molecular forms of sulfur. Both of the well-characterized modifications of S_8, monoclinic (751, 856) and orthorhombic (4, 6, 1133), as well as the rhombohedral S_6 (220, 335), are "crown"- or "chair"-shaped rings in the solid and probably also in the liquid state (356). These allotropes are well distinguished by their x-ray diagrams (220).

The crystal form of polymeric sulfur is polemical. The usual methods for preparing polymeric sulfur yield mixtures of S_8 and sulfur polymer (855, 873, 874, 892), and the interpretation of the x-ray diagram of the mixture is difficult. In addition, polymeric sulfur* may have more than

* Polymeric sulfur is usually symbolized S_x. The polymer has been interpreted as having a helical conformation in both the solid and the liquid state (858). It should be appreciated, however, that the conformations of the solid polymer and those assumed by the polymer in the more mobile liquid state need not be identical.

one crystal modification, perhaps different helical forms, which further complicates its x-ray patterns (873). According to Prins (445, 874), one modification is a helix, 10 atoms in three turns, on a cylinder of 0.92 A radius, with period length 13.7 A, angle 107°, and dihedral angle 87°. Pinkus (857, 857*a*) has suggested that the sulfur which is insoluble in carbon disulfide is a helical polymer with a conformation almost identical

Table 1-2
Sulfur molecular species

Form	Notes	References
S_8	Exists in at least three solid crystalline forms: α and β and γ. Colloidal sulfur is mainly α. Exists in the liquid as the main species from about 120 to 159° C (λ-sulfur)	286, 290, 532
S_6	Engel's or Aten's sulfur; produced by acidification of $Na_2S_2O_3$. Rhombohedral or trigonal crystal	220, 335, 335*a*
S_x	Polymeric sulfur. Exists in the solid (ϕ-sulfur) and probably has more than one crystalline modification; converts to α- or β-S_8 in a reaction increased in rate by heat or irradiation; molecular weight from 10^4 to 10^6. Exists in liquid (μ-sulfur) at 160 to 200° C	287, 489, 783, 872, 873, 892, 999
S_6, S_4	Exist in vapor at 600 to 800° C	
S_2	Predominant species in vapor above about 850° C	928
S_1	Becomes increasingly important species in the vapor above 1800° C	

to that in stacked S_8 rings. This possibility has been eliminated, however, by Donohue and Caron (334*a*) after a careful study of all the x-ray data. They find that carbon disulfide–insoluble sulfur is orthorhombic sulfur with perhaps 1% polymeric sulfur as impurity. Sulfur polymerized by light, the so called "photo-sulfur," may actually be a long-chain sulfane, H_2S_x (82).

The complex equilibria among different molecular forms in liquid sulfur are discussed in Sec. 2-1. In brief, liquid sulfur is predominantly S_8 at the melting point, about 119° C, and at the boiling point, 444.6° C. Between these two temperatures, it first polymerizes to a linear polymer and then depolymerizes. For example, the average molecule contains 5 S_8 units at 137° C, 16.4 units at 152° C, 57.9 units at 157° C, 113,900 units (the maximum reached) at 175 to 185° C, and then 5,750 units at 307° C (1055).

At the boiling point, S_8 is the principal species in the liquid and in the vapor as well. At higher temperatures, other species exist in the vapor because of dissociation reactions. Measurements of vapor density indicate that S_6, S_4, S_2, and finally S are formed as the temperature is raised

Table 1-3

Nomenclature of sulfur species

(Boldface names are used here)

Formula	Name
S cations	
RS^+	**Alkyl sulfenium ion,** sulfenyl ion, sulfonium ion
$RS_x{-}S^+$	**Alkyl polysulfenium ion,** persulfenium ion
S anions	
RS^-	**Alkyl sulfide ion, mercaptide ion,** thiolate ion
$RS_x{-}S^-$	**Alkyl polysulfide ion**
S radicals	
$RS\cdot$	**Alkyl sulfenyl radical, thiyl radical,** mercaptyl radical
$RS_x{-}S\cdot$	**Alkyl polysulfenyl radical**
S molecules, organic	
RSR	**Alkyl sulfide,** dialkyl monosulfide
RSSR	**Alkyl disulfide**
RS_xR	**Alkyl polysulfide**
RSH	**Alkanethiol, alkyl mercaptan, alkyl hydrogen sulfide**
(five-membered ring: positions 1 S, 2 S, 3 C=S, 4, 5)	**Trithione,** 1,2-dithiole-3-thione[a]
(five-membered ring: 1 S, 2, N=C 3–4, 5)	**3-Thiazoline**
S molecules, inorganic	
$HS{-}S(=O)_2{-}OH$	**Thiosulfuric acid**
$HO{-}S(=O)_2{-}S(=O)_2{-}OH$	**Dithionic acid**
$HO{-}S(=O)_2{-}S_x{-}S(=O)_2{-}OH$	**Polythionic acid**
H_2S_x	**Hydrogen polysulfide,**[b] **sulfanes**

[a] *Chemical Abstracts* uses both names but recommends the latter; the second one appears less satisfactory, however, because of its pseudo-I.U.C. sound. The name 1,2-dithia-4-cyclopentene-3-thione does not contain the confusing reference to "thiol" groups but is too bulky for convenience.

[b] For example, H_2S_4, hydrogen tetrasulfide, can be formally regarded as three sulfur atoms (polysulfide atoms) joined to a sulfide ion: $H_2S{\cdot}S_3$. Fehér and his students have synthesized and characterized these compounds through $x = 8$(376–379, 386, 392, 394, 404). They have also prepared mixtures which have average compositions up to H_2S_{120} (381, 390). Fehér has reviewed his work in two articles (375*a*,*b*). (Also see ref. 745.)

through 800° C and finally to 1800° C (172, 638). Pauling (840) and others usually imply that only even-numbered rings occur, but it is probable that species containing an odd number of sulfur atoms occur in open-chain compounds in the liquid phase and quite possibly in the vapor phase also (531, 663). The vapor-density data definitely do not eliminate S_5 and S_3, for example, as possible species (173). Donohue, Caron, and Goldish (335*a*) have calculated the strain in sulfur rings of 4, 6, 8, and 10 sulfur atoms. They find that the strain in an S_{10} ring would be similar to that in the known S_6 ring.

Unfortunately, several systems of nomenclature are used for sulfur compounds. That used here is given in Table 1-3. It was chosen to reflect usage (617, 830, 1116); to distinguish the pronunciation of the words for sulfur radicals, cations, and anions; and to make the nomenclature for organic and inorganic sulfur species consistent.

It is helpful to define a term for nucleophilicity toward sulfur. Parker and Kharasch (831) have coined the terms "S-nucleophilicity" and "C-nucleophilicity," and these seem very useful when nucleophilicity toward several atoms is being considered. Bartlett (82) uses "thiophilicity"; this term also has been used extensively here.

Finally, all rate constants are in time units of seconds and concentration units of moles per liter, abbreviated M.

2

ELEMENTAL SULFUR

Elemental sulfur and sulfur in the form of polysulfides frequently react similarly. In many reacting systems, and especially in the presence of basic catalysts, sulfur is rapidly converted to polysulfide-sulfur; in these systems the equilibrium polysulfide mixture is the reacting form of sulfur, regardless of the starting material. Different sulfur species do not always react alike, however. Two examples illustrate the extremes. The conversion of tetralin to naphthalene can be effected in about 70% yield by any of the following reagents: elemental sulfur (915), aqueous sodium or ammonium polysulfide (512), isoamyl disulfide (893), or phenyl disulfide (791). However, elemental sulfur oxidizes toluene to a complex mixture of stilbene and other products (566); aqueous sodium or ammonium polysulfide converts toluene to benzoic acid quantitatively (875, 1060).

It is apparent that an understanding of the inorganic chemistry of sulfur and the interconversions of allotropic forms of sulfur is a prerequisite to insight into the reactions of sulfur with organic compounds.

2-1. Reactions of Sulfur in Liquid Sulfur

Sulfur exists in a large number of molecular forms, including an eight-membered ring, less stable larger and smaller rings, and linear chains varying in length from 2 to over 10,000 atoms. In 1943, Bacon and Fanelli (55) measured the viscosity of extremely pure liquid sulfur as a function of temperature. They found that the viscosity increases gradually from the melting point of sulfur, 115 to 119° C (933), up to about 159° C, at which point the viscosity sharply increases ten-thousandfold (55, 1098). The viscosity reaches a maximum at 186 to 188° C and then, as the temperature is raised further, rapidly decreases to normal values. This unusual behavior was the subject of theoretical studies by Powell and Eyring (866) in 1943, Gee (358, 495) in 1952 and 1955, and Tobolsky and Eisenberg (1055) in 1959. These penetrating investigations have explained the phenomena as resulting from intraconversions between the allotropic forms of sulfur.

At 120° C, liquid sulfur exists largely in the molecular form of eight-membered rings. These low-molecular-weight species have normal viscosity. However, starting sharply at about 159° C, S_8 rings undergo thermal scission to linear sulfenyl diradicals, and these radicals attack other S_8 rings in a chain reaction which leads to polymers. The formation of polymers is indicated by the increasing viscosity of liquid sulfur (932); in addition there is ample direct evidence for sulfur polymers (55, 749, 857, page 7 of ref. 1098). Above 186 to 188° C the viscosity rapidly decreases because of cleavage of chains (495).

$$S_8\text{ (ring)} \underset{-1}{\overset{1}{\rightleftharpoons}} \cdot S{-}S_6{-}S\cdot \qquad \text{(linear diradical)} \tag{2-1}$$

$$\cdot S{-}S_6{-}S\cdot + S_8 \underset{-2}{\overset{2}{\rightleftharpoons}} \cdot S{-}S_6{-}S{-}S_8\cdot \overset{\text{etc.}}{\rightleftharpoons} \cdot S{-}S_x{-}S\cdot \tag{2-2}$$

Equations (2-1) and (2-2) explain the rapid increase in polymer concentration. From a kinetic point of view, the forward direction of Eq. (2-1) is the rate-limiting step and may have an enhanced activation energy because of the stabilization of the S_8 ring (385, 866), perhaps through the use of the *d* orbitals of sulfur [see Eq. (2-3)]. The propagation step, Eq. (2-2), has a low activation energy (3 kcal) and is fast ($k = 2 \times 10^6$ sec^{-1} M^{-1} at 45° C) (489). Thus, the polymerization of sulfur has an extremely long kinetic chain length. Temperatures at which reaction (2-1) occurs produce very high polymers. Thermodynamic calculations can be based on the equilibrium concentration of polymer as a function of temperature; this has recently been done by Tobolsky and Eisenberg (1055, 1056). Qualitatively, the sharpness of appearance of polymer and the ring-opening nature of the reaction would lead to the expectation of a high enthalpy and a positive entropy for Eq. (2-1). Tobolsky and Eisenberg calculate for Eq. (2-1), $\Delta S° = 23.0$ e.u., $\Delta H° = 32.8$ kcal, and for Eq. (2-2), $\Delta S° = 4.6$ e.u., $\Delta H° = 3.2$ kcal.

Additional confirmation of Eqs. (2-1) and (2-2) is derived from study of the postulated polysulfenyl radicals by electron paramagnetic resonance (EPR) (489). Radicals can be detected above 189° C, and they reach a maximum concentration of 1.1×10^{-3} M at 300° C. The steady-state concentration of radicals, i.e., chain ends, at 159° C is too small to be measured. The EPR data have been interpreted as localizing a free electron at either end of a linear, helical sulfur polymer (858).

The S—S bond is attacked by some electrophilic and nucleophilic species (81, 830, 1132). Consistent with this, several ionic species have been shown to open S_8 rings (84, 89, 663). Also, most free radicals attack S—S bonds (see Sec. 3-3C). Attack on S_8 by these three types of reagents is illustrated in Eqs. (2-4), (2-5), and (2-6).

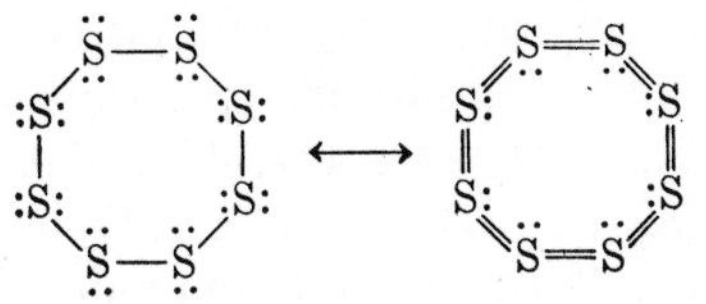

$$\text{S}_8 \text{ ring (single bonds)} \longleftrightarrow \text{S}_8 \text{ ring (alternating double bonds)} \tag{2-3}$$

$$A^+ + S_8 \longrightarrow A{-}S_7{-}S^+ \tag{2-4}$$

$$B^- + S_8 \longrightarrow B{-}S_7{-}S^- \tag{2-5}$$

$$Y\cdot + S_8 \longrightarrow Y{-}S_7{-}S\cdot \tag{2-6}$$

Because of the stability of S_8 rings, it is to be expected that any of the above open-chain polysulfide species will dissociate to radicals more easily than will the S_8 ring. The magnitude of this effect is unknown since there are no reliable estimates of the resonance of the S_8 ring. The effect, however, is undoubtedly real. This can be seen, for example, in the large enthalpy for Eq. (2-1). Also, triphenylphosphine is known to cleave open-chain polysulfides faster than it cleaves the S_8 ring. If linear polysulfides undergo homolytic scission faster than does the S_8 ring, and if ionic species convert S_8 to linear polysulfides, then these ionic species may actually catalyze the formation of polysulfenyl radicals. It is important to understand this. Although the rate of a sulfur reaction may be enhanced by an acid or a base, the over-all reaction may involve radicals. In fact, it appears that all sulfur reactions are increased in rate by added bases, but some of these reactions very likely involve radicals in some steps.* A clear-cut case is the decomposition of sulfinic acids, which involves species capable of polymerizing methyl methacrylate; nevertheless, this decomposition is catalyzed by the polar catalysts sulfonic acid and butylamine hydrochloride, as well as by radical sources such as benzoyl peroxide and dicumyl peroxide (824). Another example is the opening of S_8 rings to form polymers; here ammonia and amines have very marked effects, but the polymerizing species is a polysulfenyl radical (55).

The mechanism for the formation of polymeric sulfur, Eq. (2-2), requires that the chains be linear and not branched. Indeed, in contrast to earlier views (604, 832, 835), recent work has shown that only unbranched chains of sulfur atoms occur. Olav Foss, whose brilliant

* Base catalysis of sulfur reactions is itself a complex problem (82, 83).

insights first clarified this field (428, 429), has recently reviewed the pertinent evidence (445). Compounds studied include inorganic polysulfides (9, 382, 383, 389, 397, 429, 442, 827, 857, 863, 949); organic di- and polysulfides (56, 149, 171, 310, 311, 336, 368, 388, 437, 460, 468, 529, 642, 667, 760, 761, 822, 939, 1094, 1146, 1161); organic sulfonates and thiolsulfonates (431, 436, 438, 446, 998); trithionates (441, 452, 1168); tetrathionates (365, 432, 434, 443, 447, 448, 450, 470); pentathionates (365, 433, 439, 443, 455, 462, 463, 465, 469, 474); hexathionates (271, 365, 439, 443, 451, 456, 458, 709); sulfenyl compounds (443); sulfanes (207, 384, 391, 394–396, 398, 953, 1129, 1130); and cyanosulfanes (380, 393, 399, 400, 402, 435).

Although the structural unit $-\mathrm{S}-\overset{\overset{\mathrm{S}}{\|}}{\mathrm{S}}-\mathrm{S}-$ is unknown, oxygen branches on sulfur atoms are common, as, for example, in sulfoxides, $\mathrm{R}-\overset{\overset{\mathrm{O}}{\|}}{\mathrm{S}}-\mathrm{R}$, and sulfones (429).

2-2. Reactions of Sulfur in Hydrocarbon Solvents

The catalytic scission of S_8 rings which occurs in liquid sulfur also occurs in hydrocarbon solvents. A number of studies have been made of cleavage of S—S bonds by radicals. Radicals derived from azo compounds attack S_8 in cumene as solvent at 112° C (1051). In the absence of sulfur, the organic radicals abstract hydrogen from cumene. In the presence of sulfur, these radicals attack S_8 to form polysulfides exclusively. Aliphatic radicals from triazines, R—N=N—NH—Ar, react similarly with S_8 quantitatively to form polysulfides (25).

The S_8 ring is also cleaved by polymeric radicals present in vinyl polymerizations. Sulfur, like oxygen, inhibits polymerizations because the growing radicals attack it to form stabilized radicals (87, 624, 625). The reactions of sulfur in styrene have been studied by Bartlett and Trifan (94), who find that the initial product is a low polymer with about eight sulfur atoms per styrene unit. Thus, in the presence of sulfur, polystyryl radicals attack S—S bonds and open S_8 rings rather than adding to styrene. The relative rates for the reaction of the polystyryl radical with styrene and with S_8 are 1:100 (Table 2-1); thus sulfur is an extremely efficient radical trap. The polysulfenyl radical attacks S_8 even faster than does the styryl radical (Table 2-1). Presumably sulfenyl radicals, like sulfide ions, are exceptionally thiophilic.

The polystyryl radical attacks O_2 about 10^4 times faster than it does the S_8 ring (Table 2-1). This difference can probably be attributed, at least partially, to the stability of the S_8 ring rather than to an inherent greater reactivity of oxygen toward radicals, since S_2 (889, 955) would be expected to be much more reactive than S_8 (494). Also, radicals add to O_2, forming a new bond, whereas they displace on S_8 with cleavage of an S—S bond as the new bond is formed. The former process requires less

Table 2-1
Rate of reaction of radicals with S_8 and O_2

Reaction between		k, sec^{-1} M^{-1}	°C	References
Polysulfenyl radical	S_8	2×10^6	45	489
Polystyryl radical	S_8	*c.* 3×10^4	81	79, 94
Polystyryl radical	O_2	*c.* 10^8	50	100, 730, pages 170 and 422 of ref. 1116
Polystyryl radical	Styrene	3×10^2	81	page 95 of ref. 1116

energy than the latter. For further rate constants on the reaction of polymeric radicals with sulfur rings, see Table 3-6, page 45.

2-3. Reactions of Sulfur in Aqueous Solutions

When sulfur is heated with water, S_8 rings open and disproportionation reactions occur to form sulfide and sulfur-oxyanions; the sulfide then reacts with additional sulfur to form polysulfides. The mechanism for this process is not known in detail. The unproved assumption had gradually gained acceptance that any nucleophile could attack and open the sulfur ring. However, recent penetrating studies of this problem by Bartlett and a group of his students (81–83) have shown that triethylamine is unable to open S_8 rings unless traces of hydrogen sulfide, sulfur dioxide, or other as yet unidentified impurities are present. With this knowledge, an observation made by Bacon and Fanelli in their paper on sulfur viscosity takes on added significance (55). They reported that the viscosity of liquid sulfur is not affected by gaseous ammonia unless impurities are present. The explanation (82, 83) of these phenomena is that ammonia or triethylamine converts these impurities to very thiophilic species, which then attack S—S bonds. For example, hydrogen sulfide undoubtedly forms the bisulfide ion, which then cleaves S—S bonds.

$$R_3N + H_2S = R_3NH^+ + HS^-$$
$$HS^- + S_8 \rightarrow HS{-}S_7{-}S^-$$

Although triethylamine and ammonia do not attack S—S bonds, some general bases do. This is discussed in detail in Sec. 3-4B. At present it is not known whether or not hydroxide is able to attack S—S bonds directly. The bisulfide ion is considerably more thiophilic than is hydroxide, and if both are present most of the attack would occur by bisulfide. However, when competing nucleophiles are not present the evidence discussed below suggests that hydroxide does attack S—S bonds. (Also see pp. 59–61.)

When sulfur disproportionates in aqueous bases to sulfide and a sulfur-oxyanion, the oxyanion formed depends on the base used and the temperature of the reaction. At temperatures near 100° C in aqueous solutions of sodium or ammonium hydroxide, the disproportionation of sulfur follows Eq. (2-7) to give bisulfide and thiosulfate but not sulfate (364, 844, 849, 950, 951, 1041):

$$\tfrac{1}{2}S_8 + 4NaOH = Na_2S_2O_3 + 2NaHS + H_2O \qquad (2\text{-}7)$$

Several suggestions have been offered to explain the mechanism of this reaction, but they have not been confirmed (367, 830, 952). Thiosulfate is not always the sulfur-oxyanion formed. For example, it has been reported that magnesium hydroxide gives sulfate (292),

$$\tfrac{1}{2}S_8 + \tfrac{5}{2}Mg(OH)_2 \xrightarrow{225^\circ\,C} MgSO_4 + \tfrac{3}{2}Mg(HS)_2 + H_2O \qquad (2\text{-}8)$$

and calcium hydroxide gives sulfite (127):

$$\tfrac{3}{8}S_8 + 2Ca(OH)_2 \rightarrow CaSO_3 + Ca(HS)_2 + H_2O \qquad (2\text{-}9)$$

At 250–350° C, sodium or ammonium hydroxide (1065) produces sulfate as the sulfur-oxyanion, Eq. (2-10), although

$$\tfrac{1}{2}S_8 + 5NH_4OH = (NH_4)_2SO_4 + 3NH_4SH + H_2O \qquad (2\text{-}10)$$

under some special circumstances sulfite is also reported (127). Since the low-temperature reaction of sulfur in sodium hydroxide gives thiosulfate and the high-temperature reaction gives sulfate, it is reasonable to postulate that thiosulfate is the intermediate in the formation of sulfate. A recent study (877) has shown that sodium thiosulfate does decompose to form sulfide and sulfate at these temperatures, in contrast with the room temperature, acid-catalyzed decomposition of thiosulfate to sulfur and sulfite (304).

Since bisulfide can convert sulfur to polysulfide (33, 88, 224, 500, 849),

$$HS^- + \frac{n}{8}S_8 \leftrightharpoons HS_{n+1}^- \qquad (2\text{-}11)$$

the reactions written for the disproportionation of S_8 may actually involve polysulfide, HS_{n+1}^-. For example, Eq. (2-7) becomes:

$$NaHS_5 + 4NaOH = Na_2S_2O_3 + 3NaHS + H_2O \qquad (2\text{-}12)$$

The initial attack by aqueous base on S_8 is presumed to involve an ionic mechanism. However, this evidence for an ionic process does not eliminate the possibility that radicals and radical ions also may be present in these aqueous solutions at sufficiently elevated temperatures (see, e.g., ref. 891). The presence of polysulfenyl radicals in aqueous solutions has not been confirmed by paramagnetic resonance spectra, but two areas of study provide indirect evidence. The first is color development in polysulfide solutions, and the second is a kinetic study of the polysulfide oxidation of ring-substituted arylmethyl compounds. This latter evidence is discussed in Sec. 7-2.

Blue colors are produced when sulfur is heated in certain solvents. In this respect sulfur shows metalloid properties, since the alkali and alkali earth metals also dissolve to produce colored solutions in these solvents. The alkali metals form blue solutions which conduct electricity in ammonia, and in ether and amine solvents. In some, but not all, of these solutions, EPR reveals the presence of radicals (209, 243, 1031). The colored species, the paramagnetic species, and the species responsible for the electrical conductance need not be identical and under some circumstances, at least, are not.

In the case of sulfur, some of these colored solutions give EPR spectra. Again, however, the colored and the paramagnetic species need not be the same. In 1918, Lewis, Randall, and Bichowsky (689) reported that blue colors are produced when sulfur is heated in aqueous bases above 130° C, and that acids destroy the color. They also found that sulfur in liquid ammonia produces blue colors and that the color is destroyed by ammonium chloride, an acidic salt. Sulfur in oleum or anhydrous sulfur trioxide gives solutions which vary in color from yellow to blue, and a blue solid, believed to be $(SO_3{\cdot}S)_x$, can be isolated; both the solution and the solid are paramagnetic (490, 582, 1030). Colored solutions containing appreciable concentrations of radicals and radical ions are formed from many organic sulfides dissolved in concentrated sulfuric acid (375). A solution of sulfur in the LiCl/KCl eutectic at 400° C is blue and is paramagnetic (521). At 140° C a blue coloration is formed reversibly when sulfur is dissolved in formamide; at 150° C the solution darkens and a reaction occurs (637). Colored solutions of sulfur are also formed in boron oxide, phosphorus pentoxide, potassium thiocyanate, potassium cyanide, glycerine, ethanol, and acetone (689).

In many of these cases the species responsible for the color has not been identified. However, there is some reason to believe that sulfenyl radicals might be blue or green from colored allotropes of sulfur discovered by Rice and his students. They report that a purple, solid sulfur compound is isolated when sulfur vapor at 450° C is frozen on a liquid nitrogen cold finger (889). Rice believes this to be S_2 in a triplet state. The ground state of S_2 is known to be a triplet $^3\Sigma$, just as is that of oxygen (792), and molecular beam experiments of Shaw and Phipps (968) have shown that S_2 vapor is paramagnetic. Meyer and Schumacher (747) also believe they have isolated solid S_2. Rice (888) has also isolated a green allotrope by suspending a liquid nitrogen cold finger above liquid sulfur kept at 150° C, at which temperature liquid sulfur is mainly S_8 (888). This green compound is paramagnetic and is converted to ordinary yellow S_8 rings in 90% yield, slowly at −100° C and very rapidly at 25° C. It is believed to be a linear, open-chain S_8 diradical. Activation energies for these changes are:

$$\begin{array}{l} \text{Purple } S_2 \xrightarrow{3.1 \text{ kcal}} S_8 \text{ rings} \\ \text{Green } S_8 \xrightarrow{3.9 \text{ kcal}} S_8 \text{ rings} \end{array} \tag{2-13}$$

Radford and Rice (880) have isolated a paramagnetic species they believe to be a sulfur polymer with a free electron at each end. However, it has not been established in any of these systems that the radical species is responsible for the blue color. In fact, the colors may be due to scattering of light and diffraction by clusters of frozen molecules and may not be related to the absorption spectrum of the species in question (747, 747*a*, 880).

Some organic sulfur compounds give colored solutions when heated (thermochromism), but this is not evidence for the presence of radicals. This is discussed in Sec. 3-3A. In sulfuric acid solution thiophenol (561, 1140) and phenyl disulfide (560, 561, 1140) are paramagnetic; with $AlCl_3$ these same compounds give colored solutions that are not paramagnetic (561).

In conclusion, colored species are permissive but neither sufficient nor conclusive evidence for the presence of radicals. Further EPR studies are certainly desirable.

2-4. Reactions of Sulfur in Anhydrous Ammonia and Amine Solvents

There is evidence that polysulfides are also formed when sulfur is heated with anhydrous bases. For example, heating sulfur in liquid ammonia leads to the formation of appreciable amounts of ammonium polysulfide (124, 152). Amines also react with sulfur to give polysulfides (152). Sulfide is produced in these reactions through oxidation of the amine to a thioamide (see Sec. 5-2). Morpholine, an amine frequently used in sulfur oxidations, gives morpholine thiosulfate (850), polysulfides, and dithiooxalodimorpholide (568, 741).

Davis has found that sulfur dissolves in ethylenediamine to produce metastable, light-green solutions at 10^{-3} *M* and red-brown solutions at higher concentrations (309). These solutions conduct electricity (309, 879). Higher concentrations of sulfur in ethylenediamine produce a rapid reaction. For example, the addition of 32 g of sulfur to 100 ml of the diamine gives an extremely exothermic reaction which produces ammonia, N_4S_4, S_7NH, NH_2—CS—CH_2NH_2, NH_2—CS—CS—NH_2, and other products. Upon acid hydrolysis, formaldehyde is obtained, indicating that even the C—N bond has been cleaved. Such reactions of sulfur in amines are not completely understood, and this is a fruitful area for further research.

3

THIOLS, DISULFIDES, AND POLYSULFIDES

In this chapter some of the chemical properties and reactions associated with the S—S and the S—H bonds are discussed.

3-1. Bond Energies, Lengths, and Angles

Table 3-1 lists both bond dissociation energies and thermochemical bond strengths for S—S, S—H, and C—S bonds, as well as for some oxygen analogues.

The bond dissociation energy is the energy required (ideally at 0° K in the gas phase) to break a particular bond without breaking other bonds in the molecule. For example, the bond dissociation energy, symbolized $D(CH_3—H)$, is the energy required for the reaction: $CH_4 \rightarrow CH_3\cdot + H\cdot$. Dissociation energies are usually calculated from kinetic data. The thermochemical bond strength, or average bond strength, is assigned to each of the bonds in a molecule so that the total is equal to the heat of atomization of the molecule. Thus, the bond strength in methane is one-quarter that required for the conversion: $CH_4 \rightarrow C + 4H\cdot$, with all substances in their standard states. The required heats of atomization are usually calculated from combustion data. (See the review by Cottrell, ref. 255, pages 13, 16, 103, 123.)

The bond strength of an S—S bond in polysulfides has been studied as a function of the number of sulfur atoms in the chain. There is considerable evidence that the S—S bond strength is relatively constant in the polysulfides HS_nH for values of n between 2 and 6 (Table 3-1). The most recent and detailed calculations are those of Allen (21), who used the thermodynamic data of Fehér and coworkers (387, 405). He found that the average S—S bond strength is almost constant, rising slightly from 58.1 kcal for H_2S_2 to 62.3 kcal for H_2S_6. However, very long-chain polysulfides have a much lower bond strength; e.g., the average S—S

Table 3-1
Bond strengths

Compound	Energy, kcal	
	Bond dissociation energy[a]	Thermochemical bond strength[a]
S—S bonds:		
$CH_3S—SCH_3$	73 (255, 477)	67 (255)
$CH_3S—SC_2H_5$	72 (255, 477)	
$C_2H_5S—SC_2H_5$	70 (255, 477)	70 (255)
HS—SH	72[c] (255)	58 (21)
		63 (405)
		67 (255)
HS_3H[b]	64 (706)	61 (21)
		63 (405)
HS_4H[b]	....	62 (21)
		63 (405)
HS_5H[b]	....	62 (21)
	....	63 (405)
HS_6H[b]	....	62 (21)
		63 (405)
$—S_n—$ ($n = 5 \times 10^4$)[b]	33 (358, 489, 495)	
S_8 ring[b]	....	64 (255, 838)
S_2	101[d] (477)	
O—O bonds:		
$C_2H_5O—OC_2H_5$	32 (255)	47 (255)
HO—OH	48 (255)	35 (255)
S—H and O—H bonds:		
HS—H	89 (255)	
HO—H	116 (255)	
$CH_3S—H$	89 (477)	
$C_2H_5S—H$	87 (477)	
C—S bonds:		
$CH_3—SH$	74 (477)	
$C_2H_5—SH$	73 (477)	
i-$C_3H_7—SH$	71 (477)	
t-$C_4H_9—SH$	69 (477)	
Allyl—SH	52 (477)	
$CH_3—SCH_3$	73 (477)	
$C_2H_5—SCH_3$	72 (477)	
i-$C_3H_7—SCH_3$	67 (477)	
t-$C_4H_9—SCH_3$	65 (477)	
Allyl—SCH_3	52 (477)	
$C_6H_5S—CH_3$	60 (51)	
$C_6H_5CH_2S—CH_3$	51 (174)	

[a] Defined in text.
[b] Average S—S bond.
[c] Based on the 80 kcal value of Franklin and Lumpkin (477), but revised by Cottrell using a lower value for the heat of formation of HS (p. 227 of ref. 255). A value of 66 kcal has also been reported (706).
[d] Values of 76 and 81 kcal have been reported but the above value is preferred (491).

Table 3-2
Valence angles in sulfur compounds

Compound	Angle, degrees			References
Divalent sulfur:	S—S—S	S—S—C	C—S—C	
S_6	102	....	....	334, 335, 335*a*
$BaS_4O_6 \cdot 2H_2O$	103	....	....	448
BaS_3	103	....	....	445, 753, 1163
$BaSeS_4O_6 \cdot 2H_2O$	103	....	....	461
$K_2S_3O_6$	103	....	....	1168
$(CF_3)_2S_3$	104	....	....	167
$CH_3SO_2—S—S—SO_2CH_3$	104	....	....	997
$Na_2S_4O_6$	104	....	....	450
$(CH_3)_2S_3$	104	....	....	336
$BaS_5O_6 \cdot 2H_2O$	104	....	....	474
$BaS_4 \cdot H_2O$	104	....	....	3
S_n (helical polymer)	*c.* 105	....	....	334
S_8 (vapor)	105	....	....	704
S_8 (orthorhombic crystal)	105	....	....	1133
$C_6H_5SO_2—S—SO_2C_6H_5$	106	102	....	728
$BaS_5O_6 \cdot 2H_2O$	107	....	....	462
S_8 (orthorhombic crystal)	108	....	....	4, 220*a*
Cs_2S_6	106–110	....	....	8
$(ICH_2—CH_2)_2S_3$	113	98	....	311, 333
$(CF_3)_2S_2$	...	105	....	167
$(p\text{-}BrC_6H_4)_2S_2$	...	107	....	1078
$(CH_3)_2S_2$	...	107	....	1010
$(C_6H_5)_2S$	...	...	113	1026
$(p\text{-}BrC_6H_4)_2S$	...	...	109	1078
$(p\text{-}CH_3—C_6H_4)_2S$	...	....	109	133
Sulfones and sulfoxides:	X—S—O	X—S—X	O—S—O	
F_2SO	107	93	....	415
F_2SO_2	107	93	130	484
F_2SO_2	105	110	....	1012
Cl_2SO	106	114	....	827
Cl_2SO_2	106	111	120	827
Br_2SO	108	96	....	1011
$(CH_3)_2SO$	107	100	....	99
$(CH_3)_2SO_2$	105	115 ± 15	125 ± 15	20
$(C_6H_5)_2SO$	106	97	....	5, 7
$(p\text{-}Cl—C_6H_4)_2SO_2$	108	105	120	980
$(p\text{-}Br—C_6H_4)_2SO_2$	109	100	131	1078
$(p\text{-}I—C_6H_4)_2SO_2$	111	106	111	607
SO_3	...	....	120	827

bond energy in a chain containing 50,000 sulfur atoms is 33.4 kcal (358, 489, 495). Unfortunately, the strengths of bonds in chains of intermediate lengths between 6 and 50,000 are not known. This lowered bond energy of an S—S in a long chain presumably arises because of the delocalization of the odd electron in the radical produced in the bond scission. This delocalization probably involves expansion of the electronic octet on adjacent sulfur atoms through the use of *d* orbitals. In short chains, delocalization is apparently negligible; e.g., in H_2S_6 the average radical would be HSSS·, which has limited possibilities for resonance.

Franklin and Lumpkin point out that the C—S bond energy is relatively insensitive to the group on sulfur; either methyl or hydrogen produces about the same effect. Within these narrow limits, the group on carbon also has little effect; methyl and ethyl mercaptan have similar C—S bond energies. Allyl mercaptan, however, has a much lower C—S bond energy because of the stability of the allyl radical. Back and Sehon (51) have measured $D(C_6H_5S—CH_3)$ in a study of the pyrolysis of phenyl methyl sulfide in a stream of toluene. They found the rate to be $k = 3 \times 10^{14}e^{-60,000/RT}$ sec^{-1}, and the products to be mainly methane, thiophenol, and bibenzyl. They comment, however, that the influence of surface area was not investigated, and 60 kcal can be only tentatively identified as $D(C_6H_5S—CH_3)$. This value is 13 kcal lower than the value of Franklin and Lumpkin for $D(CH_3S—CH_3)$, and that is probably the lower limit for the delocalization energy of the C_6H_5—S· radical.

The bond angles and bond lengths in sulfur compounds were reviewed critically by Wells in 1950 (1139) and more completely by Abrahams in 1956 (7). The angle S—S—S in compounds containing chains of divalent sulfur atoms varies from 102 to 109°, if the anomalously high value for iodoethyl trisulfide is excluded (see Table 3-2). The average value is about 105°.

These sulfur chains are not planar. Compounds such as X—S—S—S—Y can exist in two isomeric conformations (1095). In the cis form, the X and Y groups are on the same side of the plane defined by the three sulfur atoms; in the trans form, X and Y are on opposite sides. If the cis form is continued for eight sulfur atoms, an S_8 ring is formed. The trans form is helical and exists in left- and right-handed screws which are enantiomeric (444). (See Fig. 3-1.)

Table 3-3 cites experimental measurements of the dihedral angle in polysulfide chains. This is the angle between the SSS and the SSX planes in Fig. 3-1. Figures 3-2 and 3-3 show sodium tetrathionate and ethyl disulfide in their lowest-energy conformation. Both these compounds have a dihedral angle of 90°.

These divalent sulfur bond angles can be explained as resulting from (1) pure *p* bonds, (2) sp^3 hybrid bonds, or (3) bonds containing *d* character.

The theory that sulfur bonds use *p* orbitals was proposed by Pauling. He theorizes that sulfur bonds are almost pure *p*, with about 1% *s* character (840). This correctly predicts an optimum bond angle of 105°.

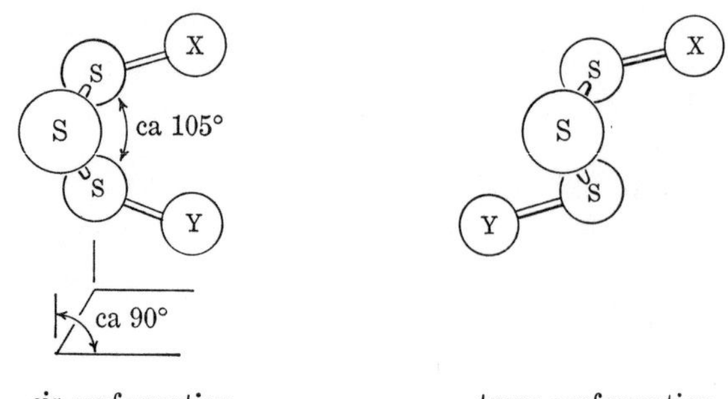

Fig. 3-1. Polysulfide chain conformations.

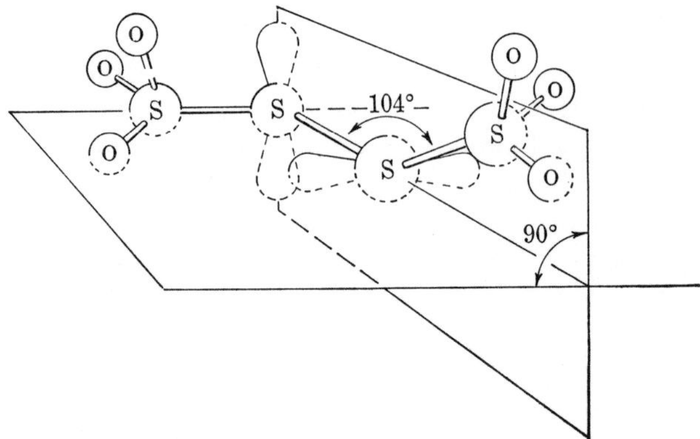

Fig. 3-2. Conformation of sodium tetrathionate (450). The postulated orthogonal *p* orbitals are shown.

The two unshared electron pairs on sulfur are then assigned to the *s* and to the remaining *p* orbital. The dihedral angle of 90° is explained as due to the repulsion between the nonbonded *p* orbitals on adjacent sulfurs (see Fig. 3-2). This model, with modifications, has been used to explain the quadruple coupling constants of S_8 (313). In a ring compound the dihedral angle is fixed by the bond angles; assuming a bond angle of 105°, Pauling then calculates the dihedral angle for a ring of 6, 8, 10, and 12 sulfur atoms. These dihedral angles are 69, 103, 119, and 129°, respectively. Pauling concludes that the S_8 ring is most stable since it

Table 3-3
Dihedral angle in polysulfide compounds

Compound	Angle, degrees	References
S_6	74	334, 335*a*
Cs_2S_6	61, 79, 82	8
$BaS_4 \cdot H_2O$	74, 77	3
$(ICH_2—CH_2)_2S_3$	82	311, 333
$Na_2S_4O_6$	90	450
H_2S_2	90	1157
S_n (helical polymer)	90	334
$(CH_3SO_2)_2S_2$	90	997
$BaS_4O_6 \cdot 2H_2O$	90	448
$(C_2H_5)_2S_2$	90	959
S_2Cl_2	92	20
$(CH_3)_2S_3$	93	336
S_8 (orthorhombic)	99	4, 220*a*
$BaS_5O_6 \cdot 2H_2O$ (triclinic)	106	462
$BaS_5O_6 \cdot 2H_2O$ (orthorhombic)	110	474
$K_2Ba(S_6O_6)_2$ (cis-cis)	108, 91, 105	453

alone has a dihedral angle in the optimum 90 to 110° range. Using Bichowsky and Rossini's thermochemical data, Pauling calculates that S_8 is more stable than is S_6 by 1.2 kcal per mole per S—S bond (335*a*). Bartlett, Meguerian, and Davis (84, 89, 302) have shown by kinetic techniques that at ordinary temperatures S_6 is unstable and is converted first to sulfur polymer and then to S_8. Only even-numbered rings were considered by Pauling; presumably Pauling believes that alternating partial double-bond resonance hybrids make even-numbered rings more stable than odd-numbered rings. There is no direct evidence that any sulfur rings other than S_6 and S_8 are stable, but a number of other sulfur ring compounds have been proposed to explain anomalies in the viscosity data of liquid sulfur (see page 6).

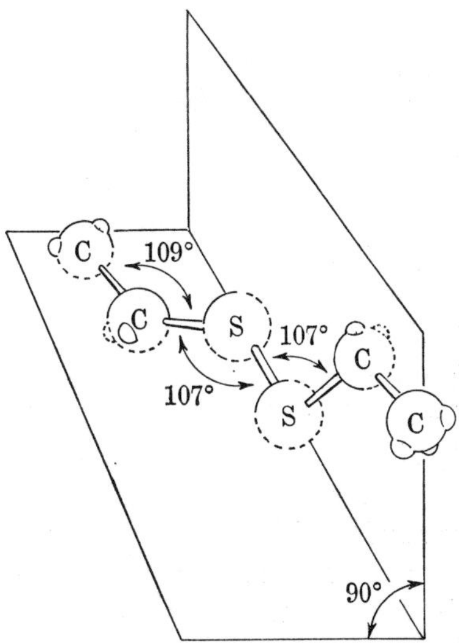

Fig. 3-3. Lowest-energy conformation of ethyl disulfide (958, 959).

Bond angles in divalent sulfur compounds can be equally well explained by sp^3 orbitals (7, 221). The bond angles in Table 3-2 are near the tetrahedral 109° angle. If sulfur is assumed to bond using sp^3 hybridization, the 90 to 110° optimum dihedral angle may be explained as arising from repulsion of nonbonding sp^3 orbitals.

The bonding can also be explained by using *d* orbitals. Kimball (627) has shown that bond angles near 110° can be constructed using 25% *s* character and anything from 0 to 75% *d* orbitals, the remainder being *p* orbital.

Thus, evidence on bond angles is not sufficient to resolve the question of the bonding orbitals in sulfur. In particular this evidence neither requires nor excludes the use of *d* orbitals.

A number of related compounds are analogous. Hydrogen sulfide, with a valence angle of 92° (266), is usually explained as pure *p* bonding. Cartmell and Fowles (221) have suggested that it can be considered a distorted tetrahedron. Burrus and Gordy (204) find that pure *p* bonds cannot explain the nuclear quadrupole coupling. They postulate bonds with 15% *s*, 15% *d*, and 70% *p* character. These three approaches parallel those described above; here also the experimental bond-angle data cannot resolve the choice between *p*, sp^3, or orbitals containing *d* character.

The interpretation of the bond angles of analogous oxygen compounds presents similar problems. A complete treatment of the stereochemistry of oxygen bonds is beyond the scope of this work, and Abrahams' review (7) should be consulted. One example will illustrate the similarities. Hydrogen peroxide has a bond angle of 97° and a dihedral angle of 94° (8, 705). Hydrogen peroxide can be treated as using pure *p* bonds (page 134 of ref. 839, 845, 846), or sp^3 bonds (221). In the oxygen compounds, of course, *d* orbitals are not available.

The bond angles between sulfur and other atoms are of interest. Abrahams (7) has tabulated all the values available; only sulfur-to-carbon and sulfur-to-oxygen bonds will be discussed here. *p*-Tolyl and *p*-bromophenyl sulfide both have C—S—C angles of 109° (see Table 3-2), in agreement with a tetrahedral sulfur. Abrahams (7) has also reviewed bond angles in sulfur heterocyclic compounds. The values for the C—S—C angle range from 65.8° for thiacyclopropane (281) to 106.5° for 1,3,5-trimethyl-2,4,6-trithiacyclohexane (548).

In trivalent sulfur compounds, the sulfur is the apex of a shallow pyramid. Thus, the trimethylsulfonium ion has C_{3v} symmetry by Raman spectroscopy (978), and is pyramidal. Dimethyl sulfoxide has a C—S—O angle of 106 to 107° (20, 99) and a C—S—C angle of 100° (99). These values for diphenyl sulfoxide are 106 and 97° (7) (see Table 3-2).

A sulfur bonded to four oxygens has nearly tetrahedral bond angles. Thus, sulfate ions are tetrahedral (676, 1139). Potassium ethyl sulfate has an O—S—O angle of 109° (588). Sodium thiosulfate pentahydrate has angles of 104 to 115° (1042). The dithionate ion (1006) and the $S_3O_{10}^{=}$ ion (353) are most likely tetrahedral. Potassium trithionate (1168) is formed of two tetrahedrons with a common corner (the middle, divalent sulfur). Sulfones are not tetrahedral, but have C—S—O angles of 105 to 107° (7) (see Table 3-2). Two exceptions are β-isoprene sulfone with 99.6° (589) and *p*-iodophenyl sulfone with 111° (607). The C—S—C angle in a sulfone is similar to that in the corresponding sulfoxide. This correspondence is so close that diphenyl sulfoxide cocrystallizes with diphenyl sulfone; even at 90% sulfoxide, the sulfone crystal remains intact, with 90% of the sulfone oxygens replaced by a sulfoxide oxygen and a pair of electrons (10). At 92% sulfoxide, the solid solution changes to the sulfoxide crystal form.

Bond lengths in divalent sulfur compounds are given in Table 3-4. The average value is 2.08 A for an S—S bond. Pauling (839) has selected 2.08 A as a normal S—S single bond. Huggins prefers 2.05 to 2.07 A (574). Since the bond in S_8 is 2.04 (6, 220*a*), it may possess some fractional double-bond character. The bond length in S_2 in its $^3\Sigma_g^-$ triplet ground state is 1.887 A by spectroscopy; as in the case of oxygen, this is probably close to the normal double-bond length (7).

In compounds containing four or more sulfur atoms in a chain, the S—S bond length is found to vary. Short bonds occur in polythionates, for example, to which 33 to 50% double-bond character has been ascribed (7). The tetra-, penta-, and hexathionate ions have been found to have the following bond lengths by Foss (445), using x-ray technique (values in angstroms):

$$^-O_3S\overset{2.12}{—}S\overset{2.02}{—}S\overset{2.12}{—}SO_3^-$$
$$^-O_3S\overset{2.12}{—}S\overset{2.04}{—}S\overset{2.04}{—}S\overset{2.12}{—}SO_3^-$$
$$^-O_3S\overset{2.10}{—}S\overset{2.04}{—}S\overset{2.04}{—}S\overset{2.04}{—}S\overset{2.10}{—}SO_3^-$$

Foss (445) believes all polythionates have longer $S—SO_3^-$ terminal bonds than central S—S bonds. Abrahams (7) states these rules for polysulfide chains in general: Chemically equivalent bonds are of equal length. In compounds with an odd number of S—S bonds, the bond lengths alternate. In compounds with an even number of bonds, the outermost bonds are the shortest, except when oxygen atoms are joined to the terminal sulfurs, in which case the S—O bond is shortened.

The C—S single-bond length is 1.82 to 1.83 A (7, 839). The C═S double-bond length has not been unambiguously determined. Thus CS_2 and COS both have C═S bonds of length 1.56 A (1016), but contributions of $\overset{-}{O}—C\equiv\overset{+}{S}$, for example, are significant (1079). Abrahams (7) has chosen 1.61 A as the best value for the carbon-sulfur double bond. In

Table 3-4a
Bond lengths; S—S bonds

Compound	Angstroms	References
S_2	1.89	579
$Na_2S_2O_3 \cdot 5H_2O$	1.97	449, 1042
$Na_2S_4O_6$	2.02	450
S_8 (orthorhombic)	2.04	4, 6, 220*a*
$(CH_3)_2S_3$	2.04	336
N,N′-Diglycyl-L-cystine·$2H_2O$	2.04	1008, 1165
H_2S_2	2.04	1010
$[(NH_2)_2C—S—]_2 \cdot X_2 \cdot H_2O$	2.04	454
Cl_2S_2	2.05	827
$(IC_2H_4)_2S_3$	2.05	311, 333
$BaS_4 \cdot H_2O$	2.02/2.07/2.02	3
Cs_2S_6	1.99/2.10/2.03/2.12/2.03	8
$BaS_4O_6 \cdot 2H_2O$	2.10/2.02/2.13	448
$BaS_5O_6 \cdot 2H_2O$ (triclinic)	2.12/2.04/2.04/2.10	462
$BaS_5O_6 \cdot 2H_2O$ (orthorhombic)	2.14/2.04/2.04/2.14	474
$K_2Ba(S_6O_6)_2$	2.10/2.04/2.04/2.04/2.10	451, 453
$(CH_3SO_2)_2S_2$	2.10/2.06/2.10	997
$(CF_3)_2S_2$	2.05	167
S_6	2.06	334, 335, 335*a*
$(CF_3)_2S_3$	2.06	167
Amorphous S	2.07	1077
Liquid S (124 to 340° C)	2.07	507, 1077
$(C_6H_5SO_2)_2S$	2.07	728
Cl_2S_2	2.07	20
Plastic S	2.08	507
$(C_6H_6SO_2—S)_2Te$	2.08	825
$NaK_5Cl_2(S_2O_6)_2$	2.08	1006
$NaK_6Cl_5S_2O_6$	2.08	1006
$(NH)_2C—S—S—C(NH)_2 \cdot 2HI$	2.09	467
$(CH_3C_6H_4SO_2—S)_2Te$	2.11	457
$(NH_4)_2TeS_4O_6$	2.11	455
$BaSeS_4O_6 \cdot 2H_2O$	2.13	461
$(CH_3—SO_2—S)_2Te$	2.14	473
$K_2S_2O_6$	2.14	1006
$K_2S_3O_6$	2.15	1168
$Na_2S_2O_6 \cdot 2H_2O$	2.16	725
S_2F_{10}	2.21	547
Na_2S_2 (β form)	2.25	425
$Na_2S_2O_4$	2.39	341

Table 3-4b; S—C bonds

Compound	Angstroms	References
CS	1.53	764
COS	1.56	1016
CS_2	1.56	548
(p-CH_3—C_6H_4)$_2$S	1.75	133
(p-BrC_6H_4)$_2$S	1.75	1078
$(C_6H_5)_2SO$	1.76	5, 7
(p-ClC_6H_4)$_2$$SO_2$	1.76	980
$(C_6H_5SO_2)_2S$	1.76	728
$(CH_3)_2S_2$	1.78	1010
CH_3—CO—SH	1.78	516
$(CH_3)_2SO_2$	1.80	693
(p-BrC_6H_4)$_2$$S_2$	1.80	1078
CH_3SH	1.81	996
$(CH_3S)_4C$	1.81	848
$(CH_3)_2SO$	1.82	99
$(CH_3)_2S$	1.82	178
$(CF_3)_2S$	1.83	167
$(CF_3)_2S_2$	1.83	167
(p-BrC_6H_4)$_2$$SO_2$	1.84	1078
$(CF_3)_2S_3$	1.85	167
(I-CH_2CH_2)$_2$$S_3$	1.86	333

many of the sulfides in Table 3-4, the C—S bond length is between the single- and the double-bond length. These shortened single bonds frequently occur in systems with unsaturated bonds on either side of sulfur. For example, p-tolyl sulfide has C—S bonds 1.75 A in length. In these compounds, the shortened bond length has been explained by resonance forms which introduce double-bond character to the C—S bonds.

$$-CH=CH-S-CH=CH- \longleftrightarrow -\overset{+}{C}H-CH=\overset{-}{S}-CH=CH-$$

These forms use the d orbitals of sulfur. This is analogous to thiophene, which has been treated from this point of view (696) and is considered to have C—S bonds with about 40% double-bond character (7). The C—S bond in thiophene is 1.74 A (940). The S—C bond lengths in dimethyl and diphenyl sulfoxide are 1.82 and 1.76 A. The diphenyl compound has a shorter than usual bond. However, dimethyl and di (p-bromophenyl) sulfone have S—C bonds of length 1.80 and 1.84 A. In these sulfones the phenyl-sulfur bond is *longer* than usual.

The sulfoxide-type S—O bond has been considered largely a covalent double bond (449, 766, 851, 1138). Jeffrey and Stadler (590) and Abrahams (7) have tabulated sulfoxide-type S—O bond distances; the bond length is fairly constant at 1.43 to 1.44 A. The S—O bond in potassium ethyl sulfate is believed to be nearly a pure single bond and is longer, having a length of 1.60 A (588). Using the Schomaker-Stevenson (941) equation, Pauling has calculated the S—O "pure" single bond as 1.70 A (839). On this basis, the sulfate S—O bonds of 1.49 A have a bond order of two (page 321 of ref. 839).

Serious theoretical objections have been raised to the concept of bond order. Wells (1138) points out that the "pure" S—O single-bond length is calculated using a number of assumptions, including the Schomaker-Stevenson equation, which have not been justified theoretically. Bauer (106*a*) has questioned whether atomic radii are known with sufficient accuracy. Walsh (1128*a*) believes resonance lowering of bond length may be a calculational artifact. Dewar (321, 322) has advanced similar arguments. In this context, the organic chemist may adopt the bond-order concept as an unproved working hypothesis. Most of the data on S—O bonds has been rationalized using this approach.* However, deductions from this working hypothesis—e.g., that sulfur uses *d* orbitals in such bonds—should be regarded as pure speculation.

The barrier to rotation around sulfur bonds has been calculated in some cases. Scott, McCullough, and coworkers (959) have measured the thermodynamic constants for methyl disulfide. They calculate the barrier for rotation around the S—S bond to be 6.8 kcal, and that for rotation around the C—S bond to be 1.5 kcal. Using this value for the S—S rotational barrier, they (571) find the skew conformation of the ethyl group in ethyl disulfide to be 0.9 kcal higher in energy than the most stable conformation shown in Fig. 3-3. The barrier in S_2Cl_2 has been calculated as 14.2 kcal (531) and that in H_2S_2 as 2.7 kcal (401), both calculations being based on measured thermodynamic data. In cyclic compounds containing S—S bonds, the optimum dihedral angle cannot be satisfied without distorting valence angles. The S—S bond in the ring of 1,2-dithiolane-4-carboxylic acid has a dihedral angle of 26.6° (472), and that of 1,2-dithiane-3,6-dicarboxylic acid has a dihedral angle of 60° (459). Neither ring is planar.

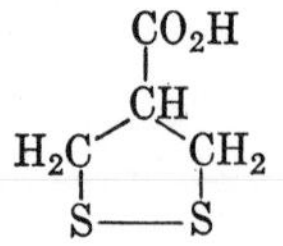

CO_2H / CH / H_2C CH_2 / S—S

HO_2C, H, S, S, H, CO_2H

1,2-Dithiolane-4-carboxylic acid 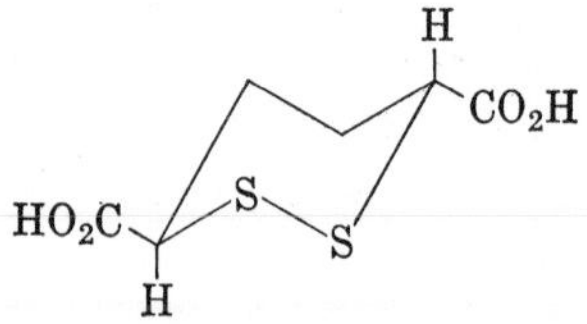   1,2-Dithiane-3,6-dicarboxylic acid

* See, for example, refs. 70, 221, 261, 262, 626, 766, 841, 851, 1018, 1032, 1033, 1109, 1110.

In thiuret hydroiodide, the ring is planar, and Foss (471) has concluded that resonance stabilization of the planar ring system may provide the energy for reduction of the normal dihedral angle. Trithiones are also planar and also may be stabilized by resonance (606) (see p. 122).

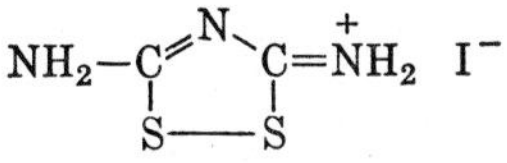

$$NH_2-C\overset{N}{\diagup\diagdown}C=\overset{+}{N}H_2 \quad I^- \quad (\text{ring closed by } S-S)$$

Thiuret hydroiodide

Bergson has reviewed the data on barrier heights for rotation around S—S bonds and has discussed several possible explanations. He favors an explanation based on molecular orbital principles (120–123).

The barrier around the S—H bond in methanethiol is estimated as 1.5 kcal, and that around the C—S bond in methyl sulfide as 2.0 kcal (296).

3-2. Use of *d* Orbitals by Sulfur

Atoms beyond the second period of the periodic table can accommodate more than eight outer-valence electrons by utilizing their *d* orbitals. Theoretic discussions of this topic have been given by Hückel (572), by Basolo and Pearson (Chap. 2 of ref. 98), and by Craig and Magnusson (263).

In particular, sulfur is able to expand its octet and delocalize electrons from adjacent centers of electron density. Cilento (238) in 1960 reviewed the extensive literature on the ability of sulfur to utilize *d* orbitals; only the more important consequences of this will be discussed here.

3-2A. Thiol and Sulfonium Sulfur. Mercapto and dialkylsulfonium groups stabilize an adjacent carbanion. This stabilization may be explained either as an inductive effect arising from the electronegativity of sulfur, or as a resonance effect in which sulfur expands its octet. The resonance forms for a carbanion stabilized by a mercapto group are shown in Eq. (3-1).

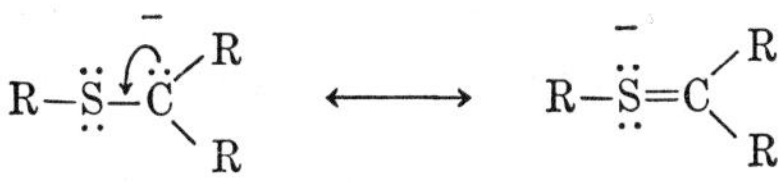

$$R-\ddot{\underset{..}{S}}-\overset{-}{\ddot{C}}R_2 \longleftrightarrow R-\ddot{\underset{..}{S}}=\overset{-}{C}R_2 \tag{3-1}$$

The resonance in dialkylsulfonium compounds is shown in Eq. (3-2).

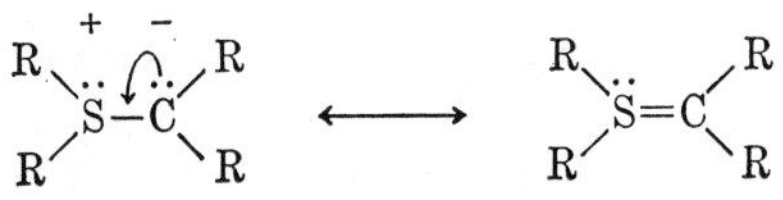

$$R_2\overset{+}{\ddot{S}}-\overset{-}{\ddot{C}}R_2 \longleftrightarrow R_2\ddot{S}=CR_2 \tag{3-2}$$

The resonance form on the right-hand side of both Eqs. (3-1) and (3-2) places 10 electrons around sulfur. If the observed stabilization of carbanions by mercapto groups is in fact partially due to such resonance forms, then atoms of the first period will be less effective than is sulfur, even though they have comparable electronegativity. Consistent with this, Doering and Hoffmann (326) found that either the trimethylsulfonium ion or the tetramethylphosphonium ion exchanges hydrogen for deuterium much faster than does the tetramethylammonium ion. Thus, hydrogens alpha to a sulfur are more acidic than those alpha to a nitrogen, presumably because of resonance.

$$CH_3-\overset{+}{\ddot{S}}(CH_3)-CH_3 \xrightarrow{\text{Base}} \left[CH_3-\overset{+}{\ddot{S}}(CH_3)-CH_2^- \longleftrightarrow CH_3-S(CH_3)=CH_2\right] \xrightarrow{D_2O} CH_3-\overset{+}{\ddot{S}}(CH_3)-CH_2D \quad (3\text{-}3)$$

$$CH_3-\overset{+}{N}(CH_3)_2-CH_3 \xrightarrow[\text{Slower}]{\text{Base}} CH_3-\overset{+}{N}(CH_3)_2-CH_2^- \xrightarrow{D_2O} CH_3-\overset{+}{N}(CH_3)_2-CH_2D \quad (3\text{-}4)$$

Another observation which indicates that sulfur stabilizes a carbanion is that mercapto groups activate a methylene group for condensation reactions (26).

$$CH_2(SC_2H_5)_2 \xrightarrow[NaNH_2, NH_3]{RCl} R{-}CH(SC_2H_5)_2 \quad (3\text{-}5)$$

The mechanism involves displacement of chloride ion by the stabilized carbanion $^-CH(SC_2H_5)_2$. If this stabilization is partly because of resonance, then sulfur should be more effective than is oxygen. Baliah (64) finds this to be the case in a related system: phenylmercaptoacetic acid condenses with benzaldehyde in acetic acid with piperidine catalysis.

$$C_6H_5S{-}CH_2{-}CO_2H + C_6H_5{-}CHO \rightarrow C_6H_5S{-}\underset{}{C}(=CH{-}C_6H_5){-}CO_2H \quad (3\text{-}6)$$

Under these conditions, the oxygen analogue does not react.

$$C_6H_5O{-}CH_2{-}CO_2H + C_6H_5{-}CHO \rightarrow \text{No reaction} \quad (3\text{-}7)$$

Similarly, Brehm and Levenson (176) find that sulfur is more activating than oxygen in an intramolecular cyclization.

$$CH_3O-\overset{\overset{O}{\|}}{C}-CH_2-[\text{ring: }C(=O)(OCH_3)-CH_2-O-CH_2-S] \xrightarrow[\text{Toluene, 80°}]{NaOCH_3} CH_3O-\overset{\overset{O}{\|}}{C}-CH[\text{ring: }C(=O)-CH_2-O-CH_2-S] \qquad (3\text{-}8)$$

Cyclization by condensation of the other ester group on the methylene group which is activated by oxygen does not occur.

$$[\text{ring: }H_2C-C(=O)(OCH_3)\ldots S-CH_2-O]\;CH_2-\overset{\overset{O}{\|}}{C}-OCH_3 \not\longrightarrow [\text{ring: }H_2C-C(=O)-CH-O-CH_2-S]\;CH-\overset{\overset{O}{\|}}{C}-OCH_3 \qquad (3\text{-}9)$$

Not formed

Doering and Schreiber have contrasted the reactions of the sulfonium ion and the ammonium ion (329). Thus, the 2-bromosulfonium ion reacts with base, Eq. (3-10), over 3,000 times faster than the comparable 2-bromoammonium ion, Eq. (3-11). Furthermore, the sulfonium ion reacts by elimination and the ammonium ion by substitution.

$$Br-CH_2-CH_2-\overset{+}{S}(CH_3)-CH_3 \xrightarrow[\text{KOH},\ k(E_2)=100]{0°C} CH_2=CH-\overset{+}{S}(CH_3)-CH_3 \qquad (3\text{-}10)$$

$$Br-CH_2-CH_2-\overset{+}{N}(CH_3)_2-CH_3 \xrightarrow[\text{KOH},\ k(S_N2)=0.036]{25°C} HO-CH_2-CH_2-\overset{+}{N}(CH_3)_2-CH_3 \qquad (3\text{-}11)$$

The difference must be ascribed to the greater acidity of the hydrogen alpha to a sulfur, and this is probably because of resonance.*

$$BrCH_2-\underset{H}{CH}-\overset{+}{S}(CH_3)_2 \longleftrightarrow BrCH_2-CH=\ddot{S}(CH_3)_2 \quad H^+ \qquad (3\text{-}12)$$

* Note, however, that α-alkoxyhalides react faster than α-mercaptohalides (147). In the γ position neither RO nor RS has much effect (148).

Nucleophiles add very rapidly to the vinyldimethylsulfonium ion (329). Thus ethanol adds at room temperature in a few minutes in the presence of a drop of 5% aqueous sodium hydroxide.

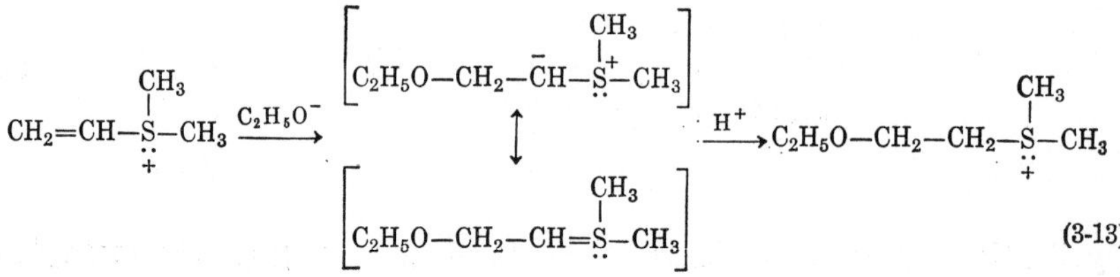

$$CH_2{=}CH{-}\overset{\overset{CH_3}{|}}{\underset{\underset{+}{\cdot\cdot}}{S}}{-}CH_3 \xrightarrow{C_2H_5O^-} \left[C_2H_5O{-}CH_2{-}\bar{C}H{-}\overset{\overset{CH_3}{|}}{\underset{\cdot\cdot}{\overset{+}{S}}}{-}CH_3\right] \updownarrow \left[C_2H_5O{-}CH_2{-}CH{=}\overset{\overset{CH_3}{|}}{\underset{\cdot\cdot}{S}}{-}CH_3\right] \xrightarrow{H^+} C_2H_5O{-}CH_2{-}CH_2{-}\overset{\overset{CH_3}{|}}{\underset{\underset{+}{\cdot\cdot}}{S}}{-}CH_3 \quad (3\text{-}13)$$

Other nucleophiles which were shown to add rapidly to the vinyldimethylsulfonium ion include water, sodium methylmercaptide, 2-mercaptoethanol, and 2-phenoxyethanol. The reaction is a general Michael-type addition, but it proceeds at an unusually fast rate because of the stabilization of the carbanion transition state by the neighboring sulfur. Under these conditions there is no evidence for any addition to the nitrogen analogue, the vinyltrimethylammonium ion. The stabilization is therefore largely due to resonance using *d* orbitals rather than to induction.

Double bonds may be isomerized by base to positions adjacent to sulfur atoms (603). Thus, Tarbell and Lovett found that an allyl sulfide is converted to a propenyl sulfide (1039).

$$CH_2{=}CH{-}CH_2{-}SR \xrightarrow[NaOC_2H_5]{3.7\ M} CH_3{-}CH{=}CH{-}SR$$

Tarbell and McCall (1040) have shown that the oxygen compound (3-14) is not isomerized in 10% sodium hydroxide whereas the sulfur compound (3-15) isomerizes to the propenyl sulfide.

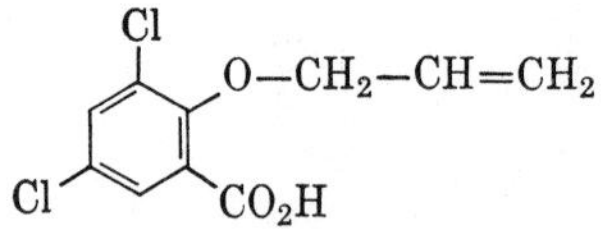

2,4-dichloro-6-carboxyphenyl ring: Cl, O$-CH_2-CH{=}CH_2$, CO_2H, Cl (3-14)

2,4-dichloro-6-carboxyphenyl ring: Cl, S$-CH_2-CH{=}CH_2$, CO_2H, Cl (3-15)

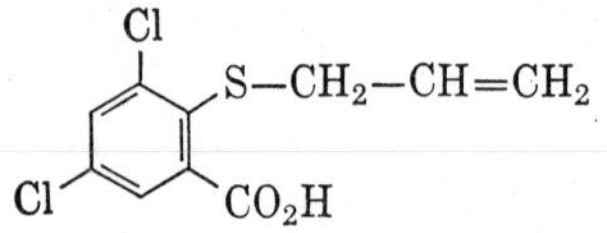

Other condensation (833, 834) and cleavage (265, 719, 902, 903) reactions are known in which di- and trivalent sulfur atoms appear to expand their valence octet.

The ultraviolet spectra of sulfur compounds frequently show that divalent sulfur is electron-withdrawing, and it appears most likely that these effects are due to resonance rather than induction (414, 587, 977). Fehnel and Carmack (408–410) have studied this in detail. For example, a para —OH or —NH_3^+ group has little effect on the spectrum of phenyl methyl sulfide. However, either a para —O^- or —NH_2 group shifts the absorption to longer wavelength and increases the intensity. Therefore, a strong electron-donating group interacts with sulfur.

$$^{-}:\ddot{O}-C_6H_4-\ddot{S}-CH_3 \longleftrightarrow :\ddot{O}=C_6H_4=\bar{\ddot{S}}-CH_3$$

Here again, nitrogen would be expected to be less effective than sulfur. In agreement with this prediction Bordwell and Boutan (155) have shown that a *p*-dimethylsulfonium group conjugates more strongly with the —O^- group than does a *p*-trimethylammonium group.

$$\bar{O}-C_6H_4-{}^{+}S(CH_3)_2 \;>\; \bar{O}-C_6H_4-{}^{+}N(CH_3)_3 \qquad (3\text{-}16)$$

Other similar examples of these spectral effects are known (56, 642, 868).

The free-electron treatment of polyenes, R—(CH═CH)$_n$—R, which predicts the correct relationship between n and the frequency of the first electronic transition (414, 860), cannot be applied to the polysulfides RS_nR (56). However, the principal band does shift to longer wavelengths in polysulfides as n increases (56), and some resonance involving d orbitals probably occurs.

Infrared spectra of divalent sulfur compounds also have been rationalized by use of d orbitals (112). A study of the infrared spectra of thiolesters, R—S—CO—R, has been reported by Baker and Harris (57). The carbonyl frequency in thiolesters is 40 to 60 cm^{-1} lower than in the corresponding ester. The thiolester carbonyl group is judged to be less basic than an ordinary ester carbonyl since it hydrogen bonds to phenylacetylene to a lesser extent. Thus the sulfur interacts with the carbonyl to remove electrons.

$$R-\ddot{S}-C(=\ddot{O}:)-R \longleftrightarrow R-\bar{\ddot{S}}=C(-\ddot{O}:^{+})-R$$

Ultraviolet spectral data support these conclusions (156, 239, 240).

The effect of a group on the acidity of benzoic acid—i.e., the σ value of the group in a Hammett $\sigma\rho$ analysis—is the classical method for determining the tendency of the group to donate or accept electrons. The methylmercapto and the methylsulfonyl groups have been studied in this way with benzoic acids, and also with phenols, thiophenols, and anilinium compounds, used as substrates. Table 3-5 collects relevant data. The sulfone data will be discussed in the following section.

Table 3-5
Hammett law analysis of the methylmercapto, methoxy, and methylsulfonyl groups

R	$R—C_6H_4—CO_2H$		$R—C_6H_4—OH$		$R—C_6H_4—SH$		$R—C_6H_4—\overset{+}{N}H_3$	
	pK_a	σ	pK_a	σ	pK_a	σ	pK_a	σ
H	5.73, 5.65[b]	0.00	9.98	0.00	7.76	0.00	....	0.00
m-CH_3O—	(5.58)[e]	+.11	9.65	.....	7.45[g]			
p-CH_3O—	6.07[d]	−.27	10.20	.....	7.99[g]	.....		
m-CH_3S—	5.53	+.14[a]	9.53	+.16[c]	....	.....	4.05	+.19[c]
p-CH_3S—	5.74, 5.72[b]	−.01[a]	9.53	+.16[c]	....	.....	4.40	+.06[c]
m-CH_3—SO_2—	4.78	+.65[f]	9.33	+.70[f]	5.88	+.71	2.68	+.69[f]
p-CH_3—SO_2—	4.68, 4.59[b]	+.72[f]	7.83	+.98[f]	5.57	+.82	1.48	+1.13[f]
Reference:	*a*	*h*	*c*	.....	*f*	*f*	*c*	

[a] Ref. 157; 25° C, 50% ethanol. [b] Ref. 1034; 25° C, 48% ethanol. [c] Ref. 157; 25° C, water. [d] Ref. 894; 25° C, 50% ethanol. [e] Interpolated using $\sigma = +.115$ (refs. 586, 736). [f] Ref. 154; 25° C, 48% ethanol. [g] Ref. 952*a*. [h] Ref. 736.

The acid-strengthening effect of groups on benzoic acid is:

$$m\text{-}CH_3S \sim m\text{-}CH_3O > H \sim p\text{-}CH_3S > p\text{-}CH_3O$$

Data on the meta compounds imply that sulfur and oxygen are about equally electron-accepting. This is a manifestation of an inductive electron-accepting tendency. In the para CH_3S group, electron-donating through resonance just balances the inductive electron-accepting effect. In p-CH_3O, a strong electron-donating resonance effect outweighs the inductive electron-withdrawing effect, and the group has a net electron-releasing tendency that is large. Therefore oxygen resonates to a larger extent with a para carboxylate group than does sulfur, but both are electron-donating in resonance. In phenols, the acid-strengthening effect of groups decreases in the order:

$$m\text{-}CH_3S \sim p\text{-}CH_3S > m\text{-}CH_3O > H > p\text{-}CH_3O$$

Both sulfur and oxygen inductively remove electron density from the phenolate group. In phenols, however, in contrast to the benzoic acids, the methylmercapto group is not electron-donating by resonance and may even be slightly electron-accepting: if the inductive effect is weaker in the para position than it is in the meta, then a resonance electron-accepting effect for the p-CH_3S group must be postulated. This effect is small, however, and these data cannot be considered strong support for the postulation of an electron-accepting resonance effect for the methylmercapto group through the use of the *d* orbitals of sulfur.

3-2B. Sulfone Sulfur. The sulfone group also stabilizes a neighboring carbanion. In this case, the effect is probably due partially to induction

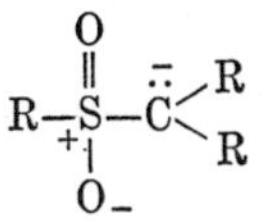

$$R-\overset{O}{\underset{O^-}{\overset{\|}{\underset{|}{S^+}}}}-\ddot{C}{<}^{R}_{R}$$

and partially to resonance forms which place more than 8 electrons around sulfur

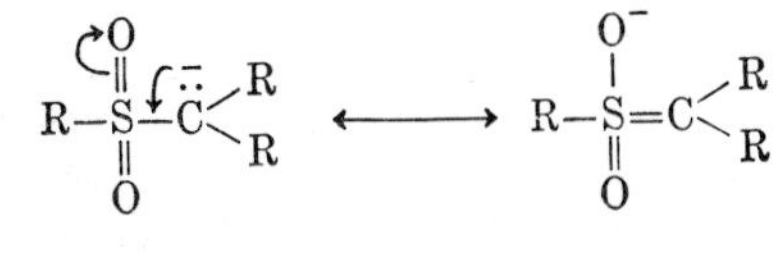

$$R-\overset{O}{\underset{O}{\overset{\|}{\underset{\|}{S}}}}-\ddot{C}{<}^{R}_{R} \longleftrightarrow R-\overset{O^-}{\underset{O}{\overset{|}{\underset{\|}{S}}}}=C{<}^{R}_{R}$$

The sulfone group is a strong electron-withdrawing group, and polysulfones are strong acids. Thus tris-(ethylsulfonyl)methane, (3-17), is about as strong an acid as hydrogen chloride (327, 920, 921).

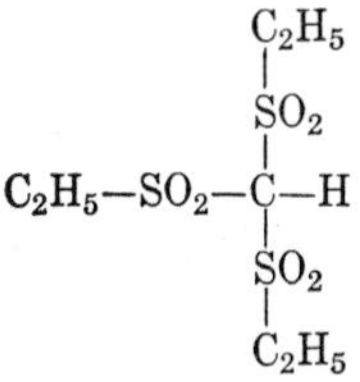

$$C_2H_5-SO_2-\overset{\overset{C_2H_5}{|}}{\underset{\underset{C_2H_5}{|}}{\overset{SO_2}{\underset{SO_2}{\overset{|}{\underset{|}{C}}}}}}-H \qquad (3\text{-}17)$$

Shriner (976) has shown that dibenzyl sulfone reacts with sodium or sodium ethoxide and is slightly soluble in 10% aqueous sodium hydroxide. The sulfoxide group is less effective than is a sulfone in stabilizing an adjacent carbanion. For example, dibenzyl sulfoxide does not react with ethoxide ion. Similarly, neither dibenzoylmethane nor bis-(phenylsulfinyl)methane, (3-18), is soluble in 10% aqueous sodium hydroxide,

$$C_6H_5\overset{O}{\overset{\|}{C}}—CH_2—\overset{O}{\overset{\|}{C}}—C_6H_5 \qquad C_6H_5—\overset{O}{\overset{\|}{S}}—CH_2—\overset{O}{\overset{\|}{S}}—C_6H_5 \tag{3-18}$$

but bis-(phenylsulfonyl)methane, (3-19), is a moderately strong acid

$$C_6H_5—SO_2—CH_2—SO_2—C_6H_5 \tag{3-19}$$

and is soluble. Dimethyl sulfone exchanges hydrogens for deuterium (562), and with a lower energy of activation than is required for the trimethylsulfonium ion. Pearson and Dillon (843) have measured the pK_a of dimethyl sulfone and found it to be 23; however, Dessy (317, 318) finds that it exchanges hydrogens with solvent 230 times *slower* than does fluorene, which has a pK_a of 25 (737, 1020).

Truce and Knospe (1085) have shown that a sulfone is effective in activating a methylene group for an aldol condensation.

$$C_6H_5—CO_2C_2H_5 + CH_3—SO_2—C_6H_5 \xrightarrow{NaOC_2H_5} \underset{28\%}{C_6H_5—\overset{O}{\overset{\|}{C}}—CH_2—SO_2—C_6H_5} \tag{3-20}$$

$$C_6H_5—CO_2C_2H_5 + CH_3—SO_2—CH_3 \xrightarrow{Na} \underset{44\%}{C_6H_5—\overset{O}{\overset{\|}{C}}—CH_2—SO_2—CH_3} \tag{3-21}$$

In liquid ammonia, benzyl chloride can be condensed with dibenzyl sulfone (549).

$$C_6H_5—CH_2—SO_2—CH_2—C_6H_5 \xrightarrow[KNH_2,\ NH_3]{C_6H_5—CH_2Cl} C_6H_5—\underset{}{\overset{CH_2—C_6H_5}{\overset{|}{C}H}}—SO_2—CH_2—C_6H_5$$

$$+\ C_6H_5—\overset{CH_2—C_6H_5}{\overset{|}{C}H}—SO_2—\overset{CH_2—C_6H_5}{\overset{|}{C}H}—C_6H_5$$

Sulfone groups activate a double bond to Michael addition (648).

$$C_6H_5—CH{=}CH—SO_2Ar + CH_2(CO_2C_2H_5)_2 \xrightarrow[C_6H_6]{Na}$$

$$C_6H_5—\underset{CH(CO_2C_2H_5)_2}{\underset{|}{C}H}—CH_2—SO_2Ar \tag{3-22}$$

Under basic catalysis, double bonds migrate to be adjacent to sulfones (603). Thus allyl benzyl sulfone is converted to propenyl benzyl sulfone (53). Another example is the equilibrium below (146).

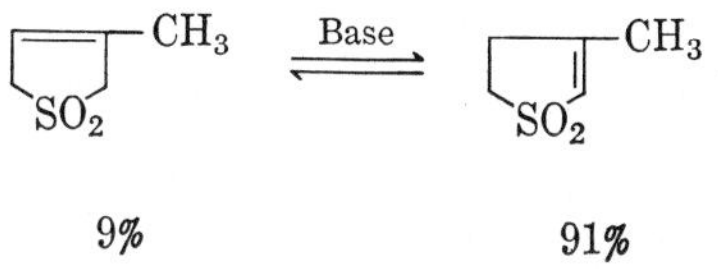

$$\text{3-methyl-3-sulfolene } (9\%) \underset{}{\overset{\text{Base}}{\rightleftharpoons}} \text{3-methyl-2-sulfolene } (91\%) \tag{3-23}$$

Table 3-5 cites data on the ability of a methylsulfonyl group to increase the acidity of benzoic acids, phenols, thiophenols, and anilinium salts. In all cases, acidity decreases in the order:

$$p\text{-}CH_3\text{—}SO_2\text{—} > m\text{-}CH_3\text{—}SO_2\text{—} > H$$

The m-CH_3—SO_2 group is electron-accepting; this is an inductive effect. The para group is even more electron-accepting, and this additional contribution must be ascribed to an electron-withdrawing resonance effect. As pointed out by Bordwell and Andersen (154), the para sulfonyl group is more acid strengthening relative to the meta to an extent which depends on the substrate examined. (This effect is also observed, but in a less pronounced manner, with the methylmercapto group; see the preceding section.) The para sulfonyl compound is more acidic than the meta by 0.10 pK units in benzoic acids, 0.31 units in thiophenols, 1.20 units in anilinium compounds, and 1.50 units in phenols. Thus the resonance electron-accepting role of the methylsulfonyl group is strongest in phenols and weakest in benzoic acids:

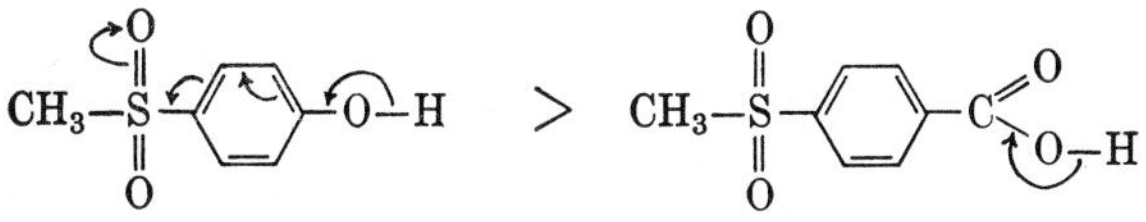

$$CH_3\text{—}SO_2\text{—}C_6H_4\text{—}O\text{—}H > CH_3\text{—}SO_2\text{—}C_6H_4\text{—}C(=O)\text{—}O\text{—}H$$

Such a variation in the electron-accepting ability of a group when the group para to it is varied is most likely a resonance effect, and this resonance can be extended to the sulfur atom if the use of d orbitals is allowed.

A number of other reactions and structures of sulfones have been rationalized by using the electron-withdrawing power and d orbitals of the sulfone group (29, 63, 153, 406, 407, 554, 659). Calculations based on group dipole moments indicate that the sulfone group is electron-attracting (276, 527, 528, 897).

Koch and Moffitt (645) have shown that a molecular orbital treatment of the sulfone group rationalizes some of these data.

3-2C. Comparison of Sulfone and Thiol Sulfur. The sulfone group is more effective in stabilizing an adjacent carbanion than is a mercapto group (158). Bonner (151) has shown that optically active 2-phenylmercaptophenylacetamide is racemized when oxidized to the sulfone. Presumably the optically active sulfone is formed and then rapidly racemizes through loss of its active hydrogen.

$$d\text{-}C_6H_5-S-\underset{\underset{CONH_2}{|}}{\overset{\overset{C_6H_5}{|}}{C}}-H \xrightarrow[100^\circ C,\ H_2O_2,\ 1\ \text{hour}]{\text{Acetic acid}} \left[d\text{-}C_6H_5-\underset{\underset{O}{\|}}{\overset{\overset{O}{\|}}{S}}-\underset{\underset{CONH_2}{|}}{\overset{\overset{C_6H_5}{|}}{C}}-H \right] \tag{3-24}$$

$$\rightleftharpoons$$

$$d,l\text{-}C_6H_5-\underset{\underset{O}{\|}}{\overset{\overset{O}{\|}}{S}}-\underset{\underset{CONH_2}{|}}{\overset{\overset{C_6H_5}{|}}{C}}-H \longleftarrow C_6H_5-\underset{\underset{O}{\|}}{\overset{\overset{O}{\|}}{S}}-\underset{\underset{CONH_2}{|}}{\overset{\overset{C_6H_5}{|}}{C^-}} + H^+ \tag{3-25}$$

The scheme shown above was not conclusively proved, since unoxidized mercaptan was not isolated from the reaction mixture and shown to retain its optical activity. However, the more rapid racemization of sulfone relative to mercaptan is in accord with the observation (151, 852) that optically active benzenesulfonylphenylacetic acid racemizes on recrystallization whereas the above mercaptans are optically stable to recrystallization.

A similar example was reported by Kipping (636). The monosulfone below can be resolved:

$$\underset{\text{Optically active}}{p\text{-}HO_2C-C_6H_4-\underset{\underset{O}{\|}}{\overset{\overset{O}{\|}}{S}}-\underset{\underset{H}{|}}{\overset{\overset{CH_3}{|}}{C}}-S-C_6H_5} \xrightarrow{[O]} \underset{\text{Racemizes}}{p\text{-}HO_2C-C_6H_4-\underset{\underset{O}{\|}}{\overset{\overset{O}{\|}}{S}}-\underset{\underset{H}{|}}{\overset{\overset{CH_3}{|}}{C}}-\underset{\underset{O}{\|}}{\overset{\overset{O}{\|}}{S}}-C_6H_5} \tag{3-26}$$

However, it is converted by oxidation to a disulfone which cannot be resolved. Roberts and Cheng (896) have found the oxidation of an optically active sulfide to the sulfone in a cyclic system also produces very rapid racemization.

An example of greater reactivity of a sulfone relative to a sulfide has been reported by Stirling (1014). He examined the reaction of the following phenyl ethers with ethoxide ion.

$$p\text{-}CH_3—C_6H_4—S—CH_2—CH_2—OC_6H_5 \xrightarrow[NaOC_2H_5, 80°C]{0.5\text{ hr., }10\%} \text{No reaction}$$

$$p\text{-}CH_3—C_6H_4—\overset{O}{\underset{O}{\overset{\|}{\underset{\|}{S}}}}—CH_2—CH_2—OC_6H_5 \xrightarrow[\text{conditions}]{\text{Same}} \underset{91\%}{p\text{-}CH_3—C_6H_4—CH_2—CH_2—OC_2H_5}$$

The mechanism is very likely a series of equilibria, displaced to the right by excess ethanol.

$$Ar—SO_2—CH_2—CH_2—OC_6H_5 \overset{C_2H_5O^-}{\rightleftharpoons}$$

$$Ar—SO_2—\bar{C}H—CH_2—OC_6H_5 \rightleftharpoons Ar—SO_2CH{=}CH_2 + C_6H_5O^-$$

$$Ar—SO_2—CH{=}CH_2 \overset{C_2H_5O^-}{\rightleftharpoons} Ar—SO_2—\bar{C}H—CH_2—OC_2H_5 \rightleftharpoons$$
$$Ar—SO_2—CH_2—CH_2—OC_2H_5$$

The sulfone reacts faster than the sulfide because its carbanion is more stable.

3-2D. Stabilization of Species Containing an Odd Electron. An odd electron is delocalized by a neighboring mercapto or sulfone group just as is an electron pair. The classical evidence that a mercapto group stabilizes an adjacent odd electron was discovered by Price and Zomlefer in 1950 (871). A vinyl sulfide undergoes free radical copolymerization with styrene faster than does a vinyl ether. Thus an α sulfur stabilizes a radical more than does an α oxygen.

$$M\cdot \xrightarrow{RS—CH{=}CH_2,\text{ fast}} M—CH_2—\overset{RS}{\underset{H}{\overset{|}{\underset{|}{C}}}}\cdot \qquad (3\text{-}27)$$

$$M\cdot \xrightarrow{RO—CH{=}CH_2,\text{ slow}} M—CH_2—\overset{RO}{\underset{H}{\overset{|}{\underset{|}{C}}}}\cdot \qquad (3\text{-}28)$$

Alfrey, Price, and coworkers (17, 18) have treated the reactivity of a monomer in copolymerization reactions as being separable into two factors: polar effects, measured by ϵ, and resonance stabilization of the radical produced, measured by Q. They assume values for Q and ϵ for styrene, and calculate values for other monomers by applying simultaneous equations to copolymerization kinetic studies. The equations are:

$$r_1 = \frac{k_{12}}{k_{11}} = \frac{Q_1}{Q_2} e^{-\epsilon_1(\epsilon_1 - \epsilon_2)}$$

$$r_2 = \frac{k_{22}}{k_{21}} = \frac{Q_2}{Q_1} e^{-\epsilon_2(\epsilon_2 - \epsilon_1)}$$

where k_{ij} = the rate constant for the attack on monomer j by a growing polymer which ends in monomer i

ϵ_i = the polar constant for monomer i

Q_i = the resonance constant for monomer i

Vinyl sulfide monomers are found to have a large Q of about 0.3 (17, 871, 956). This indicates that vinyl sulfides are reactive monomers because of resonance stabilization of the transition state (17). Divinylsulfide is an even more reactive monomer than is an alkyl vinyl sulfide and has an even higher Q value (957). The sulfonate group apparently does not appreciably stabilize a radical since butyl vinyl sulfonate is not a reactive monomer (823).

An isomerization of a double bond into conjugation with a sulfone group under irradiation has been reported (54).

R Hg arc R
SO_2 SO_2

R = methyl or *t*-butyl

The necessity for irradiation is somewhat in doubt since 1 g potassium hydroxide per gram of substrate was present.

3-2E. Stereochemistry. The requirement of coplanarity in order for resonance to occur is less severe if *d* orbitals are involved. Resonance may occur using *d* hybrid orbitals in compounds that are not planar (261, 411, 626, 639–641, 644, 806–808). Thus Doering and Hoffmann (326) found that the bicyclo-(2,2,1)-heptane-1-sulfonium ion exchanges hydrogens for deuterium.

S^+ ⇌ S^+ + H^+ (3-29)
H H H

Orbital overlap has been postulated to occur even though the sulfur is at a bridgehead. Doering and Levy (327) have shown that the bicyclic trisulfone below is a strong acid with a pK of 3.30, and that the acidic hydrogen is the one at the bridgehead.

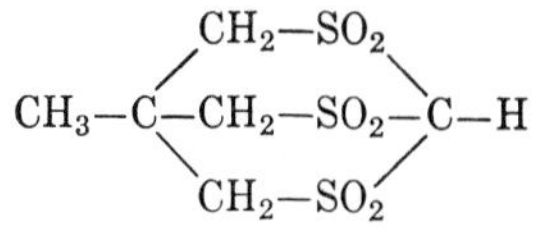

$$CH_3-C(-CH_2-SO_2-)_3C-H \qquad (3\text{-}30)$$

Further, this tricyclic sulfone is almost as acidic as the acyclic analogue, tris-(ethylsulfonyl)-methane, which has a variable but slightly larger pK.

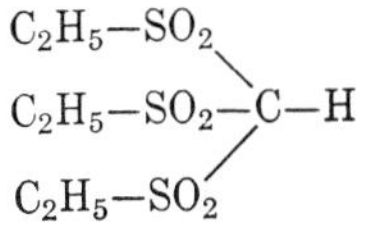

$$(C_2H_5-SO_2)_3C-H \qquad (3\text{-}31)$$

Zimmerman and Thyagarajan (1174) find that cyclopropyl phenyl sulfone has an acid dissociation constant 1.4- to 1.8-fold larger than that for isopropyl phenyl sulfone.

$$(H_3C)_2CH-SO_2-C_6H_5 \qquad (H_2C)_2CH-SO_2-C_6H_5 \qquad (3\text{-}32)$$

Again, the sulfone group stabilizes a negative charge even at a bridgehead.

These authors (1173) have also reported a study of the stereochemistry of the sulfone-stabilized carbanion based upon the direction in which model compounds protonate. They find the protonation of the conjugate base of 1-benzenesulfonyl-2-phenylcyclohexane yields from 67 to 86% of the trans isomer, depending upon the proton source and the solvent.

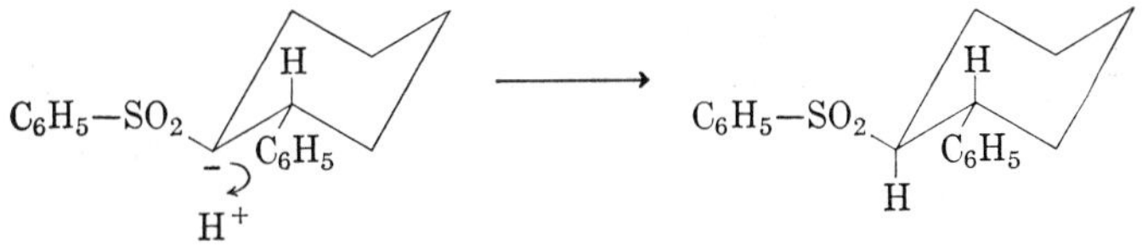

$$C_6H_5-SO_2-\bar{C}(\text{cyclohexyl, 2-H, 2-}C_6H_5) + H^+ \longrightarrow C_6H_5-SO_2-CH(\text{cyclohexyl, 2-H, 2-}C_6H_5) \qquad (3\text{-}33)$$

trans

This contrasts with the comparable enolate or *aci*-nitro carbanion, both of which give largely cis product.

$$\text{(cyclohexane, H, } C_6H_5\text{; } H^+ \curvearrowleft\ =C(-O^-)C_6H_5) \longrightarrow \text{(cyclohexane, H, H, } C_6H_5\text{; } C{=}O\text{, } C_6H_5) \text{ cis}$$

$$\text{(cyclohexane, H, } C_6H_5\text{; } H^+ \curvearrowleft\ =N(O)O^-) \longrightarrow \text{(cyclohexane, H, H, } C_6H_5\text{; } NO_2) \text{ cis} \qquad (3\text{-}34)$$

Zimmerman believes that delocalization of the electron pair is less important when the neighboring group is a sulfone than when it is a nitro or carbonyl group. Thus the sulfone-stabilized carbanion would be more tetrahedral in geometry and sp^3 in hybridization than an enolate or *aci*-nitro carbanion.

Corey and Kaiser (252) have measured both the rate of the loss of an α deuterium and the rate of racemization of optically active phenyl 2-octyl sulfone. They find that it exchanges its active hydrogen forty-one times faster than it racemizes. The rate of racemization shows no isotope effect, and therefore the cleavage of the C—H bond does not occur simultaneously with racemization. This demands the mechanism given below.

$$\text{B:} + d\text{-}C_6H_5\text{—}SO_2\text{—}\underset{CH_3}{\overset{C_6H_{13}}{C}}\text{—H} \underset{2}{\overset{1}{\rightleftharpoons}} d\text{-}C_6H_5\text{—}SO_2\text{—}\underset{CH_3}{\overset{C_6H_{13}}{C^-}} + BH^+$$

$$\qquad\qquad\qquad\qquad\qquad\qquad 3 \downarrow\uparrow 4$$

$$\text{B:} + l\text{-}C_6H_5\text{—}SO_2\text{—}\underset{CH_3}{\overset{C_6H_{13}}{C}}\text{—H} \underset{2}{\overset{1}{\rightleftharpoons}} l\text{-}C_6H_5\text{—}SO_2\text{—}\underset{CH_3}{\overset{C_6H_{13}}{C^-}} + BH^+$$

Since racemization is faster than exchange, k_2 is larger than k_3. The observed rate constant for racemization by this mechanism is equal to $(2k_1k_3)/(k_2 + 2k_3)$, where the factor of 2 corrects for two molecules racemized for each one undergoing reaction (3). The ratio of exchange to racemization is then:

$$\frac{k_1}{\left[\dfrac{2k_1k_3}{k_2+2k_3}\right]}=41$$

Therefore, k_2/k_3 is 80, and only one in 80 anions racemizes before it reverts to sulfone.

Cram, Scott, and Nielsen (264a) have studied this system also. Sulfone-stabilized carbanions are the only type yet discovered by Cram and his students which react with acids to give products with retention of configuration, rather than racemization or inversion. Cram favors an explanation for this in which the carbanion retains sp^3 hybridization and asymmetry, but the normal rate of inversion of the anion is reduced by overlap of the sp^3 orbital with the *d* orbitals on the adjacent sulfur. This explanation predicts that the stabilization of the carbanion by an adjacent sulfur would occur even at a bridgehead. These workers find that the extent of retention of configuration varies with the solvent used, so some asymmetric solvation occurs also. In some systems the amount of stereospecificity observed is striking indeed. For example, in dimethyl sulfoxide as solvent and potassium *t*-butoxide as base, hydrogen exchange occurs 1,980 times faster than racemization. Thus most protonation of the anion of phenyl 2-octyl sulfone occurs with retention.

An x-ray investigation by Lynton and Cox (713) has shown that thianthrene is not planar. The resonance energy of this molecule is not known; presumably the two benzene rings could interact even though they are not coplanar.

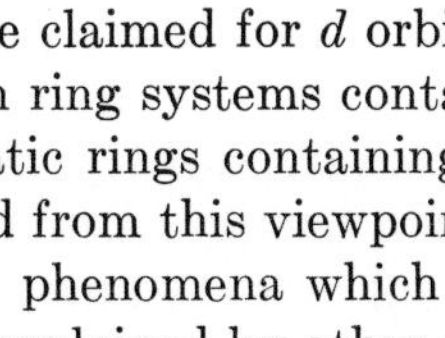

128°
S
1.76A
S

An interesting consequence claimed for *d* orbital hybridization is that aromaticity may be found in ring systems containing eight, rather than six, electrons (261). Aromatic rings containing six electrons do occur; thiophene has been examined from this viewpoint (660, 720, 940).

3-2F. Conclusion. The phenomena which have been explained by use of *d* orbitals also can be explained by other approaches; for example, no-bond resonance.

$$-\ddot{\underset{..}{S}}-\ddot{\underset{..}{S}}-\ddot{\underset{..}{S}}- \longleftrightarrow -\overset{-}{\ddot{\underset{..}{S}}}:\ \ddot{\underset{..}{S}}=\overset{+}{\underset{..}{S}}-$$

This latter explanation preserves the octet about each atom but has no other advantage. The most reasonable view is that hybrid orbitals are an extremely useful conceptual device, just as is resonance (page 219 of ref. 256). Although some of the data discussed above do not require the use of *d* orbitals, they can be most conveniently rationalized using this concept. Further, the concept has a firm theoretical basis. It should be employed, therefore, but with the reservation that it is a working hypothesis.

3-3. Homolytic Scission of the S—S Bond

Two types of homolytic scission are known: unimolecular scission, e.g.,

$$\text{RS—SR}' \xrightarrow{\text{Heat or light}} \text{RS}\cdot + \text{R}'\text{S}\cdot \tag{3-35}$$

and bimolecular, radical displacement reactions, e.g.,

$$\text{RS—SR}' + \text{R}''\cdot \rightarrow \text{RS—R}'' + \text{R}'\text{S}\cdot \tag{3-36}$$

$$\text{RS—SR}' + \text{R}''\text{—S}\cdot \rightarrow \text{RS—SR}'' + \text{R}'\text{S}\cdot \tag{3-37}$$

Unimolecular scission of some disulfides occurs at measurable rates at 80 to 160°. Bimolecular radical displacement reactions at S—S bonds are extremely fast, with rate constants as large as 2×10^6 sec^{-1} M^{-1} at 45° C (see Table 2-1 for example).

3-3A. Unimolecular, Thermal Homolytic Scission; Disulfides as Polymerization Initiators. Thermal homolysis of the S—S bonds in S_8 occurs in liquid sulfur and leads to the formation of polymers. This reaction has been studied in some detail, as was discussed in Sec. 2-1.

The most thorough study of the homolysis of S—S bonds has been made using disulfides as substrates. The weakest bond in disulfides is usually the S—S bond. Like the O—O bond in peroxides, disulfide bonds vary in strength, and consequently the temperature at which disulfides homolytically dissociate varies. It was originally thought that all disulfides thermally dissociate at 100 to 150° C, since many color reversibly when heated to temperatures in this range (643, 784, 973), and this reversible coloration was incorrectly attributed to the formation of stable radicals. However, Lecher (682) in 1945, Brand and Davidson (170) in 1956, and Davis and Perrin (308) in 1960 clearly showed that reversible coloration and homolytic dissociation may occur simultaneously but that they are not necessarily related phenomena. Unfortunately, these results have been erroneously interpreted as implying that ordinary disulfides do not dissociate at moderate temperatures.

Actually, there is excellent evidence that some disulfides do dissociate at 100 to 150° C. Although the S—S bond energy of alkyl disulfides is higher than the O—O bond energy of alkyl peroxides, very long-chain polysulfides have S—S bond energies comparable to peroxide bond energies, about 33 kcal (see Table 3-1). Also, certain organic disulfides have reduced S—S bond energies because of the resonance stabilization of the radicals formed upon dissociation. Thus several aryl disulfides have been shown to dissociate homolytically in boiling dioxane (101° C), and the percentage dissociation varies with ring substituents (678) in analogy with the behavior of aroyl peroxides (85, page 54 of ref. 202). Thiolnaphthoyl disulfide develops color reversibly at 100° C; although this is because of the undissociated molecule, a slow, concurrent irreversible dissociation to radicals also occurs (170). Benzothiazolyl disulfide, (3-38), behaves similarly (170, 308).

S S
C—S—S—C
N N
(3-38)

Benzothiazolyl disulfide was originally thought to be paramagnetic at 80° C (283), but recent electron spin resonance studies have shown that it is not (308, 964). A mixture of phenyl and pyridyl disulfides is converted to phenyl pyridyl disulfide by heating to 150° C, presumably by dissociation to radicals followed by a chain reaction which produces exchange (907). (For an opposite view, however, see refs. 679–682.) In all these cases, evidence supports the formation of stabilized sulfenyl radicals at 100 to 150° C.

The decomposition of the simplest disulfide, hydrogen disulfide, H_2S_2, has been examined. The products are hydrogen sulfide and sulfur, in analogy with the decomposition of hydrogen peroxide to water and oxygen. Fehér and Weber (403) have studied the reaction at 25 to 50° C where it is first order in H_2S_2, and they believe it is an ionic chain reaction. Tinyakova, Khrennikova, and Dolgoplosk (1052) find it is inhibited by nitric oxide at 70° C, and they postulate essentially the same chain mechanism but involving radicals instead of ions. These workers also studied the reaction of hydrogen disulfide with olefins to produce mono-, di-, and polysulfides (1052).

Some disulfides dissociate to form radicals which are capable of initiating the polymerization of certain monomers. Ferington and Tobolsky (416) have shown that tetramethylthiuram disulfide

$$(CH_3)_2N-\overset{\displaystyle S}{\overset{\|}{C}}-S-S-\overset{\displaystyle S}{\overset{\|}{C}}-N(CH_3)_2$$

is almost as efficient an initiator of methyl methacrylate at 70° C as is benzoyl peroxide. At higher concentrations it acts as a retarder and chain transfer agent; both these effects are presumably due to radical displacements on the S—S bond (see Sec. 3-3C). Tetramethylthiuram monosulfide is about as efficient an initiator as is the disulfide, but it is not a retarder (417). Ferington and Tobolsky suggest that the monosulfide may dissociate by cleavage of two bonds to form CS_2 in the primary act (417). The tetrasulfide acts only as a retarder (417), perhaps because of decomposition to give the disulfide and sulfur, a known retarder. Tetramethylthiuram disulfide is a common vulcanization accelerator; a comparison of its efficiency in vulcanization and in polymerization suggests that the former is also a radical process with this accelerator (417).

The ability of a disulfide to initiate a vinyl polymerization is conclusive evidence that dissociation to radicals occurs; however, the inability to effect polymerization of a *particular* monomer does not prove the absence of dissociation. Tetramethylthiuram monosulfide is an excellent initiator for the polymerization of methyl methacrylate at 70° C (416, 417); however, it does not cause the polymerization of styrene at 60, 80, or 120° C in the dark (819). Kern (610) has shown that tetramethylthiuram monosulfide and benzothiazolyl disulfide initiate the polymerization of acrylonitrile, methacrylonitrile, methyl acrylate, and methyl methacrylate but not of styrene or vinyl acetate at 95° C in the dark. Otsu (819) found that none of the following compounds initiates the polymerization of styrene at 60, 80, or 120° C in the dark: phenyl di-, tri-, or tetrasulfide, benzyl disulfide, benzoyl disulfide, or benzothiazolyl disulfide. This was taken as evidence that none of these compounds dissociates at 120° C. Unfortunately, Otsu did not examine the effect of these disulfides on other monomers; their failure to polymerize styrene does not establish the absence of dissociation, since even tetramethylthiuram monosulfide is ineffectual. Kharasch, Nudenberg, and Meltzer (613) found that anisyl disulfide does not initiate the emulsion copolymerization of styrene and butadiene in the dark at 50° C; they did not examine other monomers or higher temperatures.

Examination of the reactions of sulfur and thiols shows why disulfides initiate the polymerization of methyl methacrylate but not of vinyl acetate or styrene. Table 3-6 gives data demonstrating that the radical from poly(vinyl acetate) or the polystyryl radical attacks sulfur faster than it does its own monomer. This is not true of the poly(methyl methacrylyl) radical, which prefers to polymerize even in the presence of sulfur. This is probably a polar effect on these radical reactions (1116). The electron-poor poly(methyl methacrylyl) radical attacks sulfur relatively slowly; this sensitive test shows that the S—S bond is more susceptible to nucleophilic attack than to electrophilic attack. The effect is very large: the radical from poly(vinyl acetate) attacks sulfur 2×10^4 times faster than does the poly(methyl methacrylyl) radical (Table 3-6 and ref. 624). Disulfides should show this same reactivity: radical attack on the disulfide S—S bond is probably much faster for the radical from poly(vinyl acetate) than for the poly(methyl methacrylyl) radical. This rapid attack on disulfides by poly(vinyl acetate) and polystyryl radicals produces chain transfer with initiator, absence of high polymer, and destruction of the disulfide initiator. Furthermore, side reactions of the disulfides could form thiols; and polystyryl radicals undergo chain transfer with thiols thirty-three times faster than do poly(methyl methacrylyl) radicals, again because of a polar effect (page 319 of ref. 1116), and again limiting the formation of high polymer.

Table 3-6
Rate constants for the attack of polymeric radicals on sulfur

Polymeric radical from	k_s/k_p[a]	k_p[b]	k_s[c]	°C	References
Vinyl acetate	470	1,550	7.3×10^5	45	87
Styrene	*c.* 100	310	*c.* 3×10^4	81	94
Methyl methacrylate	0.075	505	3.8×10^1	44.1	624

[a] Ratio of the rate of attack of the growing polymer radical on sulfur, k_s, relative to attack on its own monomer to give chain propagation, k_p. This ratio is the "inhibitor constant" for sulfur (pp. 170–176 of ref. 1116).

[b] Values of the propagation rate constant at 45° C were interpolated from p. 95 of ref. 1116. Units for all rate constants are $sec^{-1} M^{-1}$.

[c] Rate constant for the attack of the polymeric radical on S_8, calculated from the previous columns, in $sec^{-1} M^{-1}$.

Most of the disulfides discussed above give radicals with some resonance stabilization; but Birch, Cullum, and Dean (131) find that even methyl ethyl disulfide polymerizes acrylonitrile in the dark at 150° C, but not at 100° C. Thus disulfides do initiate polymerization of some monomers at 100 to 150° C, and they therefore must undergo homolytic dissociation.

3-3B. Photolytic Dissociation. Irradiation of solutions of sulfur in benzene, toluene, carbon tetrachloride, or carbon disulfide (352) opens the S_8 ring to produce a linear diradical. These diradicals undergo a complex series of propagation and transfer reactions on S_8, and eventually terminate to form sulfur polymers, S_6, regenerated S_8, and perhaps other species (89). Sulfur rings are photolytically cleaved even in the solid state (323).

Under photolytic conditions, most disulfides initiate vinyl polymerizations at room temperature (417, 610, 613, 678, 819). Interestingly, even disulfides which do not thermally initiate the polymerization of styrene at 120° C are effective at 25° C with the use of light and are much more efficient than is benzoyl peroxide (819).

Lyons (714) has studied the quantum yield for several acyclic disulfides. He finds the value for phenyl and *o*- and *p*-tolyl disulfide to be 0.046 in 3% aqueous hydrochloric acid or in organic solvents. Cystine gives a quantum yield of 0.020 in aqueous hydrochloric acid. Lyons reports that the quantum yield is relatively insensitive to the nature of the solvent, the particular disulfide used, or the disulfide concentration. He suggests the following mechanism:

$$\mathrm{RSSR} \rightarrow [\mathrm{RSSR}]^* \tag{3-39}$$

$$[\mathrm{RSSR}]^* + \mathrm{W} \rightarrow \mathrm{RSSR} \tag{3-40}$$

$$[\mathrm{RSSR}]^* \rightarrow 2\mathrm{RS}\cdot \tag{3-41}$$

$$\mathrm{RS}\cdot + \text{solvent} \rightarrow \mathrm{RSH} \tag{3-42}$$

where [RSSR]* is a photoexcited molecule and W is an inert body or a wall. The low quantum yield implies that 44 activated molecules are deactivated by collisions before one dissociates to form a pair of thiyl radicals.

Whitney and Calvin (1150) have become interested in the photolysis of cyclic disulfides, which they believe to be an important reaction in biochemistry. They have shown that the photolysis of 6,8-thioctic acid, (3-43), and of trimethylene disulfide has a quantum yield of about unity under a variety of conditions.

$$\begin{array}{l} \mathrm{CH_2{-}CH_2{-}CH{-}(CH_2)_4{-}CO_2H} \\ \;| \qquad\qquad\;\; | \\ \mathrm{S}\text{———————}\mathrm{S} \end{array} \tag{3-43}$$

6,8-Thioctic acid

Presumably these cyclic disulfides have a larger quantum yield because of thermochemical strain in the ring (120–123, 460, 468, 948). (See the discussion on page 26.)

Walling and Rabinowitz (1126) investigated the photolysis of isobutyl disulfide in cumene. The reaction is not simple, but the chief products are isobutyl mercaptan and dicumyl. This is a dehydrogenation by a photochemically produced thiyl radical, and such reactions have been reported previously. For example, photolysis of benzothiazolyl disulfide in Tetralin or cyclohexene produces naphthalene or benzene, respectively (787, 791). Photolysis of thiophenol converts benzhydrol to benzopinacol (788).

3-3C. Radical Displacement Reactions on Disulfides and Peroxides. Disulfides as Chain Transfer Agents in Polymerization. (1) *Background.* The radical displacement reaction occupies an important position in chemistry and has fascinated both theoretical and organic chemists for many years. However, very few unambiguous examples of S_H2 reactions* are known at multivalent atoms, other than those which occur on sulfur or oxygen.† Radical displacement reactions on univalent atoms, i.e., hydrogen or halogen abstraction reactions, are well known.

$$R\cdot + R'H \rightarrow RH + R'\cdot \qquad (3\text{-}44)$$

However, electronic and stereochemical factors can be varied to only a limited extent in such reactions; therefore the bimolecular radical displacement reaction has been studied much less than its ionic counterpart, the S_N2 reaction. For this reason, the structure of the transition state for S_H2 reactions is unknown. The transition state could be the result of backside attack, as in an S_N2 Walden inversion, or attack from the side or the front.

A number of attempts have been made to calculate the geometry of the S_H2 reaction from theoretical considerations, and the conclusions from these calculations have been summarized by Glasstone, Laidler, and Eyring (pp. 88, 91, 108, 222 of ref. 508*a*). There is general agreement that the reaction of hydrogen atoms with hydrogen molecules involves a linear transition state (357, 967*a*). However, there is no agreement on the shape of the transition state when *p* electrons are present. The transition state for the reaction of chlorine atoms with hydrogen, for example, could be either linear or triangular (130*a*, 130*b*, 714*a*, 860*a*).

Attempts to determine experimentally the geometry of the transition state for S_H2 reactions have met with difficulties. Radical displacements at carbon would be ideal for studying the S_H2 reaction, but completely unambiguous examples are not known. Some limited study has been reported on organometallic substrates (887) and on epoxides (526*a*). However, the reaction studied most thoroughly is that between iodine and alkyl iodides (242, 812, 870), and recently Noyes and his students (189*a*) have reported an elegant reexamination of this reaction. They measured the exchange of radioiodine with a series of alkyl iodides in the liquid phase at 160° C, and find the following relative rates:‡ methyl

* Eliel has suggested the terms S_H1 and S_H2 for homolytic substitution reactions by analogy with S_N1 and S_N2. (See p. 142 of ref. 347.)

† A number of examples of radical reactions have been reported in which the radical adds to an unsaturated molecule, and the adduct loses a different fragment by β-scission (125, 541, 859, 1076). This is a two-step substitution reaction and does not involve an S_H2 mechanism.

‡ Noyes finds about the same rate pattern in the presence or in the absence of oxygen. He reasons that free alkyl radicals, if present, would be trapped by oxygen, and a direct displacement is therefore more likely in its presence. The data given here are those obtained in the presence of oxygen.

iodide 1.0, propyl iodide 11, isopropyl iodide 29, neopentyl iodide 2.4. Noyes believes that these exchange reactions result from direct backside attack by iodine atoms on the alkyl iodides, and have a transition state much like that for the S_N2 reaction of iodide ion with alkyl halides. However, these data indicate that methyl iodide is the slowest of the group, and that even neopentyl iodide is faster. If the attack were on carbon, the sequence should be methyl > *i*-propyl > neopentyl. The reverse trend which is observed may result from attack on the iodine. Noyes is unable to exclude this possibility, even in the presence of oxygen, owing to experimental difficulties.

Radical reactions on both sulfur and oxygen are well substantiated. In view of the difficulties in finding a suitable system in which radical attack occurs on carbon, the study of radical displacement reactions at S—S and O—O bonds assumes special interest. This is particularly true since S_N2 *ionic* reactions on sulfur appear to involve the same stereochemistry and backside attack as does the Walden inversion on carbon (see pages 62 to 64).

(2) *Studies of S_H2 Reactions at Sulfur and Oxygen.* The first study of an S_H2 reaction on an O—O or S—S bond was that on benzoyl peroxide. It was suggested as early as 1940 by Brown (184), and subsequently by a large number of other workers, that benzoyl peroxide decomposes in some solvents by a mechanism which involves two simultaneous reactions, one of the first order and one of a higher order (73, 74, 90–92, 222, 223, 805). The consensus was that this higher order, "induced" decomposition was the result of radical displacement reactions (page 137 of ref. 422, 1028). The detailed mechanism, however, was unknown. In 1946, Cass (222) reported that the products of the decomposition of benzoyl peroxide in ether solution are benzoic acid and 1-ethoxyethyl benzoate. Ether is one of the solvents in which the bimolecular, induced decomposition of benzoyl peroxide is particularly fast (92). The products suggest that this bimolecular reaction is the result of an attack on the peroxide by a radical derived from the ether solvent.

$$C_2H_5{-}O{-}\overset{\displaystyle CH_3}{\underset{\displaystyle H}{C}}\cdot + C_6H_5{-}\overset{\displaystyle O}{\overset{\|}{C}}{-}O{-}O{-}\overset{\displaystyle O}{\overset{\|}{C}}{-}C_6H_5 \longrightarrow C_2H_5{-}O{-}\overset{\displaystyle CH_3}{\underset{\displaystyle H}{C}}{-}O{-}\overset{\displaystyle O}{\overset{\|}{C}}{-}C_6H_5 + C_6H_5{-}CO_2\cdot \qquad (3\text{-}45)$$

This attack could occur either by a displacement on the peroxide bond, or by an addition of the radical to the carbonyl oxygen and subsequent

β scission of the O—O bond. The latter possibility is the mechanism that is realized when the unsaturation is olefinic rather than a carbonyl group, and therefore might be favored a priori. However, Drew and Martin in 1959 (340) and Denney and Feig in 1960 (316) have independently reexamined this reaction and they find that the mechanism actually is a direct displacement. They used O^{18}-labeled benzoyl peroxide and obtained ester labeled with O^{18} specifically in the carbonyl function.

$$C_2H_5O-\overset{\overset{\large CH_3}{|}}{\underset{\underset{\large H}{|}}{C}}\cdot + C_6H_5\overset{\overset{\large O^*}{\|}}{C}-O-O-\overset{\overset{\large O^*}{\|}}{C}C_6H_5 \longrightarrow C_2H_5O-\overset{\overset{\large CH_3}{|}}{\underset{\underset{\large H}{|}}{C}}-O-\overset{\overset{\large O^*}{\|}}{C}-C_6H_5 + C_6H_5CO_2^*\cdot \qquad (3\text{-}46)$$

$$C_6H_5CO_2^*\cdot + C_2H_5-O-C_2H_5 \longrightarrow C_6H_5CO_2^*H + C_2H_5O-\overset{\overset{\large CH_3}{|}}{\underset{\underset{\large H}{|}}{C}}\cdot \qquad (3\text{-}47)$$

Doering, Okamoto, and Krauch (328) have demonstrated that the triphenylmethyl radical displaces on benzoyl peroxide by the same mechanism.

$$(C_6H_5)_3C\cdot + C_6H_5-\overset{\overset{\large O^*}{\|}}{C}-O-O-\overset{\overset{\large O^*}{\|}}{C}-C_6H_5 \longrightarrow (C_6H_5)_3C-O-\overset{\overset{\large O^*}{\|}}{C}-C_6H_5 + C_6H_5CO_2^*\cdot$$

They isolate an 83% yield of the trityl benzoate and conclude from assay of the O^{18} that all the attack occurred on the O—O bond. Similarly, these workers have found that the same mechanism applies to the attack on benzoyl peroxide by the 2-cyclohexenyl radical.

t-Butyl peroxide also has been examined as a possible substrate for S_H2 reactions. *t*-Butyl peroxide decomposes in the gas phase by a reaction that is exclusively first order (881). However, the oxygen atoms of this peroxide are sterically hindered to bimolecular attack to the same degree as is a neopentyl carbon atom. Neat liquid *t*-butyl peroxide at 100° C reacts to give isobutylene oxide as a major product (111). Presumably this product is formed by an intramolecular displacement that is not sterically hindered.

$$t\text{-}C_4H_9O{-}OC_4H_9\text{-}t \longrightarrow 2\,t\text{-}C_4H_9O\cdot \tag{3-48}$$

$$t\text{-}C_4H_9O\cdot + t\text{-}C_4H_9O{-}OC_4H_9\text{-}t \longrightarrow t\text{-}C_4H_9O{-}O{-}\underset{\substack{|\\ CH_3}}{\overset{\substack{\cdot CH_2\\ |}}{C}}{-}CH_3 + t\text{-}C_4H_9OH \tag{3-49}$$

$$t\text{-}C_4H_9O{-}O{-}\underset{\substack{|\\ CH_3}}{\overset{\substack{\cdot CH_2\\ |}}{C}}{-}CH_3 \longrightarrow t\text{-}C_4H_9O\cdot + \overset{CH_2}{\overbrace{O{-}C}}{-}CH_3\ (\text{C bearing } CH_3) \tag{3-50}$$

The *t*-butoxy radical also decomposes to form acetone and methyl radicals. Conceivably, these methyl radicals could displace on the O—O bond of the peroxide, leading to the formation of methyl *t*-butyl ether. Such an ether has been found in only one case (880*a*). Methyl *t*-amyl peroxide decomposes in the gas phase at 195° C to give an 8% yield of methyl ethyl ether. The peroxide decomposes to form ethyl radicals, and the ether could arise from displacement on the peroxide oxygen by ethyl radicals.

$$C_2H_5\cdot + CH_3O{-}OC_5H_{11} \rightarrow C_2H_5OCH_3 + C_5H_{11}O\cdot$$

It could also result from a termination reaction between the ethyl radicals and methoxy radicals produced from the decomposition of the peroxide.

De La Mare and Rust (314) have postulated an intramolecular displacement on the O—O bond of 2-methyl-2-hexyl peroxide to explain the formation of furans and other cyclic ethers.

$$\text{(ring: } (H_3C)(CH_3)C{-}H_2C{-}H_2C{-}CH(CH_3)\text{ with } \cdot O{-}O{-}C(CH_3)_2{-}C_4H_9\text{)} \longrightarrow \text{(ring: } (H_3C)(CH_3)C{-}H_2C{-}H_2C{-}CH(CH_3){-}O\text{)} + \cdot O{-}\underset{\substack{|\\ CH_3}}{\overset{\substack{CH_3\\ |}}{C}}{-}C_4H_9 \tag{3-51}$$

An intramolecular displacement by sulfur has been postulated by Bentrude and Martin (117*a*). They find that the rates of homolytic decomposition of ortho-substituted *t*-butyl perbenzoates relative to *t*-butyl perbenzoate itself are: C_6H_5S, 2×10^4; CH_3S, 1×10^4; $t\text{-}C_4H_9$, 4. The *o*-phenoxy compound shows very little rate enhancement. The large rate enhancement due to an ortho alkylmercapto group suggests that the unshared electrons on sulfur participate in the O—O bond scission.

A number of studies of S_H2 reactions on disulfides have been reported. Walling, Basedow, and Savas (1119) have found evidence for a displacement on sulfur by a carbon radical in the reactions of triethyl phosphite with disulfides.

$$R'\cdot + RS{-}SR \rightarrow R'{-}SR + RS\cdot \qquad (3\text{-}52)$$

The thiyl radical attacks S—S bonds rapidly, and mixtures of organic disulfides exchange mercapto groups under photolytic or thermal conditions (126, 138, 251, 517, 530, 540, 678, 735, 763, 904, 905, 907, 926). The mechanism is undoubtedly a chain with a long kinetic chain length.

$$RSSR \underset{\text{initiator}}{\overset{\text{Light, heat, or}}{\rightleftharpoons}} 2RS\cdot \qquad (3\text{-}53)$$

$$RS\cdot + R'SSR' \rightleftharpoons RSSR' + R'S\cdot \qquad (3\text{-}54)$$

Most of the information on S_H2 reactions of disulfides is available from studies of disulfides as chain transfer agents in polymerizations. A chain transfer agent reacts with a growing polymer radical to terminate one molecule and rapidly start another one growing. (If the growth of the next molecule is started more slowly, retardation or inhibition results.) The mechanism is thought to involve, at least for simple alkyl disulfides, a displacement at the S—S bond by the growing polymeric radical.

$$M_n\cdot + RSSR \rightarrow M_nSR + RS\cdot \qquad (3\text{-}55)$$
$$RS\cdot + nM \rightarrow RSM_n\cdot \rightarrow \text{etc.}$$

In support of the displacement mechanism for these chain transfer reactions, Tobolsky and Baysal (1054) and Stockmayer, Howard, and Clarke (1015) have shown that when the cyclic disulfide 1-oxa-4,5-dithiacycloheptane is used as a transfer agent, molecular weight is not reduced but sulfur becomes incorporated into the polymer.

$$M_n\cdot + \overset{\frown R \frown}{S{-}S} \longrightarrow M_n{-}S{-}R{-}S\cdot \qquad (3\text{-}56)$$

$$M_n{-}S{-}R{-}S\cdot + nM \longrightarrow M_n{-}S{-}R{-}S{-}M_n\cdot \xrightarrow{\text{etc.}} \qquad (3\text{-}57)$$

The former group found up to 17 sulfur atoms incorporated into each polystyrene molecule; the latter group found up to 18 sulfur atoms in vinyl acetate. Tobolsky and Baysal also showed that an open-chain alkyl disulfide, butyl disulfide, incorporated only two sulfur atoms in each polymer chain, as the mechanism requires. Pierson, Costanza, and Weinstein (853) found that aryl disulfides also incorporate just two sulfur atoms in each polymer molecule. They used disulfides with easily analyzable end groups, and they independently measured molecular weight both by viscosity and by the number of sulfide end groups per unit weight of polymer. Using these data they can calculate the number of sulfide end groups in the average polymer molecule. For example, styrene polymerized in the presence of 2-naphthyl disulfide had an ultraviolet absorption spectrum indicating that two mercaptonaphthyl end groups were incorporated per polymer molecule.

The mechanism of chain transfer when a disulfide is used as transfer agent is formulated as below:

Initiation: $$\mathrm{I} + \mathrm{M} \xrightarrow{R_i} \mathrm{M}\cdot \qquad (3\text{-}58)$$

Propagation: $$\mathrm{M}\cdot + (n-1)\mathrm{M} \xrightarrow{k_p} \mathrm{M}_n\cdot \qquad (3\text{-}59)$$

Transfer: $$\mathrm{M}_n\cdot + \mathrm{RSSR} \xrightarrow{k_{tr}} \mathrm{M}_n\mathrm{-SR} + \mathrm{RS}\cdot \qquad (3\text{-}60)$$
$$\mathrm{RS}\cdot + n\mathrm{M} \xrightarrow{\text{fast}} \mathrm{RS-M}_n\cdot \qquad (3\text{-}61)$$

Termination: $$2\mathrm{M}_n\cdot \xrightarrow{k_t} \mathrm{M}_n\mathrm{-M}_n \qquad (3\text{-}62)$$

In a polymerization reaction, the ratio of the sum of the rates of all chain-ending steps to the rate of propagation is equal to the reciprocal of the average degree of polymerization. The degree of polymerization $\bar{P}$ is the number of repeating units in the average polymer molecule. The mechanism given in Eqs. (3-58) through (3-62) therefore yields the expression in Eq. (3-63).

$$\frac{1}{\bar{P}} = \frac{k_t(\mathrm{M}_n\cdot)^2 + k_{tr}(\mathrm{M}_n\cdot)(\mathrm{RSSR})}{k_p(\mathrm{M}_n\cdot)(\mathrm{M})} \qquad (3\text{-}63)$$

By assuming a steady-state concentration in radicals, Eq. (3-63) can be simplified to Eq. (3-64),

$$\frac{1}{\bar{P}} - \frac{(k_tR_i)^{1/2}}{(2)^{1/2}k_p(\mathrm{M})} = C\frac{(\mathrm{RSSR})}{(\mathrm{M})} \qquad (3\text{-}64)$$

where the transfer constant C for the disulfide is equal to k_{tr}/k_p. The first term, $1/\bar{P}$, is measurable, and the second is a constant at constant rate of initiation and monomer concentration. Chain transfer studies are limited to very low conversions of 5 to 10% where these conditions are met. Thus, a graph of $1/\bar{P}$ versus (RSSR)/(M) has the slope C. Since k_p can be determined from independent experiments, the absolute value of the rate constant k_{tr} for attack by the polymeric radical on the

Table 3-7
Rate constants for the attack of polymeric radicals[a] on chain transfer agents containing an O—O or an S—S bond

Transfer agent[a]	°C	$C = \frac{k_{tr}}{k_p}$	$k_{tr}{}^{b,c}$	References
Methyl disulfide	60	.0094	1.36	877*a*
Propyl disulfide	60	.0023	.34	877*a*
i-Propyl disulfide	60	.00066	.096	877*a*
n-Butyl disulfide	60	.0023	.34	877*a*
i-Butyl disulfide	60	.0020	.30	877*a*
sec-Butyl disulfide	60	.00044	.064	877*a*
t-Butyl disulfide	60	.00014	.020	877*a*
Ethyl disulfide	99	.005	2.5	324
Butyl disulfide	60	.0125	1.81	1054
Butyl disulfide	99	.0068	3.4	324
sec-Butyl disulfide	50	<.005	<.5	254
t-Butyl disulfide	50	<.005	<.5	254
Hexyl disulfide	99	.010	5.0	324
Octadecyl disulfide	99	.024	12	324
Phenyl disulfide	50	.06	6	254, 853
Phenyl disulfide	99	.14	70	324
o-Tolyl disulfide	50	.25[d]	25	853
p-Tolyl disulfide	50	.11	11	853
2,6-Dimethylphenyl disulfide	50	.69	69	853
2,3,5,6-Tetramethylphenyl disulfide	50	.73	73	853
p-Ethoxyphenyl disulfide	99	.33	165	324
p-Anisyl disulfide	50	.18	18	254
p-Carboxyphenyl disulfide	50	.11	11	853
p-Carbethoxyphenyl disulfide	50	.11	11	853
Benzyl disulfide	50	.03	3	853
Benzyl disulfide	60	.01	1.5	526
Benzyl disulfide	99	.01	5	324
Benzoyl disulfide	50	<.005	<.5	254
Benzoyl disulfide	60	.0107	1.55	877*a*
Benzoyl disulfide	99	.11	55	324
p-Chlorobenzyl disulfide	50	<.005	<.5	853
2-Naphthyl disulfide	25	.17	6.6	853
2-Naphthyl disulfide	50	.19	19	853
2-Naphthyl disulfide	75	.29	66	853
o-Tolyl disulfide	25	.22	8.6	853
o-Tolyl disulfide	50	.25[c]	25	853
o-Tolyl disulfide	75	.32	72	853
Benzoyl peroxide	60	.055	8.0	526
t-Butyl peroxide	60	.0013	.18	878*b*

Table 3-7 (Continued)

Transfer agent[a]	°C	$C = \frac{k_{tr}}{k_p}$	k_{tr}[b,c]	References
Benzothiazolyl disulfide	50	2.1	214.	853
Benzothiazolyl disulfide	99	2.7	1350.	324
Tetramethylthiuram disulfide	70	.014	2.7	416
Tetramethylthiuram disulfide (MMA)	70	.1	87.	416
Butyl disulfide (VAc)	60	<1.0	$<2.3 \times 10^3$	244*a*

[a] The monomer is styrene in every case except where noted: MMA is methyl methacrylate, VAc is vinyl acetate.

[b] The values of k_p are interpolated or extrapolated from the values at 30 and 60° C chosen by Walling (p. 95 of ref. 1116). For styrene, k_p is: 39 (25° C), 49 (30° C), 85 (45° C), 102 (50° C), 145 (60° C), 195 (70° C), 225 (75° C), 300 (80° C), 395 (90° C), 500 (99° C), 515 (100° C). For methyl methacrylate, k_p at 70° C is 87.6 M^{-1} sec^{-1}; for vinyl acetate it is 2,300 at 60° C.

[c] In sec^{-1} M^{-1}.

[d] The two values given in the reference, 0.23 and 0.28, have been averaged.

disulfide can be calculated. Gregg and Mayo (524–526, 729) use thermal initiation and the equation

$$\frac{1}{\bar{P}} = \frac{1}{\bar{P}_0} + C\,\frac{(\mathrm{RSSR})}{(\mathrm{M})} \tag{3-65}$$

where $\bar{P}_0$ = the average degree of polymerization when no transfer agent is present.

These procedures were developed extensively by Gregg and Mayo (523–526, 729) and by others (203, 488). The entire field was reviewed critically in 1957 by Walling (pages 148–158 of ref. 1116), a leading worker in this area.

Table 3-7 collects transfer constants of compounds with S—S bonds and also lists the transfer constant for *t*-butyl and benzoyl peroxide. Note that agreement among various workers suggests that these values are accurate only within a factor of about 2.

The transfer constants are reported for a range of temperatures. However, since C is a ratio of rate constants for two reactions of small and somewhat similar temperature coefficients, C does not vary greatly with small changes in temperature. Pierson, Costanza, and Weinstein (853) measured the transfer constants of six disulfide transfer agents between 25 and 75° C, and C did not vary by more than 50%. Bamford and Dewar (66, 67) found that although k_{tr} for the attack of the polystyryl radical on carbon tetrachloride increased 5.6-fold from 60 to 100° C, the ratio k_{tr}/k_p increased only 2.1-fold. Similar, but slightly larger effects were found for ethylbenzene and toluene. Thus, the differing values of C reported by different workers are frequently greater than can be accounted for by temperature variations.

In this context it is well to refer to the data of Table 2-1. Note that the polystyryl radical attacks S_8 rings about 10,000 times faster than it attacks butyl disulfide. The reason for this enormous difference has not been investigated. However, it may well be at least partially steric, with bimolecular attack occurring more easily on the cyclic compound. Radicals do attack cyclic carbon compounds faster than acyclic analogues in some cases, but the effects are not nearly this large (650, 652, 653, 748, 1154).

(3) *Radical Attack on Disulfides as a Model for the S_H2 Reaction.* These chain transfer data for disulfides have been used as a model for the S_H2 reaction (877*a*). The first seven entries in Table 3-7 show that increasing the bulk of the substituent group on sulfur decreases the rate of attack on the S—S bond. In this S_H2 reaction an *i*-propyl substituent on the sulfur undergoing attack slows the rate 14-fold and a *t*-butyl substituent slows it 66-fold. In the ionic S_N2 reaction on alkyl halides, an *i*-propyl substituent on the carbon undergoing attack slows the displacement 30-fold, and a *t*-butyl slows it by 10^5.* In ionic S_N2 reactions on sulfur, an *i*-propyl substituent slows the rate by 150-fold and a *t*-butyl substituent by approximately 10^6 (see Table 3-9). Thus, ionic displacements at sulfur respond to backside hindrance to about the same extent as do those at carbon. Radical displacements at sulfur, however, do so to only a small extent. Nor does this appear to be a special feature of S—S bonds. Table 3-7 shows that peroxides are attacked by radicals at rates very similar to the analogous disulfide. Benzoyl peroxide is attacked about 5-fold faster than is benzoyl disulfide, and *t*-butyl peroxide is attacked 10-fold faster than *t*-butyl disulfide.†

It is of interest to speculate on the direction of attack of a radical on a peroxide or disulfide. Figure 3-2 shows that the dihedral angle in a disulfide is 90° and that a *p* orbital projects away from the alkyl substituents. Figure 3-4 shows three views of a generalized disulfide. The

* The compound with a *t*-butyl substituent is a neopentyl halide. One of the prominent features of the Walden inversion is the extreme unreactivity of this compound. *t*-Butyl sulfenyl compounds should be similarly unreactive toward backside attack. For data on the S_N2 reaction see the review by Streitwieser (Table 5, ref. 1019).

† The rate constant for the S_H2 reaction of *t*-butyl peroxide has been corrected for a slow, simultaneous S_H1 reaction (878*b*). Several contradictory values for transfer constants for benzoyl disulfide have been published; the value of k_{tr} for benzoyl disulfide used here is the most recent one, determined in these Laboratories (878*a*).

direction for approach to the S—S bond which is shown in Fig. 3-4*a* and 3-4*b* is virtually free from hindrance even when the alkyl groups are *t*-butyl. If the radical attacks a sulfur atom, rather than the middle of the S—S bond, then four limiting directions need be considered. These directions are shown in Fig. 3-4*c*. They are: (1) downward attack on the sulfur atom, (2) attack at the back of the R—S bond, (3) attack at the back of the S—S bond, and (4) upward attack on the sulfur. Direction 3 is the Walden inversion direction; it places the three atoms involved in

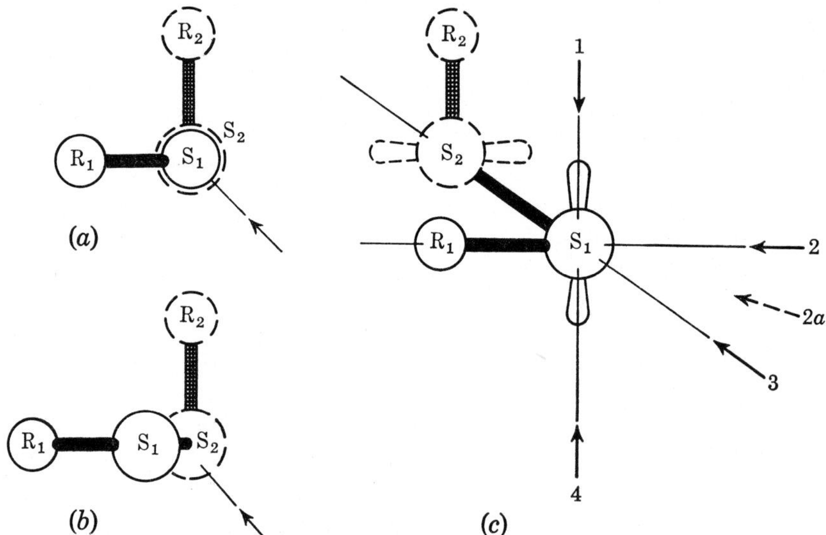

Fig. 3-4. Possible directions for attack on a disulfide by a radical.

bond making and breaking in a straight line. This direction is preferred by Bergson (122) on theoretical grounds, but the arguments are not unambiguous. Models show that hindrance to approach in these directions increases in the order: $2 < 4 \sim 3 < 1$. Direction 2*a* is a compromise between 2, the direction of low hindrance, and 3, the Walden inversion direction. Attack from directions 2 or 2*a* is as little hindered as attack on the S—S bond. Selection among these alternatives must await further information.

Finally, one difficulty must be mentioned: the chain transfer data which have been cited give the total rate of attack on the substrate by a radical, but they do not locate the site of attack. It is possible that a large percentage, or even all, of the attack in hindered compounds like *t*-butyl peroxide and disulfide is on hydrogen atoms. This point can be resolved by isolation of the products of the attack of monomeric radicals on disulfides. Such a study is in progress in these Laboratories. Until these data are available, the transfer constant for hindered disulfides given in Table 3-7 must be regarded merely as upper limits for the rate of attack on the sulfur atom itself.

3-4. Heterolytic Scission of the S—S Bond

The mechanisms by which S—S bonds undergo heterolysis are less polemic than are those involved in homolytic scission. An unambiguous example of unimolecular heterolysis has not yet been reported. The bimolecular mechanisms are of two types: catalytic electrophilic scission and nucleophilic scission.

Parker and Kharasch (830) reviewed the subject of scission of the S—S bond in 1959, concentrating especially on heterolytic scission. They particularly clarified the mechanisms by which S—S bonds cleave in the presence of electrophilic reagents.

The reactions of nucleophiles with compounds containing S—S bonds are explained by mechanisms first elaborated by Olav Foss. In 1947, Foss published a detailed monograph on nucleophilic cleavage of S—S bonds (443); this remains a modern and valuable outline of the known facts and theoretical expectations. These reactions are bimolecular nucleophilic displacements at S—S bonds; they respond to electronic and steric effects very much as do S_N2 reactions on carbon.

3-4A. Electrophilic Attack on Sulfur. Several electrophilic species are able to cleave the S—S bond of disulfides; this topic has attracted increased attention with the discovery of new examples and the attention brought to the reaction by the Parker and Kharasch review article (830).

Disulfides are cleaved in concentrated hydrochloric or sulfuric acid (919, 923, 993). For example, Benesch and Benesch (113) observed that exchange occurs between cystine and bis-(2,4-dinitrophenyl)-cystine in acid. They proposed a chain mechanism in which both protons and sulfenium ions cleave S—S bonds.

$$\mathrm{RS{-}SR} + \mathrm{H^+} \rightleftharpoons \mathrm{R{-}S{-}\underset{\displaystyle H}{\underset{|}{\overset{+}{S}}}R} \tag{3-66}$$

$$\mathrm{RS{-}\underset{\displaystyle H}{\underset{|}{\overset{+}{S}}}R} \longrightarrow \mathrm{R\overset{+}{S}} + \mathrm{RSH} \tag{3-67}$$

$$\mathrm{RS^+} + \mathrm{R'S{-}SR'} \longrightarrow \mathrm{R'S{-}SR} + \mathrm{R'S^+} \tag{3-68}$$

The exchange is catalyzed by both hydrogen peroxide and sulfenyl chlorides. This can be rationalized by the above mechanism, since both these substances lead to an increased concentration of sulfenium ions: hydrogen peroxide by oxidation of disulfides

$$RSSR + H_2O_2 + H^+ \longrightarrow RS^+ + [RSOH] + H_2O \tag{3-69}$$

and sulfenyl halides by dissociation.

$$RSCl \longrightarrow RS^+ + Cl^- \tag{3-70}$$

"Cystine disulfoxide" is also a catalyst, and Benesch and Benesch suggest, as Toennies and Lavine (677, 1058) had earlier, that it decomposes in acid to give sulfenium ions.

$$RS{-}\overset{\overset{\displaystyle O}{\|}}{\underset{\underset{\displaystyle O}{\|}}{S}}{-}R + H^+ \rightleftharpoons RS{-}\overset{\overset{\displaystyle OH}{|}}{\underset{\underset{\displaystyle O}{\|}}{S^+}}{-}R$$

$$R{-}S{-}\overset{\overset{\displaystyle OH}{|}}{\underset{\underset{\displaystyle O}{\|}}{S^+}}{-}R \longrightarrow RS^+ + RSO_2H$$

Sulfenium ions undoubtedly do cleave S—S bonds by electrophilic attack. Kharasch (616) has formulated sulfenyl compounds as electrophilic reagents. Specifically, he has shown that sulfenyl halides dissociate to sulfenium ions in concentrated sulfuric acid (619).

$$ArSCl + H_2SO_4 \rightleftharpoons ArS^+ + HCl + HSO_4^-$$

Moore and Porter (769) find that aryl sulfenyl halides cleave disulfides at 25° C.

$$ArSCl + RSSR \rightleftharpoons ArSSR + RSCl$$

The reaction is very much faster in acetic acid than in ether and is very slow in carbon tetrachloride. These results lead Moore and Porter to suggest considerable charge separation in the transition state.

$$\begin{array}{l} \quad R \\ \quad | \\ {}^{\delta+}S \\ \quad | \\ \quad S\cdots S{-}Cl^{\delta-} \\ \quad |\quad\ | \\ \quad R\ \ Ar \end{array}$$

Parker and Kharasch (830) have suggested that the chlorination of disulfides to give sulfenyl chlorides may involve an electrophilic displacement on sulfur by chlorine.

$$Cl_2 + RS{-}SR \rightarrow RS{-}Cl + RS^+ + Cl^- \qquad (3\text{-}71)$$

The reaction is catalyzed by strong acids (616, 620), which generate sulfenium ions.

$$H^+ + RS{-}SR \rightarrow RSH + RS^+ \qquad (3\text{-}72)$$

$$RS^+ + Cl_2 \rightarrow RSCl + Cl^+ \qquad (3\text{-}73)$$

$$Cl^+ + RS{-}SR \rightarrow RSCl + RS^+$$

Carbonium ions also may cleave disulfides. Although this subject has not received systematic study, a few examples may be cited. Lien, McCaulay, and Proell (690) proposed the following mechanism for the reaction between ethylene and ethyl disulfide:

$$RS{-}SR + H^+ \rightleftharpoons R\overset{+}{\underset{\substack{|\\H}}{S}}{-}SR \qquad (3\text{-}74)$$

$$R\overset{}{\underset{\substack{+|\\H}}{S}}{-}\overset{\substack{R\\|}}{S} + CH_2{=}CH_2 \longrightarrow RS{-}CH_2{-}\overset{+}{C}H_2 + RSH \qquad (3\text{-}75)$$

$$RS{-}CH_2{-}\overset{+}{C}H_2 + \underset{\substack{|\\R}}{S}{-}SR \longrightarrow RS{-}CH_2{-}CH_2{-}SR + RS^+ \qquad (3\text{-}76)$$

$$RS^+ + CH_2{=}CH_2 \longrightarrow RS{-}CH_2{-}\overset{+}{C}H_2 \qquad (3\text{-}77)$$

Challenger, Taylor, and Taylor (230, 232) have proposed that a methyl carbonium ion is the active species which methylates disulfides, using the biologically active compound betaine. Parker and Kharasch (831) have reported that 2,4-dinitrophenyl benzyl disulfide is cleaved by 2,4-dinitrophenylchloride.

$$Ar{-}S{-}S{-}CH_2C_6H_5 + Ar{-}Cl \xrightarrow{NaHCO_3} ArSAr + C_6H_5{-}CH_2SOH$$

The mechanism presumably involves electrophilic attack on sulfur by the 2,4-dinitrophenyl carbonium ion.

3-4B. Nucleophilic Attack on Sulfur. As remarked before, nucleophiles cleave compounds containing an S—S bond. These reactions have been found to be bimolecular, nucleophilic reactions (79, 89, 226, 366, 369, 371, 374, 428, 429, 440, 831, 934). In view of this, establishing the relative nucleophilicity of the common nucleophiles toward sulfur is of prime importance.

(1) *Relative Thiophilicities.* Foss, in 1947, was able to rank a number of thioanions in S-nucleophilicity using their oxidation potentials (428). Table 3-8 quotes some of these data; a nucleophile will displace the poorer nucleophiles below it from their compounds.*

Table 3-8
Potentials of sulfur anions

	E_0 (*volts*) *for* $2XS^- \rightleftharpoons XSSX + 2e^-$
$R{-}C({=}S){-}S^-$, $R{-}C({=}O){-}S^-$, RS^-	+.3
$S_2O_3^=$	−.10
$p\text{-}CH_3{-}C_6H_4{-}SO_2{-}S^-$, $(RO)_2{-}PO{-}S^-$	−.5
$C_2H_5SO_2{-}S^-$	−.54
SCN^-	−.77

From data such as these Foss was able to predict, for example, that the following reaction goes well to completion.

$$RS{-}SCN + S_2O_3^= \rightarrow R{-}S{-}S_2O_3^- + SCN^-$$

More recently, Parker and Kharasch (831) have studied thiophilicity. Using ultraviolet spectra, they have measured the position of the equilibrium of the reaction in ethanol between a series of anions and aryl disulfides. For example, the reaction in ethanol between 2,4-dinitrophenyl phenyl disulfide and cyanide ion reaches equilibrium at 90% to the right in less than 5 minutes at room temperature.

$$Ar{-}S{-}S{-}C_6H_5 + CN^- \leftrightarrows ArS^- + NC{-}S{-}C_6H_5$$

Thus, cyanide is more thiophilic than is the 2,4-dinitrophenylmercaptide ion. From this type of data the authors construct a reactivity series toward the S—S bond which is similar to that given below.

$$(C_2H_5O)_3P > R^-, HS^-, C_2H_5S^- > C_6H_5S^- > (C_6H_5)_3P, CN^- > SO_3^= > OH^-$$
$$> 2,4\text{-}(NO_2)_2C_6H_3{-}S^- > N_3^- > SCN^-, I^-, C_6H_5NH_2 \quad (3\text{-}78)$$

As Parker and Kharasch point out, this order does not coincide with nucleophilicity toward carbon. For example, Swain and Scott (1027)

* Foss (440) has extended and revised these data. (Note that his newer work uses an incorrect sign convention.)

give the order of nucleophilicity toward the carbon of methyl bromide as:

$$HS^- > CN^- > I^- > SCN^- > OH^- > N_3^-$$

The relatively high thiophilicity of the hydroxide ion is noteworthy.* Parker and Kharasch believe the reaction of hydroxide ions with disulfides involves a direct attack on the S—S bond by hydroxide to form an unstable sulfenic acid. This disproportionates to form unidentified products, shown below as disulfide and sulfonic acid (831).

$$RS{-}SR + OH^- \rightleftharpoons [RS{-}OH] + RS^-$$

$$3[RS{-}OH] \xrightarrow[\text{path}]{\text{Unknown}} RSSR + RSO_3H$$

The detailed path by which products are formed when hydroxide attacks an S—S bond is often not clear. Another example is the hydrolysis of S_8 rings by base, discussed on page 12.

In (3-78), notice that the cyanide ion is more thiophilic than is the thiocyanate ion. This is an example of a general rule first formulated by Foss (428)—namely, that thioanions are displaced by the corresponding anthioanion. Another example of the rule is the displacement of thiosulfate, $^-S{-}SO_3^-$, by sulfite, $SO_3^=$.

A few additions have been made to the sequence given by Parker and Kharasch. Sodium bisulfide cleaves phenyl disulfide (707). Therefore the bisulfide ion has been added to (3-78) before the phenyl mercaptide ion.

Carbanions are extremely thiophilic. Phenyl lithium, for example, cleaves phenyl disulfide (947).

$$C_6H_5^- + C_6H_5{-}S{-}S{-}C_6H_5 \rightarrow C_6H_5{-}S{-}C_6H_5 + C_6H_5S^- \tag{3-79}$$

Grignard reagents react with sulfur to form sulfides and polysulfides, and with ethyl disulfide and phenyl disulfide to give mercaptans (76, 615, 1162):

$$RMgX + S_8 \rightarrow R{-}S{-}S_6{-}S^- + MgX^+ \tag{3-80}$$

$$RMgX + R{-}S{-}S_6{-}S^- \rightarrow R{-}S{-}R + MgX^+ + S_7^= \tag{3-81}$$

$$RS{-}SR + R'MgX \rightarrow RS{-}MgX + R'{-}S{-}R \tag{3-82}$$

Thus carbanions rank near the beginning of Eq. (3-78).

* The nucleophilicity of the hydroxide ion is not well understood (191*a*, 284*a*). The factors upon which nucleophilicity is based are known, however. Nucleophilicity depends on basicity and polarizability. The relative importance of the latter increases as the substrate becomes more polarizable (16, note 10 in ref. 190, 191, 345, 346, 520), in agreement with theory (p. 424 of ref. 508).

Phosphorus also is extremely thiophilic. Triethylphosphite will displace the ethyl mercaptide ion (585).

$$(C_2H_5O)_3P + C_2H_3S\text{—}SC_2H_5 \rightarrow C_2H_5\text{—}S^- + C_2H_5\text{—}S\text{—}\overset{+}{P}(OC_2H_5)_3 \quad (3\text{-}83)$$

$$C_2H_5S^- + C_2H_5S\text{—}\overset{+}{P}(OC_2H_5)_3 \rightarrow C_2H_5\text{—}S\text{—}C_2H_5 + C_2H_5\text{—}S\text{—}\overset{O}{\overset{\|}{P}}(OC_2H_5)_2 \quad (3\text{-}84)$$

Triethylphosphite has therefore been added to Eq. (3-78).

Triphenylphosphine opens S_8 (89), and also displaces sulfite from thiosulfate (84). Therefore, triphenylphosphine has about the same thiophilicity as does cyanide (84, 830, 943) and has been added to Eq. (3-78).

(2) *Effect of the Leaving Group.* Parker and Kharasch (831) found that the more stable anion is lost in displacement reactions on unsymmetrical disulfides. For example, the following equation proceeds 94% to the right.

$$2,4\text{-}(NO_2)_2\text{—}C_6H_3\text{—}S\text{—}S\text{—}C_2H_5 + C_2H_5S^- \rightleftharpoons$$
$$2,4\text{-}(NO_2)_2\text{—}C_6H_3\text{—}S^- + C_2H_5S\text{—}SC_2H_5 \quad (3\text{-}85)$$

The order of leaving groups from a disulfide is therefore as follows:

$$2,4\text{-}(NO_2)_2C_6H_3S^- > 4\text{-}NO_2C_6H_4S^- > 2\text{-}NO_2C_6H_4S^- > C_6H_5S^- > \text{alkyl—}S^- \quad (3\text{-}86)$$

(3) *Stereochemical Effects.* As might be expected in these bimolecular reactions, a steric effect is observed. It is, in fact, quantitatively very similar to that observed in S_N2 reactions on carbon compounds (831). A tertiary alkyl sulfenyl compound is an analogue of a neopentyl carbon skeleton, and is similarly unreactive. For example, *t*-butylsulfenyl thiocyanate does not react with cyanide ion (558), although cyanide is more nucleophilic than is thiocyanate.

$$CH_3\text{—}\underset{CH_3}{\overset{CH_3}{C}}\text{—}S\text{—}SCN \xrightarrow{CN^-} \text{No reaction observed} \quad (3\text{-}87)$$

Compare the skeleton of *t*-butylsulfenyl thiocyanate with that of neopentyl thiocyanate, which would be predicted to react very slowly in an S_N2 reaction.

$$\mathrm{CH_3{-}\underset{\underset{CH_3}{|}}{\overset{\overset{CH_3}{|}}{C}}{-}CH_2{-}SCN \xrightarrow{CN^-} \text{Very slow reaction}} \qquad (3\text{-}88)$$

Thus the stereochemical requirements for displacement reactions at divalent sulfur are very similar to those found in similar displacements at carbon. This has been demonstrated with particular clarity by Fava and his group (369–371, 374) in a series of remarkable studies. They have compared the rate of the three exchange reactions below.

$$\mathrm{R{-}CH_2{-}X + Y^- \longrightarrow R{-}CH_2{-}Y + X^-} \qquad (3\text{-}89)$$

$$\mathrm{R{-}S{-}SO_3^- + \overset{*}{S}O_3^= \longrightarrow R{-}S{-}\overset{*}{S}O_3^- + SO_3^=} \qquad (3\text{-}90)$$

$$\mathrm{R{-}S{-}SR + R\overset{*}{S}^- \longrightarrow R{-}S{-}\overset{*}{S}R + RS^-} \qquad (3\text{-}91)$$

Reaction (3-89) is an S_N2 displacement on carbon. Streitwieser (1019) has tabulated average values for these rate constants as R is varied.* Reactions (3-90) and (3-91) are S_N2 displacements at sulfur studied by Fava. Table 3-9 shows that the rate profile as R is varied is extremely similar for all three of these reactions. Specifically, S_N2 reactions on carbon and on sulfur respond similarly to the substitution of methyl groups for hydrogen atoms beta to the site of reaction. Therefore, a *t*-butyl sulfenyl compound has a low reactivity, comparable to that of a neopentyl carbon skeleton.

* In Fava's paper, rates for an alkyl bromide exchange studied by de la Mare (723) were used as a standard for comparison.

Table 3-9
Comparison of the rate of S_N2 reactions at sulfur and at carbon (369, 371, 1019)

R	Relative rate constants for reaction		
	(3-89)	(3-90)	(3-91)
CH_3	100	100	
C_2H_5	40	50	
i-C_3H_7	3.0	0.7	
C_4H_9	40[a]	....	40
t-C_4H_9	10×10^{-4}	6×10^{-4}	0.15×10^{-4}
C_6H_5	12,000	....	75

[a] Extrapolated from R equals propyl (i. e., butyl halides).

$$\begin{array}{c} Y^- \\ CH_3 \\ CH_3-C-S-X \\ CH_3 \end{array} \quad \text{Compare with} \quad \begin{array}{c} Y^- \\ CH_3 \\ CH_3-C-CH_2-X \\ CH_3 \end{array}$$

Fava concludes that nucleophilic displacement reactions on sulfur involve attack at the backside and a 3-atoms-in-a-line transition state similar to S_N2 reactions on carbon.

Equation (3-90) is a displacement at a sulfenyl-sulfite bond, and such reactions are quite general.

$$Y^- + RS{-}SO_3^- \rightarrow YSR + SO_3^=$$

For example, thiosulfate itself reacts with sulfite (22*a*).

$$\overset{*}{S}O_3^= + HS{-}SO_3^- \rightarrow HS{-}\overset{*}{S}O_3^- + SO_3^= \qquad (3\text{-}92)$$

The thiosulfate monoanion is the simplest homologue of a thiosulfate monoester (Bunté salt), and Eqs. (3-92) and (3-90) are analogous. Cyanide ion also displaces sulfite from thiosulfate (84).

$$CN^- + \bar{S}{-}SO_3^- \rightarrow \bar{S}{-}CN + SO_3^= \qquad (3\text{-}93)$$

Similar reactions occur in polythionates and have been examined by Foss (429, 430) and by Fava (365, 372, 373). For example, sulfite can displace thiosulfite.

$$\overset{*}{S}O_3^= + {}^-SO_3{-}S_a{-}S{-}SO_3^- \longrightarrow {}^-\overset{*}{S}O_3{-}S_a{-}SO_3^- + S_2O_3^=$$

$$a = 0,\ 1,\ 2 \text{ or } 3$$

Cyanide ion can also displace thiosulfate from polythionates (306, 429).

$$\begin{array}{l} CN^- + {}^-SO_3{-}S{-}S{-}SO_3^- \longrightarrow {}^-SO_3{-}SCN + {}^-S{-}SO_3^- \\ {}^-SO_3{-}SCN + OH^- \longrightarrow HSO_4^- + SCN^- \end{array} \qquad (3\text{-}94)$$

(4) *Displacement Reactions at* S^{IV} *and* S^{VI}. The reactions considered in the previous sections have involved displacements by nucleophiles at S^{II}, i.e., divalent sulfur. However, S^{IV} and S^{VI} are also attacked; examples of these somewhat less familiar processes are given here.

The formally most simple example of displacement at S^{IV} is oxygen exchange of sulfite ions with a solvent labeled with O^{18}. Potassium sulfite exchanges oxygens with water at 100° C and the rate is retarded by hydroxide ion (534). Reasonable suggestions for the mechanism are displacement on either bisulfite or sulfurous acid by either water or hydroxide ion. That is either

$$H_2\overset{*}{O} + \overset{O}{\underset{O^-}{\overset{\|}{\underset{|}{S}}}}-OH \longrightarrow H_2\overset{+}{\overset{*}{O}}-\overset{O}{\underset{O^-}{\overset{\|}{\underset{|}{S}}}} + {}^-OH$$

$$\downarrow$$

$$H^+ + H\overset{*}{O}-\overset{O}{\overset{\|}{S}}-O^-$$

or

$$H\overset{*}{O}^- + \overset{O}{\underset{OH}{\overset{\|}{\underset{|}{S}}}}-OH \longrightarrow H\overset{*}{O}-\overset{O}{\overset{\|}{S}}-OH + {}^-OH$$

Another possibility is an S_N1 dissociation to sulfur dioxide.

$$H_2\overset{+}{O}-\overset{O}{\overset{\|}{S}}-O^- \longrightarrow H_2O + SO_2$$

$$SO_2 + H_2\overset{*}{O} \xrightarrow{\text{fast}} H_2S\overset{*}{O}_3$$

Sodium dithionite is hydrolyzed in aqueous solution in a bimolecular reaction with a positive salt effect (692, 724). The mechanism is complex and not entirely known, but a reasonable series of S_N2 displacements at sulfur can be proposed.

$$H_2O + {}^-SO_2-SO_2^- \longrightarrow [{}^-O-S-O^-] + H_2\overset{+}{O}-SO_2^-$$

$$H_2\overset{+}{O}-SO_2^- \longrightarrow SO_3^= + 2H^+$$

$$[{}^-O-S-O^-] + {}^-SO_2-SO_2^- \longrightarrow \left[{}^-O-S-O-\overset{O^-}{\underset{O^-}{\overset{|}{\underset{|}{S}}}}-SO_2^-\right] \qquad (3\text{-}95)$$

$$\left[{}^-O-S-O-\overset{O^-}{\underset{O^-}{\overset{|}{\underset{|}{S}}}}-SO_2^-\right] \xrightarrow[\text{steps}]{\text{Several}} SO_3^= + S_2O_3^=$$

The radical ion $SO_2^{\cdot-}$ has been identified in sodium dithionite (891), and an S_N1 mechanism could also be proposed.

Another example of a displacement on tetravalent sulfur which may involve an S_N2 mechanism is the attack on dimethyl sulfoxide by azide ion. The initial product loses nitrogen to form dimethylsulfonamide (116, 117).

$$CH_3-\overset{\overset{O}{\|}}{S}-CH_3 + N_3^- \longrightarrow \left[CH_3-\overset{\overset{\bar{O}}{|}}{S}-CH_3 \atop {{}^-N-{}^+N\equiv N} \right] \xrightarrow{-N_2} CH_3-\overset{\overset{O}{\|}}{\underset{\underset{{}^-N}{\|}}{S}}-CH_3 \xrightarrow{H^+} CH_3-\overset{\overset{O}{\|}}{\underset{\underset{NH}{\|}}{S}}-CH_3$$

An example of attack at S^{IV} which has been examined in detail is the hydrolysis of sulfite esters, studied by Bunton, Tillett, and their collaborators (195–198, 300, 1050) and by R. E. Davis (303). The rate law is bimolecular, being first order both in the neutral ester and in hydroxide ion. Studies with O^{18} have shown that the reaction involves S—O scission, and that the recovered starting material does not contain the heavy oxygen isotope. The rate-determining step of the mechanism must therefore be an irreversible S_N2 attack on the ester S^{IV} by hydroxide ion.

$$H\overset{*}{O}^- + \overset{\overset{O}{\|}}{\underset{\underset{OR}{|}}{S}}-OR \longrightarrow H\overset{*}{O}-\overset{\overset{O}{\|}}{S}-OR + {}^-OR$$

The attack could not be on carbon as this would lead to alkyl-oxygen scission.

A large number of reactions have been reported which can be formulated as involving an S_N2 attack on S^{VI}. In some cases the mechanism is not firmly established and could be either S_N1 or S_N2; often the exact species involved is not known. The tenor of the evidence taken as a whole suggests that some of the reactions are S_N2 displacements. One example is oxygen exchange between sulfate and water. Although it was originally reported (293) that sulfuric acid does not exchange, it is now known to do so (534, 755, 1160). The active species is not known, nor is the net charge on the activated complex. Several paths may compete

(1160). One possibility is that a neutral solvent molecule attacks the bisulfate ion as shown below.

$$H_2\overset{*}{O} + O=\underset{\substack{/\!/ \quad \backslash \\ O \quad O^-}}{\overset{O}{\overset{\|}{S}}}-OH \longrightarrow H_2\overset{+}{\overset{*}{O}}-\underset{\underset{O}{\|}}{\overset{O}{\overset{\|}{S}}}-O^- + {}^-OH$$

$$\downarrow$$

$$H^+ + H\overset{*}{O}-SO_3^-$$

Sodium thiosulfate exchanges oxygens with water (755); the reaction rate is retarded by sodium hydroxide, so presumably the mechanism involves attack by water on either the monoanion or on the neutral acid.

$$H_2\overset{*}{O} + \underset{\substack{/\!/ \quad \backslash \\ O \quad S^-}}{\overset{O}{\overset{\|}{S}}}-OH \longrightarrow H_2\overset{+}{\overset{*}{O}}-\underset{\underset{O}{\|}}{\overset{O}{\overset{\|}{S}}}-S^- + {}^-OH$$

$$\downarrow$$

$$H\overset{*}{O}-SO_2-S^-$$

At 100° C in 1N sodium hydroxide solution, thiosulfate also exchanges with radio bisulfide ion (1107, 1108). Since the sulfide ion is a very powerful nucleophile (346), it might be expected to react in an S_N2 mechanism. Voge and Libby prefer an S_N1 mechanism with unimolecular dissociation to sulfur trioxide, but the evidence does not allow an unequivocal choice to be made. The S_N2 path would be:

$$\overset{*}{S}{}^{=} + \underset{\substack{/\!/ \quad \backslash \\ O \quad O^-}}{\overset{O}{\overset{\|}{S}}}-SH \longrightarrow {}^-\overset{*}{S}-\underset{\underset{O}{\|}}{\overset{O}{\overset{\|}{S}}}-O^- + HS^-$$

At temperatures in the range of 250 to 300° C, sodium thiosulfate undergoes a third type of reaction. In aqueous buffers near neutral pH, it disproportionates to produce sulfide and sulfate (877). The reaction is first order in thiosulfate ion, has a positive salt effect, and has a first-order rate constant proportional to the proton concentration. Although several mechanisms are allowed by the kinetic evidence, the most likely was suggested to be bimolecular attack by water on the monoanion $HS-SO_3^-$.

$$H^+ + S_2O_3^{=} \rightleftharpoons HS_2O_3^-$$

$$H_2O: + \underset{O\ \ O^-}{\overset{O}{\overset{\|}{S}}}\!-\!SH \xrightarrow{\text{Slow}} H_2\overset{+}{O}\!-\!\underset{O\ \ O^-}{\overset{O}{\overset{\|}{S}}} + SH^- \tag{3-96}$$

$$\downarrow$$

$$HO\!-\!\underset{O}{\overset{O}{\overset{\|}{\underset{\|}{S}}}}\!-\!O^- + H^+$$

Another possibility which fits the kinetic data is a unimolecular decomposition of the same anion.

$$\underset{^-O\ \ O}{\overset{O}{\overset{\|}{S}}}\!-\!SH \xrightarrow{\text{Slow}} SO_3 + HS^-$$

$$SO_3 + OH^- \rightleftharpoons HSO_4^- \tag{3-97}$$

As in many of these reactions, the choice between a unimolecular and a bimolecular reaction presents the difficult problem of identifying the molecularity in the solvent. This thiosulfate disproportionation does not show buffer catalysis, and the unimolecular mechanism may be favored on that account. It was suggested that the problem could be resolved by applying the Hammett-Zucker hypothesis (695). Some solvolysis reactions of inorganic esters have been examined using this acidity function theory (194, 813, 1104). The bimolecular path, Eq. (3-96), should have a rate proportional to the molarity of the acid, and the unimolecular path, Eq. (3-97), should follow h_0. A difficulty is that the mechanism in highly acid solutions may differ from that applicable at normal pH; this actually occurs in the case of phosphoric acid exchange, discussed below (1104).

The hydrolysis of alkyl sodium sulfates has been studied by Burwell (205, 211). In acidic solution, *sec*-butyl sulfate undergoes solvolysis to produce an alcohol with retained configuration.

$$H_2O + \underset{O\ \ OH}{\overset{O}{\overset{\|}{S}}}\!-\!OC_4H_9 \longrightarrow H_2\overset{+}{O}\!-\!\underset{O\ \ OH}{\overset{O}{\overset{\|}{S}}} + {}^-OC_4H_9$$

$$\downarrow$$

$$H_2SO_4 + H^+$$

Bunton (193, 199) and Christman and Oae (237) have studied the hydrolysis of sulfonates and sulfones, for example:

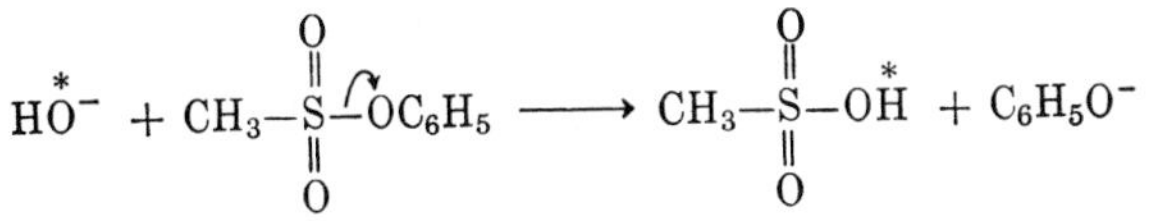

$$\overset{*}{HO}^- + CH_3{-}\underset{\underset{O}{\|}}{\overset{\overset{O}{\|}}{S}}{-}OC_6H_5 \longrightarrow CH_3{-}\underset{\underset{O}{\|}}{\overset{\overset{O}{\|}}{S}}{-}\overset{*}{O}H + C_6H_5O^-$$

No exchange with O^{18}-enriched water occurs prior to reaction, and the S—O bond is broken. The mechanism is probably S_N2 as shown.

Barker (69) has reported the reaction below:

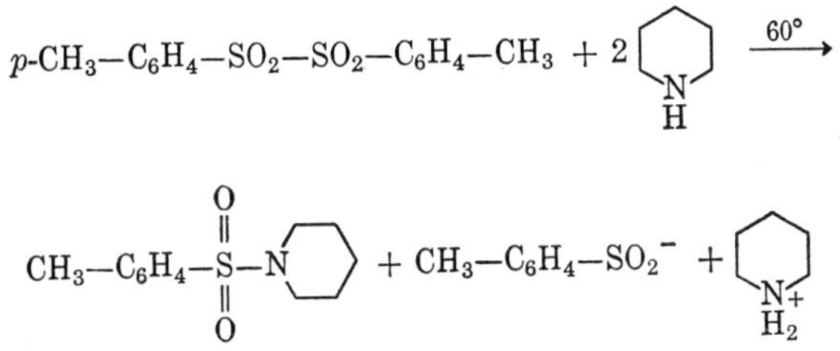

$$p\text{-}CH_3{-}C_6H_4{-}SO_2{-}SO_2{-}C_6H_4{-}CH_3 + 2\ \text{(piperidine, } C_5H_{10}NH) \xrightarrow{60^\circ}$$

$$CH_3{-}C_6H_4{-}\underset{\underset{O}{\|}}{\overset{\overset{O}{\|}}{S}}{-}NC_5H_{10} + CH_3{-}C_6H_4{-}SO_2^- + C_5H_{10}\overset{+}{N}H_2$$

The reaction mechanism most likely is S_N2 attack on a sulfone-sulfur by the piperidine; the transition state would be formulated as below.

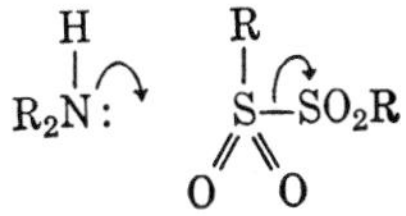

$$R_2\overset{\overset{H}{|}}{N}: \quad \overset{\overset{R}{|}}{S}{-}SO_2R \text{ (S bearing two O)}$$

Bunté salts (683) hydrolyze in aqueous hydrochloric acid at 100° C to form thiols (1145).

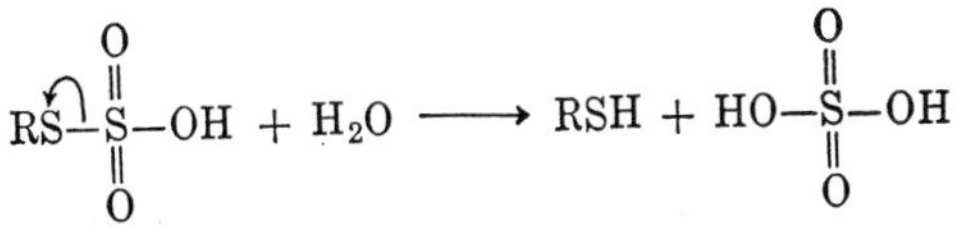

$$RS{-}\underset{\underset{O}{\|}}{\overset{\overset{O}{\|}}{S}}{-}OH + H_2O \longrightarrow RSH + HO{-}\underset{\underset{O}{\|}}{\overset{\overset{O}{\|}}{S}}{-}OH$$

The mechanism may involve S_N2 attack on S^{VI} by water.

Hydrolysis reactions of many inorganic esters undoubtedly involve nucleophilic attack at polyvalent hetero atoms. This subject has not yet been reviewed, although the hydrolysis of nitrate esters (161) and phosphates (192, 1104, 1143) has been treated separately. A complete discussion is beyond the bounds of the present work, but a few examples will suffice to show that sulfate, sulfite, and thiosulfate esters are not unique in undergoing displacement reactions.

Methyl phosphate is hydrolyzed to methanol and phosphoric acid (1104). The rate is a maximum at pH 4, where the monoanion is the chief species. When the reaction is conducted in O^{18}-labeled water, the heavy oxygen is found in one and only one of the phosphate oxygens (338, 813). The profile of this reaction rate versus pH and that for oxygen exchange by phosphoric acid versus pH are identical. Both reactions undoubtedly involve S_N2 attack by water on the monoanion.

$$H_2\overset{*}{O} + (HO)(O^-)P(=O)\text{—}OR \longrightarrow H_2\overset{+}{\overset{*}{O}}\text{—}P(=O)(OH)\text{—}O^- + {}^-OR$$

$$\downarrow$$

$$H^+ + H_2P\overset{*}{O}_4{}^-$$

A number of esters have been investigated: for R equal to hydrogen, methyl, and *p*-nitrophenyl, the rate constants are 0.1, 1, and 67. The stability of the leaving group as an anion therefore influences the rate. This reaction occurs with P—O scission at pH 4; however, in very acidic media, the scission is 50/50 C—O and P—O, and the rate follows the molarity of perchloric acid, not h_0. The acid- and base-catalyzed mechanisms are therefore distinct. The hydrolysis of a large number of other phosphate esters has been studied (71, 145), chiefly by Westheimer and his group (206, 257, 609, 664, 665, 684, 922, 1143). Thain has studied the hydrolysis of triethyl trithiolphosphate (1043).

The hydrolysis of nitrate esters has also been examined. Morrow, Cristol, and Van Dolah (780) have reported a particularly interesting example from our present viewpoint. Butyl nitrate is cleaved by S_N2 attack on nitrogen by bisulfide ions.

$$HS^- + C_4H_9O\text{—}NO_2 \longrightarrow C_4H_9O^- + [HS\text{—}NO_2]$$

$$[HS\text{—}NO_2] \longrightarrow H^+ + \tfrac{1}{8}S_8 + NO_2{}^-$$

Presumably the decomposition of the hypothetical thionitrate ion is analogous to that of thiosulfate (see page 141). A number of examples of hydrolysis of nitrates have been reported (24, 58–61, 161). These compounds can react in four ways: the nucleophile may attack nitrogen or the α carbon atom to cause hydrolysis, or it may attack either an α hydrogen or a β hydrogen atom to cause oxidation of the organic component (161).

The hydrolysis of nitrite (19, 609), hypochlorite (23), and chromate (1170) esters has been studied, as has hydrolysis of dichromate (674) and oxygen exchange in permanganate ions (1029). In many of these cases an S_N2 reaction appears to be involved, but the evidence is by no means complete. In the hydrolysis of carbonates, however, an S_N1 mechanism is likely because of the stability of CO_2 (756, 757, 815).

3-5. Thiols

Thiols are, of course, the sulfur analogues of alcohols, and their reactions might be expected to be as varied and as useful in syntheses as are those of alcohols. In fact, this appears to be the case, and the reactions of thiols are attracting increasing attention and study.

3-5A. Ionic Addition Reactions of Thiols. In basic media, thiols add to olefins which contain electron-withdrawing substituents. The basic catalyst is necessary, and the mechanism involves nucleophilic attack on the olefin by the mercaptide ion (578, 612).

$$C_2H_5SH + B:^- \longrightarrow C_2H_5S^- + BH$$

$$C_2H_5S^- + CH_2{=}CH{-}CO_2CH_3 \longrightarrow C_2H_5S{-}CH_2{-}\overset{-}{C}H{-}\overset{O}{\overset{\|}{C}}{-}OCH_3 \xrightarrow{BH} \underset{95\%}{C_2H_5S{-}CH_2{-}CH_2{-}CO_2CH_3}$$

Truce has studied base-catalyzed addition reactions of the mercaptide ion in detail. They normally involve stereospecific trans addition. For example, *p*-tolylmercaptide ion adds to vinylidene chloride, and the adduct eliminates hydrogen chloride to produce *trans*-1-tolylmercapto-2-chloroethane (1080). The reaction series shows that the initial addition is predominantly trans.

$$ArS^- + CH_2{=}CCl_2 + C_2H_5OH \longrightarrow \left[ArS^-\ \ (H)(H)C{=}C(Cl)(Cl)\right] \xrightarrow{H-OC_2H_5} ArS(H)(H)C{-}C(H)(Cl)(Cl) + {}^-OC_2H_5$$

$$\longrightarrow ArS(H)(H)C{-}C(H)(Cl)(Cl) \longrightarrow ArS(H)C{=}C(H)(Cl) + HCl$$

Favored conformation for elimination

Truce has also shown that mercaptide ions add to acetylenic bonds, usually by a mechanism that involves trans addition (1081–1084, 1086).

In acidic media, thiols and hydrogen sulfide add to olefins to give the products which would be predicted from Markovnikov's rule. The mechanism undoubtedly involves protonation of the olefinic bond to form a carbonium ion, which undergoes nucleophilic attack by sulfur to form a sulfonium ion. Thiols are excellent nucleophiles, far better in fact than their basicity would lead one to predict. Thus, the addition of thiols involves a sequence of reactions similar to the hydration of olefins, but with the sulfenium ion in place of an oxonium ion.

$$RR'C{=}CR''R''' + H^+ \rightleftharpoons RR'\overset{+}{C}{-}CHR''R'''$$

$$RR'\overset{+}{C}{-}CHR''R''' + RSH \rightleftharpoons RR'\underset{}{\overset{\overset{+}{H}SR}{|}}{C}{-}CHR''R''' \rightleftharpoons RR'\overset{SR}{\overset{|}{C}}{-}CHR''R''' + H^+$$

In this context it will be helpful to discuss some of the properties of sulfenium ions. Sulfenium ions may exist to an appreciable extent as a bridged cyclic ion.

$$>\overset{SR}{\overset{|}{C}}{-}\overset{+}{C}< \;\rightleftharpoons\; >C\overset{\overset{R}{S}}{\overset{+}{=}}C< \;\rightleftharpoons\; >\overset{+}{C}{-}\overset{SR}{\overset{|}{C}}<$$

It was postulated during the 1940s that a neighboring sulfur participates in solvolysis through formation of cyclic ions (93, 1158). Thus Bartlett and Swain (93) have shown that cyclic sulfenium ions are important in explaining the reactions of mustard gas.

$$Cl{-}CH_2{-}CH_2{-}S{-}CH_2{-}CH_2{-}Cl \longrightarrow \underset{CH_2-CH_2-Cl}{\overset{CH_2-CH_2}{\overset{\diagdown\;\diagup}{S^+}}} + Cl^-$$

In such cyclic ions, however, a larger portion of the positive charge is on carbon than might be expected. This was pointed out by Streitwieser (page 682 of ref. 1019) in a discussion of the work of Fuson, Price, and Burness (487). These authors have shown that both 2-ethylmercapto-1-propanol and 1-ethylmercapto-2-propanol give 1-ethylmercapto-2-chloropropane on treatment with hydrochloric acid. They postulated that both these alcohols form the same sulfenium ion:

$$\left.\begin{array}{l} C_2H_5S-\underset{}{\overset{CH_3}{\overset{|}{C}H}}-CH_2OH \\ C_2H_5S-CH_2-\underset{\underset{OH}{|}}{C}H-CH_3 \end{array}\right] \xrightarrow{H^+} \overset{C_2H_5}{\overset{|}{\underset{CH_2-CH-CH_3}{S^+}}} + H_2O \qquad (3\text{-}98)$$

Chloride ion then attacks this cyclic ion at the more hindered secondary carbon rather than at the primary carbon atom as might be expected. Therefore, Streitwieser suggests that the open-chain, secondary carbonium ion contributes to the resonance hydrid to an appreciable extent.

$$\left[Cl^- \curvearrowright \overset{C_2H_5}{\overset{|}{\underset{CH_2-CH-CH_3}{S^+}}} \qquad \overset{C_2H_5}{\overset{|}{\underset{CH_2-\overset{+}{C}H-CH_3}{S}}} \; Cl^- \right] \qquad (3\text{-}99)$$

$$\not\downarrow \qquad\qquad\qquad \downarrow$$

$$Cl-CH_2-\underset{}{\overset{\overset{C_2H_5}{|}}{\overset{S}{\overset{|}{C}H}}}-CH_3 \qquad\qquad \overset{C_2H_5}{\overset{|}{S}}-CH_2-\underset{\underset{Cl}{|}}{C}H-CH_3$$

Not formed — Formed

This explanation is consistent with a sulfenyl chloride addition, reported by Fuson and coworkers (487).

$$ClCH_2-CH_2-SCl + CH_2{=}CH-CH_3 \longrightarrow \overset{C_2H_4Cl}{\overset{|}{\underset{CH_2-CH-CH_3}{S^+}}} + Cl^- \qquad (3\text{-}100)$$

$$\downarrow$$

$$ClCH_2-CH_2-S-CH_2-\underset{\underset{Cl}{|}}{C}H-CH_3$$

Here again, chloride ion attacks at the secondary carbon.

Kharasch and his school (550, 618, 622) and a number of other workers (264, 268, 671, 672) have shown that sulfenyl chlorides add to olefins to give stereospecific trans addition. The cyclic sulfenium ion therefore has been postulated to be an intermediate in these reactions. For example (550, 622) *cis*- and *trans*-2-butene react with 2,4-dinitrobenzenesulfenyl chloride to give stereospecific products; e.g., the *trans*-2-butene yields an erythro adduct.

$$\mathrm{ArSCl} + \underset{\text{trans}}{\overset{\mathrm{H}\quad\quad \mathrm{CH_3}}{\underset{\mathrm{H_3C}\quad\quad \mathrm{H}}{\mathrm{C{=}C}}}} \longrightarrow \overset{\mathrm{Ar-S}}{\overset{\mathrm{H}\quad\quad \mathrm{CH_3}}{\underset{\mathrm{H_3C}\quad\quad \mathrm{H}}{\mathrm{C\overset{+}{=}C}}}} + \mathrm{Cl^-} \longrightarrow \underset{\text{erythro}}{\overset{\mathrm{Ar-S}}{\overset{\mathrm{H}\quad\quad \mathrm{CH_3}}{\underset{\mathrm{H_3C}\quad \mathrm{Cl}\quad \mathrm{H}}{\mathrm{C{-}C}}}}} \tag{3-101}$$

In sulfenyl halide additions to unsymmetric olefins, the cyclic ion opens to give both products. Thus, 2,4-dinitrobenzenesulfenyl chloride adds to propene to produce 65% secondary chloride and 15% primary (618).

$$\mathrm{ArS^+} + \mathrm{CH_2{=}CH{-}CH_3} \longrightarrow \overset{\mathrm{Ar-S}}{\mathrm{CH_2\overset{+}{=}CH{-}CH_3}} \xrightarrow{\mathrm{Cl^-}} \underset{15\%}{\mathrm{Cl{-}CH_2{-}\overset{SAr}{C}H{-}CH_3}} \quad + \quad \underset{65\%}{\mathrm{ArS{-}CH_2{-}\overset{Cl}{C}H{-}CH_3}}$$

Here again, the majority of the attack has occurred at the more hindered carbon.

Epoxides are attacked by alkoxide or hydroxide ions and by amines at the least substituted carbon. Thus carbanions (14), alkoxide ion (236, 965), amines (236), and carboxylate anions (476) all open propylene oxide to form the secondary alcohol.

$$\mathrm{Y^-} + \mathrm{H_2\overset{O}{C}{-}CH{-}CH_3} \longrightarrow \mathrm{Y{-}CH_2{-}\overset{O^-}{C}H{-}CH_3} \xrightarrow{\mathrm{H^+}} \mathrm{Y{-}CH_2{-}\overset{OH}{C}H{-}CH_3} \tag{3-102}$$

Basic catalysts are necessary to effect this reaction in the case of alcohol and water, but amines open epoxides in this direction without the addition of a further base. However, amines open thioepoxides to produce the primary thiol (536).

$$(CH_3)_2NH + \overset{\overset{S}{\diagup\,\diagdown}}{CH_2{-}CH}{-}CH_3 \longrightarrow (CH_3)_2N{-}\overset{\overset{CH_2SH}{|}}{CH}{-}CH_3$$

A cyclic sulfenium ion has been postulated to explain this, although it is not required.

$$H^+ + CH_3{-}\overset{\overset{S}{\diagup\,\diagdown}}{CH{-}CH_2} \longrightarrow \left[CH_3{-}\overset{\overset{\overset{H}{|}}{S}}{CH{\overset{+}{=}}CH_2}\right] \longrightarrow \left[CH_3{-}\overset{\overset{\overset{H}{|}}{\overset{+}{S}}}{CH{-}CH_2}\right]$$

$$H^+ + CH_3{-}\underset{\underset{N(CH_3)_2}{|}}{CH}{-}CH_2SH \longleftarrow CH_3{-}\underset{\underset{\underset{\underset{H}{|}}{{}^+N(CH_3)_2}}{|}}{CH}{-}\overset{\overset{SH}{|}}{CH_2} \xleftarrow{HN(CH_3)_2}$$

It should be pointed out that in acidic or neutral solutions, propylene oxide undergoes alcoholysis to produce both isomers (236).

$$\overset{\overset{O}{\diagup\,\diagdown}}{CH_2{-}CH}{-}CH_3 + H^+ \longrightarrow \overset{\overset{\overset{H}{|}}{O}}{CH_2^{+}{=}CH}{-}CH_3$$

(3-103)

$$C_2H_5OH + \overset{\overset{\overset{H}{|}}{O}}{CH_2^{+}{=}CH}{-}CH_3 \longrightarrow C_2H_5O{-}CH_2{-}\overset{\overset{\overset{H}{|}}{O}}{\underset{}{CH}}{-}CH_3 + C_2H_5O{-}\overset{\overset{CH_2OH}{|}}{CH}{-}CH_3$$

In neutral ethanol the ratio of secondary to primary alcohol is 3.5:1; addition of sulfuric acid lowers this ratio to about 1:1.

3-5B. Radical Addition Reactions of Thiols. The addition of thiols to olefins by a radical mechanism to produce non-Markovnikov products occurs extremely readily. Under some conditions this reaction is reversible, and thiols can be used to isomerize olefins. The thiyl radical also is an oxidant and can abstract hydrogen atoms from organic compounds. These facts make the radical reactions of thiols of considerable utility.

(1) *Background.* In 1928, Ashworth and Burkhardt (35) observed that thiophenol adds to styrene to give 1-phenyl-2-phenylmercaptoethane, the non-Markovnikov product, and that the rate depends on the

$$C_6H_5SH + C_6H_5CH{=}CH_2 \rightarrow C_6H_5S{-}CH_2{-}CH_2{-}C_6H_5$$

light intensity. In 1934 Burkhardt (201) suggested that radicals were involved in such non-Markovnikov reactions, and in 1938 Kharasch, Read, and Mayo (614) proposed the radical chain mechanism which is now accepted for such reactions. In 1939, Ipatieff and Friedman (583) found that thiols or thiolacids add to alkenes to give non-Markovnikov products if the reactants are simply heated in a sealed autoclave and no effort is made to remove air or peroxide impurities. However, under these conditions hydrogen sulfide adds in the Markovnikov direction. Jones and Reid (599) discovered that elemental sulfur effectively prevents the radical reaction; in the presence of sulfur, thiols add to olefins in the Markovnikov sense. They also showed that peroxides promote the non-Markovnikov addition. Mayo and Walling (733) reviewed the newly discovered "peroxide effect" in 1940, and showed that it provided a useful tool for the synthesis of non-Markovnikov products. At that time several features were apparent: non-Markovnikov additions of thiols to olefins occur easily in excellent yields by a radical chain mechanism; special care to remove oxygen and peroxides is necessary to achieve ionic addition of thiols; elemental sulfur inhibits the radical addition. Hydrogen sulfide, however, adds by an ionic mechanism under the usual conditions employed.

In 1942, Vaughan and Rust (1103) achieved the non-Markovnikov addition of hydrogen sulfide to olefins by use of light from a quartz mercury arc to promote the reaction. They found that hydrogen sulfide adds very rapidly. They investigated a number of olefins and gas-phase as well as liquid-phase reactions (see Secs. 10-1 and 10-4).

In 1947, Cunneen reported that thiogycolic acid (277) and thiolacetic acid (278) add to olefins in a non-Markovnikov direction. Because of the greater difficulty of achieving radical addition of hydrogen sulfide, thiolacetic acid is frequently used in an indirect synthesis of terminal mercaptans.

$$R{-}\overset{\overset{\displaystyle O}{\|}}{C}{-}SH + R'{-}CH{=}CH_2 \longrightarrow R'{-}CH_2{-}CH_2{-}S{-}\overset{\overset{\displaystyle O}{\|}}{C}{-}R$$

$$R'{-}CH_2{-}CH_2{-}S{-}\overset{\overset{\displaystyle O}{\|}}{C}{-}R \xrightarrow{\text{Hydrolyze}} R'{-}CH_2{-}CH_2{-}SH$$

The addition of alkanethiolic acids to olefins also can be used to prepare derivatives (325, 553) (see Sec. 10-5 for an example). However, the direct radical addition of hydrogen sulfide to olefins to produce non-Markovnikov products has also found use. For example, vinyl ethers add hydrogen sulfide to give non-Markovnikov products (975); the best catalyst is reported to be azobisisobutyronitrile.

The non-Markovnikov addition of thiols to olefins can also be effected by irradiation with gamma or x-rays (423, 424).

(2) *Stereochemistry.* The stereochemistry of the addition of thiyl radicals to olefins has been investigated in detail. Although it frequently occurs with some stereochemical preference, it does not always do so, and therefore bridged sulfur radicals are not involved. This contrasts with the reactions of the sulfenium cation, in which bridged, nonclassical ions may well be involved (see Sec. 3-5A).

In 1954, Cristol and Brindell (270), found that thiophenol adds to norbornene to give the exo thioether under homolytic conditions. The addition is stereospecific, and endo product is not formed, nor does a carbon-skeleton rearrangement occur.*

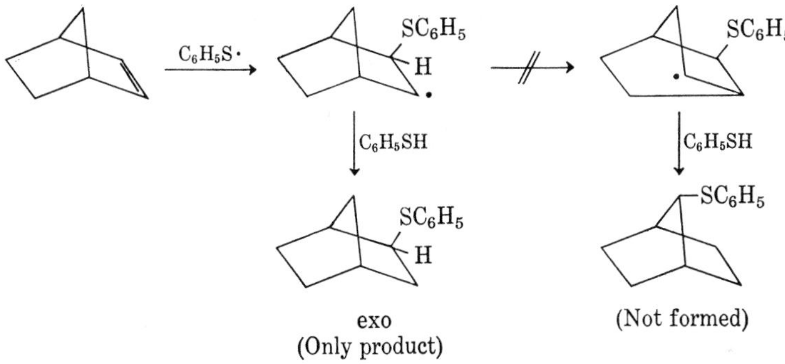

$C_6H_5S\cdot$ ⟶ SC_6H_5, H ⇸ SC_6H_5

C_6H_5SH ↓ C_6H_5SH ↓ (3-104)

SC_6H_5, H — SC_6H_5

exo (Only product) — (Not formed)

Goering, Relyea, and Larsen (511) found that thiophenol, hydrogen sulfide, or thiolacetic acid adds to 1-chlorocyclohexene to give greater than 94, 75, and 66% of the cis product, respectively. The reaction products are determined by kinetic, rather than by thermodynamic, control. The order of stereoselectivity is thiophenol > hydrogen sulfide > thiolacetic acid. These results can be explained by postulating (159) that both the thiyl radical and the thiol itself attack cyclohexene from the same direction, either axial or equatorial. Attack by both from the axial direction is shown below.

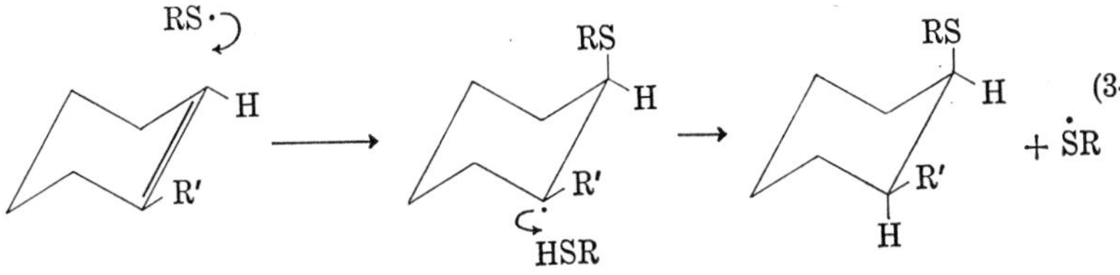

RS· H R′ ⟶ RS H R′ HSR ⟶ RS H R′ H $+\ \dot{S}R$ (3-105)

* These authors have reviewed their work (176*a*).

Abell and Chiao have discussed other mechanistic possibilities (2); at present several mechanisms appear to be equally acceptable. Part of the difficulty is that it is not known whether a carbon radical is planar or tetrahedral (159, page 140 of ref. 347).

Bordwell and Hewett (159) have found that the order of stereoselectivity in addition of thiyl radicals to 1-methylcyclohexene is thiophenol > hydrogen sulfide > thiolacetic acid. These authors also point out that since the addition is not completely stereospecific a cyclic radical cannot be involved. A cyclic radical would yield 100% stereospecificity if attack occurred solely from the backside, as in ionic S_N2 reactions* (510)

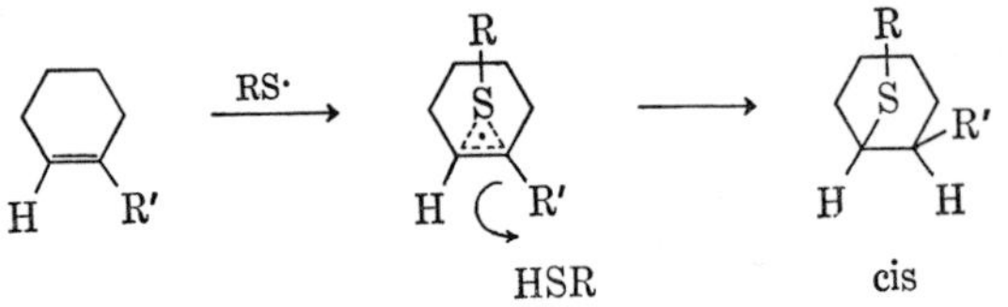

RS· ; HSR ; cis (3-106)

Goering, Relyea, and Larsen (511) found that the addition of hydrogen sulfide to 1-chlorocyclohexene varies in stereoselectivity with the concentration of the hydrogen sulfide. This implies that two classical radicals are in equilibrium and that a single mesomeric radical need not be an intermediate. The equations are given below.

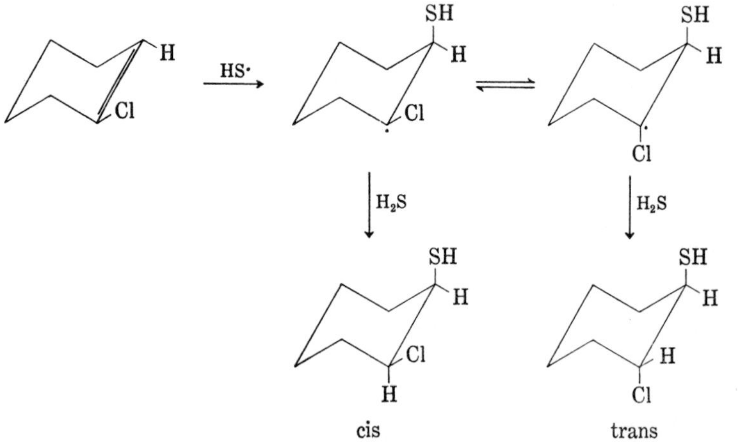

HS· (3-107)

H_2S ; H_2S ; cis ; trans (3-108)

* The ionic addition of bromine to olefins is entirely stereospecific and, for this reason, is usually assumed to involve a cyclic bromonium ion. As is often pointed out, however (e.g., on p. 523 of ref. 518), the evidence for such a cyclic ion is incomplete. Slow rotation could explain the observed stereochemical preference equally well. H. C. Brown has pointed out alternative mechanisms which do not involve bridged ions in several systems (e.g., ref. 186*a*).

Since the rate of formation of product, Eq. (3-108), depends on the hydrogen sulfide concentration whereas the unimolecular rearrangement step, Eq. (3-107), does not, it is reasonable that a greater proportion of cis product should be formed at high hydrogen sulfide concentration. Goering (511) finds that a molar equivalent of hydrogen sulfide leads to the formation of 86% cis; a fourfold excess produces 90% cis. (Material balance and duplicate determinations suggest that these differences are probably experimentally real.) Cristol and Arganbright (267) and Neureiter and Bordwell (801) have advanced stereochemical arguments for believing that a cyclic radical does not occur.

Cristol, Brindell, and Reeder (269, 270*a*) found that *p*-thiocresol adds to norbornadiene to give both unrearranged *exo*-sulfide and the product resulting from a rearrangement of the carbon skeleton.

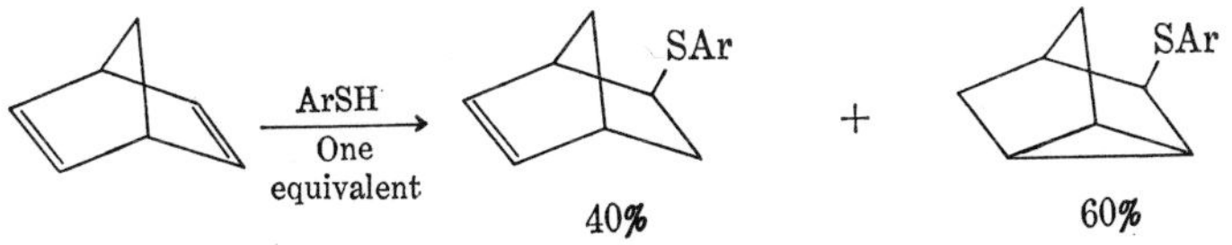

ArSH / One equivalent → SAr (40%) + SAr (60%)

They also found that the ratio of the rearranged to the unrearranged product more than doubled if the *p*-thiocresol was added dropwise rather than all at once. They conclude that the rearrangement

SAr ⇌ SAr

competes more favorably with the hydrogen transfer step

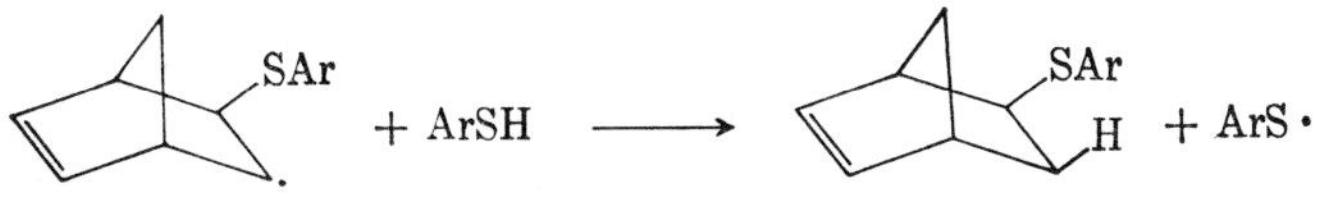

SAr + ArSH → SAr, H + ArS·

when the concentration of ArSH is kept low. This variation in the yield of the rearranged product indicates that a single mesomeric radical is not a reaction intermediate. An equilibrium between two classical radicals, as shown above, explains the data. Cristol and Reeder have confirmed this reasoning by studying the reactions of *p*-toluenesulfonyl chloride (270*b*).

In these cyclic systems, the rate of rearrangement of the intermediate radical from one conformation to another is frequently similar to the rate of hydrogen transfer from a thiol to the radical. Thus, as we have seen, changes in the concentration of transfer agent can alter the products. Skell and Allen (985) have discovered an acyclic system in which this is particularly dramatic. Deuterated methanethiol adds to either *cis*- or *trans*-2-butene at $-70°$ C to produce the same mixture of erythro and threo isomers. Thus, the isomerization of the intermediate radical is rapid relative to abstraction of a deuterium from CH_3SD, and stereochemical identity is not retained.

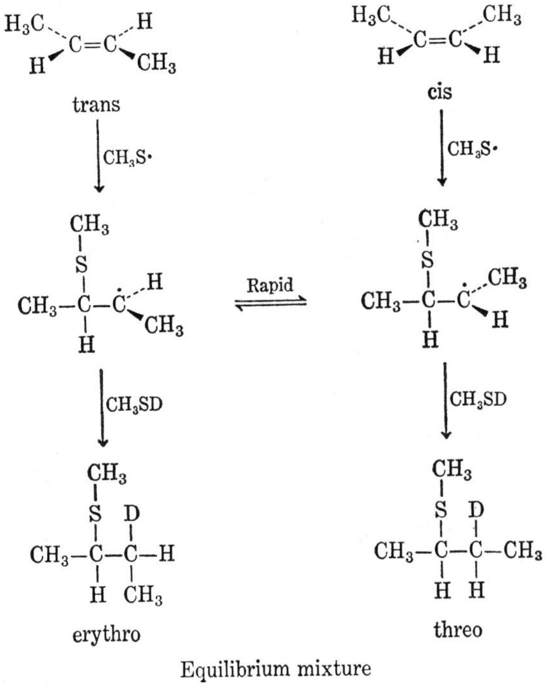

trans: $H_3C(H)C{=}C(H)CH_3$ —[$CH_3S\cdot$]→ $CH_3S{-}CH(CH_3){-}\dot{C}(H)CH_3$ —[CH_3SD]→ $CH_3{-}C(H)(SCH_3){-}C(D)(H)(CH_3)$ erythro

cis: $H_3C(H)C{=}C(H)CH_3$ —[$CH_3S\cdot$]→ $CH_3S{-}CH(CH_3){-}\dot{C}(CH_3)H$ —[CH_3SD]→ $CH_3{-}C(H)(SCH_3){-}C(D)(H){-}CH_3$ threo

The two intermediate radicals interconvert: Rapid ⇌

Equilibrium mixture (3-109)

When deuterium bromide is added, however, these sulfides are produced in stereospecific trans reactions, the *trans*-2-butene giving erythro and the cis giving threo. Therefore, abstraction of a deuterium from DBr occurs faster than the intermediate radicals can interconvert.

$$\begin{array}{ccc}
\text{trans-}CH_3CH{=}CHCH_3 & & \text{cis-}CH_3CH{=}CHCH_3 \\
\downarrow CH_3S\cdot & & \downarrow CH_3S\cdot \\
H_3C(H)C(SCH_3)\!-\!\dot{C}(H)(CH_3) & \underset{\text{to interconvert isomers}}{\overset{\text{Too slow}}{\rightleftharpoons}} & H_3C(H)C(SCH_3)\!-\!\dot{C}(CH_3)(H) \\
\downarrow \text{Fast } DBr & & \downarrow \text{Fast } DBr \\
H_3C(H)C(SCH_3)\!-\!C(H)(CH_3)(D) & & H_3C(H)C(SCH_3)\!-\!C(CH_3)(H)(D) \\
\text{erythro} & & \text{threo}
\end{array} \qquad (3\text{-}110)$$

Bromine atoms do not add, so Eq. (3-111) must be fast.

$$Br\cdot + CH_3SD \xrightarrow{\text{Fast}} CH_3S\cdot + DBr \qquad (3\text{-}111)$$

In the system above, the rate of rotation about the C—C bond has been bracketed. It must be faster than the rate of hydrogen transfer to the intermediate radical by CH_3SD and slower than transfer by DBr. The exchange reaction, Eq. (3-111), makes the rate constants difficult to measure for either one of these transfer reactions (984). The mechanism requires that Eq. (3-112) have a low activation energy not greatly different from that for rotation about a C—C bond. This is undoubtedly correct: e.g., the activation energy for Eq. (3-112) is 5 kcal when R is CH_3 and Y is CH_3S (611).

$$R\cdot + Y\text{—}H \longrightarrow RH + Y\cdot \qquad (3\text{-}112)$$

In this system, a faster hydrogen-transfer reaction was obtained by adding a better transfer agent (DBr in place of CH_3SD). In Eqs. (3-107) and (3-108), a faster transfer was obtained by increasing the concentration of the transfer agent. In either case, faster transfer of hydrogen leads to reaction of the intermediate radicals before they can interconvert and stereospecific reaction products are formed.

(3) *Reversibility.* Sivertz et al. (983) found in 1956 that the addition of methanethiol to isobutylene, propene, or ethene has an activation energy in the gas phase of from −8 to −9 kcal. This over-all negative activation energy implies a multistep mechanism for the reaction, and Sivertz therefore concluded that the addition step itself is probably reversible. Walling and Helmreich (1121) have shown that methanethiol isomerizes *cis*- to *trans*-2-butene under photolytic conditions, and Pallen and Sivertz (826) effect the same isomerization with thiophenol. Similarly, Neureiter and Bordwell (801) found that radiation and a catalytic amount of thiolacetic acid produce isomerization of either *cis*-2-chloro-2-butene or *cis*-4-methyl-2-pentene to the trans isomer at 25° C. All these addition reactions must therefore be adjudged reversible at the temperatures and concentration ratios used. In view of this reversibility, the over-all rate of appearance of thiol addition product may not be proportional to the actual rate of addition of thiyl radicals to a particular isomer of an olefin.

$$\underset{\text{trans}}{RS\cdot + R'HC{=}CHR''} \underset{k_2}{\overset{k_1}{\rightleftharpoons}} RS{-}CHR'{-}\dot{C}HR'' \underset{k_1'}{\overset{k_2'}{\rightleftharpoons}} \underset{\text{cis}}{R'HC{=}CHR'' + RS\cdot} \tag{3-113}$$

$$RS{-}CHR'{-}\dot{C}HR'' + RSH \xrightarrow{k_3} RS{-}CHR'{-}CH_2R'' + RS\cdot \tag{3-114}$$

In a sequence such as Eqs. (3-113) and (3-114), the rate of production of addition product from the trans olefin is proportional to

$$\frac{k_1}{k_2 + k_3}\,k_3$$

if $k_2' < k_3$, and is more complex if this is not the case. Despite these difficulties, Walling and Helmreich (1121) have reported the relative reactivities of a series of olefins toward dodecanethiol at 60° C (see Table 3-10). The experiments were done by competition involving as many as five olefins present simultaneously, and using gas-phase chromatography as the analytical technique. The authors show that k_2 and k_2' are probably small, and they assume an irreversible addition in calculating the rate constants.

Sivertz has reported a series of measurements of the absolute rate constants for thiyl additions. The mechanism is as below, where M is a monomer-type olefin.

$$\text{Transfer:} \quad RSH + M_n\cdot \xrightarrow{k_{tr}} RS\cdot + \text{product} \tag{3-115}$$

$$\text{Addition:} \quad RS\cdot + M \xrightarrow{k_a} RSM\cdot \tag{3-116}$$

$$\text{Propagation:} \quad RSM\cdot + (n-1)M \xrightarrow{k_p} RSM_n\cdot \tag{3-117}$$

$$\text{Termination:} \quad 2RS\cdot \xrightarrow{k_t} RSSR \tag{3-118}$$

$$2M_n\cdot \xrightarrow{k'_t} \text{products} \tag{3-119}$$

Sivertz finds a positive over-all activation energy and concludes that Eq. (3-116) is not reversible in the liquid phase and that his rate constants need not be corrected (982). His data are given in Table 3-11, with some related data of Clingman (245).

Table 3-10
Relative reactivities[a] of dodecanethiol with olefins at 60° C (1121)

Styrene	17.0
β-Methylstyrene	5.5
Vinyl butyl ether	3.9
Methyl methacrylate	2.4
Methyl acrylate	2.0
Allyl alcohol	1.5
2-Methyl-1-butene	1.2
1-Octene	(1.00)
Allylbenzene	.99
Vinyl acetate	.81
Allyl chloride	.72
Cyclopentene	.64
Allyl acetate	.59
Allyl cyanide	.37
Cyclohexene	.25
cis-Dichloroethylene	.2

[a] The assumption is made that addition is irreversible.

Cunneen (279, 280) has discovered an interesting application of the reversibility of thiol additions. He has been able to effect isomerization of either gutta-percha or rubber to the equilibrium mixture of polyisoprenes, 57% trans and 43% cis, using thiolacids.

(4) *Thiols as Chain Transfer Agents in Polymerizations. Electrophilic Character of the Thiyl Radical.* The rate constants in Table 3-11 are extremely large, and it is not surprising that thiols are excellent polymerization chain transfer agents. Thiols are employed commercially to moderate the molecular weight of the elastomer produced in the emulsion copolymerization of styrene and butadiene; in the absence of thiol the polymer reaches molecular weights so high as to prohibit the necessary milling. Representative transfer constants for thiols are given in Table 3-12.

Table 3-11
Rate constants for the addition of thiols to olefins[a]

Reaction between butanethiol and	k_{tr}	k_a	k_p	k_t	$k_t + k_t'$	References
Styrene	1.24×10^3	8×10^8 [b]	230[c]	....	5×10^8	52, 826, 982
1-Pentene[c]	1.4×10^6	6×10^7	0	5×10^{11}	6×10^{11}	816, 982
1-Octene	3.6×10^4	....	...	....	1.2×10^9	245
Isoprene	93	....	...	....	1.4×10^8	52
Cyclohexene	....	....	0	....	....	982

[a] Values in M^{-1} sec^{-1} at 25° C.

[b] Revised by Sivertz.

[c] Note k_p for polystyryl radical adding to styrene is 35 at 25° C when thiol is not present. Sivertz finds that all these rate constants depend on n in Eqs. (3-115) to (3-119). As n decreases (more chain transfer) these constants increase. Due to this, k_{tr} for 1-pentene may be 5 to 8 times too large and $(k_t + k_t')$ may be about 16 times too large (982).

Table 3-12
Chain transfer constants for thiols

Thiol	Monomer[a]	°C	C^b	References
Butanethiol	MMA	60	0.67	810, 1118
2-Propanethiol	MMA	60	0.38	810
Butanethiol	MA	60	1.6	1118
Butanethiol	VAc	60	>48	1118
Butanethiol	Sty	60	22	1118
Butanethiol	Sty	90	15.4	324
t-Butyl mercaptan	Sty	60	3.7	523
t-Butyl mercaptan	MMA	60	0.18	810
t-Butyl mercaptan	Sty	100	2.3, 3.2	523
t-Octyl mercaptan	Sty	50	4.3	744
2-Ethoxypropanethiol	Sty	60	14.1, 21.0	523
Hexanethiol	Sty	99	15.3	324
Octanethiol	Sty	50	19	744
Thiolbenzoic acid	Sty	99	>6	324
Thiolacetic acid	Sty	99	>15	324
Thiophenol	Sty	99	0.08	324
Thiophenol	MMA	60	2.7	810
p-Ethoxythiophenol	Sty	99	0.13	324
Benzyl mercaptan	Sty	99	25	324
Dodecanethiol	Sty	60	15, 19	523
Octadecanethiol	Sty	99	15	324
Ethyl thioglycolate	Sty	60	58	523

[a] MMA, methyl methacrylate; MA, methyl acrylate; VAc, vinyl acetate; Sty, styrene.

[b] The transfer constant C is defined by Eq. (3-64), page 52.

The thiyl radical, like the peroxy radical, is electrophilic.* This is because sulfur is more electronegative than carbon, and polar resonance structures contribute to the transition state of these radical reactions. For example, the transition state for the reaction of a carbon radical with a thiol has the following polar forms:

$$RSH + R'\cdot \longrightarrow \left[RS:H \;\cdot R' \longleftrightarrow R\bar{S}\!: \overset{+}{H} \;\cdot R' \longleftrightarrow R\bar{S}\!: \dot{H} \;\overset{+}{R'}\right] \qquad (3\text{-}120a)$$

Similarly, the hydrogen abstraction reaction of a thiyl radical at a C—H bond can be represented by a similar resonance hybrid.

$$RS\cdot + R'H \longrightarrow \left[RS\cdot \; H:R' \longleftrightarrow R\bar{S}\!: \overset{+}{H} \;\cdot R' \longleftrightarrow R\bar{S}\!: \dot{H} \;\overset{+}{R'}\right] \qquad (3\text{-}120b)$$

Finally, the addition of a thiyl radical to an olefin can be similarly pictured.

$$RS\cdot + CH_2{=}CHR' \longrightarrow \left[RS\cdot \; CH_2 \dot{=} CHR' \longleftrightarrow R\bar{S}\!: \overset{+}{C}H_2{-}\dot{C}HR'\right] \qquad (3\text{-}120c)$$

Thus, any of these three reactions involving the thiyl radical should be enhanced in rate by electron-donating substituents in the substrate or electron-withdrawing groups in the thiol. The prediction that electron-donating groups in the substrate enhance the rate is supported by a number of studies. Experimental evidence on the effect of electron-withdrawing groups in the thiol is somewhat contradictory.

Walling, Seymour, and Wolfstirn (1128) and Hiatt and Bartlett (557) find that thioglycolic acid reacts with α-methylstyrene to form the 1:1 adduct in the presence of a radical initiator.

$$HO_2C{-}CH_2\dot{S} + CH_2{=}\underset{\displaystyle}{\overset{\displaystyle C_6H_5\atop|}{C}}{-}CH_3 \xrightarrow{k_a} HO_2C{-}CH_2S{-}CH_2{-}\underset{\cdot}{\overset{\displaystyle C_6H_5\atop|}{C}}{-}CH_3 \qquad (3\text{-}121)$$

$$HO_2C{-}CH_2S{-}CH_2{-}\underset{\cdot}{\overset{\displaystyle C_6H_5\atop|}{C}}{-}CH_3 + HO_2C{-}CH_2SH \xrightarrow{k_{tr}}$$

$$HO_2C{-}CH_2S{-}CH_2{-}\overset{\displaystyle C_6H_5\atop|}{C}H{-}CH_3 + HO_2C{-}CH_2S\cdot \qquad (3\text{-}122)$$

Table 3-13 cites values for k_a for substituted α-methylstyrenes. It also tabulates the comparable rate constants for the addition of the radical from maleic anhydride. Electron-donating groups in the styrene increase

* See pp. 318–322 and 417 of ref. 1116. An electrophilic radical is one which attacks molecules at points of high electron availability.

the rate of reaction with the radical from both glycolic acid and maleic anhydride; however, the effect of substituents is even larger in the reaction with thioglycolic acid. Therefore, a polar contribution is even more important in the transition state for the reaction with this thiyl radical than it is with maleic anhydride. The latter forms a copolymer with styrene which is composed entirely of alternating styrene and maleic anhydride units. That is, the electron-poor maleic anhydride monomer attacks styrene exclusively, and the relatively electron-rich styryl radical attacks maleic anhydride exclusively. Walling and coworkers (1127) point out that this reasoning, originally applied to such copolymerization studies (867, 1120), can be applied equally well to addition reactions. By this standard, the thioglycolic acid radical is even more electrophilic than is the maleic anhydride radical.

Table 3-13
Rate of reaction of the radical from thioglycolic acid and from maleic anhydride with α-methylstyrenes at 60° C (1128)

Substituent in α-methylstyrene	Radical: $CO_2H{-}CH_2S\cdot$	Radical: $\cdot CH{-}CO$ / $CH_2{-}CO$ (ring closed through O)
p-OCH_3	215	18
p-CH_3	2.3	1.7
None	1.00	1.00
p-F	0.51	0.72
p-Br	0.90	0.73
m-Br	0.96	0.96

The chain transfer constants have been measured for butanethiol at 60° C with a number of monomers. These data, given in Table 3-14, have been calculated using the values for the propagation constants (page 95 of ref. 1116) and the transfer constants cited in Table 3-12. The transfer reaction, Eq. (3-115), should be increased in rate by electron-donating groups in the monomer. This is observed: k_{tr} increases in the order

$$CH_2{=}C(CH_3){-}C({=}O){-}OCH_3 \;<\; CH_2{=}CH{-}C_6H_5 \;<\; CH_2{=}CH{-}\ddot{O}{-}C({=}O)CH_3$$

This is in agreement with predictions from Eq. (3-120a). The value for k_{tr} for styrene at 60° C given in Table 3-14 compares well with the value 1.2×10^3 M^{-1} sec^{-1} at 25° C given in Table 3-11.

Table 3-14
Transfer constants for butanethiol with various monomers at 60° C

Monomer	C_{tr}[a]	k_p[b]	k_{tr}[c]
Methyl methacrylate	0.67	705	470
Styrene	22	145	1,840
Vinyl acetate	>48	2,300	1.1×10^5

[a] Values originally given by Walling (1118) and revised by him (p. 157 of ref. 1116).
[b] Values selected by Walling (p. 95 of ref. 1116).
[c] Calculated as $(k_p)(C_{tr})$ sec^{-1} M^{-1}.

Schaafsma, Bickel, and Kooyman (925) have measured the effect of ring substituents in thiophenols on the rate of the transfer reactions with 1-cyano-1-cyclohexyl radicals. Their technique involved thermal dissociation of azobis-1,1′-cyclohexylnitrile in toluene at 110° C in the presence of two thiols. It was demonstrated that hydrogen exchange from one thiyl radical to the other thiol does not interfere by showing that the relative reactivities of two thiols were independent of their mole ratios over a twelvefold range. The relative reactivity constants for the series of eight thiols studied fit Hammett's equation quite well with a value for ρ of -0.4. Thus 4-methoxythiophenol reacts with these cyanocyclohexyl radicals four times faster than does 4-nitrothiophenol. This is the reverse of the effect predicted from Eq. (3-120a), where it is predicted that electron-withdrawing groups in the thiol should increase the rate. The explanation suggested by the authors is that the cyanocyclohexyl radical is more electronegative than is the thiol.

$$(\text{CN})C_6H_{10}\text{—N=N—}C_6H_{10}(\text{CN}) \longrightarrow 2\ (\text{CN})C_6H_{10}\cdot + N_2$$

$$(\equiv R\cdot)$$

$$R\cdot + p\text{-X—}C_6H_4\text{—SH} \longrightarrow RH + p\text{-X—}C_6H_4\text{—S}\cdot$$

$$2\ p\text{-X—}C_6H_4\text{—S}\cdot \longrightarrow p\text{-X—}C_6H_4\text{—S—S—}C_6H_4\text{—X-}p$$

The transition state would then have the polar contribution below.

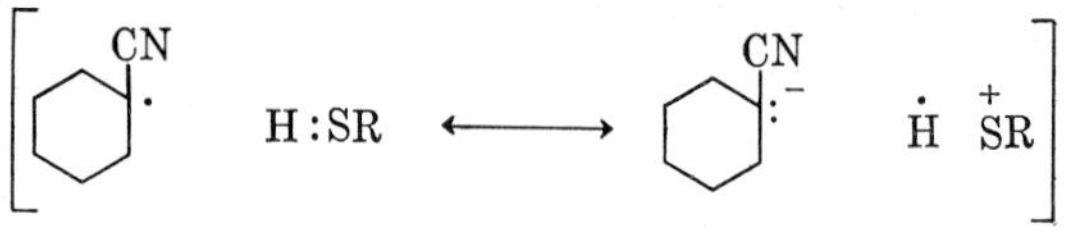

$$\left[\text{C}_6\text{H}_{11}\text{C}(\text{CN})\cdot \quad \text{H:SR} \longleftrightarrow \text{C}_6\text{H}_{11}\text{C}(\text{CN}):^- \quad \dot{\text{H}} \quad \overset{+}{\text{S}}\text{R} \right]$$

In a similar study, Bruin, Bickel, and Kooyman (188) find that the order of reactivity of thiols toward 2-cyano-2-propyl radicals is: benzyl mercaptan $\simeq$ primary aliphatic thiols > secondary aliphatic thiols > tertiary aliphatic thiols. In this case electron-donating alkyl groups on the thiol sulfur retard the reaction, as predicted from Eq. (3-120*a*).

Kerr and Trotman-Dickenson (611) have reported the relative rate for the reaction of methyl radicals with thiols in the gas phase (see Table 3-15). They photolyzed acetone in a pyrex flask in the presence of thiols. Under these conditions only the acetone is photoactivated. They calculate the activation energy of the hydrogen abstraction to be about 5 kcal, assuming a "normal" *PZ* of about $10^{11.3}$. Trotman-Dickenson and coworkers (132) deduced the same relative rate ratio from the reaction of thiols with methyl radicals produced by the homolytic decarbonylation of acetaldehyde. The results are contrary to the prediction from Eq. (3-120*a*); electron-donating alkyl groups in the thiol should slow the reaction.

Table 3-15
Relative rate of hydrogen abstraction from thiols by methyl radicals (611)

Reaction between $CH_3\cdot$ and	k_{tr}
CH_3SH	1.8
C_2H_5SH	3.5
i-C_3H_7SH	4.1
t-C_4H_9SH	5.9

Wall and Brown (1115) have measured the isotope effect in the transfer reaction of butanethiol with a polystyryl radical. The value of k_H/k_D for C_4H_9SH versus C_4H_9SD is 4.0 at 60° C and 3.8 at 70° C. These values indicate that partial rupture of the S—H bond has occurred at the transition state of the transfer reaction, Eq. (3-120*a*).

Transfer constants for thiols are not appreciably changed when emulsion- or oil-polymerization techniques are used rather than bulk polymerization (994).

Thiols are sufficiently reactive hydrogen donors to react with a number of stable radicals, including diphenylpicrylhydrazyl (355, 912), 2,2′-diketo-3,3′-diphenyl-3,3′-dicoumaranyl (698), and triphenylmethyl (942). Thiols are the only hydrogen donors yet found which act as transfer agents toward *p*-xylylene (354).

(5) *Hydrogen Abstraction by the Thiyl Radical.* Walling (1116) has concluded that the thiyl radical should be able to abstract hydrogen from a benzyl carbon atom. The S—H bond energy is about 85 kcal (see Table 3-1), and the energy of a benzyl carbon-hydrogen bond is about 77 kcal from $D(C_6H_5CH_2—H)$. Thus reaction (3-123a) should be exothermic by about 8 kcal.

$$C_6H_5CH_2—H + RS\cdot \xrightarrow{\Delta H \simeq -8 \text{ kcal}} C_6H_5CH_2\cdot + RSH \qquad (3\text{-}123a)$$

The activation energy for chain transfer of a polystyryl radical with an aliphatic thiol is 1 to 1.5 kcal less than the activation energy for propagation. Walling evaluates E_p as about 7.3 kcal; therefore E_{tr} is about 6 kcal.

$$M_n—\underset{}{\overset{C_6H_5}{\overset{|}{C}}}H\cdot + RSH \xrightarrow{E_a \simeq 6 \text{ kcal}} M_n—\overset{C_6H_5}{\overset{|}{C}}H_2 + RS\cdot \qquad (3\text{-}123b)$$

These values are not compatible, as the figure below shows.

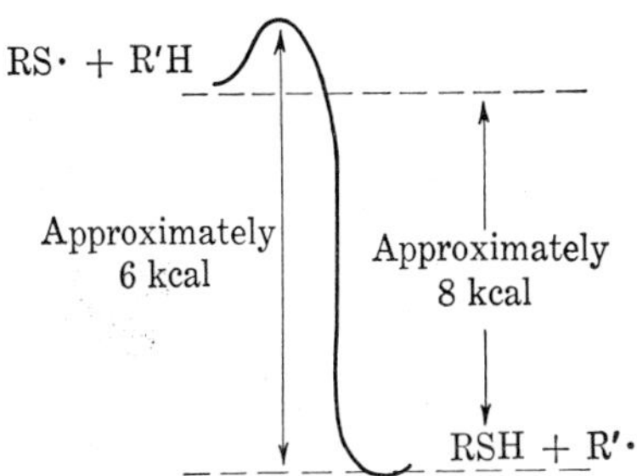

However, each has an uncertainty of ±2 kcal, and they agree within those limits. One further value is available and is in the same range: The activation energy for abstraction of a hydrogen atom from methanethiol by hydrogen atoms is about 4.6 kcal (580). Thus, the transfer reaction

$$RSH + R'\cdot \rightleftharpoons RS\cdot + R'H$$

should be exothermic to the right by 6 to 8 kcal, and should have an activation energy of less than 2 kcal in either direction when the organic fragments form fairly stable radicals. Chain transfer by thiols should be very fast, therefore.

This has been verified in a number of systems. For example, Wang and Cohen (249, 1131) find that diphenylmethyl radicals do not exchange hydrogen with radioactive diphenylmethane at 60° C.

$$(C_6H_5)_2CH{-}N{=}N{-}CH(C_6H_5)_2 \rightarrow 2(C_6H_5)_2CH\cdot + N_2$$

$$2(C_6H_5)_2CH\cdot \rightarrow \underset{\text{Inactive}}{(C_6H_5)_2CH{-}CH(C_6H_5)_2} \qquad (3\text{-}124)$$

$$(C_6H_5)_2\dot{C}H + (C_6H_5)_2\overset{*}{C}H_2 \rightarrow \text{No reaction} \qquad (3\text{-}125)$$

However, in the presence of thiophenol, the yield of dimer is reduced from 95 to 60%, and the dimer is 17% as radioactive as is the diphenylmethane starting material.

$$(C_6H_5)_2\dot{C}H + RSH \rightarrow (C_6H_5)_2CH_2 + RS\cdot \qquad (3\text{-}126)$$

$$RS\cdot + (C_6H_5)_2\overset{*}{C}H_2 \rightarrow (C_6H_5)_2\overset{*}{C}H\cdot + RSH \qquad (3\text{-}127)$$

$$(C_6H_5)_2\overset{*}{C}H\cdot + (C_6H_5)_2\dot{C}H \rightarrow (C_6H_5)_2\overset{*}{C}H{-}CH(C_6H_5)_2 \qquad (3\text{-}128)$$

Therefore, in the presence of thiophenol, 17% exchange has occurred. The exchange which does not occur directly in Eq. (3-125) is produced by Eqs. (3-126) and (3-127). Radioactive dimer is then formed through Eq. (3-128). Thiophenol reduces the amount of dimer by the transfer reaction (3-129).

$$C_6H_5SH + (C_5H_5)_2\dot{C}H \rightarrow C_6H_5S\cdot + (C_6H_5)_2CH_2 \qquad (3\text{-}129)$$

$$2C_6H_5S\cdot \rightarrow C_6H_5SSC_6H_5$$

Bickel and Kooyman (130) report that α-phenylazoethane decomposes at 125° C to give a mixture of the isomeric 2,3-diphenylbutanes.

$$C_6H_5{-}\overset{CH_3}{\overset{|}{C}H}{-}N{=}N{-}\overset{CH_3}{\overset{|}{C}H}{-}C_6H_5 \rightarrow N_2 + 2C_6H_5{-}\overset{CH_3}{\overset{|}{C}H}\cdot \rightarrow C_6H_5{-}\overset{CH_3}{\overset{|}{C}H}{-}\overset{CH_3}{\overset{|}{C}H}{-}C_6H_5 \qquad (3\text{-}130)$$

In the presence of octanethiol, ethylbenzene is formed.

$$C_6H_5{-}\overset{CH_3}{\overset{|}{C}H}\cdot + RSH \rightarrow C_6H_5{-}\overset{CH_3}{\overset{|}{C}H_2} + RS\cdot \qquad (3\text{-}131)$$

$$RS\cdot + C_6H_5{-}\overset{CH_3}{\overset{|}{C}H}{-}N{=}N{-}\overset{CH_3}{\overset{|}{C}H}{-}C_6H_5 \rightarrow RSH + C_6H_5{-}\underset{\cdot}{\overset{CH_3}{\overset{|}{C}}}{-}N{=}N{-}\overset{CH_3}{\overset{|}{C}H}{-}C_6H_5$$

$$2C_6H_5{-}\underset{\cdot}{\overset{CH_3}{\overset{|}{C}}}{-}N{=}N{-}\overset{CH_3}{\overset{|}{C}H}{-}C_6H_5 \rightarrow \text{dimer} \qquad (3\text{-}132)$$

Similarly, thiols catalyze the radical chain decomposition of aldehydes (77, 132, 542). In the absence of thiols, aldehydes decompose by the following mechanism.

$$R{-}CHO + R\cdot \rightarrow R{-}CO\cdot + RH \qquad (3\text{-}133)$$

$$R{-}CO\cdot \rightarrow R\cdot + CO \qquad (3\text{-}134)$$

Methyl azoisobutyrate is found to be only 5% effective as an initiator.

$$CH_3O_2C-\underset{CH_3}{\overset{CH_3}{\underset{|}{\overset{|}{C}}}}-N{=}N-\underset{CH_3}{\overset{CH_3}{\underset{|}{\overset{|}{C}}}}-CO_2CH_3 \rightarrow N_2 + 2CH_3O_2C-\underset{CH_3}{\overset{CH_3}{\underset{|}{\overset{|}{C}}}}\cdot \qquad (3\text{-}135)$$

However, the addition of as little as 0.5 mole % of thiophenol raises its efficiency to 80 to 90% (542). That is, Eq. (3-136) occurs more slowly

$$CH_3O_2C-\underset{CH_3}{\overset{CH_3}{\underset{|}{\overset{|}{C}}}}\cdot + RCHO \rightarrow CH_3O_2C-\underset{CH_3}{\overset{CH_3}{\underset{|}{\overset{|}{C}}}}H + RCO\cdot \qquad (3\text{-}136)$$

than does the sum of Eqs. (3-137) and (3-138).

$$CH_3O_2C-\underset{CH_3}{\overset{CH_3}{\underset{|}{\overset{|}{C}}}}\cdot + C_6H_5SH \rightarrow CH_3O_2C-\underset{CH_3}{\overset{CH_3}{\underset{|}{\overset{|}{C}}}}H + C_6H_5S\cdot \qquad (3\text{-}137)$$

$$C_6H_5S\cdot + RCHO \rightarrow C_6H_5SH + RCO\cdot \qquad (3\text{-}138)$$

Thus, in the presence of thiols, the mechanism for the decomposition of aldehydes is modified to include Eqs. (3-139) and (3-140) in place of Eq. (3-133).

$$R-CHO + R'S\cdot \rightarrow R-CO\cdot + R'SH \qquad (3\text{-}139)$$

$$R-CO\cdot \rightarrow R\cdot + CO \qquad (3\text{-}134)$$

$$R\cdot + R'SH \rightarrow RH + R'S\cdot \qquad (3\text{-}140)$$

The rate of Eq. (3-140) varies with the thiol used in the order (132):

$$H_2S < CH_3SH < C_2H_5SH < i\text{-}C_3H_7SH < t\text{-}C_4H_9SH$$

Thus electron-donating alkyl groups on the sulfur are rate-enhancing; this is contrary to the prediction from Eq. (3-120). This suggests that the carbonyl carbon is more electronegative than the sulfur atom is.

At high pressures, thiols, olefins, and carbon monoxide react to reverse reactions (3-139), (3-134), and (3-140) and form 3-mercaptoaldehydes (475). *t*-Butyl peroxide has been used as a catalyst at 130° C and 3,000 atm.

$$CH_3S\cdot + CH_2{=}CH_2 \longrightarrow CH_3S-CH_2-\dot{C}H_2 \xrightarrow{CO} CH_3S-CH_2-CH_2-\dot{C}O \qquad (3\text{-}141)$$

$$CH_3S-CH_2-CH_2-\dot{C}O + CH_3SH \longrightarrow CH_3S-CH_2-CH_2-CHO + CH_3S\cdot \qquad (3\text{-}142)$$

The hydrogen-donating ability of thiols reduces the amount of rearrangement in certain radical reactions. Winstein, Heck, Lapporte, and Baird (1159) have reported that the 2-phenyl-2-methylpropyl radical rearranges to a lesser extent if a thiol is present. Similarly, Slaugh (989) reports that 2.4 mole % thiophenol reduces the amount of rearrangement of the 1-C^{14}-2-phenylethyl radical from 5.1 to 2.3%.

Slaugh and Raley (990) found that the rearrangement of cumene to propylbenzene can be initiated at 400 to 525° C by S_8, thiols, hydrogen sulfide, alkyl disulfides, or iodine. The mechanism for the initiation is presumably homolytic scission of S—S, S—H, or I—I bonds. The high conversion (e.g., 5.3%) to rearranged products presumably results from transfer reactions.

$$C_6H_5-\underset{\underset{CH_3}{|}}{\overset{\overset{CH_3}{|}}{CH}} + RS\cdot \longrightarrow C_6H_5-\underset{\underset{CH_3}{|}}{\overset{\overset{\cdot CH_2}{|}}{CH}} + RSH \tag{3-143}$$

$$C_6H_5-\underset{\underset{CH_3}{|}}{\overset{\overset{\cdot CH_2}{|}}{CH}} \longrightarrow C_6H_5-CH_2-\dot{C}H-CH_3 \tag{3-144}$$

$$C_6H_5-CH_2-\dot{C}H-CH_3 + RSH \longrightarrow C_6H_5-CH_2-CH_2-CH_3 + RS\cdot \tag{3-145}$$

Kornblum and De La Mare (654) report that optically active 1-phenylethyl *t*-butyl peroxide reacts with thiophenol to produce optically active 1-phenylethyl alcohol.

$$C_6H_5-\underset{\underset{H}{|}}{\overset{\overset{CH_3}{|}}{C}}-O-O-C_4H_9\text{-}t \longrightarrow C_6H_5-\underset{\underset{H}{|}}{\overset{\overset{CH_3}{|}}{C}}-O\cdot + t\text{-}C_4H_9O\cdot \tag{3-146}$$

$$C_6H_5-\underset{\underset{H}{|}}{\overset{\overset{CH_3}{|}}{C}}-O\cdot \xrightarrow[?]{(3\text{-}147)} C_6H_5-\underset{\cdot}{\overset{\overset{CH_3}{|}}{C}}-O-H \xrightarrow{(3\text{-}148)}\!\!\!\!\!\!\!\!\not\;\;\; \begin{matrix}\text{Racemized products}\\ \text{(not formed)}\end{matrix}$$

C_6H_5SH (3-149) [from $C_6H_5C(CH_3)(H)O\cdot$]; C_6H_5SH (3-150) [from $C_6H_5\dot{C}(CH_3)OH$]

$$\downarrow$$

$$C_6H_5-\underset{\underset{H}{|}}{\overset{\overset{CH_3}{|}}{C}}-OH + C_6H_5S\cdot$$

Optically active alcohol
(found)

The lack of racemization in the recovered alcohol could result because the rearrangement step, Eq. (3-147), is slow relative to the transfer step, Eq. (3-149). It also could result from rearrangement occurring as in Eq. (3-147), but with step (3-150) being faster than step (3-148). This point could be clarified by deuterium labeling. Starting with C_6H_5SD could conceivably lead to the formation of 1-deutero alcohol which is nevertheless not racemized. This would then be a further example of a system in which racemization was slower than hydrogen transfer.

4

REACTION OF SULFUR WITH ALKANES

Sulfur, like oxygen itself, is a powerful enough oxidant to attack paraffinic hydrocarbons. This section discusses the reaction of sulfur and hydrocarbons in the absence of other reagents; the reactions which occur in the presence of water, aqueous bases, or amines are reviewed in the chapters which follow.

When sulfur is heated with a hydrocarbon, dehydrogenation and hydrogen sulfide evolution commence at about 150° C (809, 1102). Three useful processes have been developed from such reactions.

1. Alkanes can be dehydrogenated to olefins under controlled conditions.
2. The olefins may react with more sulfur and undergo ring closure and aromatization to form thiophenes and similar compounds.
3. Vigorous conditions lead to complete oxidation and the formation of carbon disulfide.

4-1. Dehydrogenation of Alkanes

Dehydrogenation of hydrocarbons to olefins occurs when they are pumped through molten sulfur at 300° C or above, or if S_2 vapor is allowed to react with hydrocarbons in the gas phase (884). The sulfur is always reduced to hydrogen sulfide, and this reaction is frequently used as a source of hydrogen sulfide (1106). Often the organic compound is converted to tars (708), but useful products are obtained under controlled conditions (62). For example, the reaction of butane with sulfur can be controlled so that the intermediate products, butene and butadiene, may be isolated (884). The main product is thiophene if the reaction mixture is recycled. Ethane is dehydrogenated to ethylene in the gas phase at 871° C either in the presence of gaseous sulfur as S_2 (779) or in its absence. At similar temperatures but at higher mole ratios of sulfur, acetylene is formed. Sulfur is very effective in promoting the dehydrogenation of ethane to acetylene but has little effect on the reaction forming ethylene (779). Table 4-1 gives further examples.

Table 4-1
Dehydrogenation of hydrocarbons by sulfur

Hydrocarbon	°C	Approx. reaction time, sec	Mole ratio S:compound	Product (% yield)	References
Butane	650	0.07	1.8	Thiophene (67)[a]	884
Isobutane	649	0.07	0.9	Isobutene (65)	884
Propane	704	0.1	2.8	Propene (92)	884
Ethane	760	0.1	1.8	Ethylene (95)	884
Ethane	876	2–3	0–0.8	Ethylene (50)	779
Ethane	650–930	2–3	1.4	Acetylene (50)	779
Hydrocarbons	1000	....	...	Benzene[a] + CS_2	1148
Ethylbenzene	500–700	....	...	Styrene	504

[a] See discussion of dehydrocyclization on p. 120. Yields are corrected for recovered substrate.

An investigation by Bryce and Hinshelwood (189) of the gas-phase cracking of alkanes in the presence of sulfur has demonstrated the following features: In the presence of sulfur the products remain the same, viz., lower-molecular-weight, terminal olefins. The reaction is first order in hydrocarbon and nearly zero order in sulfur vapor. Hydrogen sulfide is the main sulfur-containing product. The influence of the structure of the alkane on the rate of reaction is analogous to that observed in the thermal cracking of hydrocarbons. Since more than 1 mole of olefin is formed per mole of hydrogen sulfide, the reaction appears to be a chain process. The mechanism is probably abstraction of hydrogen atoms by radical sulfur species followed by the type of reactions known to occur in thermal cracking.

4-2. Dehydrocyclization of Alkanes

This topic is discussed in detail under aromatization, Sec. 6-2. Since sulfur is a powerful dehydrogenation agent, it has been used as a cocatalyst in vapor-phase, catalytic dehydrogenations, for example, over Al_2O_3. Sulfur dioxide and sulfur trioxide are also dehydrogenation promoters (718). However, thiophenes also may be formed (811). Thiophenes may result from the reaction of olefins, which are probably reaction intermediates (884), with hydrogen sulfide, which is a reaction product.

Olefins and hydrogen sulfide react over Al_2O_3 to produce thiophenes in fast reactions (522).

4-3. Oxidation of Alkanes to Carbon Disulfide

Complete oxidation of hydrocarbons by sulfur leads to the formation of carbon disulfide and hydrogen sulfide. This is a commercial process, and the kinetics and mechanism have been investigated (1049). When sulfur reacts with methane, the reaction is first order in S_2 and first order in hydrocarbon (421, 427). Thc conversion of S_8 or S_6 to S_2 is fast at the temperatures employed, about 600° C.

5

THE REACTION OF SULFUR WITH OLEFINS TO PRODUCE ORGANIC SULFIDES AND POLYSULFIDES

Sulfur reacts with olefins at 90 to 160° C in the liquid phase to form several types of polysulfide products. These reactions have been studied intensively because they are intrinsically interesting and useful, and also because they are models for vulcanization, an extremely complex reaction in which polysulfide chains crosslink rubber molecules.

The mechanism of the reaction of sulfur with olefins has not been established, and conflicting theories have been published. In 1947, Farmer, Shipley, and coworkers at the British Rubber Producers' Research Association published the first detailed study in this field (359, 362, 363). On the basis of their data, they proposed a mechanism that involved sulfenyl free radicals. These radicals were proposed to abstract an allylic hydrogen from an olefin to produce a carbon radical that reacts with sulfur and eventually becomes an alkyl hydrogen polysulfide, RS_xH. This species was postulated as adding to an olefin molecule in an ionic, Markovnikov addition to form the observed polysulfide products. Other studies were believed to support this mechanism (28, 963). These reactions produce a complex mixture of products, and the mechanistic evidence was incomplete at best. Nevertheless, this mechanism was widely accepted and has been frequently quoted (page 89 of ref. 202, 422, 519, page 336 of ref. 1116). It was the best working hypothesis available.

In 1958, a second group of workers at the British Rubber Producers' Research Association, including Bateman, Moore, Glazebrook, Saville, Ross, and Porter, published experiments and interpretations which conflict with the earlier work by Farmer and Shipley. The new data are the result of the application of more refined, modern analytical techniques to the complex product mixture. However, the new results are themselves not complete. The newer workers have suggested a markedly different mechanism, namely an entirely ionic, chain mechanism. As seen below, this is not unambiguously established by the data. The new evidence is the result of elegant experimental work. However, it appears that further work will be necessary to eliminate alternative possibilities.

This chapter reviews most of the data. Papers prior to 1945 are not covered, however, since they are of little current interest and have been reviewed (1144). Nor is the vast literature on the technology of rubber covered (685, 781). Craig (258) reviewed a number of aspects of the vulcanization reaction of rubber in 1957.

5-1. Reaction of Sulfur with Monoolefins

5-1A. Early Work. Research by Farmer and Shipley (359, 362, 363) and by Armstrong, Little, and Doak (28) on the reactions of olefins such as cyclohexene and isobutylene with sulfur at 100 to 140° C in the absence of other reactants established the following features:

1. The predominant products are alkyl alkenyl polysulfides, R—S_x—R′, where R is saturated and R′ contains one double bond. Equimolar mixtures of R—S_x—R and R′—S_x—R′ may also occur with isobutene but are less likely with cyclohexene and 1-methylcyclohexene. The range of x is from 1 to 6, with relatively little $x = 1$.

2. Variations in the amount of sulfur used from $\frac{1}{8}$ to $\frac{7}{8}$ gram atoms sulfur per mole of substrate affect the amount but not the nature of the products obtained (362).

3. Thioepoxides, e.g.,

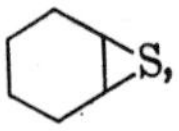

S,

are not formed (363) and indeed react very differently from the products obtained (768) (but see page 100).

4. No appreciable amounts of thiols or hydrogen sulfide are produced initially, but extensive amounts of thiols, hydrogen sulfide, and monosulfides are formed in secondary reactions if the initial products are heated to 160° C or higher. Hydrogen sulfide, therefore, is not an intermediate, and atomic sulfur is not believed to be a reaction intermediate, since it is presumed that it would react with olefins to produce thioepoxides.

5. No new C—C bonds are formed.

6. Selker and Kemp (963) found that the reaction is zero order in both

olefin and sulfur. These results are contradicted by recent findings (see page 102). These earlier workers separated products by distillation, and this is now known to decompose the primary products.

Another series of studies designed to elucidate the mechanism of the reactions of sulfur with olefins examined the reactions of olefins with hydrogen sulfide. It was shown that H_2S adds to olefins in the presence of sulfur to give Markovnikov addition in an ionic reaction (599, 798, 799, 971). For example, the products from isobutylene at 140° C include *t*-butyl mercaptan, *t*-butyl sulfide, and *t*-butyl disulfide (798). The presence of sulfur is necessary to produce Markovnikov products (599). In the absence of sulfur and with ultraviolet light, hydrogen sulfide adds to produce non-Markovnikov products in a free-radical reaction that is fast even at 0° C (733, 1103) (see Sec. 10-3).

Thiols also add to olefins to give Markovnikov products in the presence of sulfur (599). In the absence of sulfur, thiols add to olefins entirely in a non-Markovnikov direction, even in the dark (583, 584). The reaction in the presence of sulfur probably is an ionic process, with sulfur acting as an inhibitor of the radical reactions.

Tetrasulfides also react with olefins to form Markovnikov products similar to those formed from thiols. Since tetrasulfides decompose to form disulfides and sulfur when heated, the tetrasulfides themselves provide the sulfur required to achieve Markovnikov addition. For example, ethyl tetrasulfide reacts with propene in 10 hours at 180° C to give 6% of isopropyl mercaptan, 20% of isopropyl sulfide, and 15% of propanethioepoxide (599). In this reaction the ethyl tetrasulfide decomposes to ethyl disulfide and sulfur and acts as a source of sulfur; propene and S_8 react under these conditions to give 6% isopropyl mercaptan and 20% of isopropyl sulfide. Phenyl tetrasulfide reacts with 1-methylcyclohexene to give phenyl 1-methylcyclohexyl sulfide (140). The fact that the products of these reactions are those that would be predicted by Markovnikov addition of the related thiols is not sufficient evidence that the decomposition of the tetrasulfide is ionic, since the reaction is multistep and not a simple addition.

In 1947, on the basis of this information on the reaction of olefins with sulfur, hydrogen sulfide, thiols, and tetrasulfides, Farmer and Shipley (362) and Bloomfield and Naylor (144) proposed the mechanism given below for the over-all reaction of sulfur with olefins. Sulfur forms a sulfenyl radical by an unspecified pathway; this sulfenyl radical abstracts an allylic hydrogen from the olefin, forming a carbon radical; this radical attacks sulfur to produce a polysulfenyl radical which abstracts hydrogen from a second olefin molecule and then adds to a third olefin molecule in an ionic addition in the Markovnikov direction.

$$\text{Initiation by unknown mechanism} \longrightarrow YS_x\cdot \qquad \text{(5-1)}$$

$$YS_x\cdot + \underset{H_3C\quad CH_3}{\overset{CH_2}{\overset{\|}{C}}} \longrightarrow YS_xH + \underset{H_3C\quad CH_2\cdot}{\overset{CH_2}{\overset{\|}{C}}} \qquad \text{(5-2)}$$

$$\underset{H_3C\quad CH_2\cdot}{\overset{CH_2}{\overset{\|}{C}}} + S_8 \longrightarrow \underset{H_3C\quad CH_2{-}S_7{-}S\cdot}{\overset{CH_2}{\overset{\|}{C}}} \qquad \text{(5-3)}$$

$$\underset{H_3C\quad CH_2{-}S_7{-}S\cdot}{\overset{CH_2}{\overset{\|}{C}}} + \underset{H_3C\quad CH_3}{\overset{CH_2}{\overset{\|}{C}}} \longrightarrow \underset{H_3C\quad CH_2{-}S_7{-}SH}{\overset{CH_2}{\overset{\|}{C}}} + \underset{H_3C\quad CH_2\cdot}{\overset{CH_2}{\overset{\|}{C}}} \qquad \text{(5-4)}$$

$$\underset{\substack{H_3C\quad CH_2{-}S_x{-}SH \\ (x=7,\ \text{etc.})^a}}{\overset{CH_2}{\overset{\|}{C}}} + \underset{H_3C\quad CH_3}{\overset{CH_2}{\overset{\|}{C}}} \xrightarrow[\text{addition}]{\text{Ionic}} \underset{H_3C\quad CH_2}{\overset{CH_2}{\overset{\|}{C}}}{-}S_x{-}S{-}\underset{H_3C\quad CH_3}{\overset{CH_3}{\overset{|}{C}}} \qquad \text{(5-5)}$$

[a] Thermal equilibration yields a mixture of chain lengths.

The salient feature of this mechanism is that it separates the radical hydrogen abstraction steps, Eqs. (5-2) and (5-4), from the ionic addition reaction (5-5). Evidence for the radical nature of the abstraction reactions rests upon presumption; evidence for the ionic nature of the addition reaction is based solely on the isolation of Markovnikov-type products.

One difficulty with this mechanism is that the hydrogen alkyl polylsulfides RS_xH, which are postulated as intermediates, have not been isolated (106).

5-1B. Recent Work. In 1959, the reactions of sulfur with olefins were reexamined by workers at the British Rubber Producers' Research Association laboratory, and the previously published mechanism has been modified (105). The reaction of sulfur with 1-octene, cyclohexene, 2-heptene, 2-methyl-2-pentene, 1-methylcyclohexene, and 2,6-dimethyl-2-octene has been studied and the products examined by elemental analysis and chemical (30, 771) and spectroscopic methods. The main product is a mixture of polysulfides as previously reported, plus small amounts of thioepoxides which had been overlooked before (103). The polysulfide fraction consists of alkyl alkenyl polysulfides as previously reported, and also of saturated products which appear to be heterocyclic compounds.

The polysulfide products from 1-octene were shown by careful analysis to be a mixture of the compounds shown below (103).

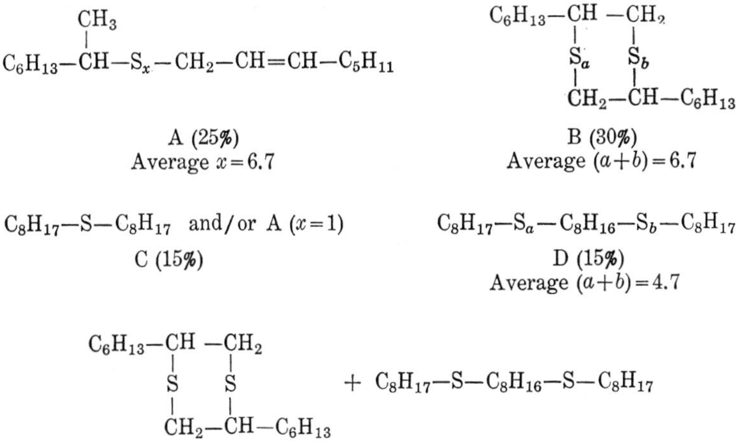

$$\begin{array}{c} CH_3 \\ | \\ C_6H_{13}-CH-S_x-CH_2-CH{=}CH-C_5H_{11} \end{array} \qquad \begin{array}{c} C_6H_{13}-CH\ -CH_2 \\ |\qquad\ | \\ S_a\quad S_b \\ |\qquad\ | \\ CH_2-CH-C_6H_{13} \end{array}$$

A (25%) Average $x=6.7$ — B (30%) Average $(a+b)=6.7$

$$C_8H_{17}-S-C_8H_{17} \text{ and/or A } (x=1) \qquad C_8H_{17}-S_a-C_8H_{16}-S_b-C_8H_{17} \tag{5-6}$$

C (15%) — D (15%) Average $(a+b)=4.7$

$$\begin{array}{c} C_6H_{13}-CH\ -CH_2 \\ |\qquad\ | \\ S\quad\ S \\ |\qquad\ | \\ CH_2-CH-C_6H_{13} \end{array} + C_8H_{17}-S-C_8H_{16}-S-C_8H_{17}$$

E (15%)

The remainder of the olefins studied give polysulfides as the major product. 1-Octene gives an anomalously low amount of alkyl alkenyl polysulfide, A, and more cyclic products, B and E, relative to the other olefins studied (see Table 5-1).

Table 5-1
Approximate distribution of the products from the reaction of various olefins with sulfur (103)

Olefin	Mole fraction			
	Alkyl-S_x-alkenyl (A)[a]	Cyclic sulfides (B)[a]	Polymer (D)[a]	Alkyl-S-alkenyl (A, x = 1)[a]
1-Octene	25	30	15	15
2,6-Dimethyl-2-octene	45	35	20	0
1-Methylcyclohexene	60	20	10	0
2-Methyl-2-pentene	80	15	0	0

[a] The letters for compounds refer to structures given in (5-6).

Thus, the earlier findings of Farmer and Shipley that substituted olefins like 1-methylcyclohexene and isobutene give mainly alkyl alkenyl polysulfides are correct. Newer data show that cyclic structures such as B also make up from 15 to 35% of the mixture, depending on the nature of the olefin.

The newer work also includes a kinetic study by Ross of the reaction of cyclohexene with sulfur between 110° and 140° C followed by dilatometry

(899). The reaction goes through three stages: (1) an accelerating rate until about 20% of the sulfur is consumed, r_a; (2) a constant, maximum rate, r_m; and (3) a decreasing rate. An induction period occurs and has increasing length at smaller initial concentrations.

The increasing rate, r_a, is proportional to the square root of the product concentration and the square root of the initial sulfur and olefin concentrations.

$$r_a = \frac{dP}{dt} = k(P)^{1/2}(S_8)_0^{1/2}(RH)_0^{1/2}$$

where P is the product, RH is cyclohexene, and subzero indicates initial concentrations. The constant rate, r_m, as measured by the time required for reaction of one-half of the sulfur, was found to be

$$r_m = k'(S_8)_0(RH)^{1/2}$$

The products formed in this reaction appear to be both cyclic sulfides and alkyl alkenyl polysulfides, and to be constant during a kinetic run.

$$C_6H_{10} \xrightarrow{S_8} C_6H_{10}\langle{S_a \atop S_b}\rangle C_6H_{10} + C_6H_{11}{-}S_x{-}C_6H_9 \qquad x = a + b$$

During the kinetic runs x remains constant over the period described by r_a and then decreases slightly.

This new evidence (106) has led to the replacement of the older mechanism for sulfur-olefin reactions, Eqs. (5-1) to (5-5), and the postulation of the ionic chain mechanism given in Eqs. (5-7) to (5-13). It is now proposed that initiation involves heterolytic scission of an S—S bond to polysulfide and polysulfenium ions. The polysulfenium ion adds to an olefin to produce a carbonium ion which either accepts a hydride ion or loses a proton.

Initiation:

$$\text{Dissociation by unknown mechanism} \longrightarrow YS_a^+ + YS_b^- \qquad (5\text{-}7)$$

$$YS_a^+ + \text{cyclohexene} \longrightarrow \text{cyclohexyl}\langle^{+}\rangle S_aY \qquad (5\text{-}8)$$

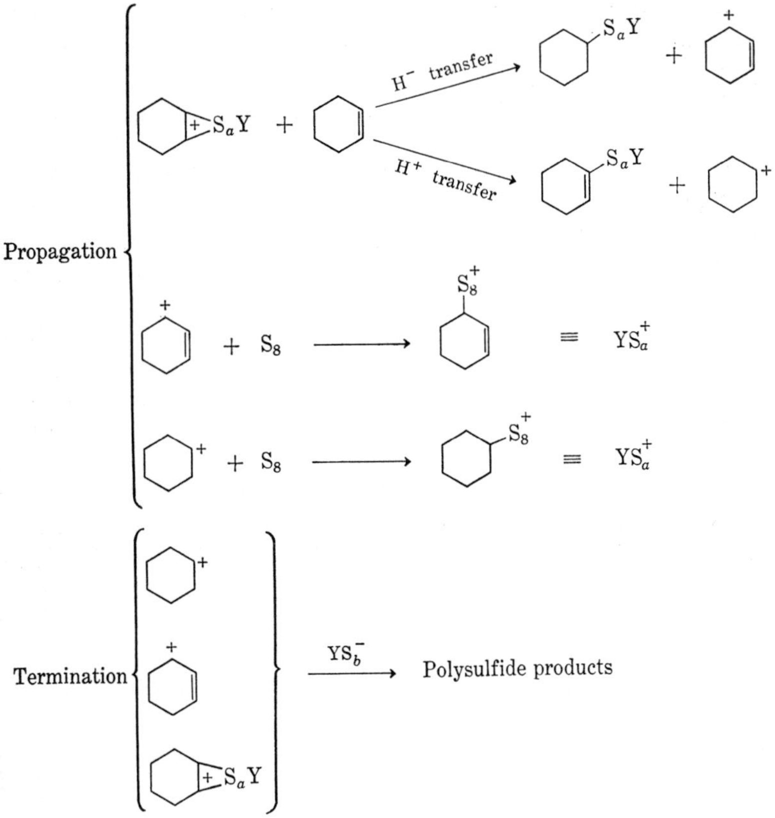

Propagation

(5-9) [cyclohexene–S_aY episulfonium ion] + cyclohexene $\xrightarrow{H^- \text{ transfer}}$ cyclohexyl–S_aY + allylic cyclohexenyl cation

(5-10) [cyclohexene–S_aY episulfonium ion] + cyclohexene $\xrightarrow{H^+ \text{ transfer}}$ cyclohexenyl–S_aY + cyclohexyl cation

(5-11) cyclohexenyl cation + S_8 $\longrightarrow$ cyclohexenyl–S_8^+ $\equiv$ YS_a^+

(5-12) cyclohexyl cation + S_8 $\longrightarrow$ cyclohexyl–S_8^+ $\equiv$ YS_a^+

Termination

(5-13) {cyclohexyl cation, cyclohexenyl cation, [cyclohexene–S_aY episulfonium ion]} $\xrightarrow{YS_b^-}$ Polysulfide products

A number of other types of reactions are possible. Reaction (5-14) may occur and lead to cyclic structures of type B, (5-6). Reaction (5-15) occurs but the authors' notation does not distinguish it. Reaction (5-16) does not occur since no new C—C bonds are formed.

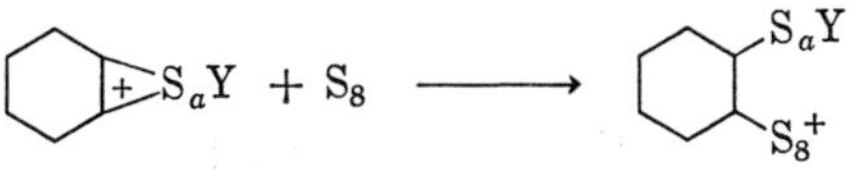

(5-14) [cyclohexene–S_aY episulfonium ion] + S_8 $\longrightarrow$ 1-S_aY-2-S_8^+-cyclohexane

$$YS_a^+ + S_8 \longrightarrow YS_{a+8}^+ \qquad (5\text{-}15)$$

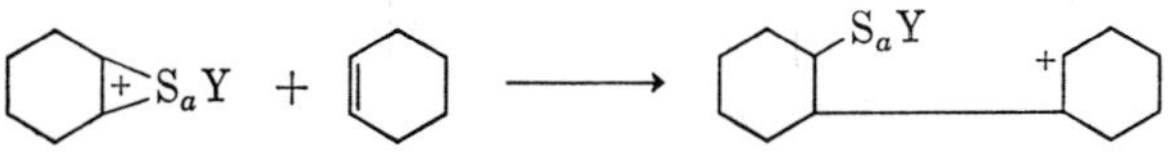

(5-16) [cyclohexene–S_aY episulfonium ion] + cyclohexene $\longrightarrow$ 2-S_aY-cyclohexyl–cyclohexyl cation

Under some conditions, e.g., in the presence of zinc salts, such as used in vulcanization, the polysulfide ion YS_b^- also is postulated to enter into these chain reactions (102).

Five areas in which the British workers find support for the ionic chain mechanism will be considered.

1. Both the old (144) and the new (106) mechanisms for the reaction of sulfur with olefins propose that the addition step is ionic and that products are those which would be predicted by the Markovnikov rule. The new data provide further examples of carefully analyzed products which have structures consistent with ionic additions.

2. The dissociation step may involve either radicals or ions. The British authors (106) prefer an ionic dissociation because they feel that no examples of thermal homolytic scission of alkyl disulfides have been reported to occur below 140° C. Their conclusion may be in error (see the discussion in Sec. 3-3A). Even if their conclusion is correct, however, it does not preclude the possibility of homolytic scission of the complex polysulfides present in sulfur-olefin reactions. The English workers suggest that the initiation does not occur by a free radical mechanism since light does not induce the reaction at 80 to 100° C (899). This also does not eliminate the possibility of radical reactions with a short chain length; sulfur is an efficient radical trap, and long kinetic chains would not be likely. Nor does it eliminate homolytic initiation at higher temperatures. Thus the presence of polysulfenyl radicals is not eliminated.

In order to have ionic initiation, polysulfenium ions must be generated. No evidence has been reported for the thermal heterolytic dissociation of a polysulfide bond.

It must be concluded that no direct evidence is available which supports dissociation of polysulfides to either ions or radicals at temperatures below 140° C. The presence of either species for the initiation step therefore rests upon supposition.

3. The authors propose the presence of bridged ions as support for an ionic mechanism. They postulate that a truer representation (106) of Eqs. (5-7) and (5-8) is nucleophilic attack on sulfur by an olefin:

$$YS_a{-}S_bY + \begin{matrix} \diagdown\ \diagup \\ C \\ \| \\ C \\ \diagup\ \diagdown \end{matrix} \longrightarrow \left[\begin{matrix} YS_{a-1} \diagdown & & \diagdown\diagup \\ & S \cdots & C \\ & & \vdots \\ S_bY \diagup & \cdots & C \\ & & \diagup\diagdown \end{matrix} \right] \longrightarrow YS_{a-1}{-}\overset{+}{S}\begin{matrix} \cdots C \\ \vdots \\ \cdots C \end{matrix} + YS_b^- \qquad (5\text{-}17)$$

Transition state

Nucleophilic attack on sulfur is observed for some, but not all, nucleophiles (81). Whether an olefin is able to accomplish this remains speculative.*

The authors point out that bridged, rather than open-chain, polysulfenium ions better explain the formation of A [see (5-6)] from 1-octene. If RS_a^+ is added directly to 1-octene in the Markovnikov direction, the ultimate product presumably would have a double bond stabilized by being adjacent to the sulfur atom.

$$YS_a^+ + CH_2{=}CH{-}C_6H_{13} \longrightarrow \underset{\displaystyle\overset{|}{YS_a}}{}CH_2{-}\overset{+}{C}H{-}C_6H_{13} \xrightarrow{-H^+} \overset{YS_a}{\overset{|}{C}H}{=}CH{-}C_6H_{13}$$

If a cyclic intermediate is involved, the observed product can be explained.

$$\overset{YS_{a-1}\text{–}S^+}{CH_2\cdots CH}{-}\underset{H}{\underset{|}{CH}}{-}C_5H_{11} \longleftrightarrow \overset{YS_{a-1}\text{–}S}{CH_2}{-}\overset{+}{CH}{-}\underset{H}{\underset{|}{CH}}{-}C_5H_{11} \xrightarrow{-H^+} \underset{A}{\overset{YS_{a-1}\text{–}S}{CH_2}{-}CH{=}CH{-}C_5H_{11}} \qquad (5\text{-}18)$$

If bridged structures are involved, they are probably ionic and not radical (986, 987). The classical structure of sulfenyl radicals was discussed on p. 78. The nonclassical, cyclic structure of sulfenium ions was considered on p. 72, where it was pointed out that the secondary carbon bears a large portion of the positive charge. Therefore, loss of a proton as in Eq. (5-18) is reasonable.

4. The authors (106, 899) find support for an ionic mechanism in the effect of additives on the rate of reaction of sulfur with cyclohexene (Table 5-2). Actually, however, the data are far from simple and do not lead to a unique conclusion. Although azo compounds are without effect, benzoquinone, iodine, and diphenylpicrylhydrazyl all have an effect, as would be consistent with a radical reaction.† Acids and bases increase

* Some evidence has been found that olefins catalyze the decomposition of peroxides in a reaction of low efficiency (521*a*, 724*a*). It is possible that olefins also catalyze the homolytic decomposition of disulfides. The catalysis of the heterolytic scission of disulfides by olefins in hydrocarbon solvents appears less likely.

† Radical chlorination by *t*-butyl hypochlorite is inhibited by hydroquinone but is accelerated by iodine (1122, 1123). The effects of iodine on reactions which are known to involve radicals are not clearly enough understood for their use as a diagnostic tool (86).

the rate; e.g., the addition of 0.3 *M* triethylamine triples the rate. These effects suggest an ionic reaction. However, catalysis by acids and amines is a common feature of sulfur reactions and occurs in several reactions which definitely involve radicals (see page 9). The effects of thiols, polysulfides, and the polysulfide product itself are not conclusive evidence for either radicals or ions. Establishing an ionic chain mechanism from the effects of additives should be expected to be difficult since no adequate model exists. For example, the effects of additives on ionic polymerizations are complex and not understood (pages 409–415 of ref. 202).

Table 5-2
The effect of additives on the reaction of sulfur with cyclohexene at 140° C (899)

Additive	Effect
1,1′-Azobisisobutyronitrile	None
1-Azobis-1-phenylpropane	None
Hydroquinone	None
Benzoquinone	Increases r_a (defined in text)
Iodine	Eliminates r_a period entirely without affecting r_m
Diphenylpicrylhydrazyl	Eliminates r_a period entirely, decreases r_m
t-Butyl alcohol	None
Pyridine	None
Dioxane	None
Trichloroacetic acid Benzoic acid Propionic acid Stearic acid	Increases rate 20 to 50% throughout course without changing products
Triethyl amine	Increases r_a and r_m and reduces activation energy with little change in products
2-Propanethiol	Increases r_a slightly
Benzyl tetrasulfide Polysulfide product	Increases r_a proportional to square root of its concentration

5. The effect of polar solvents on the rate of the reaction of sulfur with cyclohexene also has been proposed as support for the ionic mechanism (899). The over-all reaction of sulfur with cyclohexene increases 50% in rate when the solvent is changed from cyclohexane to nitromethane (dielectric increase from 2 to 39, see ref. 727). If the two neutral molecules, sulfur and cyclohexene, were to react to produce a transition state with considerable charge separation, then a solvent effect much larger than this would be expected (80, 1172). For example, in the radiochloride exchange reaction between triphenylmethyl chloride and tetra-

butylammonium chloride, the rate increases, 1,620-fold when 6.8 *M* nitromethane is added to the benzene solvent (575).

A further comparison can be made using data on the reactions of triphenylphosphine discussed on pages 159 and 160. The reaction of this phosphine with S_8 increases 208-fold in rate when the solvent dielectric is increased from 2.0 to 5.7. Bartlett and Meguerian (89) concluded that the reaction is ionic with considerable charge separation in the transition state. The reaction of the same phosphine with 2-butene episulfide increases 45% in rate when the dielectric is increased from 2.4 to 37.6, and Denney and Boskin (315) conclude that this reaction is molecular rather than ionic and involves very little charge separation. In the sulfur-olefin reaction, Bateman, Moore, and Porter (106) observe a small solvent effect very similar to that observed in the 2-butene episulfide reaction. They correctly conclude that the transition state involves little charge separation, and they formulate it as in Eq. (5-17). However, they then propose that fully ionic species are formed after the transition complex. This appears unlikely.

The effect of solvents on the ionic chain mechanism given in Eqs. (5-7) to (5-13) is difficult to predict. The mechanism involves an initiation step in which charges develop in the transition state, propagation steps in which charges are dispersed, and termination steps in which charges are reduced. (For elaboration of terminology see page 347 of ref. 581.) The solvent effect on ionic polymerizations, although not an exact analogy, is relevant, and the effects are much larger than those observed here (499). For example, the polymerization of α-methylstyrene catalyzed by stannic chloride increases in rate by a factor of 1,000 on changing the solvent from cyclohexane to nitrobenzene (847).

The solvent effect on chain reactions involving free radicals is usually smaller than solvent effects observed in ionic reactions (page 236 of ref. 202, page 60 of ref. 1057). However, measuring the over-all rate effect of solvents on a vinyl polymerization, for example, is complicated by changing amounts of chain transfer to the different solvents (68). The rate of the initiation step (65, pages 60 and 73 of ref. 1057) has been examined separately; it is insensitive to change in solvent. The rate of the chain-transfer step is also relatively insensitive to the dielectric constant of the solvent; e.g., the abstraction of bromine atoms from CBr_4 by a polystyryl radical increases 10% in rate when the dielectric constant of the medium is increased from 2 to 37 (486).

It must be concluded that the solvent effect does not lend strong support to an ionic mechanism for sulfur-olefin reactions. The 50% increase in over-all rate with a twentyfold increase in dielectric constant is more consistent with a radical mechanism. However, an ionic mechanism with very small charge development or with cancellation of effects in various steps is conceivable.

5-2. Reaction of Sulfur with Monoolefins in the Presence of Amines

Amines profoundly affect both the rate of sulfur-olefin reactions and the nature of the products. For example, at 140° C, in the presence of diethylamine, sulfur and cyclohexene form cyclohexyl sulfide. This product contrasts sharply with the cyclohexyl cyclohexenyl polysulfides obtained in the absence of amine (771). Sulfur and amines form complexes at room temperature (110, 687, 688). It has been suggested that the mechanism for the accelerating effect of amines on sulfur-olefin reactions involves this complex (661, 960), but this has been discounted because these complexes do not react with cyclohexene at 80° C (771); the reaction at 140° C has not been investigated. Instead, Moore and Saville (771) have proposed that H_2S is the active sulfur species. Cyclohexyl sulfide is one of the products formed in the reaction of cyclohexene with H_2S in the presence of amines (798).

Moore and Saville (771) suggest the following mechanism. At 140° C, the α carbon atom of an amine is oxidized by sulfur in a reaction which produces hydrogen sulfide. The hydrogen sulfide then reacts with more amine to form a salt (168, 563, 628, 630, 686, 742, 771, 773).

$$R-CH_2-\overset{\overset{\large H}{|}}{N}-CH_2R + \tfrac{1}{4}S_8 \longrightarrow R-CH_2-\overset{\overset{\large H}{|}}{N}-\overset{\overset{\large S}{\|}}{C}-R + H_2S \qquad (5\text{-}19)$$

$$H_2S + R-CH_2-\overset{\overset{\large H}{|}}{N}-CH_2R \longrightarrow [RCH_2-NH_2-CH_2R]^+\ HS^- \qquad (5\text{-}20)$$

Both the thioamide and the ammonium salt have been isolated from the reaction of sulfur with diethylamine (771). If this is the mechanism of the reaction, then the amine is not a catalyst but a reagent and is converted to the thioamide. For example, the reaction of cyclohexene, diethylamine, and sulfur has been formulated by Moore and Saville as Eqs. (5-19) and (5-20), followed by Eqs. (5-21) and (5-22).

$$(C_2H_5)_2NH_2^+\ SH^- + \text{cyclohexene} \longrightarrow \text{cyclohexyl-SH} + (C_2H_5)_2NH \qquad (5\text{-}21)$$

$$\text{cyclohexyl-SH} + \text{cyclohexene} \longrightarrow \text{cyclohexyl-S-cyclohexyl} \qquad (5\text{-}22)$$

Either the thiol or the monosulfide is postulated to be oxidized by more sulfur to disulfide in a fast reaction (142, 758, 759). The reaction of sulfur and amines with 1-methylcyclohexene yields 1-methylcyclohexyl disulfide as a product. Since the addition follows Markovnikov's rule, it has been postulated to involve an ionic reaction (772).

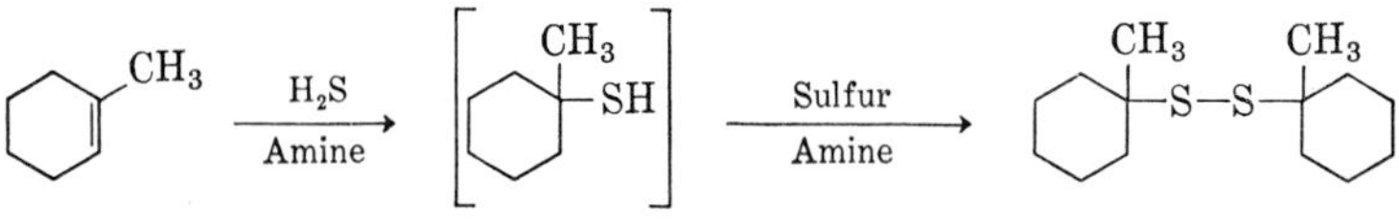

$$\text{1-methylcyclohexene} \xrightarrow[\text{Amine}]{H_2S} \left[\text{1-methylcyclohexanethiol } (CH_3,\ SH)\right] \xrightarrow[\text{Amine}]{\text{Sulfur}} \text{(1-methylcyclohexyl)}{-}S{-}S{-}\text{(1-methylcyclohexyl)} \tag{5-23}$$

Dimethylaniline, which does not liberate H_2S when heated with sulfur, does not change the products of sulfur-olefin reactions (771). The Moore-Saville mechanism does not make clear why dimethylaniline does not react as in Eq. (5-19). (See page 157.)

The *N*,*N*′-dithiobisamines, for example *N*,*N*′-dithiobismorpholine, are superior vulcanizing agents, and it has been suggested that they function through a similar mechanism (771). However, the products obtained from the reaction of such compounds with simple olefins are complex (924).

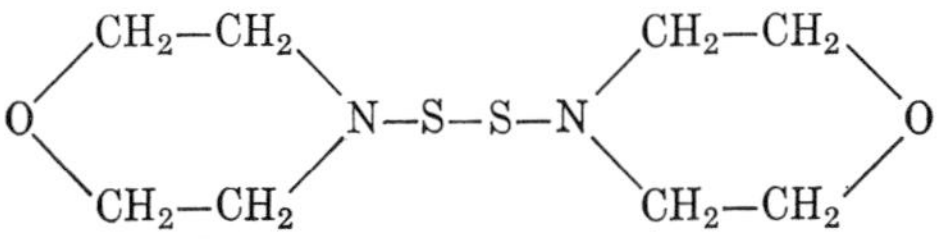

$$O\left\langle\begin{matrix}CH_2{-}CH_2\\ CH_2{-}CH_2\end{matrix}\right\rangle N{-}S{-}S{-}N\left\langle\begin{matrix}CH_2{-}CH_2\\ CH_2{-}CH_2\end{matrix}\right\rangle O$$

N,*N*′-Dithiobismorpholine

5-3. Reaction of Sulfur with Monoolefins in the Presence of Vulcanization Additives

The effect on sulfur-olefin reactions of various compounds used in vulcanization recipes has been studied. Such additives usually produce varied effects and may interact so that the combined effects of a mixture of additives are greater than the sum of the separate effects (28). For example, isobutylene reacts with sulfur to give alkyl alkenyl polysulfides, $R{-}S_x{-}R'$, with values of x from 1 to 6 (362). Organic vulcanization accelerators such as mercaptobenzothiazole increase the rate but do not alter the product (814). However, with a zinc soap plus an accelerator, the main products are dialkenyl mono- and disulfides (27, 28, 361, 814).

5-4. Reaction of Sulfur with Di- and Polyenes

5-4A. Reaction of Sulfur with Dienes. 2,6-Dimethyl-2,6-octadiene has been used as a low-molecular-weight model for the isoprenoid structure of rubber. The original work on the reaction of sulfur with 2,6-dimethyl-2,6-octadiene showed that linear polysulfides and a cyclic monosulfide were formed. Thiols were postulated as intermediates in the formation of the cyclic compound, as in Eq. (5-24) (144, 362). However, the structure of F was not conclusively established.

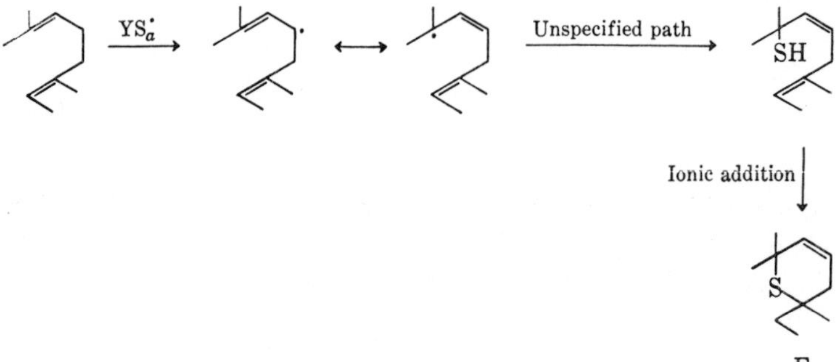

YS$_a^{\cdot}$ → ↔ Unspecified path → SH

Ionic addition ↓ (5-24)

S

F

More recent work (102, 104, 106, 509) has indicated that the products (101) consist of compounds with structures G through O, as shown in (5-25).

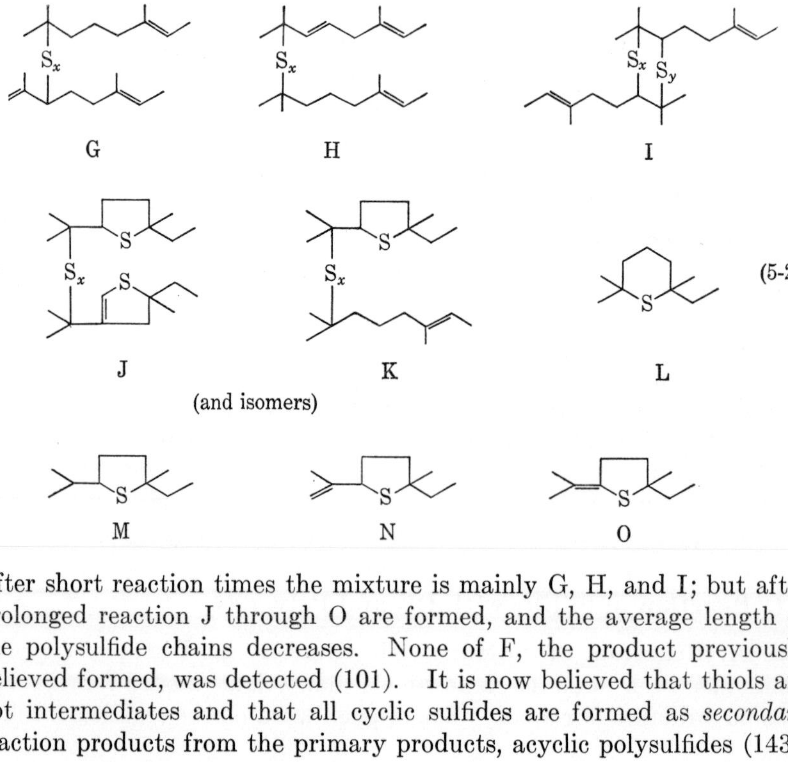

S_x S_x S_x S_y

G H I

S S_x S S S_x S (5-25)

J K L

(and isomers)

S S S

M N O

After short reaction times the mixture is mainly G, H, and I; but after prolonged reaction J through O are formed, and the average length of the polysulfide chains decreases. None of F, the product previously believed formed, was detected (101). It is now believed that thiols are not intermediates and that all cyclic sulfides are formed as *secondary* reaction products from the primary products, acyclic polysulfides (143).

A scheme has been suggested which is analogous to the ionic chain mechanism postulated to explain the reaction of monoolefins with sulfur. Equations (5-26) through (5-29) show how this scheme explains (106) the formation of typical open-chain polysulfide and cyclic monosulfide products given in (5-25).

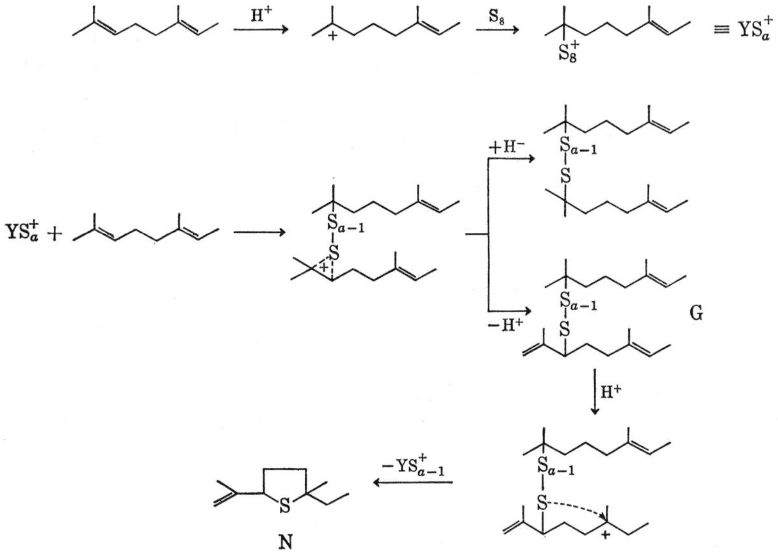

$\xrightarrow{H^+}$ $\xrightarrow{S_8}$ S_8^+ $\equiv YS_a^+$ (5-26)

$+H^-$ S_{a-1} S (5-27)

$YS_a^+ +$ $\longrightarrow$ S_{a-1} S +

$-H^+$ S_{a-1} S G (5-28)

H^+

$-YS_{a-1}^+$ S N S_{a-1} S + (5-29)

The mechanism requires protonation for the formation of cyclic products, Eq. (5-28). In agreement with this, the rate of formation of rings in the vulcanization of rubber is proportional to the activity of added protons (515).

5-4B. Reaction of Sulfur with Terpenes. Although the reaction of sulfur with terpenes has been known for some time (789, 790, 913, 981), its mechanism remains uncertain. Weitkamp has reported a careful study of the reactions of sulfur with limonene, terpinolene, and α-terpinene (1135). When these terpenes are heated to 170° C for 2 hours with a 15% molar excess of sulfur, several types of products are formed (Table 5-3).

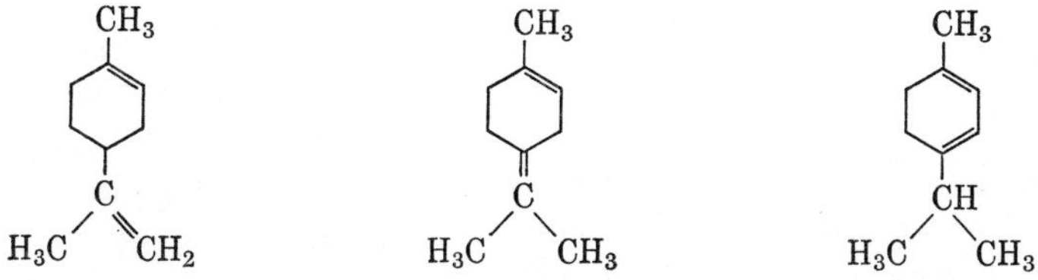

CH_3	CH_3	CH_3	
C	C	CH	(5-30)
H_3C CH_2	H_3C CH_3	H_3C CH_3	
Limonene	Terpinolene	α-Terpinene	

Table 5-3
Products of the terpene-sulfur reaction (1135)

Terpene	Mole %						
	Unreacted	P	Q	R	S	Volatile sulfur compounds	Poly-sulfides
d-Limonene	6	4	10	0	<0.1	36	44
Terpinolene	0	2	47	4	12	Trace	35
α-Terpinene	0	0	50	4	6	Trace	40

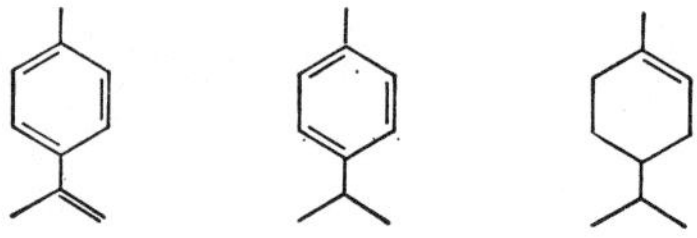

P Q R S (5-31)

In another experiment, limonene was refluxed with a 50% molar excess of sulfur for 1 hour, and the products consisted of 2% P, 5% Q, 56% polysulfides, 5% recovered limonene, and 31% of the volatile sulfur compounds T through W.

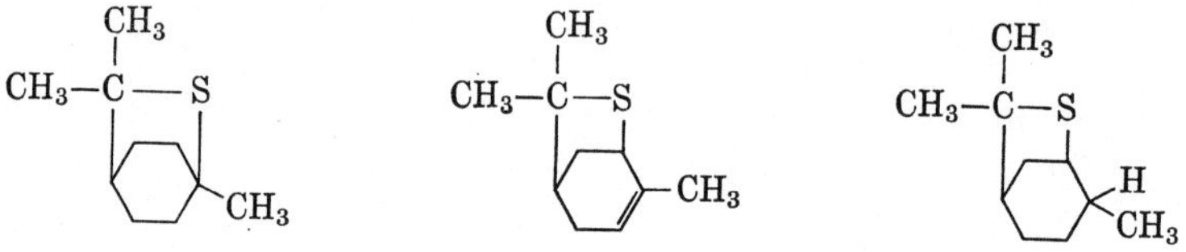

CH_3 CH_3—C—S CH_3

T, 2%

CH_3 CH_3—C—S CH_3

U, 6%

CH_3 CH_3—C—S H CH_3

V, 22% (98% trans) (5-32)

S C—CH_3 CH

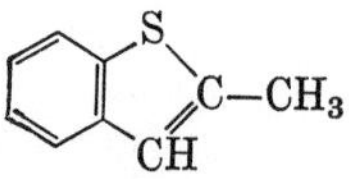

W, 0.4%

The structures of these products are consistent with ultraviolet, infrared, and mass spectral data, elemental analysis, optical activity, and the nature of their desulfurization products (1136). The percentage conversion of limonene at 140° C has been reported for 2-, 4-, and 8-hour reaction times (1137); the limited data indicate that limonene disappears at a first-order rate. (These calculations were made using the method of R. E. Powell, page 156 of ref. 485.)

A stereochemical investigation has related the cyclic monosulfide product U to *d*-limonene (699).

(5-33)

The conversion of *d*-limonene to U requires an allylic shift. The products can be explained (699) by an ionic addition to the ring followed by ionic or free radical reactions as shown in Eqs. (5-34) through (5-36). Moore and Porter have shown that these data also are consistent with the completely ionic mechanism for sulfur-olefin reactions (770).

(5-34)

(5-35)

(5-36)

5-4C. Reaction of Sulfur with Polyenes. Squalene has been studied as an example of a poly-isoprenoid compound that does not present the difficulties inherent in the polymeric rubber hydrocarbon. Squalene reacts with sulfur to form products similar to those found in the reaction of sulfur with mono- and diolefins (139, 141). A considerable fraction of the sulfur incorporated is in intramolecular rings rather than in polysulfide crosslinks (139). This phenomenon also occurs in rubber and lowers the efficiency of sulfur as a crosslinking agent.

5-4D. Reaction of Sulfur with Rubber. (1) *Vulcanization.* A review of all the literature on vulcanization is beyond the scope of this monograph; however, some of the salient features of this important and complex reaction should be pointed out. For a more detailed treatment, the 1957 review of D. Craig is recommended (258).

Rubber reacts with sulfur to give intramolecular polysulfides (rings) and intermolecular polysulfides (crosslinks) (142, 143). In distinction to older beliefs (360, 493), all crosslinks formed in vulcanization are polysulfide links and no new C—C bonds are detected (332, 767, 814, 962, 1024). The use of accelerators in vulcanization favors intermolecular crosslinking (143).

Until very recently when the ionic chain mechanism for sulfur-olefin reactions was published, it was implicit in all discussions of vulcanization that radicals are involved in at least some steps. However, no conclusive proof for this assumption has been published, although a number of studies with indicative evidence may be cited (259, 330, 331, 417, 577, 842). For example, Shelton and McDonel (970) examined the effect of a series of radical trapping compounds on the rate of crosslinking by several commercial vulcanization systems. They conclude that some of these systems react by radical and some by ionic mechanisms. In most systems, the evidence they are able to adduce is inconclusive. This absence of completely unequivocal evidence for either ionic or radical mechanisms, despite the enormous industrial importance and theoretical interest in vulcanization, exists because of the overwhelming complexity of the systems used. Optimum vulcanization of rubber requires the addition of all four ingredients: sulfur, an accelerator, zinc oxide, and a zinc soap (28). This makes a mechanistic study of rubber vulcanization difficult, since many interactions are possible (114, 115, 576). For example, tetramethylthiuram disulfide, sulfur, and zinc oxide interact to form 14 products in the absence of rubber (670). Hydrogen sulfide, a secondary product (1053), interacts to give further compounds (668, 669) (see also Sec. 5-3).

Amines catalyze the vulcanization of rubber. In a related series of amines, e.g., aniline, methylaniline, and dimethylaniline, the effectiveness of the amine as a catalyst is proportional to its base strength (662). However, this relationship does not hold when comparisons are made between amines of different structures (662). That is, when the amount of combined sulfur in a vulcanized rubber is plotted as a function of the base strength of the amine catalyst, anilines, toluidines, and guanidines each lie on separate lines. Base strength alone does not determine the effectiveness of the catalyst; sodium hydroxide is about half as effective as is aniline (662).

A large number of kinetic studies of vulcanization have been reported. Both the rate of combination of sulfur and the rate of formation of crosslinks have been measured; the latter can be obtained from measurements of the modulus (496) or from the extent of swelling of the rubber by a solvent (pages 576–580 of ref. 422). Crosslinking may actually occur more rapidly than the total rate of incorporation of sulfur under some conditions (496). Another complication is that a chain scission reaction occurs simultaneously, probably by typical β-scission reactions, and may be initiated by sulfur.

The rate of combination of sulfur with natural rubber has the following features, as summarized by Craig (258): The reaction is autocatalytic and has an induction period. Zinc oxide and certain other additives may greatly shorten the induction period (929–931). At low sulfur concentrations the reaction is zero order in sulfur; with excess sulfur present (e.g., a tenfold excess) the reaction is first order in sulfur. The zero-order rate constant increases with increasing sulfur concentrations, but zinc oxide has no effect. The dependence on the rubber molecule is usually zero order. Rubbers other than natural rubber behave similarly but not identically. The rate-determining step in several systems has been proposed to be opening of the S_8 ring (513, 514).

The rate of development of crosslinks as measured by increasing modulus or by extent of swelling is second order and appears to depend on both sulfur and rubber concentration (258). An optimum temperature may exist for vulcanization. Craig has interpreted this to mean that at low temperatures crosslinking "sites" are too dilute for reaction and at higher temperatures scission preferentially occurs. The rate of disappearance of sulfur is equal to the rate of appearance of crosslinks if the system includes rubber, sulfur, and accelerator (697).

The Arrhenius activation energy for vulcanization is about 30 to 32 kcal, but accelerators and additives decrease this to as low as 18 kcal (247, 501).

(2) *The Nature of the Crosslinks in Rubber and Analogies with Some Oxygen Reactions.* It was originally supposed that the crosslinks formed in rubber during vulcanization involved C—C bonds. This misconception probably arose because some reactions of sulfur compounds do lead to new C—C bonds. For example, irradiation of a mixture of a disulfide

and cumene leads to dicumyl (1126). However, sulfur is an extremely effective radical trap (see Sec. 2-2), and if it were present, no dicumyl would be expected (see, for example, ref. 1051). Radicals react with S_8 much faster than they abstract benzyl hydrogen. Radicals also react faster with S_8 than they add to olefins. Table 2-1 shows that the polystyryl radical attacks sulfur 10^2 times faster than it adds to styrene. Thus, at vulcanization temperatures (100 to 120° C), radical reactions lead to new C—S bonds in preference to new C—C bonds if sulfur is present.

Analogous reactions involving oxygen are known. Under certain conditions oxygen can cause cumene to dimerize (854). However, C—O bonds are usually formed when organic compounds are heated with oxygen (100, 134, 150, 909), because radicals are trapped by O_2 before they can dimerize (730, 732). An oxygen reaction very similar to vulcanization is the air drying of oils; i.e., oxygen-induced crosslinking of unsaturated esters. At usual oxygen concentrations, no new C—C bonds are formed and crosslinks are through peroxy bonds (731).

6

DEHYDROGENATION BY SULFUR AT ELEVATED TEMPERATURES

Sulfur abstracts hydrogen from organic compounds at 200 to 300° C to produce fragments which ultimately give stable products by aromatization, ring formation, or dimerization. Sulfur may become incorporated in the product. The oxidation of the organic substrate is balanced by the reduction of sulfur to hydrogen sulfide.

$$\text{cyclohexane} \xrightarrow[300°C]{S_8} \text{benzene} \qquad (6\text{-}1)$$

$$\text{2,2'-dimethylbiphenyl } (H_3C\ CH_3) \xrightarrow{S_8} \text{phenanthrene (50\%)} \qquad (6\text{-}2)$$

$$CH_3CH_2CH_2CH_3 \xrightarrow{S_8} \text{thiophene} \qquad (6\text{-}3)$$

$$CH_2{=}CH{-}CH_3 \xrightarrow{S_8} \text{1,2-dithiole-3-thione} \qquad (6\text{-}4)$$

$$2\ C_6H_5CH_3 \xrightarrow{S_8} C_6H_5CH{=}CHC_6H_5 \qquad (6\text{-}5)$$

The mechanism of these dehydrogenation reactions by sulfur remains speculative. The question of whether radical species are involved is of particular interest since it arises in all the reactions of sulfur. Four lines of evidence support a mechanism involving sulfenyl radicals:

1. Thiyl and polysulfenyl radicals abstract hydrogen from carbon atoms in facile reactions (1121). Unequivocal examples of hydrogen abstraction by either sulfenium or sulfide ions are not known.

2. These dehydrogenation reactions occur at temperatures where sulfenyl radicals are definitely present in liquid sulfur (489); this has led to the assumption that radicals are also present in these reaction mixtures.

3. Analogy with the reaction of peroxides with toluene suggests that dimerizations like Eq. (6-5) involve the coupling of radicals. However, the mechanism of Eq. (6-5) is controversial and the role of radicals has not been established (see below).

4. Conclusive evidence for radicals has been established in the gas-phase dehydrogenation of aliphatic hydrocarbons by sulfur at 320 to 350° C; the products are unrearranged terminal olefins typical of radical cracking processes (189).

Table 6-1 gives data showing that dehydrogenations by sulfur are catalyzed by many polar substances. This is most likely because of their ability to open sulfur rings and should not be taken as proof of the ionic nature of the hydrogen abstraction reactions involved (see page 9).

Table 6-1
Catalysts for dehydrogenation reactions

Reaction between S_8 and	Product	°C	Catalyst	References
Cyclohexanol	Phenol	150	Silicates	233
Tetralin	Naphthalene	200	Organic sulfides and polysulfides	1141
Tetralin	Naphthalene	200	Amines	595
Tetralin	Naphthalene	140	Na_2S	594
Dicyclohexyl[a]	Diphenyl	. . .	Sulfur compounds	15
Cumene	4-Phenyltrithione	150	Guanidines	418
Diphenylmethane	Thiobenzophenone	180	Aniline	1088, 1091
Diphenylmethane	Thiobenzophenone	180	Sulfides and polysulfides	1092, 1093, 1096
Styrene	Diphenylthiophenes	. . .	2-Mercaptobenzothiazole	538

[a] Dehydrogenation over Raney Ni.

The occurrence of dimeric products is consistent with radical reactions; however, the absence of dimers does not preclude a radical mechanism. *p*-Toluic acid dimerizes when heated with sulfur to produce 4,4′-stilbenedicarboxylic acid (1075); in aqueous solution these same reactants produce terephthalic acid (1060). In the latter case, the dimer would not be expected to be stable, even if formed, since ethylbenzene is oxidized to benzoic acid.

6-1. Aromatization

Dehydrogenation of hydroaromatic compounds by sulfur, sometimes called the Vesterberg procedure (1105), was discovered in 1874 (282). The reaction originally was used as a degradative tool for structure proofs, and much of this original work has been reviewed by Ruzicka (913). More recent reviews are those of Linstead in 1936 (691) and Plattner in 1946 (861).

Physical methods of structure proof have largely replaced the use of this reaction. However, some recent applications include (1) Tetralin dehydrogenation to naphthalene (595, 1141);* (2) the conversion of thiazolines to thiazoles (47); (3) the conversion of tetrahydrothiophene and related compounds to thiophenes (483, 566, 657); (4) dehydrogenation of 2,5-dihydro-3-phenylfuran to 3-phenylfuran (1164); and (5) conversion of cyclohexane and substituted cyclohexanes to benzene and substituted benzenes (179).

Frequently sulfur gives fewer side reactions than other dehydrogenation reagents (246, 818):

H_5C_2 CH_3 CH_3 CH_3 $\xrightarrow[220°C]{S_8}$ H_5C_2 CH_3 CH_3 CH_3 80% (6-6)

Se, 350°C → CH_3 CH_3 CH_3 (6-7)

C_6H_5—C(=O)— $\xrightarrow[58\%]{S_8\ 270°C}$ C_6H_5—C(=O)— (6-8)

Pd–C, 220-320°C: 16%; 66% → C_6H_5—CH_2— (6-9)

* See Sec. 10-6.

However, unsaturated side chains are sometimes reduced when sulfur is used (691), and methyl groups on tertiary carbon atoms are eliminated (691). Cycloalkenes are more readily dehydrogenated than are cycloalkanes (179). The precise location of the unsaturation in isomeric compounds can have an enormous effect on the yield of aromatic products (see Table 5-3).

6-2. Aromatization with the Formation of a New Ring (Dehydrocyclization)

The prototype dehydrocyclization (535) reaction, viz., the conversion of hexane to benzene, has not yet been effected by sulfur in good yield (see page 95). However, other examples are known. Some involve the formation of new C—C bonds and some, new C—S bonds.

6-2A. New C—C Bond Formed. The structure of the substrate determines whether ring formation will occur. Frequently isomers which differ only in the location of double bonds give very different products. An example from the sesquiterpene series is zingiberene X, which gives the naphthalene derivative, cadalene Y when heated with sulfur (914, 916–918).

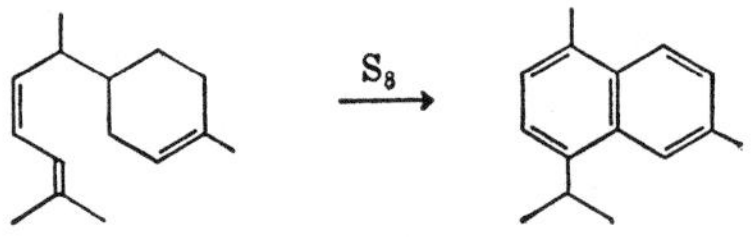

S_8 (6-10)

X Y

However, the isomeric bisabolene Z gives a benzene derivative, identified as AA from its oxidation product.

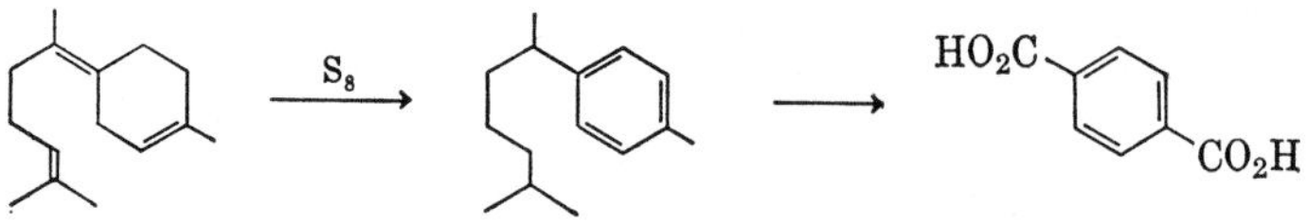

S_8 HO_2C CO_2H (6-11)

Z AA

The ability of sesquiterpenes to give naphthalenes is related to their tendency to cyclize to tetralins with acid catalysis (913). This may indicate that an ionic alkylation process is involved in the ring-closure step.

An intriguing dehydrocyclization reaction is the conversion of 2,2′-

dimethylbiphenyl to phenanthrene by sulfur at 250° C in 50% yield (119, 974), Eq. (6-2). Selenium does not give the reaction (119), and palladium at 450° C leads to the formation of 4-methylfluorene instead of phenanthrene (817).

$$\text{2,2'-dimethylbiphenyl} \xrightarrow[450°C]{Pd-C} \text{4-methylfluorene} \quad (6\text{-}12)$$

6-2B. New C—S Bond Formed. (1) *Thiophene Formation.* Many organic compounds cyclize to form thiophenes when heated with sulfur or H_2S (545). The uncatalyzed, vapor-phase reaction of sulfur with butane at 700° C to give a 70% yield of thiophene is a commercial process (537, 885, 886). In this case, butenes and butadiene are believed to be intermediates (page 55 of ref. 545, 884). Acetylene and ethylene also react with sulfur or H_2S to give thiophene (241, 503, page 47 of ref. 545). Substituted thiophenes can be synthesized; e.g., hexane gives dimethylthiophene, styrene is converted to diphenylthiophene, and stilbene to tetraphenylthiophene. Isooctane is converted to 2,2,4,4-tetramethylthiophane by sulfur at 285° C (482). Sulfur converts toluene to tetraphenylthiophene and a large number of other products (566), possibly via stilbene as an intermediate (1074). 1-Phenylbutane, 1-phenylbutenes, and 1-phenylbutadiene give 2-phenylthiophene when heated with sulfur (Table 6-2) (see Sec. 10-7). Cinnamic acid gives both 2,4- and 2,5-diphenylthiophene (882). All the isomeric methylphenylthiophenes have been prepared from the appropriate phenylpentene or phenylpentane (180–183, 1112, 1114).

Table 6-2
Synthesis of thiophenes (1113)

Reactant	2-Phenylthiophene, % yield	°C
1-Phenylbutane	5	195–200
1-Phenyl-1-butene	35	200–250
1-Phenyl-2-butene	15	200–250
1-Phenyl-3-butene	26	200–250
1-Phenylbutadiene	8	200–250

Parham and Harper (829) have utilized these cyclization reactions to synthesize substituted thiophenes, e.g.:

$$CH_3O{-}C_6H_4{-}CH_2{-}CH{=}C(CH_3){-}C_6H_5 \xrightarrow[50\text{ hr., }200^\circ C]{S_8} CH_3O{-}C_6H_4{-}C{=}CH{-}C(C_6H_5){=}CH \ (\text{ring closed through } S) \qquad (6\text{-}13)$$

Parham and Gadsby have synthesized thienothianaphthenes (828).

$$\text{benzothiophene}{-}C(CH_3)(OH){-}C_6H_5 \xrightarrow[220^\circ C,\ 1.5\text{ hr.}]{S_8} \text{thienothianaphthene}{-}C_6H_5 \quad 16\% \qquad (6\text{-}14)$$

$$\text{benzothiophene}{-}C(OH)(CH_3){-}C_6H_5 \xrightarrow[240^\circ C,\ 4\text{ hr.}]{S_8} \text{thienothianaphthene}{-}C_6H_5 \quad 33\% \qquad (6\text{-}15)$$

(2) *Trithione Formation.* The formation of trithiones, Eq. (6-4), was first reported in 1947 (166, 699, 700, 1111). Trithione itself has been synthesized (935, 1142), as have a number of substituted trithiones (see Table 6-3).* The reaction appears to be general, but it has not received

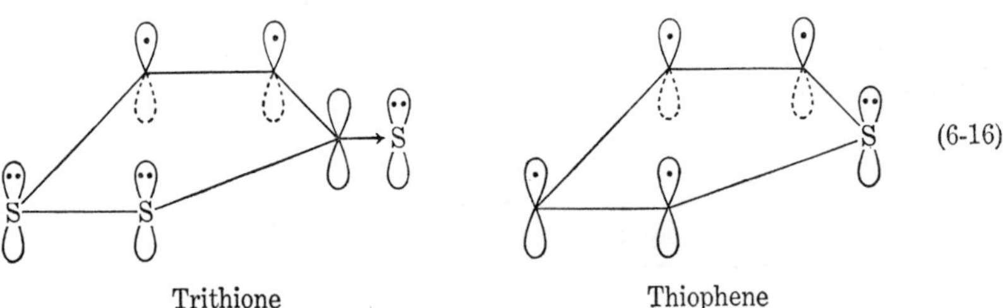

extensive study. Some compounds give both trithiones and thiophenes. Both these heterocyclics have six π electrons in orbitals of ring atoms and may have similar resonance energy (120, 121, 573, 606, 711, 895, 1149); see (6-16). Trithiones withstand temperatures up to about 250° C and are stable to acid, but they decompose in the presence of base with the formation of sulfur (937).

* See Secs. 10-8 through 10-10 for specific procedures.

Table 6-3

Synthesis of trithiones, [structure: 1,2-dithiole-3-thione ring, positions 1–5, =S at 3], by heating olefins with sulfur

Sulfur reacts with	Conditions		Substituted trithione produced	% yield	References
	Hr.	°C			
Propene	...	....	(Unsubstituted)[b]	1	712
Isobutene	1	170°	4-Methyl-[b]	38	1001
3-Methyl-1-butene	2	210°	4,5-Dimethyl-	4	710
2-Methyl-2-butene	2	210°	4,5-Dimethyl-	7	710
2,4,4-Trimethyl-1-pentene	1	170°	4-(2,2-Dimethylpropyl)-	17	1001
			4-Methyl-5-*t*-butyl-	11	
2,4,4-Trimethyl-2-pentene	1	170°	4-(2,2-Dimethylpropyl)-	20	1001
			4-Methyl-5-*t*-butyl-	10	
1-Methylcyclohexene	1	205°	4,5-Benzo-	...	702
1-Phenylpropene	1	240°	5-Phenyl-	25	166
1-Phenylpropene	25	190°	5-Phenyl-	30	1111
2-Phenylpropene	1	240°	4-Phenyl-	30	166
2-Phenylpropene	12	215°	4-Phenyl-	42	1111
3-Phenylpropene	1	240°	5-Phenyl-	25	166
1-Phenyl-2-methylpropene	10	210°	4-Methyl-5-phenyl-	80	1111
1-(2-Thienyl)-propene	2	200°	5-(2-Thienyl)-	...	703
1-(1-Naphthyl)-propene	...	....	5-(1-Naphthyl)-	62	165
1-(4-Anisyl)-propene	1	240°	5-(4-Anisyl)-[a]	50	166
1-(4-Anisyl)-propene	...	....	5-(4-Anisyl)-	...	936
1-(4-Dimethylaminophenyl)-propene	...	....	5-(4-Dimethylaminophenyl)-	...	701
3-(4-Anisyl)-propene	...	....	5-(4-Anisyl)-	16	165
1-Phenylpropyne	...	....	5-Phenyl-	...	701
Cinnamyl alcohol	15	215°	5-Phenyl-	4	1111
Cinnamaldehyde	...	....	5-Phenyl-	...	1111
1,2-Diphenylpropene	...	....	4,5-Diphenyl-	...	938
1,2-Diphenylpropene	24	190°	4,5-Diphenyl-	80	1111
Triisobutylene	...	200°	4-Neopentyl-5-*t*-butyl-	72	675

[a] Plus 20% dimethyl-di-*p*-anisylthiophene.
[b] Also see refs. 728*a* and 1142.

An example which illustrates the complexity of the reaction and the simultaneous formation of more than one product is the reaction of acetylene with sulfur (231).

$$HC{\equiv}CH \xrightarrow[S_8]{450°C} H_2S + CS_2 + \underset{S}{\square} + \underset{\underset{S}{\|}}{S\!-\!C\!-\!S} + \underset{S-S}{\square\!-\!C{=}S} \qquad (6\text{-}17)$$

Some sulfides and disulfides also give trithiones in reactions with sulfur at 200° C. Rearrangements may occur in the process; e.g., both amyl and isoamyl disulfide give 4,5-dimethyltrithione (1142).

$$\left.\begin{array}{l}(CH_3{-}CH_2{-}CH_2{-}CH_2{-}CH_2{-}S{-})_2 \\ \phantom{(CH_3{-}}CH_3 \\ (CH_3{-}\overset{|}{C}H{-}CH_2{-}CH_2{-}S{-})_2\end{array}\right\rangle \xrightarrow[200°C]{S_8} \begin{array}{l}CH_3{-}C{-\!-\!-}C{=}S \\ \phantom{CH_3{-}}\| \qquad\; | \\ CH_3{-}C\diagdown_{S}\diagup S\end{array} \qquad (6\text{-}18)$$

The mechanism of this reaction has not been investigated, but two reasonable paths have been suggested. Ring closure may either precede (163) or follow (875, page 339 of ref. 1116) oxidation to form a thiocarbonyl function.

(3) *Friedel-Crafts-type Reactions.* New bonds are formed in cyclization reactions when a number of types of compounds are heated with sulfur and a Friedel-Crafts catalyst such as aluminum chloride or even iodine. For example, benzene gives some thianthrene, thiophenol, and phenylsulfide (480).

$$C_6H_6 + S_8 \xrightarrow[80°C]{AlCl_3} C_6H_5{-}S{-}C_6H_5 + C_6H_5{-}SH + \text{(thianthrene)} \qquad (6\text{-}19)$$

Biphenyl in the presence of sulfur and aluminum chloride reacts to give good yields of dibenzothiophene (506) (see Sec. 10-11).

$$C_6H_5{-}C_6H_5 + S_8 \xrightarrow[10\text{ hr. }240°C]{AlCl_3} \text{(dibenzothiophene)} \quad 70\% \qquad (6\text{-}20)$$

Phenyl ether yields phenoxathiin (13, 1025).

$$C_6H_5{-}O{-}C_6H_5 + S_8 \xrightarrow[4\text{ hr. }100°C]{AlCl_3} \text{(phenoxathiin)} \quad 87\% \qquad (6\text{-}21)$$

Analogously, diphenylamine yields phenothiazene (11, 12).

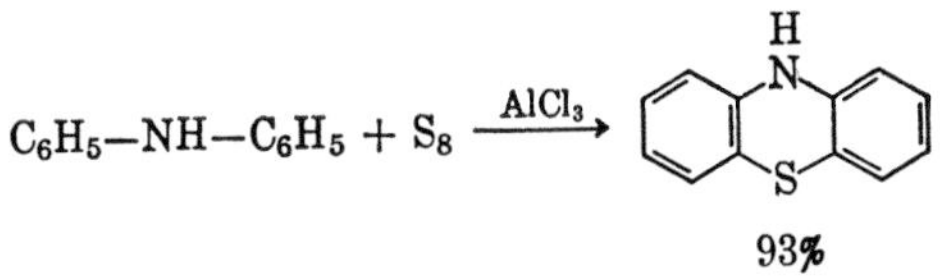

$$C_6H_5{-}NH{-}C_6H_5 + S_8 \xrightarrow{AlCl_3} \text{phenothiazene (93\%)} \qquad (6\text{-}22)$$

Nothing has been reported concerning the mechanism of any of these reactions, but they probably involve electrophilic substitution reactions.

6-2C. Dimerization of Alkylaromatic Compounds. When alkylaromatic compounds, BB, are heated at 200 to 350° C with sulfur, products of the type CC through FF are formed.

$Ar{-}CH_3$	$Ar{-}CH_2{-}CH_2{-}Ar$	$Ar{-}CH{=}CH{-}Ar$	2,3,4,5-tetraarylthiophene (Ar, Ar, Ar, Ar, S)	More complex products	
BB	CC	DD	EE	FF	(6-23)

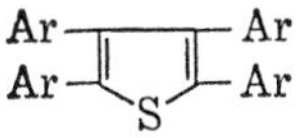

Toluene ($Ar = C_6H_5{-}$) reacts with sulfur to give DD, EE, and FF (566). The following have also been identified as products: *o*-bitolyl, 1,2,3,4-tetraphenylbutane, and 2-phenylthianaphthene (566).

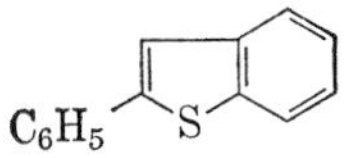

2-Phenylthianaphthene

p-Toluic acid ($Ar = p\text{-}CO_2H{-}C_6H_4{-}$) gives DD and EE (1075); in the presence of excess hydrogen sulfide, the products are CC and DD (1074). *p*-Xylene (Ar = *p*-tolyl) gives CC, DD, and EE (34). 4-Picoline (Ar = 4-pyridyl) gives CC, DD, EE, and FF (350, 608, 1044, 1045).

Diphenylmethane reacts with sulfur at 230 to 300° C to form tetraphenylethylene. Moreau (774) reports that the reaction sequence involves thiobenzophenone and tetraphenylethane as isolable intermediates. Diphenylmethanethiol is not isolable and is eliminated as an intermediate by a study of its reactions in the presence of sulfur (775). Thiobenzophenone reacts with diphenylmethane at 230 to 270° C to produce tetraphenylethane first, followed by tetraphenylethylene (776). The mechanism of the condensation of diphenylmethane and thiobenzophenone to form tetraphenylethane and tetraphenylethylene is not known; however, Moreau has shown that at 230° C no H_2S is evolved until 90% of the tetraphenylethylene has been formed (777, 1089).

Moreau (778) concludes that the reaction of diphenylmethane with sulfur involves thiobenzophenone as a critical intermediate in the formation of tetraphenylethylene, but the exact path is not known.

At 180° C the chief product of the reaction of diphenylmethane with sulfur is benzhydryl polysulfide and hydrogen sulfide (778, 1089, 1097). At this low temperature, neither tetraphenylethylene nor tetraphenylethane is formed. The rate of the reaction has been followed by measuring hydrogen sulfide evolution, and the kinetic order in the initial S_8 concentration was found to be 0.5 at 160° C, 0.53 at 180° C, and 0.7 at 200° C (1090). Amines catalyze the reaction with an effect proportional to their base strength (1091); i.e., they obey the Brønsted catalysis law. The reaction is also catalyzed by the vulcanization accelerators 2-mercaptobenzothiazole (1096) and 2,2′-benzothiazolyl disulfide (1092, 1093). Light increases the rate to a small extent; for example, at 180° C the time required for formation of 2% of the H_2S is 21 hours in the dark, 15 hours in diffuse light, and 8 hours in sunlight (1087).

7

OXIDATION BY POLYSULFIDE SOLUTIONS TO FORM ALDEHYDES, CARBOXYLIC ACIDS, OR CARBOXAMIDES

7-1. Oxidation of Compounds Containing a Functional Group (Including the Willgerodt Reaction)

7-1A. Nature of the Reaction. Definition of the Willgerodt Reaction. The reactions discussed in Chaps. 4, 5, and 6 usually involve sulfur as the only reactant. This section reviews reactions which involve sulfur in the form of inorganic polysulfides in aqueous solution or in an amine solvent; the solvent is a reagent and becomes incorporated into the substrate through hydrolysis reactions which influence the course of the reaction and the nature of the products.

In 1887 Willgerodt discovered that aryl methyl ketones are converted to arylacetamides by aqueous ammonium polysulfide* (1151, 1152).

$$\text{Ar—}\overset{\overset{\text{O}}{\|}}{\text{C}}\text{—CH}_3 \xrightarrow[\substack{(\text{NH}_4)_2\text{S}_x \\ 200\text{-}300°\text{C}}]{\text{Aqueous}} \text{Ar—CH}_2\text{—}\overset{\overset{\text{O}}{\|}}{\text{C}}\text{—NH}_2$$

In 1940, Fieser and Kilmer (419) discovered a more convenient procedure† for the reaction, and in 1946 a review article by Carmack and Spielman (219) attracted general attention to the reaction. Depending on the nature of the polysulfide solution used, the product may be isolated as the amide, thioamide, as the acid itself, or as a mixture.

Subsequent research has shown that polysulfide oxidants are capable of oxidizing an organic compound containing any functional group to a

* See Sec. 10-14.
† See Sec. 10-13.

carboxylic acid derivative, and in the past decade more severe conditions have been found under which even saturated aliphatic and alkylaromatic hydrocarbons are oxidized to acids. The Willgerodt reaction of ketones should be regarded as simply one example of oxidation by polysulfide solutions. This section reviews the oxidation of compounds containing an activating functional group; the oxidation of aliphatic and alkylaromatic hydrocarbons is treated in Sec. 7-2.

The Willgerodt reaction is defined as an oxidation by a polysulfide solution in which a carbonyl function is reduced to a methylene group, and a terminal carbon atom is oxidized to a carboxyl or carboxamide group. This definition is essentially the same as that given in previous reviews of the reaction (219, 478, 601, 743). Note that the polysulfide oxidation of compounds such as styrene, toluene, pentane, 1-phenylethanol, and 2-phenylethanol is not a Willgerodt reaction in terms of this definition, although it occasionally is so called. In this monograph the term *Willgerodt reaction* will be limited in meaning to the definition given above, and the reaction will be treated as a special case of oxidation of organic compounds to carboxylic acids by polysulfide solutions.

7-1B. Structure of the Substrate. Many types of compounds can be oxidized by polysulfide. The compound need not contain an aromatic nucleus, although best yields are obtained if part of the molecule is resistant to oxidation* (225). Heterocyclic compounds are satisfactory.† Chapter 11 gives data concerning all compounds which have been subjected to polysulfide oxidation since a 1946 review (219).

Although yields may vary, compounds with the same carbon skeleton give the same product. For example, acetophenone (219), styrene (219), phenylacetylene (219), phenylacetaldehyde (219), 1-phenylethanol (218, 632), 2-phenylethanol (218), 1-phenylethanethiol (632), 2-phenylethyl disulfide (742), and 1-phenylethylamine (502) all give phenylacetic acid derivatives.

The Willgerodt reaction of ketones has been studied extensively. In going from methyl ketones to higher homologues the yields progressively decrease; they apparently are negligible for pentyl ketones [$n = 4$ in Eq. (7-1)]. Studies with branched-chain ketones indicated that a rearrange-

$$\mathrm{Ar{-}\overset{\displaystyle O}{\overset{\|}{C}}{-}(CH_2)_n{-}CH_3} \xrightarrow{(NH_4)_2S_x} \mathrm{Ar{-}CH_2{-}(CH_2)_n{-}CO_2H} + \mathrm{Ar{-}CH_2{-}(CH_2)_n{-}\overset{\displaystyle O}{\overset{\|}{C}}NH_2} \qquad n = 0-3 \tag{7-1}$$

* See Sec. 10-15.

† See Secs. 10-16 and 10-17.

ment of the carbon skeleton does not occur (218, 219, 1153). Similar studies with isotopically labeled straight-chain ketones have demonstrated this conclusively (186, 295, 297, 298, 966). Therefore, the oxidized site migrates down the unrearranged carbon chain by some multistep process.

The effect of ring substituents on the rate of reaction of acetophenones conceivably could lead to information about the electronic nature of the attacking oxidant in the Willgerodt reaction. This approach was used successfully in a study of the polysulfide oxidation of substituted toluenes (876), but no such rate study has been made of the oxidation of acetophenones. However, a less satisfactory method has been reported (Table 7-1), in which the effect of substituents on yields of products was

Table 7-1
Yields of products from the Willgerodt reaction on substituted acetophenones

Substituents in acetophenone	% yield of substituted product	
	Phenylacetamide (ammonium polysulfide)[a]	Phenylacetic acid (after hydrolysis) (sulfur-morpholine)[b]
Unsubstituted	94[c]	
4-Chloro	35[c]	28
4-Iodo	12	
4-Methyl	63	
4-Hydroxy	...	50
4-Methoxy	25	68[d]
4-Amino	...	66
4-Acetamido	...	70
2,4-Dichloro	45[c]	
2,5-Dichloro	35	
3-Methyl-4-bromo	68	
3-Methyl-6-bromo	79[c]	
3-Methyl-4-chloro	73	
3-Methyl-6-chloro	93[c]	
4-Methyl-2-chloro	75	
2-Methyl-4-methoxy	60	
3-Methyl-4-methoxy	62	
2,4,5-Trimethyl	42	

[a] Conditions: 4 hours, 170°, ammonium polysulfide in dioxane-water (95).

[b] Conditions: Reflux 2 hours in morpholine. Isolate crude thioacetomorpholide and hydrolyze (635).

[c] Of this yield 4 to 7% is isolated as the acid.

[d] Of this, 28% is isolated as *p*-hydroxyphenylacetic acid.

measured (95, 635). The two reagents which have been studied give conflicting results. However, even if the two sets of data are examined separately, conclusions about the effect of substituents are not clear. All substituents lead to lower yields in a way not related to their electronic nature. Disubstituted thiophenes are formed from several acetophenones where yields of phenylacetamide are low (95). Since it is not known whether these thiophenes are formed from the Willgerodt products in further reactions, or directly from the original ketone in a side reaction, the relation between the yield of Willgerodt products and the total rate of reaction of the ketone is not clear.

In a Willgerodt reaction on a ketone with two different alkyl groups, both possible products are isolated:

$$CH_3\text{—}R\text{—}CO\text{—}R'\text{—}CH_3 \rightarrow CO_2H\text{—}R\text{—}CH_2\text{—}R'\text{—}CH_3 + CH_3\text{—}R\text{—}CH_2\text{—}R'\text{—}CO_2H$$

It is significant that the isolation of the product of oxidation of both alkyl groups in the same molecule, i.e., $CO_2H\text{—}R\text{—}CH_2\text{—}R'\text{—}CO_2H$, has never been reported. A study of C^{14}-labeled methyl alkyl ketones (227) has shown that proportionally more of the oxidation occurs toward the methyl group as the alkyl group increases in size (Table 7-2).

Table 7-2
Oxidation products from the Willgerodt reaction on labeled methyl ketones[a] (227)

Ketone	Product, % total yield	% of oxidation which occurred at methyl group
$\overset{*}{C}H_3\text{—}CH_2\text{—}CO\text{—}CH_3$	Butanamide, 10	60
$CH_3\text{—}CH_2\text{—}CH_2\text{—}CO\text{—}\overset{*}{C}H_3$	Pentanamide, 25	68
$C_5H_{11}\text{—}CO\text{—}\overset{*}{C}H_3$	Heptanamide, 30	86

[a] Asterisk shows location of C^{14} in ketone.

7-1C. Effect of Reaction Variables. The effects of molar ratio of reactants, temperature, solvent, and nature of the base catalyst on polysulfide oxidations have been examined.

For the conversion of acetophenone to phenylacetamide by aqueous ammonium hydroxide and sulfur, a thorough investigation (319) of the effect of initial ratios of reactants indicates the following: Increasing the molar ratio of sulfur to acetophenone increases yields until a 10:1 ratio is reached, after which more sulfur has no effect. Increasing the ratio of ammonium hydroxide to acetophenone also increases the yield. The addition of hydrogen sulfide decreases the yield.

The reaction rate increases with temperature. For example (319), acetophenone is converted to phenylacetamide in 14% yield by ammonium polysulfide in 4 hours at 130° C; 4 hours at 158° C increases the yield to 62%. However, in some cases an optimum temperature exists, beyond which yields again fall, probably because of oxidative degradation. This phenomenon is clearly seen in the thiophene series, where the nucleus is degraded above 150° C (136) (Table 7-3).

Table 7-3
Effect of temperature on the yields of products in the Willgerodt reaction on thiophene compounds[a]

°C	% yield of thienylacetamides from		
	2-Thienyl methyl ketone	3,4-Dimethyl-2-thienyl methyl ketone	2,5-Dimethyl-3-thienyl methyl ketone
130	40[b]	14	27
150	47	32	80
160	43	30	95
170	...	28	53
190	0[b]	1	19

[a] Oxidant is ammonium polysulfide in dioxane-water (136).
[b] Interpolated or extrapolated from authors' data.

Cosolvents may cause a small increase in yield. In the oxidation of acetophenone (319) at 158° C with aqueous ammonium polysulfide, the addition of dioxane increases the yield from 62 to 76%. In the same reaction, a change in solvent from ethanol-water to pyridine-water increases the yield from 60 to 77%.

Virtually any base is effective in catalyzing polysulfide oxidation. Aqueous inorganic and organic bases and anhydrous amines (631, 635, 1073) all work satisfactorily. Reagents commonly used are ammonium polysulfide in water, aqueous dioxane, aqueous ethanol, or aqueous pyridine; sodium polysulfide in water; sulfur in anhydrous amines (usually morpholine); sulfur in liquid ammonia (629); and sulfur in water (1060).

7-1D. By-products and Possible Intermediates. At temperatures lower than those required for complete oxidation, sulfur compounds can be isolated from polysulfide oxidations. These sulfur compounds have been suggested as possible oxidation intermediates, since they can be further oxidized to the usual acid and amide product. Isobutyl disulfide and trisulfide are isolated from the reaction of isobutene, sulfur, and aqueous ammonia at 150 to 200° C; at 220 to 250° C these sulfides can be further oxidized to isobutyramide (796). Similar results are obtained with 2-methyl-2-butene (1000). Thiols and disulfides have been isolated from the polysulfide oxidation of cyclohexanone (1166), and similar sulfur compounds have been postulated as intermediates in the Willgerodt reaction of acetophenone (1167).

If sufficient sulfur is not present to oxidize the substrate to an acid or amide, partial oxidation to ketones or aldehydes may occur. In morpholine, 1 mole of 2-phenylethyl disulfide is converted by 1 gram atom of sulfur to phenylacetaldehyde instead of phenylacetic acid (742). Styrene under similar conditions is converted to about 6% acetophenone and 29% phenylthioacetomorpholide (742). Benzyl alcohols are converted by one gram atom of sulfur in the absence of solvent to a number of products:

$$\text{Ar—CH}_2\text{OH} + \tfrac{1}{8}\text{S}_8 \xrightarrow{200°\text{C}} \text{ArCH}_2\text{—O—CH}_2\text{Ar} + \text{ArCHO} + \text{Ar—CO}_2\text{H} + \text{ArCH}_2\text{—CH}_2\text{Ar} + \text{ArCH}{=}\text{CHAr} + \text{sulfur compounds} \quad (7\text{-}2)$$

where Ar can be *o*-, *m*-, or *p*-tolyl (1036), α- or β-naphthyl (1035).

By-products may be formed through degradative side reactions if the temperature is too high (31, 32, 218, 741, 1152, 1153). 1,2,3,4-Tetrahydro-6-propionylnaphthalene gives some degradation at 125° C (32).

$$\text{C}_{10}\text{H}_{11}\text{—C(=O)—CH}_2\text{—CH}_3 \xrightarrow[\text{2. Saponify}]{\text{1. S}_8\text{, morpholine, 11 hr., 125°C}} \text{C}_{10}\text{H}_{11}\text{—CH}_2\text{—CH}_2\text{—CO}_2\text{H}\ (65\%) + \text{C}_{10}\text{H}_{11}\text{—CO}_2\text{H}\ (6\%) \quad (7\text{-}3)$$

2-Phenylpropene gives phenylacetamide and 2-phenylpropionamide in a 1:2 ratio when oxidized by ammonium polysulfide at 190° C (837). Degradation may be the major reaction; e.g., at 290° C diisobutylene is oxidized to pivalic acid (1067), and acetophenone gives benzoic acid (1073).

Frequently in polysulfide oxidations, one part of the substrate is reduced and another is oxidized; e.g., the conversion of acetophenone or 1-phenylethanol to phenylacetic acid. In some cases reduction is the only reaction. For example, 1-acetylacenaphthene is reduced to 1-ethylacenaphthene in 67% yield by ammonium polysulfide at 160° C, and very little of the expected Willgerodt product, 1-acenaphtheneacetamide, is formed (419). 9-Propionylanthracene is reductively cleaved to give an 85% yield of anthracene in 6 hours at 160° C (319). Reduction of a carbonyl group by inorganic sulfides may occur even at room temperature (107).

$$C_6H_5-\overset{\overset{\large O}{\|}}{C}-CH_3 \xrightarrow[\text{8 days, 25°C}]{NH_4HS} C_6H_5-\overset{\overset{\large CH_3}{|}}{C}H-S-S-\overset{\overset{\large CH_3}{|}}{C}H-C_6H_5$$

Cyclic compounds may also be formed (214, 479, 715).

$$R_2C{=}O \xrightarrow[\text{0°C, 3 days}]{Na_2S_2\,+\,NH_4Cl,\ \text{Ethanol-water}} R_2C\langle{}^{S_a}_{S_b}\rangle CR_2 \qquad (7\text{-}4)$$

Equation (7-4) has been demonstrated to occur with several ketones, and one product slowly precipitates in each case. Values of a and b between 1 and 3 are observed for different ketones; e.g., acetone (R = methyl) gives 5% of the product with $a = b = 2$. A number of ketones and aldehydes give 1,3,5-trithiacyclohexanes (213, 215); formaldehyde is converted to trithiane in 98% yield (162). Under high pressure, hydrogen sulfide converts ketones to *gem*-dithiols and to sulfides (210).

$$R_2C{=}O \xrightarrow[\text{30-120°C}]{H_2S,\ \text{30-8500 atm.}} R_2C(SH)_2 + R_2HC-S_n-CHR_2 \qquad (7\text{-}5)$$

Further examples of reactions between hydrogen sulfide and carbonyl compounds are given in a review by Campaigne (214*a*).

Facile oxidation reduction undoubtedly is effected on many substrates by sulfur oxidants, but attempts to isolate such products have not always been made. When polysulfide oxidation is used in synthesis, usually no attempt is made to isolate anything but the desired, expected product, and fractions are discarded that would not contain it. Bible (129), however, has isolated an interesting compound from the oxidation product of methyl *O*-methyl-7-propionylpodocarpate. Oxidation by anhydrous morpholine and sulfur produces a reaction mixture which is extracted into ether. The expected thiomorpholide is obtained in 43% yield upon concentration of the ether. The mother liquors are then chromatographed over alumina and yield an unexpected β-ketone in 10% yield.

$$\text{Ar—}\overset{\overset{\displaystyle O}{\|}}{C}\text{—CH}_2\text{—CH}_3 \xrightarrow[\text{Reflux 10 hr.}]{S_8,\text{ morpholine}} (?) \xrightarrow{\text{Recryst. from ether}} \underset{43\%}{\text{Ar—CH}_2\text{—CH}_2\text{—}\overset{\overset{\displaystyle S}{\|}}{C}\text{—NR}_2} + [\text{liquors}] \xrightarrow{\text{Alumina chromatography}} \underset{\substack{10\% \\ \beta\text{-Ketone}}}{\text{Ar—CH}_2\text{—}\overset{\overset{\displaystyle O}{\|}}{C}\text{—CH}_3} \qquad (7\text{-}6)$$

A β-ketone, not a β-thioketone, is obtained. The oxidation reagent does not contain oxygen, and the source of this keto-oxygen must be explained. There are two alternatives: the β-ketone could have been produced from hydrolysis of the corresponding β-thioketone during the alumina chromatography, or it could result from a *direct* migration of the oxygen atom in the original ketone via a totally unknown mechanism. Carmack and Berchtold have found that such a 1,2-migration of an oxygen atom occurs in some systems, and their evidence is discussed in the following paragraph. Regardless of whether the unexpected product is originally formed as a thioketone or a ketone, it appears that the oxidized site migrates down the carbon chain one atom at a time, since the β-ketone was shown to be oxidized to the thiomorpholide final product in about the same yield as was the original compound. It is therefore both a possible and a reasonable precursor, although the evidence does not prove it to be a necessary precursor.

$$\text{Ar—CH}_2\text{—}\overset{\overset{\displaystyle O}{\|}}{C}\text{—CH}_3 \xrightarrow[\text{as in (7-6)}]{\text{Same conditions}} \underset{41\%}{\text{Ar—CH}_2\text{—CH}_2\text{—}\overset{\overset{\displaystyle S}{\|}}{C}\text{—NR}_2} \qquad (7\text{-}7)$$

Berchtold and Carmack (118) have found that the ketone function wanders when a carbonyl compound is subjected to mild sulfur oxidation conditions:

$$R-\overset{\overset{\displaystyle O}{\|}}{C}-CH_2-CH_2-CH_2-R' \xrightarrow[\text{Reflux 8 hr.}]{S_8,\ \text{morpholine}}$$

$$\underset{3.3\%}{R-CH_2-CH_2-CH_2-\overset{\overset{\displaystyle O}{\|}}{C}-R'} + \underset{0.5\%}{R-CH_2-\overset{\overset{\displaystyle O}{\|}}{C}-CH_2-CH_2-R'}$$

where R = 4-chlorophenyl and R′ = phenyl. Also 28% of the starting ketone was recovered. The solvent is anhydrous, and these compounds were isolated by chromatographic techniques. Therefore, as in the case reported by Bible, the oxygen in the new ketone could be either the original keto-oxygen which has migrated, or an oxygen from the solvent used to work up the reaction mixture. However, Carmack and Berchtold have shown in another system that the oxygen migrates directly. They found that 1,3-diphenyl-2-propanone is equilibrated in part to 1,3-diphenyl-1-propanone by anhydrous morpholine and sulfur at 85 to 100° C. They used infrared spectroscopy and analyzed directly for the presence of the 1-ketone in the reaction solutions. Since the solvent is anhydrous, it is clear that the oxygen atom in the 1-ketone must be the original keto-oxygen. This surprising 1,2-migration of an oxygen under extremely mild oxidative conditions cannot be accommodated by any mechanism yet proposed for the Willgerodt reaction. This is discussed further in the following section.

7-1E. The Mechanism of Polysulfide Oxidation of Compounds Containing a Functional Group. A general mechanism for polysulfide oxidation cannot be formulated as yet, but several excellent studies have clarified some of the problems involved. Research on several aspects of the mechanism will be reviewed: (1) the site of the initial attack on ketones by polysulfide oxidants, (2) the migration of the oxidized site to the terminal carbon atom, and (3) the oxidation of the terminal functional group to the carboxylic acid level.

1. The site of initial attack in the polysulfide oxidation of ketones, the Willgerodt reaction, is not known. Under mild conditions polysulfide solutions attack ketones at either the carbonyl carbon or the carbon alpha to it (see pages 133 and 153). It is reasonable to suppose, therefore, that under the more rigorous Willgerodt conditions the initial attack could occur at either one of these two positions. Although some evidence limits the mechanistic possibilities, it is not yet possible to choose between these alternatives.

One limitation which may be set is as follows. A ketothiomorpholide, a possible product of attack at the α carbon atom, is not an intermediate in the reaction of acetophenone, since the ketothiomorpholide is reduced to the Willgerodt product more slowly than this product is formed directly from acetophenone (78).

$$C_6H_5-\overset{\overset{O}{\|}}{C}-CH_3 \xrightarrow{S_8,\ morpholine} C_6H_5-\overset{\overset{O}{\|}}{C}-\overset{\overset{S}{\|}}{C}-NR_2 \text{ (Small amounts isolated)}$$

$$C_6H_5-\overset{\overset{O}{\|}}{C}-\overset{\overset{S}{\|}}{C}-NR_2 \xrightarrow[Slow]{S_8,\ morpholine} C_6H_5-CH_2-\overset{\overset{S}{\|}}{C}-NR_2$$

$$C_6H_5-\overset{\overset{O}{\|}}{C}-CH_3 \xrightarrow[Fast]{S_8,\ morpholine} C_6H_5-CH_2-\overset{\overset{S}{\|}}{C}-NR_2$$

This does not preclude attack at the α carbon atom if reduction of the carbonyl were to occur at an intermediate stage. Dauben and Rogan have shown that the hindered carbonyl group of methyl mesityl ketone is not reduced by polysulfide, but oxidation nevertheless occurs at the α carbon atom and the ketothiomorpholide is the major product (299). Furthermore, this reaction also occurs with other alkyl mesityl ketones

$$O=C(-(CH_2)_n-CH_3)-C_6H_2(CH_3)_3 \xrightarrow[Morpholine]{S_8} O=C(-(CH_2)_n-\overset{\overset{S}{\|}}{C}-NR_2)-C_6H_2(CH_3)_3 \qquad n=0,\ 1,\ 2$$

in a fashion reminiscent of the normal Willgerodt reaction. Apparently attack at the α carbon atom can lead to migration of the oxidized site and to oxidation of the terminal carbon without reduction of the carbonyl function. Thus it is possible that the Willgerodt reaction proceeds either by initial attack at the α carbon followed by reduction of the carbonyl at some intermediate stage, or by initial attack at the carbonyl carbon itself. However, simultaneous oxidation of both alkyl groups of a dialkyl ketone has not been reported. This implies that if attack is at the α position, the keto function is rapidly reduced at an intermediate stage before the second α position is attacked.

2. Another problem in polysulfide oxidations is the mechanism by which the site of oxidation is transferred to the terminal carbon atom. In the special case of the Willgerodt reaction, three suggestions have been made for the mechanism of this migration, and they all involve initial attack at the carbonyl carbon. These are illustrated below in abbreviated form using acetophenone. Each can be extended to explain migration in compounds with longer side chains.

Amine mechanism (218, 219)

$$C_6H_5-\overset{\overset{O}{\|}}{C}-CH_3 \rightleftharpoons C_6H_5-\underset{\underset{NR_2}{|}}{\overset{\overset{OH}{|}}{C}}-CH_3 \rightleftharpoons C_6H_5-\underset{\underset{NR_2}{|}}{C}=CH_2 \rightleftharpoons$$

$$C_6H_5-C\equiv CH \rightleftharpoons C_6H_5-CH=CH-NR_2 \longrightarrow C_6H_5-CH_2-\overset{\overset{S}{\|}}{C}-NR_2$$

Thiol (or sulfide) mechanism (228, 632, 633, 742)

$$C_6H_5-\overset{\overset{O}{\|}}{C}-CH_3 \rightleftharpoons C_6H_5-\overset{\overset{SH}{|}}{C}H-CH_3 \rightleftharpoons C_6H_5-CH=CH_2 \rightleftharpoons$$

$$C_6H_5-CH_2-CH_2SH \longrightarrow C_6H_5-CH_2-\overset{\overset{S}{\|}}{C}-NR_2$$

Thioepoxide mechanism (796, 1166)

$$C_6H_5-\overset{\overset{O}{\|}}{C}-CH_3 \rightleftharpoons C_6H_5-\underset{\underset{SH}{|}}{C}H-CH_3 \rightleftharpoons C_6H_5-\underset{\underset{S_x-SR}{|}}{C}H-CH_3 \rightleftharpoons$$

$$C_6H_5-\underbrace{CH-CH_2}_{S_x} \rightleftharpoons C_6H_5-CH_2-CH_2-S_x-SR \longrightarrow C_6H_5-CH_2-\overset{\overset{S}{\|}}{C}-NR_2$$

The amine mechanism cannot be a general path since polysulfide oxidations can be accomplished by sodium polysulfide (1153). In addition, in some systems at least, a triple bond is definitely not the functional group that is transferred since methyl branches do not interfere. For example, isobutyl phenyl ketone gives 2-methyl-4-phenylbutanamide and phenylacetamide (218).

$$C_6H_5-\overset{\overset{O}{\|}}{C}-CH_2-\underset{\underset{CH_3}{|}}{C}H-CH_3 \longrightarrow$$

$$C_6H_5-CH_2-CH_2-\underset{\underset{CH_3}{|}}{C}H-\overset{\overset{O}{\|}}{C}-NH_2 + C_6H_5-CH_2-\overset{\overset{O}{\|}}{C}-NH_2$$

In addition, $C_6H_5—CO—CH_2—CD_2—CH_2—CH_3$ is oxidized to phenylpentanoic acid and the product contains 5% of the original deuterium (228). This is consistent with several addition-elimination sequences involving a double bond, but it does not permit elimination to a triple bond. When the starting material is an acetylene, it has been postulated that prior conversion to a ketone is not required, but rather that acetylenes undergo polysulfide oxidation by a mechanism entirely distinct from that which applies to the Willgerodt oxidation of ketones (218). However, phenylacetylene and acetophenone give virtually identical yields of product (218, 319) and may react by a similar path under some conditions.

The thiol mechanism requires hydrogen sulfide addition in both the Markovnikov and the reverse direction. Non-Markovnikov addition of hydrogen sulfide to olefins has not been demonstrated to occur in the presence of sulfur (see page 76). However, the ratio of non-Markovnikov to Markovnikov addition can be small; addition in the non-Markovnikov direction produces an intermediate which is irreversibly converted to the final product (633).

The thioepoxide mechanism was originally suggested by Yukawa and Kishi to avoid the postulation of styrene as an intermediate in the reaction of acetophenone, as is necessary in the thiol mechanism. These workers discovered conditions under which styrene was converted to phenylacetamide in lower yield than was acetophenone itself (1166, 1167). However, under different conditions Carmack and DeTar have reported that the yields of phenylacetamide from styrene (218) and from acetophenone (319) are 64 and 77%, respectively. Considering that this is yield of isolated, purified product and that conditions were not identical (e.g., temperatures were 160 ± 5° C and 157 ± 6° C), such evidence does not eliminate styrene as a reaction intermediate in the Willgerodt oxidation of acetophenone under all conditions. In a recent study aimed at this (118), Carmack and Berchtold have shown that in morpholine plus sulfur, 1,3-diphenyl-2-propanone reversibly isomerizes to the thermodynamic mixture of 1-one and 2-one.

$$C_6H_5-CH_2-\overset{\overset{\displaystyle O}{\|}}{C}-CH_2-C_6H_5 \rightleftarrows C_6H_5-\overset{\overset{\displaystyle O}{\|}}{C}-CH_2-CH_2-C_6H_5$$

A number of compounds which represent potential intermediates were subjected to the reaction conditions. Both 1,3-diphenyl-2-mercaptopropane and 1,3-diphenylpropyne were converted to this mixture too slowly to be intermediates, and neither 1,3-diphenyl-2-propanol nor 1,3-diphenylpropene was converted to carbonyl compounds at all. This demonstrates that a carbonyl migration can occur under conditions where an olefin, acetylene, thiol, or alcohol is not an intermediate. These new facts cannot be accommodated by any of the mechanisms postulated.

3. After the unknown functional group has been transferred to the terminal carbon, irreversible oxidation and hydrolysis occur to form the acid and amide product. The mechanism of this oxidation has not been studied. The only related work is a study of the oxidation of the methyl group in methylaromatic compounds. This reaction is believed to involve oxidation of the methyl group to intermediate oxidation levels, possibly including thiols, followed by fast oxidation to the carboxyl level. A radical mechanism is most consistent with kinetic data on the conversion of the methyl to intermediate oxidation stages. The over-all kinetic data provide no information on the mechanism of the subsequent fast oxidation of these intermediates. However, the assumption has been made that these steps also involve radicals at 250 to 300° C (876).

7-2. Oxidation of Aliphatic and Alkylaromatic Compounds

Early attempts at polysulfide oxidation of a saturated hydrocarbon side chain on an aromatic nucleus failed (219). However, Toland at the California Research Corporation (1061) and Naylor at du Pont subsequently discovered that under more vigorous conditions alkanes and aralkyl hydrocarbons are oxidized to acid derivatives (793, 794, 797, 1062). Saturated side chains on most heterocyclic rings are readily oxidized. These reactions have been developed into useful synthetic methods (1073).*

7-2A. Nature of the Reaction. Structure of the Substrate. The oxidation of methyl groups on aromatic rings has been studied intensively. The reaction is

$$R\text{-}C_6H_4\text{-}CH_3 \xrightarrow[250\text{-}350°C]{\text{Sulfur + base}} R\text{-}C_6H_4\text{-}CO_2H \quad \text{(and amides)}$$

The substituent R is limited to groups that are not destroyed by these vigorous oxidative and reductive conditions. Such resistant groups are carboxyl and sulfonic acid groups. Longer side chains may or may not be degraded: ethylbenzene gives both benzamide and phenylacetamide (797). In the heterocyclic series, 4-ethylpyridine gives amides of 4-pyridylacetic acid (864).

Table 7-4 gives data showing the utility of this reaction. *m*-Xylene and *p*-xylene are converted to iso- or terephthalic acids by sulfur plus either sodium or ammonium hydroxide. *o*-Xylene is oxidized by sulfur

* See Secs. 10-21 through 10-24.

and water to phthalic acid in lower yields. The toluic acids behave similarly. In the case of *p*-toluenesulfonic acid, quantitative yields are obtained if excess base is used above that necessary to neutralize all the sulfobenzoic acid formed. If the reaction medium becomes acidic, the —SO_3H group is lost (1073). Table 7-4 also shows that acetophenone under these severe conditions (260 to 300° C for 1 hour) is cleaved to give benzoic acid in poor yield, whereas under more mild Willgerodt conditions good yields of phenylacetamide are obtained.

Table 7-4
Oxidation of aralkyl compounds by aqueous sulfur oxidants[a]

Substrate	Base[b]	Acid product(s)	Yield, %	References
Toluene	None[c]	Benzoic	86	1060
Toluene	$CaCO_3$, 2.0	Benzoic	61	1073
o-Toluic	None[c]	Benzoic, phthalic	16, 47	1060
m-Toluic	None[c]	Isophthalic	100	1060
m-Toluic	NaOH, 1.0–8.5	Isophthalic	100	1073
p-Toluic	None	Terephthalic	92	1060
p-Toluic	NaOH, 1.0–8.5	Terephthalic	100	1073
o-Xylene	None	Phthalic, benzoic	45, 8	1060
m-Xylene	None	*m*-Toluic, isophthalic	12, 79	1060
m-Xylene	NaOH, 2.0	Isophthalic	61	1073
m-Xylene	Na_2CO_3, 1.3	Isophthalic, benzoic	71, 10	1073
m-Xylene	NH_4OH, 10	Isophthalic	87	1073
p-Xylene	None	Terephthalic, benzoic	66, 4	1060
p-Xylene	NaOH, 2.0	Terephthalic	77	1073
p-Xylene	Na_2CO_3, 2.4	Terephthalic	86	1073
p-Xylene	$Na_2B_4O_7$	Terephthalic	76	1073
p-Xylene	NH_4OH, 10	Terephthalic	96	1073
p-Toluene sulfonic acid	NaOH, 2.0	*p*-Sulfobenzoic	95	1073
Acetophenone	None	Benzoic	41	1060
Acetophenone	NaOH, 2.0	Benzoic	28	1073

[a] Conditions are about 30% excess sulfur above theoretical, temperatures 300 to 330° C.
[b] Formula and moles used per mole of substrate are given.
[c] Substrate and sulfur mixed only after both are dissolved in water. See discussion in text.

The oxidant in these reactions is probably water-soluble inorganic polysulfides (875, 878). These polysulfides are produced by disproportionation reactions of sulfur which are base-catalyzed (see pages 11–13). If sulfur and water are used as the oxidant without added base, special care must be taken to allow these disproportionation reactions to occur and the sulfur to form water-soluble polysulfides before the organic compound is added (1060). If the substrate is allowed to contact a separate sulfur phase, dimerization and dehydrogenation reactions occur to form tars (see page 94), and yields of acids decrease. For example, 39% of benzoic acid is formed if sulfur, toluene, and water are mixed cold and heated together to 335° C. If toluene and sulfur are preheated to 335° C and allowed to dissolve in water separately before the two aqueous solutions are mixed, an 85% yield of benzoic acid is obtained.

An interesting variation of this reaction is the use of a pair of sulfur anions which give polysulfide *in situ;* for example, ammonium sulfate plus sulfide (1059, 1066). A reasonable mechanism by which sulfide and sulfate interact to form polysulfide is as follows: Sulfuric acid and bisulfide react to form thiosulfuric acid (877).

$$HO-S(=O)_2-OH + SH^- \rightleftharpoons HO^- + HO-S(=O)_2-SH \tag{7-8}$$

The thiosulfuric acid then decomposes to produce sulfur and sulfite, a reaction which is known to occur in acidic solution and which probably has the following mechanism (304):

$$^-O-S(=O)_2-S^- + HS-SO_3^- \rightleftharpoons {}^-O-S(=O)_2-S-SH + SO_3^= \tag{7-9}$$

$$^-O-S(=O)_2-S_x-S^- + HS-SO_3^- \rightleftharpoons {}^-O-S(=O)_2-S_x-SH + SO_3^= \tag{7-10}$$

$$^-O-S(=O)_2-S_x-S(-S^-) \rightleftharpoons SO_3^= + \text{cyclo-}(S_x-S-S) \tag{7-11}$$

The sulfur formed in Eq. (7-11) then may react with bisulfide ion to give polysulfide ion (88):

$$S_8 + HS^- \rightleftharpoons HS-S_7-S^- \tag{7-12}$$

or, alternatively, polysulfide may be formed directly:

$$^{-}O-\underset{\underset{O}{\|}}{\overset{\overset{O}{\|}}{S}}-S-S_x-SH + SH^{-} \rightleftharpoons \begin{cases} SO_3^{=} + HS-S-S_x-SH \\ ^{-}O-\underset{\underset{O}{\|}}{\overset{\overset{O}{\|}}{S}}-SH + ^{-}S-S_x-SH \end{cases}$$

Other sulfur species oxidize alkylaromatic compounds: sodium bisulfite plus hydrogen sulfide (739), sodium or ammonium thiosulfate (1059, 1071), sulfur dioxide (212, 1072), sodium or ammonium sulfite (212, 1059), and sulfur dioxide plus hydrogen sulfide (1017). Sulfur dioxide reacts with toluene over vanadium oxide to give good yields of benzoic acid at 410° C and benzaldehyde at 315° C (1022, 1023).

When anhydrous ammonia is the solvent rather than water, nitriles and thioamides are obtained. Sulfur in liquid ammonia at 315° C converts *p*-xylene to *p*-tolunitrile and terephthalonitrile in excellent yields if hydrogen sulfide is removed as it is formed (1069). If the hydrogen sulfide is not removed, thioamides are produced (1070). The mechanism of these oxidations is probably similar to that in aqueous solution, and hydrolysis and ammonolysis reactions give nitrogen derivatives of acids.

Aliphatic hydrocarbons are oxidized by polysulfide oxidants. However, the high temperatures necessary to initiate the reaction may cause degradation of the initial products. Isobutane is oxidized to isobutyramide in 21% yield by aqueous ammonium polysulfide in 2 hours at 320 to 333° C; propane under similar conditions gives small amounts of acetamide and formamide (795). Hexane and octane are degraded to CO_2 and mixtures of acids (1068). If no portion of the substrate is resistant to oxidation, complete degradation to CO_2 or CS_2 may occur, as in the reaction of alkanes with sulfur (see page 96).

7-2B. Mechanism. The mechanism of the polysulfide oxidation of methylaromatic compounds has been investigated from a kinetic point of view. It was found that *m*-toluic acid, the substrate studied in most detail (875, 878), is oxidized quantitatively to isophthalic acid by aqueous solutions of sodium or ammonium polysulfide at 250 to 290° C. No

$$m\text{-}CH_3C_6H_4CO_2^{-} \xrightarrow[(NH_4)_2S_x]{Na_2S_x \text{ or}} m\text{-}C_6H_4(CO_2^{-})_2$$

by-products or intermediates could be isolated using a sensitive technique. The oxidation can be accomplished by either preformed sodium or ammonium polysulfide or by generating sodium polysulfide *in situ* with sodium hydroxide and sulfur. The reaction appears to be homogeneous since the rate is independent of agitation.

The oxidant has been identified as polysulfide although several other sulfur species are also present. In solutions of sodium polysulfide at 250 to 300° C, the following species have been identified: sulfide, polysulfide, thiosulfate, and sulfate. Sodium sulfate (1066) and sodium thiosulfate are eliminated as oxidants since neither is capable of oxidizing *m*-toluic acid alone (878). Sulfide, of course, cannot be an oxidant since it is the lowest possible valence state of sulfur.

The rate of the oxidation of *m*-toluic acid by excess sodium polysulfide depends on the first power of the concentration of *m*-toluic acid and the square root of the polysulfide concentration:

$$\frac{d(\text{IP})}{dt} = -\frac{d(m\text{-T})}{dt} = k(m\text{-T})(\text{HS}_{n+1}^{-})^{1/2} \quad (7\text{-}13)$$

where IP is isophthalic acid or its ion, *m*-T is *m*-toluic acid or its ion, HS_{n+1}^{-} is the chief polysulfide species, and n is the average chain length of the polysulfide oxidant and is a constant in any kinetic run. If n is varied in different kinetic runs and the *concentration* of HS_{n+1}^{-} is held constant, the rate is found to be proportional to n. Therefore, to determine the effect of the concentration of HS_{n+1}^{-} in a series of kinetic runs, n must be held constant. This treatment gives the square root dependence, as shown in Eq. (7-13) (878).

A mechanism consistent with the above rate expression involves reversible cleavage of a polysulfide molecule into two polysulfenyl radicals. These radicals abstract hydrogen atoms from the substrate in the rate-determining step.

$$Y_2S_{a+b} \underset{k_2}{\overset{k_1}{\rightleftharpoons}} YS_a\cdot + YS_b\cdot \quad (7\text{-}14)$$

$$YS_a\cdot \text{ (or } YS_b\cdot) + ArCH_3 \xrightarrow[\text{slow}]{k_3} YS_aH + Ar\dot{C}H_2 \quad (7\text{-}15)$$

$$Ar\dot{C}H_2 \xrightarrow[\text{polysulfide}]{\text{Rapid steps in excess}} [ArCH_2S_aY] \quad (7\text{-}16)$$

$$[ArCH_2S_aY] \xrightarrow{\text{Fast}} [ArCH(S_aY)_2] \quad (7\text{-}17)$$

$$[ArCH(S_aY)_2] \xrightarrow{\text{Fast}} [ArC(S_aY)_3] \xrightarrow{\text{Rapid hydrolysis}} ArCO_2H \quad (7\text{-}18)$$

In these equations Y can be H, Na, $ArCH_2$, etc. Hydrolysis may occur at any stage after Eq. (7-15), but for simplicity only the final hydrolysis is shown.

If a steady-state concentration of $YS_a\cdot$ is assumed, a rate equation can be derived from this mechanism which reduces to the experimentally observed rate equation, Eq. (7-13). This mechanism also predicts an energy of activation which is in agreement with the experimentally determined values of 29 to 34 kcal.

The fact that the rate of oxidation depends on the chain length of the polysulfide molecule is also explained by this mechanism. There are n S—S bonds in HS_{n+1}^-. Since all these bonds have the same energy (see page 16), the rate of scission of these bonds, Eq. (7-14), and consequently the over-all rate of oxidation, depends on the number of such bonds.

Although homolytic scission of the S—S bond is assumed, one involving ionic scission would agree equally well with kinetic data regardless of whether the active oxidant was the sulfide or the sulfenium ion, or both. At these high temperatures and in the presence of sulfur, the usual techniques for proving the presence of free radicals are not applicable. This problem was resolved indirectly by determining the effect of ring substituents on the rate.

The rate of polysulfide oxidation of substituted toluenes was compared to model reactions representing the three possible mechanisms:

Carbonium ion: $$Z^+ + ArCH_3 \rightarrow ZH + ArCH_2^+ \qquad (7\text{-}19)$$

Carbanion: $$Z^- + ArCH_3 \rightarrow ZH + ArCH_2^- \qquad (7\text{-}20)$$

Radical: $$Z\cdot + ArCH_3 \rightarrow ZH + ArCH_2\cdot \qquad (7\text{-}21)$$

$$ArCH_2^+,\ ArCH_2^-,\ \text{or}\ ArCH_2\cdot \xrightarrow{\text{fast}} \text{products}$$

In these models the rate of the bimolecular attack is assumed to equal the rate of product formation. For sulfur oxidation, Z^+ is the polysulfenium ion YS_a^+, Z^- is the polysulfide ion YS_a^-, and $Z\cdot$ is the polysulfenyl radical $YS_a\cdot$.

An approximate model for the Z^+ reaction is unimolecular solvolysis, Eq. (7-22) (1019). This is not an exact model since it replaces H^- with

$$ArCH_2X \rightarrow ArCH_2^+ + X^- \qquad (7\text{-}22)$$

X^-; but it is the only equation for which data are available, and it is satisfactory for predicting qualitative trends. The model for a Z^- reaction is the abstraction of a proton from toluene-α-d by lithium cyclohexylamide in cyclohexylamine where Z^- is RNH^- (1021). The reactions used as models for a radical mechanism are oxidation and chlorination, where Z· is ROO· and Cl·, respectively (908, 1125).

Table 7-5 gives relative rates for these model reactions and compares them with the rates for polysulfide oxidation. The rate sequence for a mechanism involving carbanion intermediates is the reverse of that found for polysulfide oxidation (compare columns 2 and 4, Table 7-5). Thus an anion such as YS_a^- cannot be the active oxidant.

Table 7-5
Relative rate constants[a] (876)

	1		2	3		4	
Mechanism:	Carbonium ion		Car-banion	Radical		Polysulfide oxidation	
	Solvolysis[b]						
X in $X-C_6H_4-CH_3$	Benzyl tosylates	Benzyl chlorides	Benzyl deuterium loss[c]	Oxidation by O_2[d]	Chlorination[e]	NaOH + S	$(NH_4)_2S_{1.7}$
H	1.0	1.00	1.00	1.00	1.00	1.00	1.00
m-CH_3	2.6	1.2	0.68	1.16	1.33	....	1.27
p-CH_3	56.5	8.7	0.29	1.60	1.62	....	1.67
o-CO_2^-	....	......	....	....	....	1.71	
m-CO_2^-	....	......	....	....	....	1.83	1.78
p-CO_2^-	....	(1)	....	....	....	1.88	
p-SO_3^-	....	(0.65)	....	....	....	1.14	
p-Cl	....	0.59	....	0.84	0.72		

[a] All rates are per methyl group.

[b] Table 20 (1019). Solvolysis of $X—C_6H_4—CH_2OTs$ in acetic acid and $X—C_6H_4—CH_2Cl$ in 50% aqueous acetone. Values in parentheses are calculated from Hammett $\sigma\rho$ law, using σ from ref. (736) and ρ from ref. (586).

[c] Rate of abstraction of deuterium from $ArCH_2D$ by lithium cyclohexylamide in cyclohexylamine (1021).

[d] Rate is proportional to removal of benzyl hydrogen by ROO· (908).

[e] Rate is proportional to removal of benzyl hydrogen by Cl· (1125).

A carbonium ion mechanism is excluded since it predicts that the substituents p-CO_2^- and p-SO_3^- would give slower rates than those found in the polysulfide oxidation (compare columns 1 and 4, Table 7-5). This mechanism also is excluded by the ease of oxidation of methylpyridines. 2-Methylpyridine and 4-methylpyridine are oxidized by polysulfide solutions at temperatures 100° C lower than are required for the oxidation of toluene. The 3 isomer is oxidized more slowly (Table 7-6). This can be rationalized if the mechanism involves either carbanions or radicals. That a carbanion intermediate may be involved is supported by the fact that the acidity of the methyl hydrogens in the three methylpyridines is

Table 7-6
Polysulfide oxidation of alkylpyridines

Alkylpyridine	Base[a]	Hours	°C	% yield	Product	References
2-Methyl	M	10.5	150	20	2-Pyridinethio- carboxomorpholide	786
3-Methyl	M	13	170	2	3-Pyridinethio- carboxomorpholide	786
4-Methyl	M	9	170	52	4-Pyridinethio- carboxomorpholide	786
2-Methyl	M	14	150	22	2-Pyridinethio- carboxomorpholide	864
4-Methyl	M	12	170	40	4-Pyridinethio- carboxomorpholide	864
2-Methyl	A	12	160	63	2-Pyridinethio- carboxanilide	864
3-Methyl	A	24	200	0	3-Methylpyridine recovered (80%)	864
4-Ethyl	M	8	160	50	4-Pyridinethio- acetomorpholide	864
2-Methyl	O	20	143	87	*N-t*-octyl-2-pyri- dinecarboxamide	721
2,4-Dimethyl	O	8	164	90	4-Methyl-*N-t*- octyl-2-pyridine- carboxamide	721
2,6-Dimethyl	O	4	190	82	6-Methyl-*N-t*-octyl- 2-pyridine- carboxamide	721

[a] M = morpholine, A = aniline, O = mixture of *t*-octylamines (primary amines).

greater than is that of toluene (187, 782). The stability of these carbanions can be explained in the case of 2- and 4-methylpyridine by resonance forms, e.g.,

$$\text{(2-pyridyl)}\overset{-}{C}H_2 \longleftrightarrow \text{(1,2-dihydropyridin-2-ylidene, } \ddot{\text{N}}^{-}\text{)}=CH_2$$

Radical intermediates also would be expected to be stabilized for 2- and 4-methylpyridine (721).

The rapid oxidation of the methylpyridines relative to toluene cannot be explained by a carbonium ion intermediate.

The mechanism most consistent with the observed substituent effects involves radical intermediates. The data for the substituents H, *m*-CH_3, and *p*-CH_3 are in excellent agreement with known radical reactions (compare columns 3 and 4, Table 7-5). Electron-withdrawing substituents would be expected to decrease the rate of attack by the sulfenyl radical through a polar effect (page 318 of ref. 1116). However, the carboxylate and sulfonate groups can increase the rate through a resonance effect; e.g., for *p*-CO_2^- (569, 570, 836):

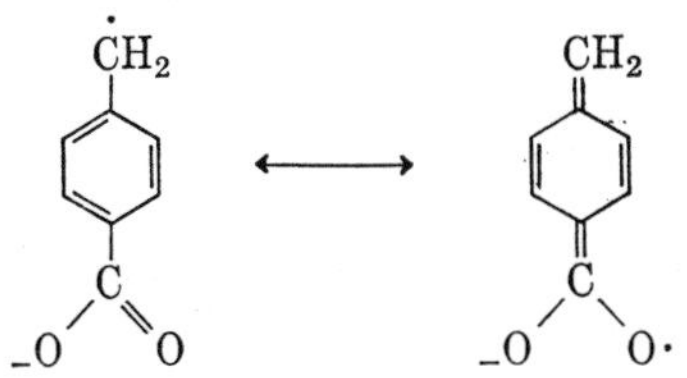

Opposing polar and resonance effects have been discussed in similar radical reactions (320, 555, 559, 734, 910, 911, 1037, 1124).

The similar rates for the three toluic acids could not have been predicted from any of the three mechanisms. This is most easily rationalized, however, by a free radical mechanism (876).

This polysulfide oxidation has been concluded to involve the polysulfenyl radical because of the effect that ring substituents have on the rate of oxidation of toluene. If this rate effect is examined in detail, more can be learned about the nature of the polysulfenyl radical (876). Relative rate patterns for abstraction of a benzyl hydrogen atom by an electrophilic radical, Q·, fall into two classes (734, 908, 910, 911, 1124).

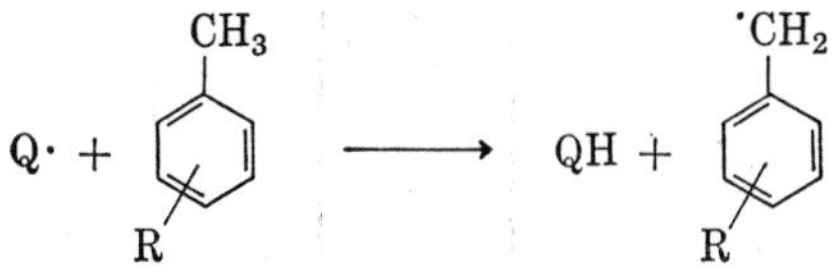

$$Q\cdot + RC_6H_4CH_3 \longrightarrow QH + RC_6H_4\dot{C}H_2 \qquad (7\text{-}23)$$

In one, relatively little C—H bond breaking has occurred at the transition state, and the effect of substituents, R, can be correlated using Hammett's law with normal σ values. In the second, bond breaking has proceeded further, some charge separation occurs in the transition state, and the rate pattern is predicted more precisely using σ^+. Chlorine atoms and peroxy radicals (597, 908) are examples of the first class, and bromine atoms of the second (910). The relative rate pattern for the trichloromethyl (578*a*, 651), *t*-butoxy (1117, 1154), *N*-succinimidyl radicals (651), and methyl radicals (748) has also been measured. The relative rate pattern has not yet been determined for the important and useful thiyl radical, and Walling has shown that there are difficulties in attempting to determine it (1126). However, if Eqs. (7-15) and (7-23) are compared, it can be seen that the relative rates for abstraction of a benzylic hydrogen by the polysulfenyl radical are proportional to the rate constants for the polysulfide oxidation given in column 4 of Table 7-5. The data of Table 7-5 show that the polysulfenyl radical follows a normal σ_p law. This is probably also true of the thiyl radical.

Sulfur therefore is analogous to oxygen. In both cases, normal values of σ best correlate the oxidation data. The total rate of oxidation of substituted toluenes by oxygen is proportional to the rate of abstraction of a benzylic hydrogen atom by ROO· (908); for sulfur, the total rate is proportional to the rate of abstraction of a hydrogen atom by the polysulfenyl radical (876).

In an independent study of the oxidation of some potential intermediates, an alcohol was found to be oxidized sixty times faster than the related methyl compound (876).

$$\begin{array}{l} m\text{-}CH_3\text{—}C_6H_4\text{—}CH_3 \quad (1) \\ m\text{-}CH_3\text{—}C_6H_4\text{—}CH_2OH \quad (60) \end{array} \xrightarrow[200°C]{(NH_4)_2S_x} m\text{-}CH_3\text{—}C_6H_4\text{—}CO_2H$$

If reaction (7-16) is assumed to be irreversible, these rates imply that the steady-state concentration of alcohol would reach a maximum of 1.5% if it were an intermediate. Less than 0.2% of intermediates was found.

Table 7-7

Oxidation of thiols and alcohols by sulfur[a]

Compound	Oxidant	°C	Hours	Yield, %	References
1-Phenylethyl alcohol	b	210	4	48	634
1-Phenylethyl mercaptan	b	210	4	44	632
1-Phenylethyl alcohol	c	160	5	0	218
2-Phenylethyl alcohol	b	205	4	0	633
2-Phenylethyl mercaptan	b	205	4	95	633

[a] Conditions given in Sec. 10-18. Also see Secs. 10-19 and 10-20.
[b] Ammonium polysulfide in water.
[c] Ammonium polysulfide in dioxane-water.

Therefore, either the kinetic scheme is more complex than that given in Eqs. (7-14) to (7-18) or the actual intermediates are oxidized more rapidly than are benzyl alcohols. Thiols are likely intermediates, but Table 7-7 cites data showing that benzyl alcohols and thiols are oxidized at about the same rate. (Notice that in the 2-phenylethyl system, thiols are oxidized much faster than alcohols are.) It appears likely that Eqs. (7-16) to (7-18) are rapid and reversible such that the total concentration of sulfur containing intermediates is very small.

7-3. Conversion of Nitrotoluenes to Aminobenzaldehydes

Aqueous alcoholic solutions of sodium polysulfide convert *o*- or *p*-nitrotoluene to *o*- or *p*-aminobenzaldehyde at 80° C. Examples of this reaction were first reported in German patents in 1896 (497, 498).

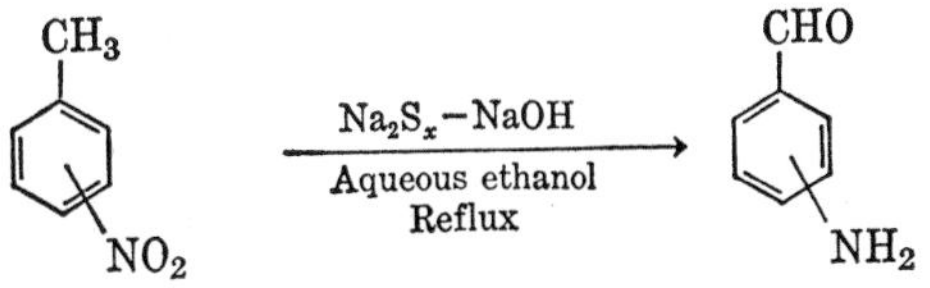

CH_3, NO_2 —[Na_2S_x—NaOH; Aqueous ethanol; Reflux]→ CHO, NH_2

60-80%

The meta isomer recently has been found to react similarly to give derivatives of the unstable *m*-aminobenzaldehyde (877*b*). The reaction also has been extended to the synthesis of aminoketones (694).

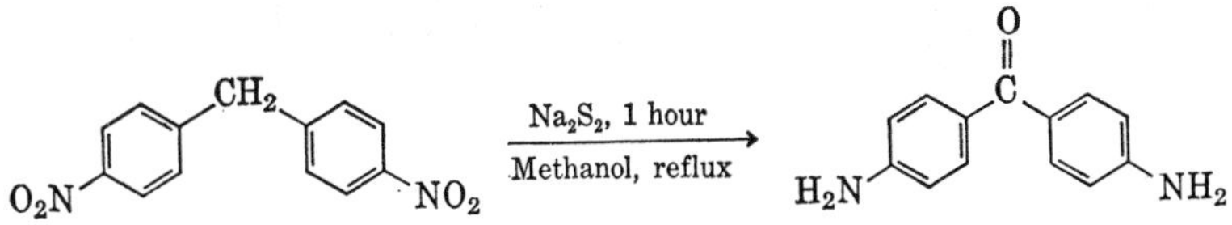

O_2N, CH_2, NO_2 —[Na_2S_2, 1 hour; Methanol, reflux]→ H_2N, C=O, NH_2

90%

This remarkable reaction is the best synthetic route to the aminobenzaldehydes and gives excellent yields.* The reaction is completely unexpected; toluene, for example, is unaffected by polysulfide solutions below about 250° and at that temperature is converted to benzoic acid, not to benzaldehyde. The mechanism of this reaction is therefore of unusual interest, but it has not been studied in detail and is not known with certainty.

The effects of changes in some of the reaction variables have been examined, however. A critical variable is the ratio of sulfur to sulfide

* See Sec. 10-25.

(108); a composition near Na_2S_4 gives the highest yield of *p*-aminobenzaldehyde (see Table 7-8). DeGarmo and McMullen (312) have recently

Table 7-8
Reaction of *p*-nitrotoluene with polysulfide (108)

Na_2S_x	*% yield of p-aminobenzaldehyde*
$x = 1$	40
2	45
3	53
4	72
5	Contaminated with by-products

reported that yields are improved if additional sulfur is added continuously as the reaction proceeds to keep the composition at the optimum Na_2S_3 to Na_2S_4. This at first sight seems surprising, since the balanced equation shows that sulfur is produced rather than consumed by the reaction.

$$NO_2—C_6H_4—CH_3 + NaHS \rightarrow NH_2—C_6H_4—CHO + \tfrac{1}{8}S_8 + NaOH$$

Consistent with this equation, Table 7-8 shows that sodium sulfide can effect this reaction without added elemental sulfur. The table also shows that elemental sulfur is necessary for optimum yields of aldehyde. The reason for this is not known. The disproportionation of sulfur will be a concurrent side reaction in these basic solutions.

$$6NaOH + \tfrac{1}{2}S_8 \rightarrow 2Na_2S + Na_2S_2O_3 + 3H_2O$$

Since this side reaction consumes sulfur, and since sulfur is required for optimum yields of amino-aldehyde, make-up sulfur must be added as the reaction proceeds.

Reduction is a competing process to oxidation-reduction, and aminotoluenes are frequently found as by-products. Since polysulfide solutions are known to be capable of reducing a nitro to an amino group (251*a*, 564, 883, 898, 972, 1156), this is expected. In the case of *p*-nitrotoluene (108) the relative amounts of reduction to an amine and oxidation-reduction to an amino-aldehyde depend on the ratio of sulfur to sulfide. Compositions near Na_2S_4 give mainly amino-aldehyde, but compositions nearer Na_2S give up to 50% yields of toluidine.

The effect of varying the solvent composition has been examined; aqueous ethanol gave the largest yields (108). The reactants were sodium tetrasulfide, sodium hydroxide, and *p*-nitrotoluene, and the yields of amino-aldehyde in the solvents examined were: water, 32%; aqueous methanol, 53%; aqueous ethanol, 75%; aqueous propanol, 59%. (All aqueous alcoholic solutions were ⅓ alcohol by volume.) The reason for this large solvent effect has not been studied.

A brief investigation of the mechanism by Shchukina and Predvoditeleva (969) supports the reasonable supposition than an interaction between the two functional groups is involved in the oxidation-reduction reaction. Equations (7-24) and (7-25) show transformations postulated by these Russian authors for *o*-nitrotoluene. It is known that aqueous alcoholic base converts *o*-nitrotoluene to anthranil nitrone, and that further heating with concentrated base yields anthranilic acid, probably via the *β*-lactam. The Russian workers have made the reasonable suggestion that the nitrone is also an intermediate in the formation of the amino-aldehyde. However, when the nitrone is subjected to the conditions which convert nitrotoluene to aminobenzaldehyde, it is converted to anthranilic acid as well as *o*-aminobenzaldehyde, as shown in Eq. (7-26). Therefore, the reaction sequence given in Eq. (7-25), although reasonable, must await further proof.

CH_3, NO_2 —NaOH, heat→ CH, N→O (Anthranil nitrone) —NaOH, heat→ [C=O, N—H] —H_2O→ CO_2H, NH_2 (Anthranilic acid) (7-24)

—S_8, NaOH→ CH, N→O ⟶ [CH, N] —H_2O→ CHO, NH_2 (7-25)

CH, N→O —S_8, NaOH→ CO_2H, NH_2 + CHO, NH_2 (7-26)

Equations (7-27) and (7-28) show similar reactions postulated for *p*-nitrotoluene. Heating in strong base leads to an intractable polymer which was identified as a polyamide by its infrared spectrum. This polyamide is assumed to arise by rearrangement of a polynitrone (1038). The polynitrone itself has not been isolated and is assumed to be present by analogy with Eq. (7-25). It is a reasonable intermediate for the reactions which occur in base alone and in polysulfide. However, more evidence is required to substantiate the mechanism.

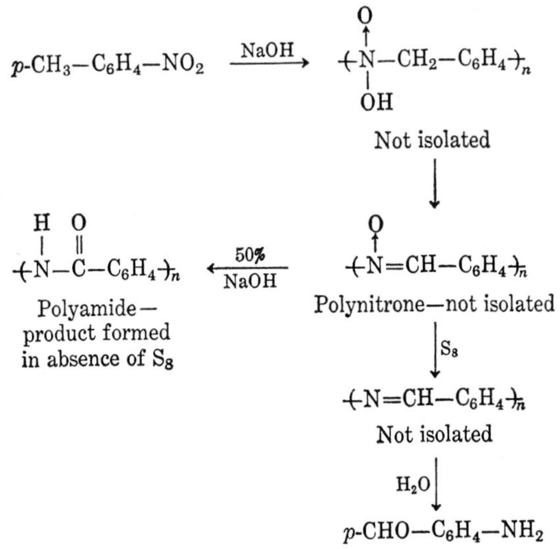

$$p\text{-}CH_3-C_6H_4-NO_2 \xrightarrow{NaOH} \left[\overset{\overset{O}{\uparrow}}{\underset{\underset{OH}{|}}{N}}-CH_2-C_6H_4 \right]_n \qquad (7\text{-}27)$$

Not isolated

$$\downarrow$$

$$\left[\overset{H}{\overset{|}{N}}-\overset{O}{\overset{\|}{C}}-C_6H_4 \right]_n \xleftarrow[NaOH]{50\%} \left[\overset{\overset{O}{\uparrow}}{N}=CH-C_6H_4 \right]_n$$

Polyamide—product formed in absence of S_8 | Polynitrone—not isolated

$$\downarrow S_8$$

$$\left[N=CH-C_6H_4 \right]_n \qquad (7\text{-}28)$$

Not isolated

$$\downarrow H_2O$$

$$p\text{-}CHO-C_6H_4-NH_2$$

A patent has been issued which claims that benzyl alcohols are converted to benzaldehydes by refluxing in a nitrobenzene-xylene solvent in the presence of sodium hydroxide (750). This may be an intermolecular example of this oxidation-reduction; the patent does not state whether the nitrobenzene is reduced to aniline.

8

OXIDATION OF KETONES TO THIAZOLINES AND α-MERCAPTOKETONES

The oxidation of ketones to thiazolines by sulfur and ammonia was reported by Asinger in 1956 (36, 41, 43, 45). This is the only known sulfur oxidation at a carbon atom that has an appreciable rate at 25° C. The detailed mechanism of this interesting transformation is unknown. The generalized equation is:

$$\begin{matrix} R-C=O \\ | \\ R'-CH_2 \end{matrix} + \tfrac{1}{8}S_8 \underset{}{\overset{\text{Base}}{\rightleftharpoons}} \left[\begin{matrix} R-C=O \\ | \\ R'CH-SH \end{matrix}\right] \tag{8-1}$$

$$\left[\begin{matrix} R-C=O \\ | \\ R'-CH-SH \end{matrix}\right] + NH_3 + O=C\begin{matrix} \diagup R \\ \diagdown CH_2R' \end{matrix} \longrightarrow \begin{matrix} R-C=\!=\!=N^{3} \\ |\qquad\quad | \\ R'-HC\diagdown_{S_1}\diagup C\begin{matrix} \diagup R \\ \diagdown CH_2R' \end{matrix} \end{matrix} \tag{8-2}$$

3-Thiazoline

The reaction is usually performed under anhydrous conditions: 1 mole of sulfur is slurried with 2 moles of ketone, and gaseous ammonia is blown through the mixture. The solution gradually warms, darkens in color, and becomes homogeneous. If water is present, yields are lowered. In the case of diethyl ketone (44), aqueous sodium polysulfide plus ammonia gives an 18% yield (corrected for recovered ketone), while the anhydrous procedure gives 85% of the same product, 2,2,4-triethyl-5-methyl-3-thiazoline.

Most of the ketones which have been studied react similarly. These include diethyl ketone (44), methyl ethyl ketone (37, 40), cyclohexanone (42), methyl cyclohexyl ketone (46), and diisopropyl ketone (48). Acetone gives a small yield of 2,2,4-trimethyl-3-thiazoline plus several other compounds (1046).

Hydrolysis of the thiazoline with acid reverses Eq. (8-2) to give 1 mole each of ketone, α-mercaptoketone, and ammonia (44). If the α-mercaptoketone is warmed to 60° C with small amounts of an amine, Eq. (8-1) is reversed to give sulfur and the ketone (44):

$$\text{(2,2-diethyl-4-ethyl-5-methyl-3-thiazoline)} \xrightarrow{\text{HCl, 25°C}} C_2H_5{-}C(=O){-}CH(CH_3){-}SH + NH_3 + C_2H_5{-}C(=O){-}C_2H_5 \qquad (8\text{-}3)$$

$$\xrightarrow[\text{Amine catalyst}]{60°\text{C}} C_2H_5{-}C(=O){-}C_2H_5 + \tfrac{1}{8}S_8 \qquad (8\text{-}4)$$

A recent review (1134) of this reaction has pointed out the relationship between it and the reaction of sulfur with phenols or anilines:*

$$\text{phenol} \rightleftharpoons \text{cyclohexadienone} + \tfrac{1}{8}S_8 \xrightarrow{\text{NaOH}} [\text{2-mercaptocyclohexadienone}] \longrightarrow \text{bis(2-hydroxyphenyl) disulfide } (S{-}S)$$

$$\text{aniline} \rightleftharpoons \text{cyclohexadienimine (NH)} + \tfrac{1}{8}S_8 \longrightarrow [\text{2-mercapto imine (NH, SH)}] \longrightarrow \text{bis(2-aminophenyl) disulfide } (S{-}S)$$

Some inferences can be drawn about the mechanism of Eqs. (8-1) and (8-2). An α-mercaptoketone is a likely intermediate (44, 1047), although it is not an isolable product when sulfur and a ketone are allowed to react with ammonia. If, however, an α-mercaptoketone is allowed to react with ammonia and the related ketone, the same thiazoline is obtained as when the ketone, sulfur, and ammonia react in one step (38, 44).

Equation (8-1) is the more interesting transformation; Eq. (8-2) undoubtedly occurs via intermediates typical of carbonyl-amine condensation reactions. Reaction (8-1) may involve the enolate ion.

$$R{-}\overset{O}{\overset{\|}{C}}{-}CH_2{-}R' + NH_3 = R{-}\overset{O}{\overset{\|}{C}}{-}\overset{-}{C}H{-}R' + NH_4^+ \qquad (8\text{-}5)$$

$$R{-}\overset{O}{\overset{\|}{C}}{-}\overset{-}{C}H{-}R' + S_8 \rightleftharpoons R{-}\overset{O}{\overset{\|}{C}}{-}CH(S{-}S_6{-}S^-){-}R' \overset{+H^+}{\rightleftharpoons} R{-}\overset{O}{\overset{\|}{C}}{-}CH(S{-}S_6{-}SH){-}R'$$

$$R{-}\overset{O}{\overset{\|}{C}}{-}\overset{-}{C}H{-}R' + R{-}\overset{O}{\overset{\|}{C}}{-}CH(S{-}S_6{-}SH){-}R' \rightleftharpoons R{-}\overset{O}{\overset{\|}{C}}{-}CH(S{-}S_6^-){-}R' + R{-}\overset{O}{\overset{\|}{C}}{-}CH(SH){-}R'$$

* See Sec. 10-27.

The general equation is

$$\mathrm{R{-}\overset{\displaystyle O}{\overset{\|}{C}}{-}\bar{C}H{-}R' + R{-}\overset{\displaystyle O}{\overset{\|}{C}}{-}\underset{\displaystyle S_x{-}SH}{\underset{|}{C}H}{-}R' \rightleftharpoons R{-}\overset{\displaystyle O}{\overset{\|}{C}}{-}\underset{\displaystyle SH}{\underset{|}{C}H}{-}R' + R{-}\overset{\displaystyle O}{\overset{\|}{C}}{-}\underset{\displaystyle S_x^-}{\underset{|}{C}H}{-}R'}$$

This mechanism requires that the substrate form a carbanion which is able to attack sulfur. It predicts, through microscopic reversibility, that Eq. (8-4), which is the reverse of Eq. (8-1), involves the same carbanion. The mechanism of this intriguing desulfuration would then be:

$$\mathrm{R{-}\overset{\displaystyle O}{\overset{\|}{C}}{-}\underset{\displaystyle S^-}{\underset{|}{C}HR'} + R{-}\overset{\displaystyle O}{\overset{\|}{C}}{-}\underset{\displaystyle SH}{\underset{|}{C}HR'} \longrightarrow R{-}\overset{\displaystyle O}{\overset{\|}{C}}{-}\underset{\displaystyle S{-}SH}{\underset{|}{C}HR'} + R{-}\overset{\displaystyle O}{\overset{\|}{C}}{-}\bar{C}HR'} \qquad (8\text{-}6)$$

followed by protonation of the enolate ion as in the reversal of Eq. (8-5). Equation (8-6) may be generalized as:

$$\mathrm{R{-}\overset{\displaystyle O}{\overset{\|}{C}}{-}\underset{\displaystyle S^-}{\underset{|}{C}HR'} + R{-}\overset{\displaystyle O}{\overset{\|}{C}}{-}\underset{\displaystyle S_xH}{\underset{|}{C}HR'} \longrightarrow R{-}\overset{\displaystyle O}{\overset{\|}{C}}{-}\underset{\displaystyle S{-}S_xH}{\underset{|}{C}HR'} + R{-}\overset{\displaystyle O}{\overset{\|}{C}}{-}\bar{C}HR'}$$

followed by

$$\mathrm{R{-}\overset{\displaystyle O}{\overset{\|}{C}}{-}\underset{\displaystyle S{-}S_x^-}{\underset{|}{C}HR'} + \longrightarrow R{-}\overset{\displaystyle O}{\overset{\|}{C}}{-}\bar{C}HR' + S\frown S_x}$$

This mechanism predicts that stable anions can be eliminated from thiols. Notice the formal similarity between these equations and Eqs. (7-9) to (7-11), which were suggested to explain the decomposition of thiosulfate, where the stable anion HSO_3^- is eliminated. Another example may be diphenylmethanethiol, which cleaves to form diphenylmethane and sulfur at 200° C (775, 1007).

9

OXIDATIONS AT ATOMS OTHER THAN CARBON

9-1. Sulfur

Two oxidations at sulfur by sulfur have been reported. In one, sulfides or polysulfides are converted to higher polysulfides (vol. 2 of ref. 886*a*).

$$RS_nR + \frac{m}{8} S_8 \rightarrow RS_{n+m}R \qquad (9\text{-}1)$$

The reaction has not been investigated in detail and has little utility.

A more useful reaction is the oxidation of thiols to disulfides by sulfur (142, 759).*

$$2RSH + \tfrac{1}{8}S_8 \xrightarrow{130°C} RSSR + H_2S \qquad (9\text{-}2)$$

Polysulfides are also produced. The reaction is base-catalyzed, probably by a general base-catalyzed path obeying the Brønsted law. The mechanism can be formulated as involving nucleophilic attack on sulfur by the mercaptide ion, followed by homolytic reactions to produce dimers, etc.

$$RSH + B: \rightarrow RS^- + BH^+ \qquad (9\text{-}3)$$

$$RS^- + S_8 \rightarrow RS{-}S{-}S_6{-}S^- \rightleftharpoons RS\cdot + \cdot S{-}S_6{-}S^- \qquad (9\text{-}4)$$

$$2RS\cdot \rightarrow RSSR \qquad (9\text{-}5)$$

$$RS{-}S{-}S_6{-}S^- \rightarrow RS{-}S\cdot + \cdot S_6{-}S^- \qquad (9\text{-}6)$$

$$RS{-}S\cdot + RS\cdot \rightarrow RS_3R, \text{ etc.} \qquad (9\text{-}7)$$

Alternatively, the mechanism can be written as involving nucleophilic displacements on polysulfides by mercaptide ions.

$$RS{-}S{-}S_6{-}S^- + RS^- \rightarrow RSSR + {}^-S{-}S_6{-}S^- \qquad (9\text{-}8)$$

* See Sec. 10-28.

9-2. Nitrogen

Sulfur oxidation at nitrogen atoms yields a variety of sulfur nitrides, or nitrogen sulfides (109, 765, 967). Ammonia is oxidized by sulfur to nitrogen tetrasulfide, N_4S_4, a solid with mp 179° C.

$$\tfrac{10}{8}S_8 + 16NH_3 \rightarrow N_4S_4 + 6(NH_4)_2S \qquad (9\text{-}9)$$

Nitrogen tetrasulfide is hydrolyzed by water to pentathionate, sulfur, and ammonia, and by alkali to thiosulfate, sulfite, and ammonia. It reacts with sulfur at 125° C to form nitrogen disulfide, NS_2, which is an unstable liquid at room temperature. A number of nitrogen derivatives of sulfuric acid are known, such as amine sulfonic acids and sulfonamides, but these compounds are not prepared by sulfur oxidations.

The reactions of sulfur with amines constitute an important area of sulfur chemistry, the understanding of which will contribute to a better insight into many sulfur oxidations which are catalyzed by amines. Bartlett and his group (82, 83) have shown that amine catalysis of sulfur reactions does not result, at least in the case of tributylamine, from a direct attack by the amine on sulfur. Davis and Nakshbendi (307*a*) have shown that primary and secondary amines react with sulfur rapidly to form a charge transfer complex, $R_2\overset{+}{N}H\cdot S_8^-$. This complex reacts with another amine molecule in a subsequent slower reaction to produce ammonium and polysulfide ions.

$$R_2NH + R_2\overset{+}{N}H\cdot S_8^- \rightarrow R_2\overset{+}{N}H_2 + R_2N{-}S_8^-$$

Tertiary amines cannot react by this mechanism. This explains the failure of dimethylaniline to react with S_8 to liberate hydrogen sulfide. It also accounts for the fact that such tertiary amines are poor catalysts for sulfur-olefin reactions (see Sec. 5-2, page 109).

Amines also may undergo oxidation at a carbon atom in a reaction which produces hydrogen sulfide (593, 967). These reactions were discussed on page 108.

9-3. Phosphorus

Both elemental and bound phosphorus react readily with sulfur and with sulfur compounds. Phosphorus burns in sulfur to form phosphorus sulfides, four molecular modifications of which are known: P_4S_3, P_4S_5, P_4S_7, and P_4S_{10} (765). Phosphorus compounds frequently abstract sulfur atoms from sulfur-containing substrates to yield the desulfurized substrate and a thiophosphorus compound. It is apparent that phosphorus-sulfur reactions will be many, varied, and complex. Only a few of them have been investigated; the clarification of this area of sulfur chemistry, like that of sulfur-nitrogen reactions, is just beginning. Only the more thoroughly studied and better-understood reactions between phosphorus and sulfur are discussed below.

Elemental sulfur oxidizes phosphines and phosphites.

$$8R_3P + S_8 \rightarrow 8R_3P{=}S$$

$$8(RO)_3P + S_8 \rightarrow 8(RO)_3P{=}S$$

Phenylphosphine, an example of a primary phosphine, is oxidized to $C_6H_5PSH_2$ and $(C_6H_5)_3P_3S_2$ by sulfur (647). The first compound may be a thiophosphinous acid.

$$8C_6H_5PH_2 + S_8 \rightarrow 8C_6H_5\overset{\overset{\displaystyle S}{\|}}{\underset{\underset{\displaystyle H}{|}}{P}}{-}H$$

Peters (850*a*) has studied the oxidation of secondary phosphines with sulfur in an inert solvent.

$$8R{-}\underset{\underset{\displaystyle R'}{|}}{P}{-}H + S_8 \xrightarrow{CCl_4} 8R{-}\overset{\overset{\displaystyle S}{\|}}{\underset{\underset{\displaystyle R'}{|}}{P}}{-}H$$

The crude product is obtained in excellent yields, but it decomposes upon distillation. These phosphine sulfides have an active hydrogen, and they add to carbonyl compounds in base-catalyzed aldol condensation reactions. Further oxidation by sulfur converts the phosphine sulfides to dithiophosphinic acids.

$$8R{-}\overset{\overset{\displaystyle S}{\|}}{\underset{\underset{\displaystyle R'}{|}}{P}}{-}H + S_8 \rightarrow R{-}\overset{\overset{\displaystyle S}{\|}}{\underset{\underset{\displaystyle R'}{|}}{P}}{-}SH$$

Dithiophosphinic acids can also be produced directly from the phosphines by oxidation by sulfur (250, 717).

The reaction of tertiary phosphines with sulfur has been studied in detail by Bartlett and his students. Bartlett and Meguerian (89) studied the reaction of triphenylphosphine with sulfur.

$$8(C_6H_5)_3P + S_8 \rightarrow 8(C_6H_5)_3P{=}S$$

Electron-donating substituents in the aryl rings lead to a large rate enhancement, and the data fit Hammett's law with a rho of −2.5. The mechanism therefore involves nucleophilic attack on sulfur by phosphorus. Ionizing solvents greatly increase the rate; an increase in the dielectric constant from 2.0 to 5.7 (cyclohexane to chlorobenzene) produces a rate increase of 208-fold. Therefore the rate-determining step is formulated as involving charge separation. The reaction is first order in sulfur and in phosphine.

$$(C_6H_5)_3P + S_8 \xrightarrow{\text{Slow}} (C_6H_5)_3\overset{+}{P}{-}S{-}S_6{-}S^- \xrightarrow[7\,(C_6H_5)_3P]{\text{Rapid}} 8(C_6H_5)_3P{=}S \qquad (9\text{-}10)$$

The reaction of triphenylphosphine with sulfur is catalyzed very strongly by some acids and bases. Bartlett, Cox, and Davis (83) have reported a painstaking and extremely thorough investigation of the mechanism of the catalysis by triethylamine. They observed that the catalytic effect of the amine depended on the purity of the reagents used. If they used sulfur purified by ordinary techniques and solutions prepared in the light, then triethylamine produced erratic rate effects. If the benzene solution of triphenylphosphine was allowed to age for 4 to 6 days under diffuse light, the rate was faster than if fresh solutions were used. However, if scrupulously pure reagents were used and all work was done in the dark, triethylamine was found to have virtually no effect on the rate of reaction between sulfur and triphenylphosphine. This suggests that a material which is an impurity in ordinary sulfur reacts with the amine to form a powerful catalyst for the sulfur-phosphine reaction. Bartlett, Cox, and Davis confirmed this by showing that very pure sulfur does not react with triethylamine, as judged by the fact that the spectrum of the mixture is merely the sum of that of the separate components. The mixture showed the normal ultraviolet and infrared spectrum of S_8. Further, both hydrogen sulfide and sulfur dioxide were shown to be powerful cocatalysts for the phosphine reaction, and these species are known to be impurities in ordinary sulfur. As little as 3 molecules of hydrogen sulfide, or 1 molecule of sulfur dioxide, per 75,000 atoms of sulfur produces an observable rate enhancement. From these data it is clear that triethylamine does not attack the S_8 ring directly, but that some amine-hydrogen sulfide product does. Finally, these workers showed that S_6 rings oxidize triphenylphosphine 25,000 times faster than does S_8 at 7° C.

The reaction of phosphites and elemental sulfur has been studied by

Chernick, Pedley, and Skinner (235). They measured the heat of reaction between three trialkyl phosphites and S_8, obtaining an observed heat of −26.6, −27.6, and −27.5 kcal/mole for ethyl, propyl, and butyl phosphite, respectively. From these values they calculate $D(R_3P{=}S)$ as 91 kcal. Chernick and coworkers used the value of 66 kcal for the heat of formation of sulfur. Three values have been reported for this heat of formation: 65 to 66, 57, and 53 kcal. Cottrell (page 163 of ref. 255) has reviewed all the pertinent evidence and concludes that 57 kcal is the best choice at present, although Herzberg prefers 65 and the National Bureau of Standards uses 53 kcal. Using Cottrell's value for the heat of formation of sulfur, $D(R_3P{=}S)$ is calculated as 82 kcal. The values for $D(R_3P{=}O)$ are much higher, being in the range of 120 to 135 kcal (page 214 of ref. 255). Chernick concludes from this and related evidence that the P=O bond has a higher bond order than the P=S bond.

Phosphines are thiophilic enough to react with molecularly bound sulfur as well as elemental sulfur, and they are therefore powerful desulfurizing agents. Triaryl phosphines react with thiosulfate (302), tetrathionates (302), thioepoxides, and organic disulfides (943).

$$Ar_3P + S_2O_3^{=} \longrightarrow Ar_3P{=}S + SO_3^{=}$$

$$2\,Ar_3P + S_4O_6^{=} \longrightarrow 2\,Ar_3P{=}S + 2\,SO_3^{=}$$

$$Ar_3P + R_2C\overset{S}{\triangle}CR_2 \longrightarrow Ar_3P{=}S + R_2C{=}CR_2$$

$$Ar_3P + RSSR \longrightarrow Ar_3P{=}S + RSR$$

Neureiter and Bordwell (800) have studied the reaction of *cis*- and *trans*-2-butene episulfide with phosphines and have shown that the reaction is stereospecific. *Trans*-2-butene episulfide yields *trans*-2-butene, and the *cis*-episulfide yields the *cis*-olefin.

$$R_3P + S\langle\begin{matrix} C(H)(CH_3) \\ | \\ C(H)(CH_3) \end{matrix} \longrightarrow R_3P{=}S + \begin{matrix} C(H)(CH_3) \\ \| \\ C(H)(CH_3) \end{matrix}$$

Denney and Boskin (315) have confirmed this and have also found that the reaction rate is insensitive to variations in the dielectric constant. Changing the solvent from xylene to dimethylformamide (dielectric increase from 2.4 to 37.6) results in a rate increase of only 45%. The authors conclude that the mechanism is a single-step displacement on sulfur and that an intermediate with some charge separation, such as shown below, does not accurately represent the transition state (also see ref. 305).

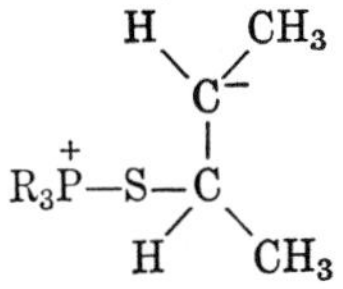

$$R_3\overset{+}{P}-S-C(H)(CH_3)-\overset{-}{C}(H)(CH_3)$$

Culvenon, Davies, and Heath (275) point out that the sulfur in a thioepoxide cannot usually be oxidized above the S^{II} level. Attempts to do so may lead to desulfuration. For example, oxidation of thioepoxides by hydrogen peroxide, permanganate, or nitric acid does not produce a cyclic sulfoxide or sulfone. The reaction product of nitric acid oxidation of ethylene thioepoxide has been identified as $HO_3S—CH_2—CH_2—S—CH_2—CO_2H$. The reaction of thioepoxides with methyl iodide produces desulfuration.

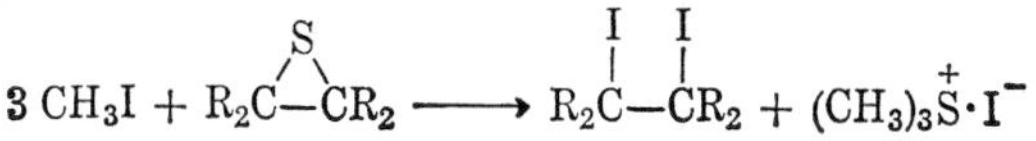

$$3\,CH_3I + R_2C\overset{S}{\frown}CR_2 \longrightarrow R_2C(I)-C(I)R_2 + (CH_3)_3\overset{+}{S}\cdot I^-$$

10

EXPERIMENTAL PROCEDURES FOR SELECTED SULFUR REACTIONS

Experimental procedures are given in this chapter in sufficient detail to illustrate conditions required to effect some of the reactions described in earlier chapters. The yield of product has been corrected to allow for unconsumed starting material if such data are given. Many of the examples given are taken from the review by Wegler, Kuehle, and Schaefer (1134); these authors checked and confirmed most of the procedures they cite.

10-1. Addition of Hydrogen Sulfide to 1-Butene Initiated by Irradiation (1103)

1-Butene (2.46 g, 0.044 mole) and hydrogen sulfide (3.0 g, 0.088 mole) are sealed in a quartz tube of 10-mm ID and illuminated at 0° C for 4 minutes with a quartz mercury arc. The tube is then cooled and opened, and unreacted materials are allowed to evaporate. The product (3.8 ml) is washed with 10% aqueous sodium hydroxide. The top layer (0.5 ml) is removed; it is butyl sulfide, n_D^{20} 1.4530. The aqueous solution is acidified with hydrochloric acid, and the top layer is removed and distilled. It is 1-butanethiol, bp 98.0, n_D^{20} 1.4431. These conditions give an 80% conversion to 85% 1-butanethiol and 15% butyl sulfide.

At −78° C, the same conditions lead to a 40% conversion.

10-2. Addition of Hydrogen Sulfide to Propene Initiated by Irradiation (1103)

This is similar to Procedure 10-1. Irradiation of a mixture of 6.5 ml of propene and hydrogen sulfide in quartz leads to a 95% conversion in 6 minutes. The product is 65% 1-propanethiol, bp 67.5° C, n_D^{20} 1.4351; 35% propyl sulfide, bp 141.5° C, n_D^{20} 1.4480.

If 0.5 ml acetone is added, the reaction can be run in pyrex. In this case the same conditions produce a 75% conversion to 80% 1-propanethiol and 20% propyl sulfide.

10-3. Addition of Hydrogen Sulfide to 1-Chlorocyclohexene Initiated by Irradiation (511)

A tubular reaction flask is fitted with a coaxial quartz Hanovia SC-2537 lamp (which generates 85% of its light in the 2,537 A band) and with a reflux condenser. Hydrogen sulfide (300 ml, 9.0 moles) is distilled into the graduated reaction flask, which is immersed in a dry ice–acetone bath. 1-Chlorocyclohexene (15.5 g, 0.10 mole) is added, the lamp and reflux condenser are inserted, and the mixture is irradiated at −60 to −80° C for 2 hours, during which time the hydrogen sulfide is allowed to reflux gently (bp −60° C). The product is allowed to warm, and the unreacted hydrogen sulfide is evaporated. The material is distilled and gives 2.30 g (15%) of recovered 1-chlorocyclohexene (bp 48 to 50° C/20 mm), 12.41 g (62%) of a mixture of *cis*- and *trans*-2-chlorocyclohexanethiol (bp 93 to 96° C/12 mm), and 3.94 g (22%) of 2-chlorocyclohexyl sulfide (bp 170 to 173° C/1 mm). The thiol is more than 90% cis, as shown by rates of solvolysis in ethanol.

10-4. Addition of Propanethiol to Propene to Form Propyl Sulfide, Initiated by Irradiation (1103)

A quartz tube is filled with equimolar amounts of 1-propanethiol and propene, evacuated, cooled in liquid nitrogen, evacuated, and sealed. The tube is irradiated at 0° C for 6 minutes with a 400-watt mercury arc lamp placed 20 cm from the tube. The tube is cooled and opened, and unconverted propene is allowed to escape. The liquid remaining is washed with 10% sodium hydroxide and water, and distilled. A 95% yield of propyl sulfide, bp 141.5° C, n_D^{20} 1.4480, is obtained. The reaction may be carried out in a pyrex tube if 0.5 ml acetone is added.

10-5. Addition of Thiolacetic Acid to 2-Chloro-2-Butene (801)

A mixture of either *cis*- or *trans*-2-chloro-2-butene (12.8 g, 0.142 mole), thiolacetic acid (10.8 g, 0.142 mole), and about 20 drops of Lucidol Corp. *t*-butyl hydroperoxide is placed in a flask equipped with a reflux condenser. The flask is irradiated for 1 hour with a 100-watt bulb 2 cm distant. The mixture warms within 5 to 10 minutes and reaches a maximum temperature of 89°. Distillation gives a 66 to 78% yield of 2-(2-chlorobutyl) thiolacetate, bp 80 to 84° C/13 mm. Under these conditions thiolacetic acid isomerizes the olefins, and the equilibrium mixture of about 75% threo and 25% erythro is obtained from either cis or trans.

Alternatively, the reaction may be conducted at −78° C. Under these conditions the starting olefins are not isomerized, but the same mixture of about 90% threo and 10% erythro is produced from either isomer because of the rapid interconversion of the intermediate radical species. At this lower temperature, a Hanovia ultraviolet lamp arranged coaxially inside a pyrex reaction tube is used; the more powerful irradiation obviates the necessity for the peroxide. The chlorobutene (14.0 g, 0.155 mole) is placed in the flask and cooled to −70° C while protected from moisture by a drying tube. Thiolacetic acid (9.4 g, 0.124 mole) is added, the reactants are mixed, the lamp is inserted, and the flask is cooled in dry ice–acetone. The mixture is irradiated for 50 minutes, and then about 5 g sodium bicarbonate and a few milliliters of water are added to retard isomerization. The mixture is warmed, more water is added, sodium sulfate is added, and the layers are separated. The organic layer is washed with water, dried, and distilled. Chlorobutene is recovered (about 2.4 g, 17%) unchanged, and the 1:1 adduct, bp 96 to 98° C/28 mm, $n_D^{29.7}$ 1.4822, obtained in about 80% yield.

10-6. Reaction of Tetralin with 3-Methylbutyl Disulfide to Produce Naphthalene (893)

Tetralin (26.4 g, 0.186 mole) and 3-methylbutyl disulfide (82.4 g, 0.400 mole) are added to a flask equipped with distillation column. The flask is held at 250 to 260° C as long as 3-methylbutanethiol (bp 115° C) distills (about 10 hours). A slow, continuous distillation is obtained by gradually increasing the temperature from 250 to 260° C. The yield of thiol (75 g) indicates 88% dehydrogenation. The flask is cooled, and the dark solid is steam-distilled to give naphthalene (18 g, 70%).

10-7. Reaction of 1-Phenylbutene with Sulfur to Produce 2-Phenylthiophene (1113)

1-Phenylbutene (39.3 g, 0.32 mole) and sulfur (28.9 g, 0.90 gram atom) are heated to 200 to 250° C for 15 hours, until no further hydrogen sulfide is evolved. The product cools to a black tar. Distillation gives 2.6 g of hydrocarbon, bp 48 to 60° C/3 mm, 16.85 g (35%) 2-phenylthiophene, bp 80 to 105° C/3 mm, and 24.2 g of residue. The hydrocarbon is 1-phenylbutane, sulfonamide derivative, mp 94 to 95° C. The thiophene solidifies to yellow crystals which are recrystallized from alcohol-water (it tends to oil out of undiluted organic solvents). The recrystallized

2-phenylthiophene has silver lamellar crystals, mp 34.0 to 34.5° C, bp 256.1° C/760 mm, n_D^{35} 1.6320.

10-8. Reaction of *p*-Cymene with Sulfur to Produce 5-(*p*-Tolyl)trithione (418, 1134)

p-Cymene (1,108 g, 8.25 mole), sulfur (400 g, 12.5 gram atom), and ditolyl guanidine (8.2 g, 0.034 mole) are heated for 21 hours at reflux, 185° C. Hydrogen sulfide is evolved. The mixture is cooled and held at 5° C for 2 hours to allow the product to crystallize to a red slurry which is collected on a filter, washed with 400 ml of 1:3 benzene/hexane, dried, and then recrystallized from benzene to give crude 5-(*p*-tolyl)trithione (355 g, 38% yield based on sulfur), mp 119 to 120° C. One recrystallization from benzene raises the mp to 122.5 to 123° C.

10-9. Reaction of 1-Phenyl-2-methylpropene with Sulfur to Form 4-Methyl-5-phenyltrithione (1111)

1-Phenyl-2-methylpropene (31.7 g, 0.24 mole) and sulfur (15.4 g, 0.48 gram atom) are heated at 190 to 210° C for 10 hours in a flask equipped with a thermometer and a reflux condenser. Hydrogen sulfide is evolved. The reaction product is cooled and solidifies to a black mass. Distillation gives 13.6 g recovered hydrocarbon, bp 53 to 55° C/4 mm, and a dark-red liquid, bp 204 to 210° C/1.5 mm, which crystallizes to a red solid. The solid is recrystallized from acetone to give small orange crystals, which are washed with hot ether, dissolved in hot alcohol, and treated with silver to remove elemental sulfur, and allowed to crystallize. A 19.0 g yield (80%) of $C_{10}H_8S_3$, mp 104.5 to 104.8° C, is obtained. The orange-red, elongated platelets are identified as 4-methyl-5-phenyltrithione.

CH_3 — =S
C_6H_5 S–S

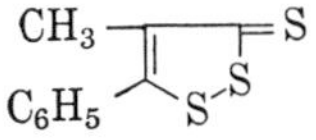

10-10. Reaction of 4-Propenylanisole with Sulfur to Form 6-(*p*-Anisyl)trithione (166, 1134)

4-Propenylanisole (103.2 g, 0.70 mole) and sulfur (89.9 g, 2.8 gram atom) are gently stirred and heated under an inert atmosphere in a flask equipped with a distillation head. At 175° C evolution of hydrogen sulfide starts. The reaction effervesces, and the temperature rapidly rises from 175 to 240° C as 3.8 g of a colorless oil distills. (This oil is mainly 4-propenyl- and 4-propylanisole.) Stirring is continued for

1 hour after the temperature drops to 220° C. The total loss of weight during the reaction is 34.2 g. The solution is cooled, diluted with 200 ml acetone, and allowed to stand. Crude 4-anisyltrithione (80.4 g, 48%) crystallizes. This product also contains sulfur and 2,5-dimethyl-3,4-dianisylthiophene, etc.; it is sublimed at 10^{-3} mm and 90° C, at which temperature only the trithione sublimes. Alternatively, sulfur can be removed by recrystallization from carbon disulfide, and final purification accomplished by recrystallization from butyl acetate. The product forms orange-red prisms of mp 111° C.

10-11. Reaction of Biphenyl with Sulfur and Aluminum Chloride to Form Dibenzothiophene (506)

Biphenyl (500 g, 3.24 mole) and sulfur (208 g, 6.5 gram atoms) are melted together in a 5-liter flask held at 115 to 120° C. Anhydrous aluminum chloride (25 g) is added over 75 minutes. The temperature is held at 120° C for another 105 minutes, and then gradually allowed to increase to 240° C by the eighth or ninth hour. The mixture is cooled and extracted three times by boiling gently with 500 ml water, cooling, and decanting the water. The organic material is then extracted with eight 1,000-ml portions of ethanol by boiling and decanting while hot. The combined alcohol is carbon-treated, filtered hot, and cooled. Almost colorless needles of dibenzothiophene (70%), mp 98° C, crystallize. Distillation (bp 152 to 154° C/3 mm) and recrystallization from alcohol give colorless needles of mp 99° C.

10-12. Reaction of Dibutylamine with Sulfur to Form *N*-Butylthiobutanamide (686, 1134)

Dibutylamine (97 g, 0.75 mole) and sulfur (48 g, 1.5 gram atoms) are refluxed in 200 ml pyridine for 10 hours with stirring. The solution is diluted with 400 ml chloroform, washed with water, dilute aqueous hydrochloric acid, and water, and is distilled. *N*-Butylthiobutanamide (67.2 g, 53%), bp 142 to 144° C/6 mm, is obtained as a light-yellow oil.

10-13. Willgerodt Oxidation of 1-Acetylacenaphthene (419, 1134)

This is the procedure Fieser and Kilmer developed for improved yields in the Willgerodt reaction.

1-Acetylacenaphthene (19.2 g, 0.10 mole), an ammonium polysulfide solution (96 g) prepared by saturating concentrated ammonium hydroxide with hydrogen sulfide gas and then adding 10% sulfur by weight, and 17 ml dioxane are heated for 18 hours, at 175 to 180° C. On cooling, acenaphthene-1-carboxamide (6.8 g, 33%) crystallizes. The filtrate is washed with benzene and the aqueous layer acidified to produce acenaphthene-1-carboxylic acid (0.43 g, 2.1%) mp 159 to 160° C; an additional amount (0.38 g, 1.7%) is recovered from the benzene. The benzene is distilled and 1-ethylacenaphthene (8.3 g, 47%) is obtained, mp 34.8 to 35.1° C.

10-14. Willgerodt Oxidation of Acetophenone (319)

Acetophenone (25.0 g, 0.21 mole), sulfur (37.5 g, 1.17 gram atoms), 50 ml concentrated ammonium hydroxide, and 30 ml pyridine are sealed in a 22-mm OD glass tube and heated at 157 ± 6° C for 4.5 hours. The tube is opened and the reaction product evaporated to dryness in an evaporating dish. The solid is leached with 500 ml boiling water in several portions, the liquid is carbon treated, and cooled to precipitate phenylacetamide (20.0 g), mp 156 to 158° C. A second crop of 2.7 g is obtained. Evaporation to dryness gives an additional 0.32 g amide and 1.2 g phenylacetic acid (4.2%). The combined yield of acid and amide is 85.8%. The acid, after recrystallization from water, has a melting point of 76.3 to 77.3° C.

10-15. Willgerodt Oxidation of *t*-Butyl Methyl Ketone (Pinacolone) (225, 1134)

This reaction produces an excellent yield of amide from an aliphatic ketone which can be oxidized to only one product.

Ammonium sulfide is prepared by bubbling hydrogen sulfide into concentrated ammonium hydroxide and is 12 *M* in ammonia and 7 *M* in sulfide. This solution (16 ml) is mixed with dioxane (8 ml), and *t*-butyl methyl ketone (4.0 g, 0.04 mole) and sulfur (12.8 g, 0.40 gram atom) are added. The mixture is sealed in a pyrex ampoule and held at 210 ± 5° C for 6 hours. The tube is cooled and opened. The product is filtered at 0° C and the solid recrystallized from water to give 3,3-dimethylbutanamide in three crops. The first (1.52 g) has mp 134.0 to 134.2° C, the second (0.59 g) has mp 133 to 134° C, and the last (0.57 g) has mp 129 to 130° C. The combined yield is 58%.

10-16. Reaction of 4-Methylpyridine with Sulfur to Produce 1,2-Dipyridylethane (1045, 1134)

4-Methylpyridine (279 g, 3.0 mole) and sulfur (48 g, 1.5 gram atoms) are heated at 140 to 155° C for 12 hours, and hydrogen sulfide is allowed to escape. Unreacted methylpyridine (131 g, 47%) is recovered by distillation, and the distillation residue is poured into an ice–50% sulfuric acid mixture. Sulfur is filtered off, and the filtrate is made alkaline with 30% sodium hydroxide. The oil phase is separated, the aqueous phase is extracted with benzene, and the combined organic phases are distilled. A 60% yield of 1,2-di-(4-pyridyl)ethane is obtained, bp 164 to 174° C/3 mm, which can be recrystallized from cyclohexane-benzene (3:1) to mp 110 to 111° C. Also obtained are 1,2-di-(4-pyridyl)ethene, 4%, bp 175 to 205° C/2 mm, mp (benzene recrystallization) 151 to 152° C; and 1,2,3-tri-(4-pyridyl) propane, 14%, bp 230 to 242° C/2 mm, mp (ethyl acetate recrystallization) 110 to 111° C.

10-17. Reaction of 4-Methylpyridine with Sulfur and Morpholine (1134)

Sulfur (96.2 g, 3.0 gram atoms) is suspended in a mixture of 4-methylpyridine (93.1 g, 0.90 mole) and morpholine (130.7 g, 1.26 mole). The mixture is held at 170° C for 12 hours, and hydrogen sulfide is allowed to evolve. The product is cooled, dissolved in 500 ml hot absolute ethanol, and chilled. Small, black needles separate and are carbon treated and recrystallized from 2 liters of absolute ethanol. This gives 66.2 g pyridine-4-thiocarboxymorpholide (38%) as a first crop. Two subsequent crops bring the amount to 83.1 g (47%) of material, mp 141 to 147° C.

10-18. Oxidation of 2-Phenylethanethiol under Conditions Where 2-Phenylethanol Does Not React (633)

2-Phenylethanethiol (1.0 g, 0.0073 mole) and an ammonium polysulfide solution (5.0 g), prepared by saturating concentrated ammonium hydroxide with hydrogen sulfide and then adding 10% sulfur by weight, are held at 205° C for 4 hours. The contents of the tube are evaporated to dryness and leached with hot ethanol, and phenylacetamide (0.93 g, 95%), mp 153 to 154° C, is obtained. Under these conditions 2-phenylethanol is recovered quantitatively.

10-19. Oxidation of Decanethiol with Sulfur (635, 1134)

Decanethiol (174 g, 1 mole), sulfur (64 g, 2 gram atoms), and 300 ml concentrated ammonium hydroxide are held at 200° C for 12 hours in a steel autoclave. A quantitative yield of decanamide, mp 97 to 98° C, is isolated.

10-20. Oxidation of 2-Phenylethyl Disulfide to Phenylacetic Acid (742)

2-Phenylethyl disulfide (2.74 g, 0.01 mole), morpholine (3.48 g, 0.04 mole), and sulfur (1.28 g, 0.04 gram atom) are refluxed for 1 hour. The reaction mixture is cooled and diluted with chloroform. This solution is washed with water, dilute hydrochloric acid, and water, and concentrated under vacuum. The organic product was refluxed for 5 hours with 50% sulfuric acid to give phenylacetic acid (1.90 g, 70%), mp 73 to 75° C.

10-21. Oxidation of Xylene with Sulfur Dioxide and Ammonium Sulfide (1062, 1134)

Xylene (106 g, 1.0 mole) (ortho, para, or a mixture), sulfur dioxide (96 g, 1.5 moles), ammonia (51 g, 3.0 moles), and hydrogen sulfide (51 g, 1.5 moles) in 1 liter of water are heated in a 316-type stainless steel autoclave at 315° C for 1 hour. The pressure reaches approximately 2,700 psi. The autoclave is cooled, and the product is slurried with carbon and filtered. A 96% conversion is obtained of material having a 101 neutralization number.

10-22. Oxidation of *m*-Xylene with Ammonium Thiosulfate (1071, 1134)

m-Xylene (75 g, 0.70 mole) is placed in a large glass test tube and the test tube is stood upright in a 2.5-liter rocking autoclave. A 60% solution of ammonium thiosulfate (262 g) is placed directly in the autoclave. [The solution is prepared by dissolving 1.06 moles of $(NH_4)_2S_2O_3$ in 658 g water.] The charge is heated to 315° C, at which point the rocking is started, dumping the xylene into the aqueous solution. The autoclave is held at 315° C for another 1.5 hours, cooled, and the gases are vented (20 g obtained). The liquid product is filtered, heated with sodium hydroxide (60 g), acidified to pH 6, carbon-treated, filtered, and finally acidified to pH 1 to 2; the product, isophthalic acid, is collected (112 g, 90%).

10-23. Oxidation of *m*-Xylene to Isophthalic Acid by Ammonium Sulfate (1059)

m-Xylene (225 g, 2.12 moles), ammonium sulfate (463 g, 3.5 moles), sulfur (32.0 g, 1.0 gram atom), and water (955 ml) are added to a 2.5-liter stainless steel rocking autoclave. The mixture is heated to 315° C, the rocking is started, and the mixture is held at that temperature for 1 hour.

The autoclave is cooled and opened. The contents plus sodium hydroxide (187 g, 4.65 moles) are heated in a beaker on the steam bath until no further ammonia is evolved (vapor no longer turns wet litmus paper blue). The product is carbon-treated and filtered, and hydrochloric acid is slowly added with stirring. At pH 4.5, sulfur is filtered (58.9 g). At pH 1 to 2, isophthalic acid (312 g, 89%) is precipitated.

10-24. Oxidation of *p*-Toluenesulfonic Acid to *p*-Sulfobenzoic Acid (1073)

p-Toluenesulfonic acid monohydrate (190 g, 1.0 mole), sodium hydroxide (80.0 g, 2.0 moles), sulfur (100 g, 3.1 gram atoms), and water (900 ml) are placed in a 4.5-liter 316-type stainless steel rocking autoclave and heated at 315° C for 2 hours. The maximum pressure developed is 2,100 psi. Steam distillation to remove a small amount of oil, carbon treatment, and evaporation to dryness give disodium sulfobenzoate (243 g, 95%). Use of only 1.0 mole of sodium hydroxide leads to loss of the sulfonic acid group and formation of more than a 30% yield of benzoic acid.

10-25. Reaction of *p*-Nitrotoluene with Sulfur to Form *p*-Aminobenzaldehyde (312, 1134)

Ethanol (187 ml), water (400 ml), sodium sulfide nonahydrate (54.0 g, 0.222 mole), and sulfur (7.5 g, 0.234 gram atom) are stirred together as sodium hydroxide (40.0 g, 1.00 mole) is added. *p*-Nitrotoluene (90.0 g, 0.665 mole) is added, and the heterogeneous mixture is refluxed for 2 hours, during which time additional sulfur (15 g, 0.47 gram atom) is added. Refluxing is continued for 2 hours, the alcohol is removed by distillation, and the residue is subjected to steam distillation. The organic distillate is cooled to 2° C and *p*-aminobenzaldehyde (81 g, 100%) separates as a noncrystalline product.

10-26. Reaction of Diethyl Ketone with Sulfur to Form 2,2,4-Triethyl-5-methylthiazoline (44)

Diethyl ketone (430 g, 5.0 moles) and sulfur (80 g, 2.5 gram atoms) are placed in a 2-liter, 3-neck flask equipped with stirrer, reflux condenser, and gas inlet tube. A vigorous stream of ammonia is passed through the inlet tube for 7 hours. The mixture quickly darkens, and the temperature rises to 50 to 60° C; after 3 hours the temperature again drops. At the end of the 7 hours the mixture is dark brown, all the sulfur has dissolved, and water separates as a bottom layer. Either the entire reaction mixture can be steam-distilled, or the organic phase can be extracted with ether and the ether washed and evaporated. The former method gives purer products; both give similar yields. Distillation of the organic material from either of these methods separates unreacted ketone (85 g, 19.8%) and 2,2,4-triethyl-5-methylthiazoline (315 g, 80%), bp 96° C/12 mm, n_D^{20} 1.4862.

10-27. Reaction of Phenol with Sulfur (1134)

Phenol (28.2 kg, 300 moles), sulfur (9.6 kg, 300 gram atoms), and sodium hydroxide (0.45 kg, 11.2 moles) are stirred into 1,350 ml water, and then refluxed at 120 to 122° C for 15 hours. Hydrogen sulfide (3.6 kg) escapes. The reaction mass is cooled and distilled under vacuum at a flask temperature of 60 to 130° C. The distillate is 10.05 kg and is mainly phenol. Heating the mixture further for 8 hours more at 130° C and 4 mm causes another 4.8 kg to distill. The residue is 31.6 kg of a dark polymer with softening point of 60° C. The use of more sulfur yields polymers of higher softening point.

10-28. Oxidation of 2-Phenylethanethiol to 2-Phenylethyl Disulfide (742)

2-Phenylethanethiol (69 g, 0.50 mole) and 1 ml of an amine (either morpholine or butylamine) are stirred as sulfur (10 g, 0.31 gram atom) is added slowly. Hydrogen sulfide is evolved. The solution is stirred for an hour after all the sulfur is added, and then is allowed to stand overnight. Benzene (100 ml) is added, the solution is filtered, washed successively with water, dilute hydrogen chloride, dilute sodium hydroxide, and water, concentrated, and distilled. Unconverted thiol (11 g, 16%), bp 55 to 59° C/1 mm, and disulfide (49 g, 71%), bp 168 to 180° C/1.5 mm, are isolated. The disulfide on redistillation boils at 172 to 175° C/0.8 mm.

11

COMPOUNDS WHICH HAVE BEEN OXIDIZED BY SULFUR OR POLYSULFIDE (1947–1957)

Explanatory Notes

(*a*) Each compound is listed under the *last* classification in which it fits; e.g., *p*-anisyl-1-propene is listed as an aromatic olefin (part 11 in Table 11-1), not as an aromatic oxygen compound (part 10 in Table 11-1); β-nitrostyrene is listed in part 15, not 11. However, compounds in a related series are classed together, even if this violates the rule; e.g., all ring-substituted acetophenones are listed as aromatic ketones, including 4-methoxy-, 4-methylmercapto-, 4-carbethoxy-, and 4-nitroacetophenone.

(*b*) The following tables in the text contain related material which is not repeated in this chapter: 5-3, 6-1, 6-2, 6-3, 7-1 through 7-4, 7-6, 7-7.

(*c*) The oxidants are coded as follows:

A Aqueous ammonium polysulfide or ammonium hydroxide plus sulfur
B Ammonium polysulfide in dioxane-water
C Ammonium polysulfide in pyridine-water
D Morpholine plus sulfur
E Sodium hydroxide plus sulfur
F Ammonium polysulfide in ethanol-water
G Amine (name) plus sulfur
H Sulfur
I Sulfur plus another reagent (name)
J Ammonium polysulfide in pyridine-water plus added compound (name)

(*d*) Refl. = Refluxed
Flow = Flow system, in some cases with recycle
R = Some products recycled
Only the highest temperature is given if a range is reported; only the longest time is cited if a time range is reported.

(*e*) PAM = Phenylacetamide
PAA = Phenylacetic acid

PTAM = Phenylthioacetomorpholide
No Rx = No reaction occurs

(*f*) Nomenclature is that of *Chemical Abstracts.* Alternate names are used if they make relationships in the table more apparent. The following references to *Chemical Abstracts* are especially pertinent: rules 157, 182, 204–208, 210, and 212 (as revised by rule 13 *l*, page 6R, subject index to *Chem. Abstracts,* **51,** 1957) on pages 5896–5898 of the subject index to *Chem. Abstracts,* **41,** 1945. Also in the subject index, see *Chem. Abstracts,* **51,** 1957, rules 1, 4, 9, page 5R. For example:

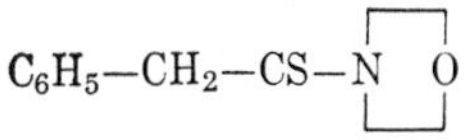

$C_6H_5—CH_2—CS—N\ O$ — Phenylthioacetomorpholide

$C_6H_5—(CH_2)_4—CS—N\ O$ — 5-Phenylthiopentanomorpholide

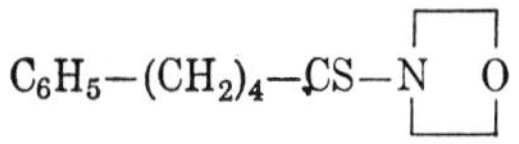

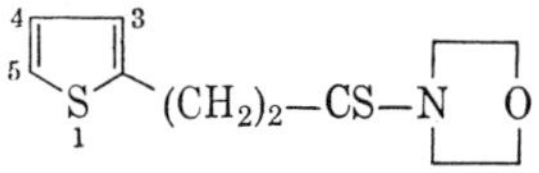

4, 3, 5, S, 1 $(CH_2)_2—CS—N\ O$ — 2-Thiophenethiopropanomorpholide

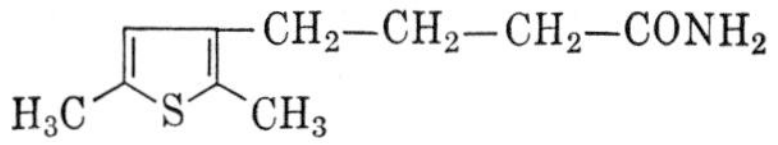

$CH_2—CH_2—CH_2—CONH_2$, H_3C, S, CH_3 — 2,5-Dimethyl-3-thiophenebutanamide

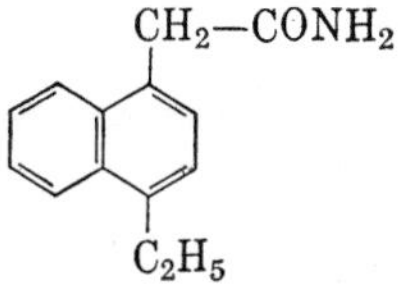

$CH_2—CONH_2$, C_2H_5 — 4-Ethyl-1-naphthaleneacetamide

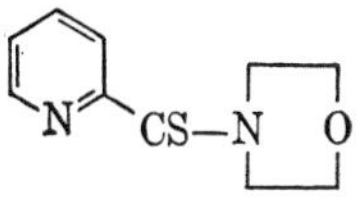

N, $CS—N\ O$ — 2-Pyridinethiocarboxomorpholide

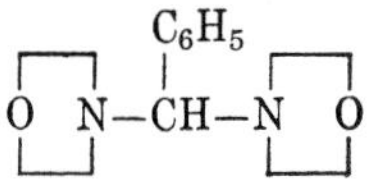

C_6H_5, $O\ N—CH—N\ O$ — α,α-Dimorpholinotoluene

(*g*) Yields reported are seldom the maximum obtainable. Frequently only the amide product is isolated and appreciable amounts of the related acid are discarded. The product listed is the first compound which was purified and characterized, not necessarily the first formed. Conv. = conversion.

Table 11-1

Compound oxidized[a,b]	Oxidant[c]	°C	Hours[d]	Product, %[e,f,g]	Refs.
1. Aliphatic ketones:					
Acetone	A	210	4	Propanamide, 5	634
Acetone	E	177	2	Acetic acid, 4	1064, 1073
2-Butanone-4-C-14	B	170	5	Butanamide, 10	227
2-Pentanone-1-C-14	B	170	5	Pentanamide, 25	227
3-Pentanone	A	200	6	Pentanamide, 43	634
4-Methyl-2-pentanone	A	200	4	4-Methylpentanamide, 88	634
4-Methyl-2-pentanone	A	210	4	4-Methylpentanamide, 20	635
4-Methyl-2-pentanone	B	180	3	4-Methylpentanamide, 60	552
Cyclohexanone	B	200	4	Cyclohexanethiol, 28; cyclohexyl disulfide, 2; adipic acid, <1	1166
Cyclohexanone	D	...	.....	*p*-Phenylene-*N*-*N'*-dimorpholine	75
Cyclohexanone	G (piperidine)	...	.....	*p*-Phenylene-*N*,*N'*-dipiperidine	75
3-Methylcyclohexanone	B	200	4	3-Methylcyclohexanethiol, 16; 3-methylcyclohexyl disulfide, 6	1166
2-Heptanone-1-C-14	B	170	5	Heptanamide, 30	227
4-Heptanone	A	200	24	Heptanamide, 9	634
5-Nonanone	A	200	24	Nonanamide, 1	634
2-Undecanone	A	210	4	Undecanamide, 5	634
2-Undecanone	D	Refl.	10	Undecanoic acid, 75	342
Dihydro-β-ionone	D	...	.....	2,6,6-Trimethyl-1-cyclohexenylbutanoic acid, 45	420
Dihydro-α-ionone	D	...	.....	2,6,6-Trimethyl-1-cyclohexenylbutanoic acid, 45	420
2. Aliphatic aldehydes:					
Paraformaldehyde	D	Refl.	5	Morpholinium morpholine-4-carbodithioate, 74	742
3. Aliphatic compounds containing oxygen (non-carbonyl):					
1-Butanol	E	290	2	Propanoic acid, 16; acetic acid, 19	1073
1-Butanol	H	325	4	Butyl butanoate	567
t-Butanol	A	210	4	Isobutanamide, 1	635

Table 11-1 (Continued)

Compound oxidized[a,b]	Oxidant[c]	°C	Hours[d]	Product, %[e,f,g]	Refs.
1,1-Dimethoxy-pentane	B	160	12	Butanamide, 80	591
1,1,3-Trimethoxy-butane	B	160	12	Butanamide, 80	592
3-Pentanol	A	215	4	Pentanamide, 1	634
4-Heptanol	A	220	5	Butyramide, 1	634
5-Nonanol	A	225	5	Butanamide, 1	634
4. Aliphatic olefins:					
Propylene	A	250	1 R	Propanamide, 75	796
Propylene	A	250	0.5	Propanamide, 46	1017
Propylene	I(KSH)	230	1.5	Propanoic acid, 12; acetic acid, 7	1073
Isobutylene	A	250	.....	Isobutanamide, 70	796
2-Pentene	A	200	5	Pentanamide, 1	634
Cyclohexene	A	220	4	Tar	796
1-Heptene	J [$(NH_4)_2S_2O_3$]	155	4	Heptanamide, 15	837
3-Heptene	A	200	14	Heptanamide, 1	634
1-Octene	A	200	6	Octanamide, 4	634
4-Nonene	A	200	14	Nonanamide, 1	634
1-Decene	A	210	4	Decanamide, 3	635
1-Decene	A	200	6	Decanamide, 6	634
1,1-Di-neopentyl-ethylene	C	210	5	Neopentylacetamide, 8	837
1-Tetradecene	A	200	6	Tetradecanamide, 1	634
Butadiene	A	200	2 R	Butanamide, 20	796
Vinylcyclohexene	A	220	2	Tar	796
5. Aliphatic acetylenes:					
1-Heptyne	C	145	4	Heptanamide, 35	837
6. Aliphatic compounds containing sulfur:					
Ethanethiol	A	200	14	Acetamide, 19	634
1-Propanethiol	A	200	12	Propanamide, 9	634
2-Propanethiol	A	200	12	Propanamide, 6	634
1-Butanethiol	A	200	12	Butanamide, 24	634
2-Butanethiol	A	200	14	Butanamide, 0.5	634
Isobutanethiol	A	200	14	Isobutanamide, 15	634
t-Butanethiol	A	200	14	Isobutanamide, 0.5	634
3-Pentanethiol	A	200	12	Pentanamide, 5	634
4-Heptanethiol	A	200	12	Heptanamide, 1	634
1-Octanethiol	A	200	5	Octanamide, 6	634
5-Nonanethiol	A	200	12	Nonanamide, 1	634
1-Decanethiol	A	200	5	Decanamide, 8	634
1-Decanethiol	A	210	4	Decanamide, 100	635
1-Dodecanethiol	A	200	12	Dodecanamide, 62	634

Table 11-1 (Continued)

Compound oxidized[a,b]	Oxidant[c]	°C	Hours[d]	Product, %[e,f,g]	Refs.
7. Aliphatic compounds containing nitrogen:					
Methylene-bis-(4-morpholine)	H	150	.....	Morpholinium morpholine-4-carbodithioate, 70	742
Morpholine-4-methanethiol	D	160	1	Morpholinium morpholine-4-carbodithioate, 72	742
Butylamine	A	200	.....	Butanamide, 20	796
Dibutylamine	G (pyridine)	Refl.	10	*N*-butyl thiobutanamide	686
1-Nitro-1-pentene	C	180	6	Pentanamide, 11	412
4-Methyl-2-pentanone oxime	H	200	2	4-Methylpentanoic acid, 9	1002
N-methylene-*t*-octylamine	G (*t*-octylamine)	155	1	*t*-Octylisothiocyanate, 61	722
N-methylenecyclohexyl amine	H	Refl.	0.1	*N*,*N'*-dicyclohexylthiourea, 37	961
2-Octanone oxime	H	200	2	Octanoic acid, 10	1002
2-Undecanone oxime	H	200	2	Undecanoic acid	1002
1,3,5-trimethylhexahydro-*s*-triazine	H	150	0.5	*N*,*N'*-dimethylthiourea, 62	722
8. Aromatic ketones:					
Acetophenone	A	158	4	PAM, 72	319
Acetophenone	A	210	2	PAM, 62	635
Acetophenone	A	130	4	PAM, 45	319
Acetophenone	B	170	4	PAM, 88; PAA, 6	95
Acetophenone	B	158	4	PAM, 76	319
Acetophenone	B	200	4	PAM, 75	1166
Acetophenone	C	158	4	PAM, 86	319
Acetophenone	D	Refl.	8	PTAM, 72	216
Acetophenone	E	300	1	Benzoic acid, 28	1073
Acetophenone	F	158	4	PAM, 90	319
Acetophenone	F	170	Flow	PAM, 92	492
Acetophenone-carbonyl-C-14	C	165	4	PAM, 80; PAA, 2	186
Acetophenone-carbonyl-C-13	D	Refl.	3	PAA, 52	966
4-Bromoacetophenone	D	Refl.	8	4-Bromophenylacetic acid, 51	954
4-Chloroacetophenone	D	Refl.	8	4-Chlorophenylacetic acid, 47	954

Table 11-1 (Continued)

Compound oxidized[a,b]	Oxidant[c]	°C	Hours[d]	Product, %[e,f,g]	Refs.
4-Chloroaceto-phenone	D	175	2	4-Chlorophenylacetic acid, 28	635
2-Hydroxyaceto-phenone	A + *i*-propanol	...	.....	2-Hydroxyphenylacetic acid, 81	821
2-Hydroxyaceto-phenone	D	175	2	2-Hydroxyphenylacetic acid, 59	635
3-Hydroxyaceto-phenone	A + *i*-propanol	160	12	3-Hydroxyphenylacetic acid, 41	821
3-Hydroxyaceto-phenone	D	175	2	4-Hydroxyphenylacetic acid, 66	635
4-Hydroxyaceto-phenone	A + *i*-propanol	160	12	4-Hydroxyphenylaceta-mide, 67	821
4-Hydroxyaceto-phenone	D	Refl.	6	4-Hydroxyphenylacetic acid, 42	954
4-Hydroxyaceto-phenone	D	175	2	4-Hydroxyphenylacetic acid, 50	635
2-Methoxyaceto-phenone	D	175	2	2-Methoxyphenylacetic acid, 70	635
3-Methoxyaceto-phenone	D	175	2	3-Methoxyphenylacetic acid, 82	635
4-Methoxyaceto-phenone	D	Refl.	5	4-Methoxyphenylacetic acid, 75	954
4-Methoxyaceto-phenone	D	175	2	4-Methoxyphenylacetic acid, 36; 4-hydroxy-phenylacetic acid, 28	635
2,3-Dimethoxy-acetophenone	G (piperi-dine)	200	4	2,3-Dimethoxyphenyl-acetic acid, 50	1003
2,5-Dimethoxy-acetophenone	D	Refl.	7	2,5-Dimethoxyphenyl-acetic acid, 64	1
4-Methylmercapto-acetophenone	D	Refl.	14	4-Methylmercapto-phenylacetic acid, 43	253
3-Acetoxyaceto-phenone	D	175	2	3-Hydroxyphenylthio-acetomorpholide, 70	635
4-Phenoxyaceto-phenone	D	Refl.	14	4-Phenoxyphenyl-acetic acid	253
3-Nitroaceto-phenone	D	175	2	3-Nitrophenylthio-acetomorpholide, 30	635
3-Aminoaceto-phenone	D	175	2	3-Aminophenylacetic acid, 61	635
4-Aminoaceto-phenone	D	Refl.	8	4-Aminophenylacetic acid, 44	954
4-Aminoaceto-phenone	D	175	2	4-Aminophenylacetic acid, 66	635
2-Acetamidoaceto-phenone	D	175	2	2-Acetamidophenylthio-acetomorpholide, 75	635

Table 11-1 (Continued)

Compound oxidized[a,b]	Oxidant[c]	°C	Hours[d]	Product, %[e,f,g]	Refs.
3-Acetamidoaceto- phenone	D	175	2	3-Acetamidophenyl- acetic acid, 68	635
4-Acetamidoaceto- phenone	D	175	2	4-Acetamidophenyl- acetic acid, 70	635
2-Carboxyaceto- phenone	D	Refl.	5	Homophthalic acid, 10	954
2-Carbethoxyaceto- phenone	D	Refl.	6	Homophthalic acid, 32	954
4-Methylaceto- phenone	D	...	.....	4 Methylphenylthio- acetomorpholide, 85	1169
2,5-Dimethylaceto- phenone	D	...	.....	2,5-Dimethylphenyl- thioacetomorpholide, 63	1169
4-*t*-Butylaceto- phenone	D	135	16	4-*t*-Butylphenylacetic acid	253
4-*t*-Amylaceto- phenone	D	135	14	4-*t*-Amylphenylacetic acid	253
3-Trifluoromethyl- acetophenone	D	135	16	3-Trifluoromethyl- phenylacetic acid, 89	253
3-Phenylaceto- phenone	D	Refl.	7	3-Biphenylylacetic acid, 51	1100
4-Phenylaceto- phenone	D	...	.....	4-Biphenylylthio- acetomorpholide, 82	1169
4-Phenylaceto- phenone	D	Refl.	8	4-Biphenylylthio- acetomorpholide, 94	954
4-Phenylaceto- phenone	B	160	6	4-Biphenylylacetamide, 84	319
4-Benzoylaceto- phenone	D	Refl.	2.5	4-Benzoylphenylacetic acid, 47	1171
4-Styrylaceto- phenone	D	Refl.	2	4-Styrylphenylthio- acetomorpholide, 46	649
Acetylmesitylene	D	Refl.	8	*N*-(mesitoylthio- formyl)morpholine, 33 (48 conv.)	299
Propiophenone	D	Refl.	2	3-Phenylpropanoic acid, 67	742
Propiophenone	D	Refl.	6	3-Phenylpropanoic acid, 65	954
Propiophenone	C	165	5	3-Phenylpropanamide, 82	319
4-Hydroxypropio- phenone	D	Refl.	8	4-Hydroxyphenyl- propanoic acid, 27	954
4-Hydroxypropio- phenone	B	160	12	4-Hydroxyphenyl- propanoic acid, 42	821
Propionylmesitylene	D	Refl.	9	*N*-(α-Mesitoylthio- acetyl)morpholine, 30	299

Table 11-1 (Continued)

Compound oxidized[a,b]	Oxidant[c]	°C	Hours[d]	Product, %[e,f,g]	Refs.
Butyrophenone	D	Refl.	15	4-Phenylbutanoic acid, 36	954
Butyrophenone	C	165	5	4-Phenylbutanamide, 42	319
Isobutyrophenone	A	200	5.5	2-Methyl-3-phenyl propanamide, 3	633
Isobutyrophenone	D	Refl.	2	No Rx, 89% recovered	742
n-Butyrylmesitylene	D	Refl.	7	*N*-(β-mesitoylthio-propionyl)-morpholine, 9	299
Butyl phenyl ketone	D	Refl.	15	5-Phenylpentanoic acid, 14	954
Butyl phenyl ketone	C	165	5	5-Phenylpentanamide, 29	319
Butyl phenyl ketone-β-d_2	C	170	5	5-Phenylpentanamide	228
Isobutyl phenyl ketone	A	200	24	2-Methyl-4-phenyl-butanamide, 6	633
Isobutyl phenyl ketone	C	160	4	PAM, 12	218
Isobutyl phenyl ketone	C	190	4	2 Methyl-4-phenyl-butanamide	218
t-Butyl phenyl ketone	A	205	30	Neopentylbenzene, 66	633
Phenylacetone	A	210	5	3-Phenylpropanamide, 60	632
Phenylacetone	C	160	4	3-Phenylpropanamide, 72	218
4-Methoxyphenyl-acetone	D	Refl.	5	4-Methoxyphenylthio-acetomorpholide, 37	655
Benzoylacetone	B	175	3	Benzamide; 3-phenyl-propanoic acid	1167
Benzalacetone	D	Refl.	4	4-Phenyl-3-thio-butenomorpholide, 35	804
4-Methyl-4-Phenyl-pentanone-2	D	Refl.	20	4-Methyl-4-phenyl-thiopentano-morpholide, 62	217
1-Acetylnaphthalene	F	165	5	1-Naphthalene-acetamide, 84	96
1-Acetylnaphthalene	B	170	4	1-Naphthalene-acetamide, 88	95
2-Acetylnaphthalene	D	Refl.	16	2-Naphthalenethio-acetomorpholide, 90	802
2-Acetylnaphthalene	G (piperi-dine)	Refl.	6	2-Naphthalenethio-acetopiperidide, 38	655

Table 11-1 (Continued)

Compound oxidized[a,b]	Oxidant[c]	°C	Hours[d]	Product, %[e,f,g]	Refs.
4-Methyl-1-acetyl-naphthalene	B	170	4	4-Methyl-1-naphthaleneacetamide, 86	95
4-Ethyl-1-acetyl-naphthalene	B	170	4	4-Ethyl-1-naphthaleneacetamide, 41	95
4-Propyl-1-acetyl-naphthalene	B	170	4	4-Propyl-1-naphthaleneacetamide, 40	95
4-Butyl-1-acetyl-naphthalene	B	170	4	4-Butyl-1-naphthaleneacetamide, 34	95
4-Methoxy-1-acetyl-naphthalene	B	170	4	4-Methoxy-1-naphthaleneacetamide, 20	95
6-Methoxy-2-acetyl-naphthalene	D	140	18	6-Methoxy-2-naphthaleneacetic acid, 67	598
1-Cyclopentyl-4-acetylnaphthalene	B	172	24	4-Cyclopentyl-1-naphthaleneacetamide, 91	50
2-Acetyl-phenanthrene	B	160	6	2-Phenanthrene-acetamide, 72	319
2-Acetyl-phenanthrene	D	160	15	2-Phenanthreneacetic acid, 81	598
3-Acetyl-phenanthrene	D	160	15	3-Phenanthreneacetic acid, 84	598
2-Methyl-9-acetyl-1,2,3,4-tetrahydro-phenanthrene	B	...	.....	2-Methyl-1,2,3,4-tetrahydro-9-phen-anthreneacetamide, 61	49
9-Propionyl-anthracene	B	160	6	Anthracene, 85	319
2-Propionylphen-anthrene	B	160	6	2-Phenanthrene-propanamide, 66	319
3-Acetylretene	D	Refl.	5	3-Retenethioaceto-morpholide, 75	343
2-Acetyl-phenoxathiin	B	160	10	4-Phenoxathiin-acetamide, 68	505
Methyl *O*-methyl-7-propionylpodo-carpate	D	Refl.	10	Methyl *O*-methyl-7-acetonylpodocarpate, 10	129
Methyl *O*-methyl-7-acetonylpodo-carpate	D	...	.....	Methyl *O*-methyl-7-(β-thiopropano-morpholide)podo-carpate, 41	129
4,4′-Diacetyl-biphenyl	D	Refl.	10	4,4′-Biphenyldiacetic acid, 76	954
1,3,5-Triacetyl-benzene	D	Refl.	14	1,3,5-Benzenetriacetic acid, 75	803
Benzophenone	D	180	3	Diphenylmethane, 85; benzhydryl disulfide	1004
9-Fluorenone	D	180	4	9,9′-Bifluorene, 49	1005

Table 11-1 (Continued)

Compound oxidized[a,b]	Oxidant[c]	°C	Hours[d]	Product, %[e,f,g]	Refs.
9-Fluorenone	G (Piperidine)	175	2	Fluorene	1005
Acetylferrocene	B	Refl.	18	Ferrocenethioacetomorpholide, 35	890
1,1′-Diacetyl ferrocene	B	Refl.	18	1,1′-Ferrocenediacetic acid, 13	890
Propionylferrocene	B	Refl.	18	Ferrocenepropanoic acid, 3	890
9. Aromatic aldehydes:					
Phenylacetaldehyde	C	160	4	PAM, 48	218
3-Phenylpropanol	C	160	4	3-Phenylpropanamide, 48	218
Salicyaldehyde	D	...	.....	Salicylthiomorpholide	229
10. Aromatic compounds containing oxygen (noncarbonyl):					
1-Phenylethanol	B	160	5	No Rx	218
1-Phenylethanol	A	210	4	PAM, 33	635
1-Phenylethanol	A	210	4	PAM, 48	632
2-Phenylethanol	A	205	4	No Rx	633
2-Phenylethanol	B	160	5	No Rx	218
Methylbenzylcarbinol	B	160	5	No Rx	218
Dimethylphenylcarbinol	C	190	4	2-Phenylpropanamide and PAM, 38	837
Methyldiphenylcarbinol	C	210	5	Diphenylacetamide, 14	837
1-Phenyl-2-methylpropanol	A	200	6	2-Methyl-3-phenylpropanamide, 2	633
α,α-Dimethoxytoluene	B	160	12	Benzamide, 75	591
Styrene oxide	B	175	3	PAM, 65	1167
Styrene oxide	B	170	7	PAM, 87	502
α-Hydroxyacetophenone	B	200	4	PAM, 30	1166
11. Aromatic olefins:					
Styrene	A	210	4	PAM, 49	632
Styrene	A	210	4	PAM, 61; PAA, 32	635
Styrene	B	200	4	PAM, 33	1166
Styrene	C	165	4	PAM, 64	218
Styrene	D	Refl.	2.5	Acetophenonesemicarbazone, 6; PTAM, 29	742
Styrene	D	Refl.	2	PAA, 84	635
Styrene	G (piperidine)	Refl.	2	PAA, 58	635

Table 11-1 (Continued)

Compound oxidized[a,b]	Oxidant[c]	°C	Hours[d]	Product, %[e,f,g]	Refs.
Styrene	G (cyclo-hexyl-amine)	Refl.	2	PAA, 47	635
Styrene	G (aniline)	Refl.	2	PAA, 23	635
Styrene	G (heptyl-amine)	Refl.	2	PAA, 59	635
2-Chlorostyrene	D	175	2	2-Chlorophenylacetic acid, 63	635
2,5-Dichlorostyrene	D	175	2	2,5-Dichlorophenyl-acetic acid, 61	635
4-Chlorostyrene	D	175	2	4-Chlorophenylacetic acid, 59	635
1-Phenylpropene	C	160	4	3-Phenylpropanamide, 74	218
4-Anisyl-1-propene	D	160	3	4-Anisylthiopro-panomorpholide, 54	938
2-Phenylpropene	C	190	4	2-Phenylpropanamide and PAM, 55 to 61	837
2-Phenylpropene	A	200	5	2-Phenylpropanamide, 3	633
3-Phenylpropene	A	205	5	3-Phenylpropanamide, 50	633
1-Phenyl-2-methyl-propene	A	200	6	2-Methyl-3-phenyl-propanamide, 1 to 2	633
1,1-Diphenyl-ethylene	C	230	6	Diphenylacetamide, 37	837
2-Vinylnaphthalene	C	145	4	2-Naphthalene-acetamide, 24	837
β-Phenylvinyl methyl ketone	B	175	3	Benzoic acid, 3-phenyl-propanoic acid	1167
12. Aromatic acetylenes:					
Phenylacetylene	C	160	4	PAM, 72	218
1-Phenylpropyne	A	205	5	3-Phenylpropanamide, 50	633
1-Phenylpropyne	C	160	4	3-Phenylpropanamide, 90	218
Propionylphenyl-acetylene	D	...	.....	Tar	804
Acetylphenyl-acetylene	D	Refl.	4	4-Phenylthiobutano-morpholide, 51	804
13. Aromatic compounds containing halogen:					

Table 11-1 (Continued)

Compound oxidized[a,b]	Oxidant[c]	°C	Hours[d]	Product, %[e,f,g]	Refs.
Benzyl chloride	A	190	3.7	Benzamide, 60	797
1-Phenylethyl bromide	B	170	7	PAM, 40	502
2-Phenylethyl bromide	B	170	7	PAM, 66	502
α-Bromoacetophenone	B	200	4	PAM, 26	1166
β-Bromostyrene	B	170	7	PAM, 80	502
14. Aromatic compounds containing sulfur:					
α-Toluenethiol	A	200	12	Benzamide, 53	634
1-Phenylethanethiol	A	200	4	PAM, 44; PAA, 18	634
2-Phenylethanethiol	A	205	4	PAM, 95	633
2-Phenylethanethiol	A	210	4	PAM, 92	635
2-Phenylethanethiol	D	Refl.	4	Phenylacetaldehyde-semicarbazone	742
Benzyl disulfide	D	Refl.	1	Thiobenzomorpholide	742
2-Phenylethyl disulfide	D	Refl.	1	PAM, 70	742
2-Phenylethyl disulfide	D	Refl.	2	Phenylacetaldehyde semicarbazone, 12	742
Styryl disulfide	B	200	4	PAM, 99	1166
2-Mercapto-5-phenylthiazolidine	B	175	3	PAM, 59	1167
Thioacetophenone trimer	D	150	7.5	PTAM, 83	216
3-Phenyl-2-thioxo-propanoic acid	B	175	3	PAA, 97	1167
Phenacyl sulfide	B	200	4	PAM, 82	1166
Ammonium α-aceto-phenonesulfonate	B	175	3	PAM, 17; benzoic acid, 4	1167
Sodium benzyl thiosulfate	D	...	.....	Thiobenzomorpholide	754
15. Aromatic compounds containing nitrogen:					
Benzylamine	D	160	1	*N*-benzylthiobenz-amide, 41	740
Benzylamine	H	Refl.	0.75	*N*-benzylthiobenz-amide, 91	740
N-methyleneaniline	H	240	1.9	*N,N'*-diphenylthiourea	605
N-methylbenzyli-denimine	H	200	.....	*N*-methylthiobenz-amide	164
1-Phenylethylamine	B	170	7	PAM, 61	502
2-Phenylethylamine	B	170	7	PAM, 32	502
2-Phenyl-2-chloro-ethylamine hydrochloride	B	175	3	PAM, 64	1167

Table 11-1 (Continued)

Compound oxidized[a,b]	Oxidant[c]	°C	Hours[d]	Product, %[e,f,g]	Refs.
Acetophenoneoxime	H	200	2	PAA, 22	1002
β-Nitrostyrene	C	180	6	PAM, 38	412
α-Cyanoacetophenone	B	175	3	Benzamide, 13; benzoic acid, 7	1167
N,N-dimethyl-1-phenylethylamine	B	170	7	PAM, 31	502
N-methyl-1-phenylpropylenimine	B	175	3	Benzoic acid; 3-phenylpropanoic acid	1167
N-(2-hydroxyethyl)-1-phenylethylamine	B	170	7	PAM, 63	502
N,N-di-(2-hydroxyethyl)-1-phenylethylamine	B	170	7	PAM, 66	502
1-Acetamido-2-hydroxy-2-phenylethane	B	175	3	PAM, 54	1167
N-(5-chloroamyl-benzamide	C	160	6	5-Benzamidopentanamide, 43	413
α-Morpholinoacetophenone	B	170	7	PAM, 72	502
Phenacylpyridinium iodide	B	170	7	PAM, 53	502
α-Anilinoacetophenone	B	200	4	PAM, 35	1166
α,α-Dimorpholinotoluene	H	145	.....	Thiobenzomorpholide, 98	742
16. Aromatic and aliphatic acids and derivatives:					
2-Bromobutanoic acid	C	185	.....	Propanamide, 18	906
2-Mercaptobutanoic acid	C	185	.....	Propanamide, 19	906
Leucine	C	185	.....	3-Methylbutanamide, 16	906
Ethyl levulinate	B	150	4	Pentanamide, 15	539
2-Nonenoic acid	C	160	4.5	Octanamide, 69	301
Undecylenic acid	$C+(NH_4)_2S_2O_3$	160	4	Nonane-1,9-dicarboxylic acid, 35	837
α-Bromophenylacetic acid	C	185	.....	Benzamide, 64	906
Methyl salicylate	E	320	10	Heptanoic acid, 93	602
Cinnamic acid	B	170	5.5	PAM, 77	301
Trans-α-methylcinnamic acid	C	170	5	Phenylpropanamide, 63	301
Ethyl 3-acetylphenylacetate	D	Refl.	8	3-Phenylenediacetic acid, 61	954

Table 11-1 (Continued)

Compound oxidized[a,b]	Oxidant[c]	°C	Hours[d]	Product, %[e,f,g]	Refs.
Ethyl 4-acetyl-phenylacetate	D	Refl.	6	4-Phenylenediacetic acid, 70	954
α-Acetoxyaceto-phenone	B	200	4	PAM, 39	1166
β-Phenylethyl acetate	B	160	5	No Rx	218
9-Anthraceneacrylic acid	B	170	5	Anthracene, 50	301
2-Phenylglycine	C	185	.....	Benzamide, 75	906
Phenylalanine	C	180	.....	PAM, 32	906
17. Tetralin and related compounds:					
1-Tetralone	D	135	8	2-Morpholino-naphthalene, 50	568
1-Tetralone	D	...	.....	2-Morpholino-naphthalene	75
1-Tetralone	G (pyrrolidene)	...	.....	2-(*N*-pyrrolidyl) naphthalene	75
1-Tetralone	G (piperidine)	...	.....	2-(*N*-piperidyl) naphthalene	75
2-Tetralone	D	...	.....	2-Morpholino-naphthalene	75
2-Tetralone	G (piperidine)	...	.....	2-(*N*-piperidyl)-naphthalene	75
2-Tetralone	G (pyrrolidine)	...	.....	2-(*N*-pyrrolidyl)-naphthalene	75
7-Methyl-1-tetralone	G (pyrrolidine)	...	.....	7-Methyl-2-(*N*-pyrrolidyl)-naphthalene	75
7-Methyl-1-tetralone	G (piperidine)	...	.....	7-Methyl-2-(*N*-piperidyl)-naphthalene	75
6-Methoxy-1-tetralone	D	140	8	6-Methoxy-2-morpholinonaphthalene, 30	294
2-Morpholino-1-tetralone	D	Refl.	8	1-Naphthol, 77	294
6-Methyl-2-tetralone	D	...	.....	6-Methyl-2-morpholinonaphthalene	75
7-Methyl-2-tetralone	D	...	.....	7-Methyl-2-morpholinonaphthalene	75
1,4-Dihydronaphthalene	D	Refl.	8	2-Morpholinonaphthalene, <1; naphthalene, 88	294

Table 11-1 (Continued)

Compound oxidized[a,b]	Oxidant[c]	°C	Hours[d]	Product, %[e,f,g]	Refs.
1,2-Dihydronaphthalene	D	Refl.	8	2-Morpholinonaphthalene, 0.6	294
1,2,3,4-Tetrahydro-6-acetylnaphthalene	D	Refl.	14	1,2,3,4-Tetrahydro-6-naphthalene acetic acid	598
1,2,3,4-Tetrahydro-6-propanoylnaphthalene	D	125	11	1,2,3,4-Tetrahydro-6-naphthalenepropanoic acid, 65; 1,2,3,4-tetrahydro-6-naphthoic acid, 6	32
18. Thiophenes:					
Thiophane	A	232	3	Succinic acid, 20	1073
Thiophene	A	232	2	Succinic acid, 19; acetic acid, 9	1063
2-Thienyl methyl ketone	B	142	1	2-Thiopheneacetamide, 68	285
2-Thienyl methyl ketone	B	140	12	2-Thiopheneacetamide, 53	136
3-Thienyl methyl ketone	B	160	12	3-Thiopheneacetamide, 13	135
3-Methyl-2-thienyl methyl ketone	B	160	12	3-Methyl-2-thiopheneacetamide, 29	135
5-Methyl-2-thienyl methyl ketone	B	160	12	5-Methyl-2-thiopheneacetamide, 54	135
5-Ethyl-2-thienyl methyl ketone	B	160	12	5-Ethyl-2-thiopheneacetamide, 55	135
5-*t*-Butyl-2-thienyl methyl ketone	D	Refl.	10	Methyl 5-*t*-butyl-2-thiopheneacetate	426
3,4-Dimethyl-2-thienyl methyl ketone	B	160	12	3,4-Dimethyl-2-thiopheneacetamide, 34	135
3,4-Dimethyl-2-thienyl methyl ketone	B	150	12	3,4-Dimethyl-2-thiopheneacetamide, 32	136
2,5-Dimethyl-3-thienyl methyl ketone	B	160	12	2,5-Dimethyl-3-thiopheneacetamide, 95	136
2,5-Dimethyl-3-thienyl methyl ketone	B	160	12	2,5-Dimethyl-3-thiopheneacetamide, 95	185
2,5-Dimethyl-3-thienyl methyl ketone	D	Refl.	12	2,5-Dimethyl-3-thiophenethioacetomorpholide, 66	185
2,5-Diethyl-3-thienyl methyl ketone	B	160	12	2,5-Diethyl-3-thiopheneacetamide, 52	135

Table 11-1 (Continued)

Compound oxidized[a,b]	Oxidant[c]	°C	Hours[d]	Product, %[e,f,g]	Refs.
2,3-Dimethyl-5-thienyl methyl ketone	B	160	12	2,3-Dimethyl-5-thiopheneacetamide, 55	135
2,5-Dimethyl-3-ethyl-4-thienyl methyl ketone	B	160	12	2,5-Dimethyl-3-ethyl-4-thiophene-acetamide, 52	746
2-Thienyl ethyl ketone	B	140	12	2-Thiophene-propanamide, 42	136
2,5-Dimethyl-3-thienyl ethyl ketone	B	160	12	2,5-Dimethyl-3-thiophene-propanamide, 80	185
2,5-Diethyl-3-thienyl ethyl ketone	B	160	12	2,5-Diethyl-3-thiophenethio-propanomorpholide, 40	185
2,5-Dimethyl-3-thienyl ethyl ketone	D	...	.....	2,5-Dimethyl-3-thiophenepropanoic acid	208
2-Thienyl propyl ketone	B	140	12	2-Thiophene-butanamide, 37	136
2,5-Dimethyl-3-thienyl propyl ketone	B	160	12	2,5-Dimethyl-3-thiophenebutanamide, 27	185
2,5-Dimethyl-3-thienyl propyl ketone	D	...	.....	2,5-Dimethyl-3-thiophenebutanoic acid	208
2,5-Dimethyl-3-thienyl butyl ketone	B	160	12	2,5-Dimethyl-3-thiophene-pentanamide, 7.8	185
2-Thienylacetone	B	160	12	2-Thiophene-propanamide, 28	135
2-Thienylcarbox-aldehyde	B	160	12	2-Thiophenecarbox-amide, 70	135
1-(2-Thienyl)-ethanol	B	169	12	2-Thiopheneacetamide, 35	135
2-Vinylthiophene	B	160	12	2-Thiopheneacetamide, 30	135
19. Pyridines:					
2-Picoline	D	160	6	2-Pyridinethio-carboxomorpholide, 44	938
2-Picoline	D	150	14	2-Pyridinethiocarboxo-morpholide, 22	864
2-Picoline	D	150	10.5	2-Pyridinethiocarboxo-morpholide, 20	786
2-Picoline	G (aniline)	220	16	2-(2-Pyridyl)-benzothiazole; 2-pyridinethio-carboxoanilide	752

Table 11-1 (Continued)

Compound oxidized[a,b]	Oxidant[c]	°C	Hours[d]	Product, %[e,f,g]	Refs.
2-Picoline	G (aniline)	160	12	2-Pyridinethiocarboxomorpholide, 63	864
2-Picoline	G (*t*-octylamine)	143	20	2-*N*-*t*-Octylpyridinecarboxamide, 85	721
3-Picoline	D	170	13	3-Pyridinethiocarboxomorpholide, 2.5	786
3-Picoline	G (aniline)	200	24	Tar	864
4-Picoline	D	170	9	4-Pyridinethiocarboxomorpholide, 52.2	786
4-Picoline	D	170	12	4-Pyridinethiocarboxomorpholide, 40	864
4-Picoline	D	Refl.	.....	4-Pyridinethiocarboxomorpholide	938
4-Picoline	G (aniline)	Refl.	40	4-Pyridinethiocarboxanilide	351
4-Picoline	G (aniline)	220	24	2-(4-Pyridyl)-benzothiazole; *N*,*N'*-diphenylpyridinethiocarboxanilide	752
2,4-Dimethylpyridine	G (*t*-octylamine)	190	4	4-Methyl-2-*N*-*t*-octylpyridinecarboxamide, 82	721
2,6-Dimethylpyridine	G (*t*-octylamine)	164	8	2-Methyl-6-*N*-*t*-octylpyridinecarboxamide, 90	721
4-Ethylpyridine	D	160	8	4-Pyridinethioacetomorpholide, 50	864
2-Methyl-5-ethyl pyridine	G (*t*-octylamine)	200	8	5-Ethyl-2-*N*-*t*-octylpyridinecarboxamide, 90	721
2-Vinylpyridine	B	150	4	2-Pyridineacetamide, 31	837
2-Vinylpyridine	C	150	4	2-Pyridineacetamide, 38	837
2-Vinylpyridine	C [plus $(NH_4)_2S_2O_3$]	150	4	2-Pyridineacetamide, 31	837
2-Pyridyl methyl ketone	D	Refl.	12	2-Pyridinethioacetomorpholide, 63	716
3-Pyridyl methyl ketone	B	170	6	3-Pyridineacetamide	544
3-Pyridyl methyl ketone	D	Refl.	12	3-Pyridinethioacetomorpholide, 80	716
3-Pyridyl methyl ketone	D	Refl.	6	3-Pyridinethioacetomorpholide, 65	954
4-Pyridyl methyl ketone	D	Refl.	12	4-Pyridinethioacetomorpholide, 76	716

Table 11-1 (Continued)

Compound oxidized[a,b]	Oxidant[c]	°C	Hours[d]	Product, %[e,f,g]	Refs.
2-Pyridinecarboxaldehyde	D	170	14	2-Pyridinethiocarboxomorpholide, 55.2	786
3-Pyridinecarboxaldehyde	D	170	12	3-Pyridinethiocarboxomorpholide, 37	786
4-Pyridinecarboxaldehyde	D	170	14.5	4-Pyridinethiocarboxomorpholide, 84	786
2-Pyridinemethanol	D	180	11	2-Pyridinethiocarboxomorpholide, 70	786
3-Pyridinemethanol	D	170	10	3-Pyridinethiocarboxomorpholide, 6	786
4-Pyridinemethanol	D	180	10.5	4-Pyridinethiocarboxomorpholide, 91.3	786
20. Pyrroles and carbazoles:					
2,4-Dimethyl-3-acetyl-5-carbethoxypyrrole	D	Refl.	2	2,4-Dimethyl-5-carbethoxy-3-pyrrolethioacetomorpholide, 26	1099
2-Acetylcarbazole	B	...	.....	2-Carbazoleacetamide, 58	505
3-Acetylcarbazole	B	160	12	3-Carbazoleacetamide, 85	505
21. Furans and dibenzofurans:					
Tetrahydrofuran	A	232	4	Succinic acid, 4; acetic acid, 17	1063
Furan	A	232	4	Succinic acid, 30	1073
2-Furaldehyde	B	100	12	2-Furancarboxamide, 26	137
2-Methyl-5-furyl methyl ketone	B	100	12	2-Methyl-5-furanacetamide, 10	137
2,5-Dimethyl-3-furyl methyl ketone	B	100	12	2,5-Dimethyl-3-furanacetamide, 27	137
2-Acetyldibenzofuran	B	160	10	2-Dibenzofuranacetamide, 70	505
2,8-Diacetyldibenzofuran	B	160	12	2,8-Dibenzofurandiacetic acid, 53	505
22. Quinolines:					
2-Methylquinoline	D	Refl.	.....	2-Quinolinethiocarboxomorpholide	938
2-Methylquinoline	G (piperidine)	Refl.	.....	2-Quinolinethiocarboxopiperidide	938
6-Ethoxy-2-methylquinoline	D	180	1	6-Ethoxy-2-quinolinethiocarboxomorpholide	938
2,4-Dimethylquinoline	D	180	1	4-Methyl-2-quinolinethiocarboxomorpholide, 64	938

Table 11-1 (Continued)

Compound oxidized[a,b]	Oxidant[c]	°C	Hours[d]	Product, %[e,f,g]	Refs.
3-Acetylquinoline	A	150	20	3-Quinolineacetic acid, 19	598
6-Acetylquinoline	D	Refl.	24	6-Quinolineacetic acid, 88	598
2-Phenyl-4-acetyl-quinoline	D	Refl.	5	2-Phenyl-4-quino-linethioaceto-morpholide, 78	954
23. Other heterocyclic compounds:					
Morpholine	H	158	4	Oxalodimorpholide, 32	568
4-Methyl-5-acetyl-thiazole	B	175	7	4-Methyl-5-thia-zoleacetamide, 84	337
1-Phenyl-4-(thio-butanoyl)-piperazine *Note:* (Forty-seven other substituted piperazines have also been reported)	D	. . .	. . . . .	1-Phenyl-4-piper-azinethiobutano-morpholide, 29	862
Ethyl 3-acetyl-1,4-dimethylpyrazole-5-carboxylate	D	150	1	5-Carbethoxy-1,4-dimethyl-3-pyrazolethio-acetomorpholide, 50	169

REFERENCES

1. Abbott, L. D., and Smith, J. D.: *J. Biol. Chem.*, **179,** 365 (1949).
2. Abell, P. I., and Chiao, C.: *J. Am. Chem. Soc.*, **82,** 3610 (1960).
3. Abrahams, S. C.: *Acta Cryst.*, **7,** 423 (1954).
4. Abrahams, S. C.: *Acta Cryst.*, **8,** 661 (1955).
5. Abrahams, S. C.: *Acta Cryst.*, **10,** 417 (1957).
6. Abrahams, S. C.: *Acta Cryst.* (in press).
7. Abrahams, S. C.: *Quart. Revs. (London)*, **10,** 424 (1956).
8. Abrahams, S. C., Collin, R. L., and Lipscomb, W. N.: *Acta Cryst.*, **4,** 15 (1951).
9. Abrahams, S. C., and Grison, E.: *Acta Cryst.*, **6,** 206 (1953).
10. Abrahams, S. C., and Silverton, J. V.: *Acta Cryst.*, **9,** 281 (1956).
11. Ackermann, F.: German patent 222,879 (May 27, 1909); *Chem. Abstracts*, **4,** 2882 (1910).
12. Ackermann, F.: German patent 224,348 (July 9, 1909); *Chem. Abstracts*, **5,** 210 (1911).
13. Ackermann, F.: German patent 234,743 (May 19, 1910); *Chem. Abstracts*, **5,** 2912 (1911).
14. Adams, R. M., and VanderWerf, C. A.: *J. Am. Chem. Soc.*, **72,** 4368 (1950).
15. Adkins, H., Rae, D. S., Davis, J. W., Hager, G. F., and Hoyle, K.: *J. Am. Chem. Soc.*, **70,** 381 (1948).
16. Aksnes, G.: *Acta Chem. Scand.*, **14,** 1515 (1960).
17. Alfrey, T., Bohrer, J. J., and Mark, H.: "Copolymerization," Interscience Publishers, Inc., New York (1952).
18. Alfrey, T., and Price, C. C.: *J. Polymer Sci.*, **2,** 101 (1947).
19. Allen, A. D.: *Nature*, **172,** 301 (1953).
20. Allen, P. W., and Sutton, L. E.: *Acta Cryst.*, **3,** 46 (1950).
21. Allen, T. L.: *J. Chem. Phys.*, **31,** 1039 (1959).
22. Alphen, J. van: *Rev. gén. caoutchouc*, **27,** 529 (1950); *Chem. Abstracts*, **44,** 10369a (1950).

22*a*. Ames, D. P., and Willard, J. E.: *J. Am. Chem. Soc.*, **73,**164 (1951).

23. Anbar, M., and Dostrovsky, I.: *J. Chem. Soc.*, **1954,** 1094.
24. Anbar, M., Dostrovsky, I., Samuel, D., and Yoffe, A. D.: *J. Chem. Soc.*, **1954,** 3603.
25. Andakushkin, V. Ya., Dolgoplosk, B. A., and Radchenko, I. I.: *J. Gen. Chem. U.S.S.R.* (Eng. transl.), **26,** 3307 (1956).
26. Arens, J. F., Fröling, A., and Fröling, M.: *Rec. trav. chim.*, **78,** 663 (1959).
27. Armstrong, R. T.: U.S. patent 2,446,072 (July 27, 1948).
28. Armstrong, R. T., Little, J. R., and Doak, K. W.: *Ind. Eng. Chem.*, **36,** 628 (1944).

29. Armstutz, E. D., Hunsberger, I. M., and Chessick, J. J.: *J. Am. Chem. Soc.*, **73,** 1220 (1951).
30. Arnold, R. C., Lien, A. P., and Alm, R. M.: *J. Am. Chem. Soc.*, **72,** 731 (1950).
31. Arnold, R. T., and Rondestvedt, E.: *J. Am. Chem. Soc.*, **67,** 1265 (1945).
32. Arnold, R. T., Schultz, E., and Klug, H.: *J. Am. Chem. Soc.*, **66,** 1606 (1944).
33. Arntson, R. H., Dickson, F. W., and Tunell, G.: *Science*, **128,** 716 (1958).
34. Aronstein, M. L., and Van Nierop, A. S.: *Rec. trav. chim.*, **21,** 448 (1902).
35. Ashworth, F., and Burkhardt, G. N.: *J. Chem. Soc.*, **1928,** 1791.
36. Asinger, F.: *Angew. Chem.*, **68,** 413 (1956).
37. Asinger, F., *et al.*: U.S.S.R. patent 121,791.
38. Asinger, F., Thiel, M., and Esser, G.: *Ann.*, **610,** 33 (1957).
39. Asinger, F., Thiel, M., and Horingklee, W.: *Ann.*, **610,** 1 (1957).
40. Asinger, F., Thiel, M., and Kaltwasser, H.: *Ann.*, **606,** 67 (1957).
41. Asinger, F., Thiel, M., Kaltwasser, H., and Reckling, G.: U.S. patent 2,865,924 (Dec. 23, 1958); *Chem. Abstracts*, **53,** 8165a (1959).
42. Asinger, F., Thiel, M., and Kalzendorf, I.: *Ann.*, **610,** 25 (1957).
43. Asinger, F., Thiel, M., and Lipfert, G.: *Ann.*, **627,** 195 (1959).
44. Asinger, F., Thiel, M., and Pallas, E.: *Ann.*, **602,** 37 (1957).
45. Asinger, F., Thiel, M., and Pallas, E.: U.S. patent 2,888,487 (May 26, 1959).
46. Asinger, F., Thiel, M., Peschel, G., and Meinicke, K. H.; *Ann.* **619,** 145 (1958).
47. Asinger, F., Thiel, M., and Schroder, L.: *Ann.*, **610,** 49 (1957).
48. Asinger, F., Thiel, M., and Tesar, V.: *Ann.*, **619,** 169 (1958).
49. Bachmann, W. E., and Anderson, A. G.: *J. Org. Chem.*, **13,** 297 (1948).
50. Bachmann, W. E., and Klemm, L. H.: *J. Am. Chem. Soc.*, **72,** 4911 (1950).
51. Back, M. H., and Sehon, A. H.: *Can. J. Chem.*, **38,** 1076 (1960).
52. Back, R., Trick, G., McDonald, C., and Sivertz, C.: *Can. J. Chem.*, **32,** 1078 (1954).
53. Backer, H. J., and Jong, G. J. de: *Rec. trav. chim.*, **67,** 884 (1948).
54. Backer, H. J., and Strating, J.: *Rec. trav. chim.*, **54,** 618 (1935).
55. Bacon, R. F., and Fanelli, R.: *J. Am. Chem. Soc.*, **65,** 639 (1943).
56. Baer, J. E., and Carmack, M.: *J. Am. Chem. Soc.*, **71,** 1215 (1949).
57. Baker, A. W., and Harris, G. H.: *J. Am. Chem. Soc.*, **82,** 1923 (1960).
58. Baker, J. W., and Easty, D. M.: *J. Chem. Soc.*, **1952,** 1193.
59. Baker, J. W., and Heggs, T. G.: *Chem. & Ind.* (*London*), **1954,** 464.
60. Baker, J. W., and Heggs, T. G.: *J. Chem. Soc.*, **1955,** 616.
61. Baker, J. W., and Neale, A. J.: *J. Chem. Soc.*, **1955,** 608.
62. Baker, R. B., and Reid, E. E.: *J. Am. Chem. Soc.*, **51,** 1566 (1929).
63. Baliah, V., and Shanmuganathan, Sp.: *J. Phys. Chem.*, **63,** 2016 (1959).
64. Baliah, V., and Varadachari, R.: *Current Sci.* (*India*), **23,** 19 (1954); *Chem. Abstracts*, **49,** 3076c (1955).
65. Bamford, C. H., Barb, W. G., Jenkins, A. D., and Onyon, P. F.: "Kinetics of Vinyl Polymerizations by Radical Mechanisms," Academic Press, Inc., New York (1958).
66. Bamford, C. H., and Dewar, M. J. S.: *Discussions Faraday Soc.*, **2,** 310 (1947).
67. Bamford, C. H., and Dewar, M. J. S.: *Discussions Faraday Soc.*, **2,** 314 (1947).
68. Bamford, C. H., and Dewar, M. J. S.: *Proc. Roy. Soc.* (*London*), **A193,** 309 (1948).
69. Barker, H. J.: *Rec. trav. chim.*, **70,** 254 (1951).
70. Barnard, D., Fabian, J. M., and Koch, H. P.: *J. Chem. Soc.*, **1949,** 2442.
71. Barnard, P. W. C., Bunton, C. A., Llewellyn, D. R., Oldham, K. G., Silver, B. L., and Vernon, C. A.: *Chem. & Ind.* (*London*), **1955,** 760.
72. Barnes, W. H., and Wending, A. V.: *Z. Krist.*, **99,** 153 (1938).

73. Barnett, B., and Vaughan, W. E.: *J. Phys. & Colloid Chem.*, **51,** 926 (1947).
74. Barnett, B., and Vaughan, W. E.: *J. Phys. & Colloid Chem.*, **51,** 942 (1947).
75. Barone, R. P. (with Carmack, M.): *Dissertation Abstr.*, **13,** 174 (1953).
76. Baroni, A.: *Atti accad. Lincei*, **11,** 905 (1930); *Chem. Abstracts*, **25,** 69 (1931).
77. Barrett, K. E. J., and Waters, W. A.: *Discussions Faraday Soc.*, **14,** 221 (1953).
78. Barrett, P. A.: *J. Chem. Soc.*, **1957,** 2056.
79. Bartlett, P. D.: unpublished data quoted in D. M. Gardner and G. K. Fraenkel, *J. Am. Chem. Soc.*, **78,** 3279 (1956).
80. Bartlett, P. D., and Altschul, R.: *J. Am. Chem. Soc.*, **67,** 816 (1945).
81. Bartlett, P. D., Colter, A. K., Cox, E. F., Davis, R. E., and Roderick, W. R.: Abstracts of Papers, ACS Meeting, p. 9-M, (April, 1960).
82. Bartlett, P. D., Colter, A. K., Davis, R. E., and Roderick, W. R.: *J. Am. Chem. Soc.*, **83,** 109 (1961).
83. Bartlett, P. D., Cox, E. F., and Davis, R. E.: *J. Am. Chem. Soc.*, **83,** 103 (1961).
84. Bartlett, P. D., and Davis, R. E.: *J. Am. Chem. Soc.*, **80,** 2513 (1958).
85. Bartlett, P. D., and Hiatt, R. R.: *J. Am. Chem. Soc.*, **80,** 1398 (1958).
86. Bartlett, P. D., and Kwart, H.: *J. Am. Chem. Soc.*, **72,** 1051 (1950).
87. Bartlett, P. D., and Kwart, H.: *J. Am. Chem. Soc.*, **74,** 3969 (1952).
88. Bartlett, P. D., Lohaus, G., and Weis, C. D.: *J. Am. Chem. Soc.*, **80,** 5064 (1958).
89. Bartlett, P. D., and Meguerian, G.: *J. Am. Chem. Soc.*, **78,** 3710 (1956).
90. Bartlett, P. D., and Nozaki, K.: *J. Am. Chem. Soc.*, **68,** 1686 (1946).
91. Bartlett, P. D., and Nozaki, K.: *J. Am. Chem. Soc.*, **68,** 1495 (1946).
92. Bartlett, P. D., and Nozaki, K.: *J. Am. Chem. Soc.*, **69,** 2299 (1947).
93. Bartlett, P. D., and Swain, C. G.: *J. Am. Chem. Soc.*, **71,** 1406 (1949).
94. Bartlett, P. D., and Trifan, D. S.: *J. Polymer Sci.*, **20,** 457 (1956).
95. Baskakov, Yu. A., and Mel'nikov, N. N.: *J. Gen. Chem. U.S.S.R.* (Eng. transl.), **23,** 905 (1953); *Chem. Abstracts*, **48,** 4477a, 12730i (1954).
96. Baskakov, Yu. A., and Mel'nikov, N. N.: *Zhur. Priklad. Khim.*, **28,** 1016 (1955); *Chem. Abstracts*, **50,** 4880h (1956).
97. Basolo, F., Gray, H. B., and Pearson, R.: *J. Am. Chem. Soc.*, **82,** 4200 (1960).
98. Basolo, F., and Pearson, R. G.: "Mechanisms of Inorganic Reactions," John Wiley & Sons, Inc., New York (1958).
99. Bastiansen, O., and Viervoll, H.: *Acta Chem. Scand.*, **2,** 702 (1948).
100. Bateman, L.: *Quart. Revs.*, **8,** 147 (1954).
101. Bateman, L., Glazebrook, R. W., and Moore, C. G.: *J. Chem. Soc.*, **1958,** 2846.
102. Bateman, L., Glazebrook, R. W., and Moore, C. G.: *J. Applied Polymer Sci.*, **1,** 257 (1959).
103. Bateman, L., Glazebrook, R. W., Moore, C. G., Porter, M., Ross, G. W., and Saville, R. W.: *J. Chem. Soc.*, **1958,** 2838.
104. Bateman, L. C., Glazebrook, R. W., Moore, C. G., and Saville, R. W.: *Proceedings of the Third Rubber Technology Conference*, p. 298, London, June, 1954 (Publ. 1956); *Chem. Abstracts*, **50,** 16167e (1956).
105. Bateman, L., and Moore, C. G.: Reactions of Sulfur with Olefins, in "Organic Sulfur Compounds," vol. I, Pergamon Press, London (1961).
106. Bateman, L., Moore, C. G., and Porter, M.: *J. Chem. Soc.*, **1958,** 2866.
106*a*. Bauer, S. H.: *J. Am. Chem. Soc.*, **69,** 3104 (1947).
107. Baumann, E., and Fromm, E.: *Ber.*, **28,** 907 (1895).
108. Beard, H. G., Hodgson, H. H., and Davies, R. R.: *J. Chem. Soc.*, **1944,** 4.
109. Becke-Goehring, M.: "Advances in Inorganic Chemistry and Radiochemistry," vol. 2, edited by H. J. Emeleus and A. G. Sharp, Academic Press, Inc., N.Y. (1960).

110. Bedford, C. W.: *India Rubber World,* **64,** 572 (1921).
111. Bell, E. R., Rust, F. R., and Vaughan, W. E.: *J. Am. Chem. Soc.,* **72,** 337 (1950).
112. Bellamy, L. J.: The Infrared Spectra of Organo-Sulfur Compounds, in "Organic Sulfur Compounds," vol. I, Pergamon Press, London (1961).
113. Benesch, R. E., and Benesch, R.: *J. Am. Chem. Soc.,* **80,** 1666 (1958).
114. Beniska, J., and Dogadkin, B.: *Rubber Chem. and Technol.,* **32,** 774 (1959).
115. Beniska, J., and Dogadkin, B.: *Rubber Chem. and Technol.,* **32,** 780 (1959).
116. Bentley, H. R., and Whitehead, J. K.: *J. Chem. Soc.,* **1950,** 2081.
117. Bentley, H. R., and Whitehead, J. K.: *J. Chem. Soc.,* **1952,** 1572.
117*a*. Bentrude, W. G., and Martin, J. C.: (in press).
118. Berchtold, G. A., and Carmack, M.: *Dissertation Abstr.,* **20,** 1162 (1959).
119. Berger, H.: *J. prakt. Chem.,* **133,** 331 (1932).
120. Bergson, G.: *Arkiv Kemi,* **12,** 233 (1958).
121. Bergson, G.: *Arkiv Kemi,* **16,** 315 (1958).
122. Bergson, G.: *Arkiv Kemi* (in press).
123. Bergson, G., and Schotte, L.: *Arkiv Kemi,* **13,** 43 (1958).
124. Bergstrom, F. W.: *J. Am. Chem. Soc.,* **48,** 2319 (1926).
125. Berson, J. A., Olsen, C. J., and Walia, J. S.: *J. Am. Chem. Soc.,* **82,** 5000 (1960).
126. Bertozzi, E. R.: *J. Polymer Sci.,* **19,** 17 (1956).
127. Bertozzi, E. R.: U.S. patent 2,796,325 (June 18, 1957); *Chem. Abstracts,* **51,** 14220h (1957).
128. Bertozzi, E. R., Davis, F. O., and Fettes, E. M.: *J. Polymer Sci.,* **19,** 17 (1956).
129. Bible, R. H.: *J. Am. Chem. Soc.,* **79,** 3924 (1957).
130. Bickel, A. F., and Kooyman, E. C.: *Nature,* **170,** 211 (1952).
130*a*. Bigeleisen, J., Klein, F. S., Weston, R. E., and Wolfsberg, M.: *J. Chem. Phys.,* **30,** 1340 (1959).
130*b*. Bigeleisen, J., and Wolfsberg, M.: *J. Chem. Phys.,* **23,** 1535 (1955).
131. Birch, S. F., Cullum, T. V., and Dean, R. A.: *J. Inst. Petroleum,* **39,** 206 (1953).
132. Birrell, R. N., Smith, R. F., Trotman-Dickenson, A. F., and Wilkie, H.: *J. Chem. Soc.,* **1957,** 2807.
133. Blackmore, W. R., and Abrahams, S. C.: *Acta Cryst.,* **8,** 329 (1955).
134. Blanchard, H. S.: *J. Am. Chem. Soc.,* **81,** 4548 (1959).
135. Blanchette, J. A., and Brown, E. V.: *J. Am. Chem. Soc.,* **73,** 2779 (1951).
136. Blanchette, J. A., and Brown, E. V.: *J. Am. Chem. Soc.,* **74,** 1066 (1952).
137. Blanchette, J. A., and Brown, E. V.: *J. Am. Chem. Soc.,* **74,** 2098 (1952).
138. Blokh, G. A.: *Rubber Chem. and Technol.,* **31,** 1035 (1958).
139. Bloomfield, G. F.: *J. Chem. Soc.,* **1947,** 1546.
140. Bloomfield, G. F.: *J. Chem. Soc.,* **1947,** 1547.
141. Bloomfield, G. F.: *J. Polymer Sci.,* **1,** 312 (1946).
142. Bloomfield, G. F.: *J. Soc. Chem. Ind.* (*London*), **67,** 14 (1948).
143. Bloomfield, G. F.: *J. Soc. Chem. Ind.* (*London*), **68,** 66 (1949).
144. Bloomfield, G. F., and Naylor, R. F.: *Proceedings of the XI International Congress of Pure and Applied Chemistry,* vol. 2, p. 7, London (1947).
145. Blumenthal, E., and Herbert, J. B. M.: *Trans. Faraday Soc.,* **41,** 611 (1945).
146. Böeseken, J., and Roy van Zuydewijn, E. de: *Proc. Acad. Sci.* (*Amsterdam*), **40,** 23 (1937); *Chem. Abstracts,* **31,** 4953[7] (1937).
147. Böhme, H.: *Ber.,* **74,** 248 (1941).
148. Böhme, H., and Sell, K.: *Ber.,* **81,** 123 (1948).
149. Böhme, H., and Zinner, G.: *Ann.,* **585,** 142 (1954).
150. Bollard, J. L.: *Quart. Revs.,* **3,** 1 (1949).
151. Bonner, W. A.: *J. Am. Chem. Soc.,* **76,** 6350 (1954).

152. Borchers, Gebr., A.-G.: British patent 753,667 (July 25, 1956); *Chem. Abstracts*, **51**, 8127h (1957).
153. Bordwell, F. G., and Albisetti, C. J.: *J. Am. Chem. Soc.*, **70**, 1558 (1948).
154. Bordwell, F. G., and Andersen, H. M.: *J. Am. Chem. Soc.*, **75**, 6019 (1953).
155. Bordwell, F. G., and Boutan, P. J.: *J. Am. Chem. Soc.*, **78**, 87 (1956).
156. Bordwell, F. G., and Boutan, P. J.: *J. Am. Chem. Soc.*, **78**, 854 (1956).
157. Bordwell, F. G., and Cooper, G. D.: *J. Am. Chem. Soc.*, **74**, 1058 (1952).
158. Bordwell, F. G., Cooper, G. D. and Morita, H.: *J. Am. Chem. Soc.*, **79**, 376 (1957).
159. Bordwell, F. G., and Hewett, W. A.: *J. Am. Chem. Soc.*, **79**, 3493 (1957).
160. Bordwell, F. G., and McKellin, W. H.: *J. Am. Chem. Soc.*, **73**, 2251 (1951).
161. Boschan, R., Merrow, R. T., and Van Dolah, R. W.: *Chem. Revs.*, **55**, 485 (1955).
162. Bost, R. W., and Constable, E. W.: "Organic Syntheses," collective vol. 2, p. 610, John Wiley & Sons, Inc., New York (1943).
163. Böttcher, B.: *Ber.*, **81**, 376 (1948).
164. Böttcher, B., and Bauer, F.: *Ann.*, **568**, 218 (1950).
165. Böttcher, B., and Bauer, F.: *Ber.*, **84**, 458 (1951).
166. Böttcher, B., and Luttringhaus, A.: *Ann.*, **557**, 89 (1947).
167. Bowen, H. J. M.: *Trans. Faraday Soc.*, **50**, 452 (1954).
168. Brace, N. O.: *J. Am. Chem. Soc.*, **75**, 357 (1953).
169. Brain, E. G., and Finar, I. L.: *J. Chem. Soc.*, **1957**, 2356.
170. Brand, J. C. D., and Davidson, J. R.: *J. Chem. Soc.*, **1956**, 15.
171. Brandt, G. R. A., Emeléus, H. J., and Haszeldine, R. N.: *J. Chem. Soc.*, **1952**, 2549.
172. Braune, H., Peter, S., and Neveling, V.: *Z. Naturforsch.*, **6A**, 32 (1951).
173. Braune, H., and Steinbracher, E.: *Z. Naturforsch.*, **7A**, 486 (1952).
174. Braye, E. H., Sehon, A. H., and Darwent, B. deB.: *J. Am. Chem. Soc.*, **77**, 5282 (1952).
175. Bredt, J.: *Ann. Acad. Sci. Fennicae*, **29A**, No. 2 (1927); *Chem. Abstracts*, **22**, 1152 (1928).
176. Brehm, W. J., and Levenson, T.: *J. Am. Chem. Soc.*, **76**, 5389 (1954).
176*a*. Brindell, G. D., and Cristol, S. J.: Additions of Thiols and Related Substances to Bridged Bicyclic Olefins, in "Organic Sulfur Compounds," vol. 1, Pergamon Press, London (1961).
177. Briske, C., and Hartshorne, N. H.: *Discussions Faraday Soc.*, **23**, 196 (1957).
178. Brockway, L. O., and Jenkins, H. O.: *J. Am. Chem. Soc.*, **58**, 2036 (1936).
179. Broun, A. S., and Ioffe, B. V.: *Nauch. Byull. Leningrad. Gosudarst. Univ.*, **20**, 11 (1948); *Chem. Abstracts*, **43**, 5376e (1949).
180. Broun, A. S., and Voronkov, M. G.: *Nauch. Byull. Leningrad. Gosudarst. Univ.*, **20**, 6 (1948); *Chem. Abstracts*, **43**, 2614i, 5392f (1949).
181. Broun, A. S., and Voronkov, M. G.: *Zhur. Obshcheĭ Khim.*, **17**, 1162 (1947); *Chem. Abstracts*, **42**, 1591a (1948).
182. Broun, A. S., Voronkov, M. G., and Gol'dburt, F. I.: *Nauch. Byull. Leningrad. Gosudarst. Univ.*, **18**, 14 (1947); *Chem. Abstracts*, **43**, 5392d (1949).
183. Broun, A. S., Voronkov, M. G., and Shlyakhter, R. A.: *Nauch. Byull. Leningrad. Gosudarst. Univ.*, **18**, 11 (1947); *Chem. Abstracts*, **43**, 5392d (1949) and **42**, 1591a (1948).
184. Brown, D. J.: *J. Am. Chem. Soc.*, **62**, 2657 (1940).
185. Brown, E. V., and Blanchette, J. A.: *J. Am. Chem. Soc.*, **72**, 3414 (1950).
186. Brown, E. V., Cerwonka, E., and Anderson, R. C.: *J. Am. Chem. Soc.*, **73**, 3735 (1951).

186*a*. Brown, H. C., and Ichikawa, K.: *Tetrahedron,* **1,** 221 (1957).
187. Brown, H. C., and Murphey, W. A.: *J. Am. Chem. Soc.,* **73,** 3308 (1951).
188. Bruin, P., Bickel, A. F., and Kooyman, E. C.: *Rec. trav. chim.,* **71,** 1115 (1952).
189. Bryce, W. A., and Hinshelwood, C.: *J. Chem. Soc.,* **1949,** 3379.
189*a*. Bujake, J. E., Pratt, M. W. T., and Noyes, R. M.: *J. Am. Chem. Soc.,* **83,** 1547 (1961).
190. Bunnett, J. F.: *J. Am. Chem. Soc.,* **79,** 5969 (1957).
191. Bunnett, J. F., and Bassett, J. Y.: *J. Am. Chem. Soc.,* **81,** 2104 (1959).
191*a*. Bunnett, J. F., and Davis, G. T.: *J. Am. Chem. Soc.,* **76,** 3011 (1954).
192. Bunton, C. A.: *Ann. Repts. Chem. Soc.,* **55,** 190 (1958).
193. Bunton, C. A., and Frei, Y. F.: *J. Chem. Soc.,* **1951,** 1872.
194. Bunton, C. A., Lewis, T. A., Llewellyn, D. R., and Vernon, C. A.: *J. Chem. Soc.,* **1955,** 4419.
195. Bunton, C. A., de la Mare, P. B. D., Greaseley, P. M., Llewellyn, D. R., Pratt, N. H., and Tillett, J. G.: *J. Chem. Soc.,* **1958,** 4751.
196. Bunton, C. A., de la Mare, P. B. D., Lennard, A., Llewellyn, D. R., Pearson, R. B., Pritchard, J. G., and Tillett, J. G.: *J. Chem. Soc.,* **1958,** 4761.
197. Bunton, C. A., de la Mare, P. B. D., Llewellyn, D. R., Pearson, R. B., and Pritchard, J. G., *Chem. & Ind. (London),* **1956,** 490.
198. Bunton, C. A., de la Mare, P. B. D., and Tillett, J. G.: *J. Chem. Soc.,* **1958,** 4754.
199. Bunton, C. A., and Welch, V. A.: *J. Chem. Soc.,* **1956,** 3240.
201. Burkhardt, G. N.: *Trans. Faraday Soc.,* **30,** 18 (1934).
202. Burnett, G. M.: "Mechanism of Polymer Reactions," Interscience Publishers, Inc., New York (1954).
203. Burnett, G. M., and Melville, H. W.: *Discussions Faraday Soc.,* **2,** 322 (1947).
204. Burrus, G. A., and Gordy, W.: *Phys. Rev.,* **92,** 274 (1953).
205. Burwell, R. L.: *J. Am. Chem. Soc.,* **74,** 1462 (1952).
206. Butcher, W. W., and Westheimer, F. H.: *J. Am. Chem. Soc.,* **77,** 2420 (1955).
207. Butler, K. H., and Maass, O.: *J. Am. Chem. Soc.,* **52,** 2184 (1930).
208. Buu-Hoï and Nguyen-Hoán: *Rec. trav. chim.,* **68,** 5 (1949); *Chem. Abstracts,* **43,** 4665b (1949).
209. Cafasso, F., and Sundheim, B. R.: *J. Chem. Phys.,* **31,** 809 (1959).
210. Cairns, T. L., Evans, G. L., Larchar, A. W., and McKusick, B. C.: *J. Am. Chem. Soc.,* **74,** 3982 (1952).
211. Calhown, G. M., and Burwell, R. L.: *J. Am. Chem. Soc.,* **77,** 6441 (1955).
212. California Research Corp.: British patent 776,161 (June 5, 1957).
213. Campaigne, E.: *Chem. Revs.,* **39,** 1 (1946).
214. Campaigne, E.: *J. Am. Chem. Soc.,* **66,** 684 (1944).
214*a*. Campaigne, E.: Additions of Thiols or Hydrogen Sulfide to Carbonyl Compounds, in "Organic Sulfur Compounds," vol. 1, Pergamon Press, London (1961).
215. Campaigne, E., Reid, W. B., and Pera, J. D.: *J. Org. Chem.,* **24,** 1229 (1959).
216. Campaigne, E., and Rutan, P. V.: *J. Am. Chem. Soc.,* **69,** 1211 (1947).
217. Campbell, R. D., and Cromwell, N. H.: *J. Am. Chem. Soc.,* **77,** 5169 (1955).
218. Carmack, M., and DeTar, D. F.: *J. Am. Chem. Soc.,* **68,** 2029 (1946).
219. Carmack, M., and Spielman, M. A.: "Organic Reactions," edited by R. Adams, vol. III, John Wiley & Sons, Inc., New York (1946).
220. Caron, A., and Donohue, J.: *J. Phys. Chem.,* **64,** 1767 (1960).
220*a*. Caron, A., and Donohue, J.: *Acta Cryst.,* **14,** 548 (1961).
221. Cartmell, E., and Fowles, G. W. A.: "Valency and Molecular Structure," Academic Press, Inc., New York (1956).
222. Cass, W. E.: *J. Am. Chem. Soc.,* **68,** 1976 (1946).

223. Cass, W. E.: *J. Am. Chem. Soc.*, **69,** 500 (1947).
224. Caujolle, F., Meynier, D., and Payssot, P.: *Ann. inst. hydrol. et climatol.*, **23,** 73 (1952); *Chem. Abstracts,* **47,** 5834c (1953).
225. Cavalieri, L., Pattison, D. B., and Carmack, M.: *J. Am. Chem. Soc.*, **67,** 1783 (1945).
226. Cecil, R., and McPhee, J. R.: *Biochem. J.*, **60,** 496 (1955).
227. Cerwonka, E., Anderson, R. C., and Brown, E. V.: *J. Am. Chem. Soc.*, **75,** 28 (1953).
228. Cerwonka, E., Anderson, R. C., and Brown, E. V.: *J. Am. Chem. Soc.*, **75,** 30 (1953).
229. Chabrier, P., and Renard, S. H.: *Compt. rend.*, **228,** 850 (1949).
230. Challenger, F.: *Quart. Revs.*, **9,** 255 (1955).
231. Challenger, F., Mason, E. A., Holdsworth, E. C., and Emmott, R.: *Chem. & Ind.* (*London*), **1952,** 714.
232. Challenger, F., Taylor, P., and Taylor, B.: *J. Chem. Soc.*, **1942,** 48.
233. Charonnat, R., and Girard, M.: *Bull. soc. chim. France,* **1949,** 208.
234. Chateau, H., and Pouradier, J.: *Science et inds. phot.*, **27,** No. 2, 465 (1956).
235. Chernick, C. L., Pedley, J. B., and Skinner, H. A.: *J. Chem. Soc.*, **1957,** 1851.
236. Chitwood, H. C., and Freure, B. T.: *J. Am. Chem. Soc.*, **68,** 680 (1946).
237. Christman, D. R., and Oae, S.: *Chem. & Ind.* (*London*), **1959,** 1251.
238. Cilento, G.: *Chem. Revs.*, **60,** 147 (1960).
239. Cilento, G.: *J. Am. Chem. Soc.*, **75,** 3748 (1953).
240. Cilento, G.: *J. Org. Chem.*, **24,** 413 (1959).
241. Clapham, P. H., and Emmott, R.: *J. Inst. Petroleum,* **34,** 922 (1948).
242. Clark, D., Pritchard, H. O., and Trotman-Dickenson, A. F.: *J. Chem. Soc.*, **1954,** 2633.
243. Clark, H. C., Horsfield, A., and Symons, M. C. R.: *J. Chem. Soc.*, **1959,** 2478.
244. Clark, V. M., and Todd, A. R.: *J. Chem. Soc.*, **1950,** 2023.
244*a*. Clark, J. T., Howard, R. O., and Stockmayer, W. H.: *Makromol. Chem.*, **44–46,** 427 (1961).
245. Clingman, W. H.: *J. Phys. Chem.*, **64,** 1355 (1960).
246. Cocker, W., Cross, B. E., and McCormick, J.: *J. Chem. Soc.*, **1952,** 72.
247. Coe, W. S.: *Ind. Eng. Chem.*, **31,** 1481 (1939).
248. Coffman, D. D.: U.S. patent 2,410,401 (Oct. 29, 1946); *Chem. Abstracts,* **41,** 2086h (1947).
249. Cohen, S. G., and Wang, C. H.: *J. Am. Chem. Soc.*, **77,** 4435 (1955).
250. Cohours, A., and Hofmann, A. W.: *Ann.*, **104,** 1 (1857).
251. Colodny, P. C., and Tobolsky, A. V.: *J. Appl. Polymer Sci.*, **2,** 39 (1959).
251*a*. Cope, O. J., and Brown, R. K.: *Can. J. Chem.*, **39,** 1695 (1961).
252. Corey, E. T., and Kaiser, E. T.: *J. Am. Chem. Soc.*, **83,** 490 (1961).
253. Corse, J. W., Jones, R. G., Soper, Q. F., Whitehead, C. W., and Behrens, O. K.: *J. Am. Chem. Soc.*, **70,** 2837 (1948).
254. Costanza, A. J., Coleman, R. J., Pierson, R. M., Marvel, C. S., and King, C.: *J. Polymer Sci.*, **17,** 319 (1955).
255. Cottrell, T. L.: "The Strength of Chemical Bonds," Academic Press, Inc., New York (1954).
256. Coulson, C. A.: "Valence," Oxford University Press, New York (1953).
257. Cox, J. R., Wall, R. E., and Westheimer, F. H.: *Chem. & Ind.* (*London*), **1959,** 929.
258. Craig, D.: *Rubber Chem. and Technol.*, **30,** 1291 (1957).
259. Craig, D., Diller, D., and Rowe, E. H.: *J. Polymer Sci.*, **28,** 435 (1958).

260. Craig, D., Juve, A. E., Davidson, W. L., Semon, W. L., and Hay, D. C.: *J. Polymer Sci.*, **8,** 321 (1952).
261. Craig, D. P.: Symposium on Recent Work on the Inorganic Chemistry of Sulfur, Bristol, 1958, in *Special Publication No.* 12, p. 343, The Chemical Society, London (1958).
262. Craig, D. P., Maccoll, A., Nyholm, R. S., Orgel, L. E., and Sutton, L. E.: *J. Chem. Soc.*, **1954,** 332.
263. Craig, D. P., and Magnusson, E. A.: *J. Chem. Soc.*, **1956,** 4895.
264. Cram, D. J.: *J. Am. Chem. Soc.*, **71,** 3884 (1949).
264*a*. Cram, D. J., Scott, D. A., and Nielsen, W. D.: *J. Am. Chem. Soc.*, **83,** 3696 (1961).
265. Crane, C. W., and Rydon, H. N.: *J. Chem. Soc.*, **1947,** 766.
266. Crawford, B. L., and Cross, P. C.: *J. Chem. Phys.*, **5,** 371 (1937).
267. Cristol, S. J., and Arganbright, R. P.: *J. Am. Chem. Soc.*, **79,** 6039 (1957).
268. Cristol, S. J., Arganbright, R. P., Brindell, G. D., and Heitz, R. M.: *J. Am. Chem. Soc.*, **79,** 6035 (1957).
269. Cristol, S. J., and Brindell, G. D.: ACS Meeting Abstract **128,** 35N (1955).
270. Cristol, S. J., and Brindell, G. D.: *J. Am. Chem. Soc.*, **76,** 5699 (1954).
270*a*. Cristol, S. J., Brindell, G. D., and Reeder, J. A.: *J. Am. Chem. Soc.*, **80,** 635 (1958).
270*b*. Cristol, S. J., and Reeder, J. A.: *J. Org. Chem.*, **26,** 2182 (1961).
271. Croatto, U., and Fava, A.: *Gazz. chim. ital.*, **82,** 552 (1952); *Chem. Abstracts*, **47,** 7884d (1953).
272. Cullis, C. F., and Ladbury, J. W.: *J. Chem. Soc.*, **1955,** 1407.
273. Cullis, C. F., and Ladbury, J. W.: *J. Chem. Soc.*, **1955,** 2850.
274. Cullis, C. F., and Ladbury, J. W.: *J. Chem. Soc.*, **1955,** 4186.
275. Culvenon, C. C. J., Davies, W., and Heath, N. S.: *J. Chem. Soc.*, **1949,** 282.
276. Cumper, C. W. N., and Walker, S.: *Trans. Faraday Soc.*, **52,** 193 (1956).
277. Cunneen, J. I.: *J. Chem. Soc.*, **1947,** 36.
278. Cunneen, J. I.: *J. Chem. Soc.*, **1947,** 134.
279. Cunneen, J. I., Higgins, G. M. C., and Watson, W. F.: *J. Polymer Sci.*, **40,** 1 (1959).
280. Cunneen, J. I., and Watson, W. F.: *J. Polymer Sci.*, **38,** 533 (1959).
281. Cunningham, G. L., Boyd, A. W., Myers, R. J., Gwinn, W. D., and LeVan, W. I.: *J. Chem. Phys.*, **19,** 676 (1951).
282. Curie, P.: *Chem. News*, **30,** 189 (1874).
283. Cutforth, H. C., and Selwood, P. W.: *J. Am. Chem. Soc.*, **70,** 278 (1948).
284. Daly, N. D., Kruger, G., and Miller, J.: *Australian J. Chem.*, **11,** 290 (1958).
284*a*. Daneky, J. P., and Kreuz, J. A.: *J. Am. Chem. Soc.*, **83,** 1109 (1961).
285. Dann, O., and Distler, H.: *Ber.*, **84,** 423 (1951).
286. Das, S. R.: I.U.P.A.C. Münster, "Colloquium on Silicon, Sulfur, and Phosphates," p. 82, Verlag Chemie, G. m. b. H., Weinheim/Bergstrasse (1955).
287. Das, S. R.: *Indian J. Phys.*, **12,** 163 (1938); *Chem. Abstracts*, **32,** 8233[9] (1938).
288. Das, S. R., and Das-Gupta, K.: *Nature*, **143,** 332 (1939).
289. Das, S. R., and Ghosh, K.: *Indian J. Phys.*, **13,** 91 (1939); *Chem. Abstracts*, **33,** 7173[5] (1939).
290. Das, S. R., and Ghosh, K.: *Science and Culture*, **4,** 132 (1938); *Chem. Abstracts*, **32,** 8880[8] (1938).
291. Das, S. R., and Ray, K.: *Science and Culture*, **2,** 650 (1937); *Chem. Abstracts*, **31,** 7306[9] (1937).

292. Datta, J.: *J. Indian Chem. Soc.*, **29,** 101 (1952); *Chem. Abstracts*, **46,** 9004*f* (1952).
293. Datta, S. C., Day, J. N. E., and Ingold, C. K.: *J. Chem. Soc.*, **1937,** 1968.
294. Dauben, W. G., Ciula, R. P., and Rogan, J. B.: *J. Org. Chem.*, **22,** 362 (1957).
295. Dauben, W. G., and Coad, P.: *J. Am. Chem. Soc.*, **71,** 2928 (1949).
296. Dauben, W. G., and Pitzer, K.: Conformational Analysis, in "Steric Effects in Organic Chemistry," edited by M. S. Newman, John Wiley & Sons, Inc., New York, 1956.
297. Dauben, W. G., Reed, J. C., Yankwich, P. E., and Calvin, M.: *J. Am. Chem. Soc.*, **68,** 2117 (1946).
298. Dauben, W. G., Reed, J. C., Yankwich, P. E., and Calvin, M.: *J. Am. Chem. Soc.*, **72,** 121 (1950).
299. Dauben, W. G., and Rogan, J. B.: *J. Am. Chem. Soc.*, **78,** 4135 (1956).
300. Davies, E. D., and Tillett, J. G.: *J. Chem. Soc.*, **1958,** 4766.
301. Davis, C. H., and Carmack, M.: *J. Org. Chem.*, **12,** 76 (1947).
302. Davis, R. E.: Thesis, Harvard University, Cambridge, Mass. (1958).
303. Davis, R. E.: *Proc. Indiana Acad. Sci.*, **70,** 106 (1961); *J. Am. Chem. Soc.* (in press).
304. Davis, R. E.: *J. Am. Chem. Soc.*, **80,** 3565 (1958).
305. Davis, R. E.: *J. Org. Chem.*, **23,** 1767 (1958).
306. Davis, R. E.: *J. Phys. Chem.*, **62,** 1599 (1958).
307. Davis, R. E.: Private communication.
307*a*. Davis, R. E., and Nakshbendi, H. F.: (in press).
308. Davis, R. E., and Perrin, C.: *J. Am. Chem. Soc.*, **82,** 1590 (1960).
309. Davis, R. E., and Schmidt, F. C.: Private communication from R. E. Davis.
310. Dawson, I. M., Mathieson, A. M., and Robertson, J. M.: *J. Chem. Soc.*, **1948,** 322.
311. Dawson, I. M., and Robertson, J. M.: *J. Chem. Soc.*, **1948,** 1256.
312. DeGarmo, O., and McMullen, E. J.: U.S. patent 2,795,614 (June 11, 1957).
313. Dehmelt, H. G.: *Phys. Rev.*, **91,** 313 (1953).
314. De La Mare, H. E., and Rust, F. F.: *J. Am. Chem. Soc.*, **81,** 2691 (1959).
315. Denney, D. B., and Boskin, M. J.: *J. Am. Chem. Soc.*, **82,** 4736 (1960).
316. Denney, D. B., and Feig, G.: *J. Am. Chem. Soc.*, **81,** 5322 (1959).
317. Dessy, R. E., Grannen, E., and Okazumi, Y.: Abstracts of Papers, ACS Meeting, p. 32P, New York (Sept., 1960).
318. Dessy, R. E.: Personal communication.
319. DeTar, D. F., and Carmack, M.: *J. Am. Chem. Soc.*, **68,** 2025 (1946).
320. Dewar, M. J. S.: "The Electronic Theory of Organic Chemistry," Oxford University Press, New York (1949).
321. Dewar, M. J. S., and Schmeising, H. N.: *Tetrahedron*, **5,** 166 (1959).
322. Dewar, M. J. S., and Schmeising, H. N.: *Tetrahedron*, **11,** 96 (1960).
323. Dhar, N. R., and Raghaven, B. V. S.: *Proc. Nat. Acad. Sci., India*, **17A, 7** (1948); *Chem. Abstracts*, **46,** 2948d (1952).
324. Dinaburg, V. A., and Vansheidt, A. A.: *J. Gen. Chem. U.S.S.R.* (Eng. transl.), **24,** 839 (1954).
325. Dodson, R. M., and Tweit, R. C.: *J. Am. Chem. Soc.*, **81,** 1224 (1959).
326. Doering, W. E., and Hoffmann, A. K.: *J. Am. Chem. Soc.*, **77,** 521 (1955).
327. Doering, W. E., and Levy, L. K.: *J. Am. Chem. Soc.*, **77,** 509 (1955).
328. Doering, W. E., Okamoto, K., and Krauch, H.: *J. Am. Chem. Soc.*, **82,** 3579 (1960).

329. Doering, W. E., and Schreiber, K. C.: *J. Am. Chem. Soc.*, **77**, 514 (1955).
330. Dogadkin, B. A.: *J. Polymer Sci.*, **30**, 351 (1958).
331. Dogadkin, B. A., and Belyaeva, E. N.: *Rubber Chem. and Technol.*, **33**, 199 (1960).
332. Dogadkin, B. A., Tarasova, Z. N., Kaplunov, M. Ia., Karpov, V. L., and Klauzen, N. A.: *Rubber Chem. and Technol.*, **32**, 785 (1959).
333. Donohue, J.: *J. Am. Chem. Soc.*, **72**, 2701 (1950).
334. Donohue, J.: The Structure of Elemental Sulfur, in "Organic Sulfur Compounds," vol. I, Pergamon Press, London (1961).
334*a*. Donohue, J., and Caron, A.: *J. Polymer Sci.*, **50**, 517 (1961).
335. Donohue, J., Caron, A., and Goldish, E.: *Nature*, **182**, 518 (1958).
335*a*. Donohue, J., Caron, A., and Goldish, E.: *J. Am. Chem. Soc.*, **83**, 3748 (1961).
336. Donohue, J., and Shomaker, V.: *J. Chem. Phys.*, **16**, 92 (1948).
337. Dornow, A., and Petsch, G.: *Ber.*, **86**, 1404 (1953).
338. Dostrovsky, I., and Halmann, M.: *J. Chem. Soc.*, **1956**, 1004.
339. Draves, C. Z., and Tartar, H. V.: *J. Am. Chem. Soc.*, **48**, 1527 (1926).
340. Drew, E. H., and Martin, J. C.: *Chem. & Ind. (London)*, **1959**, 925.
341. Dunitz, J. D.: *Acta Cryst.*, **9**, 579 (1956).
342. Dupont, G., Dulou, R., Clément, G., and Martinez, N. G.: *Compt. rend.*, **239**, 178 (1954).
343. Dynesen, E.: *Acta Chem. Scand.*, **13**, 360 (1959).
344. Eastman, R. H., and Wagner, R. M.: *J. Am. Chem. Soc.*, **71**, 4089 (1949).
345. Edwards, J. O.: *J. Am. Chem. Soc.*, **76**, 1540 (1954).
346. Edwards, J. O.: *J. Am. Chem. Soc.*, **78**, 1819 (1956).
347. Eliel, E. L.: Substitution at Saturated Carbon Atoms, in "Steric Effects in Organic Chemistry," edited by M. S. Newman, John Wiley & Sons, Inc., New York (1956).
348. Elkeles, H.: *Acta Chem. Scand.*, **7**, 1012 (1953).
349. Elkeles, H.: *Acta Chem. Scand.*, **8**, 1557 (1954).
350. Emmert, B., and Groll, M.: *Ber.*, **86**, 205 (1953).
351. Emmert, B., and Holz, A.: *Ber.*, **87**, 676 (1954).
352. Erämetsä, O., and Suonuuti, H.: *Suomen Kemistilehti*, **32B**, 47 (1959); *Chem. Abstracts*, **53**, 18611d (1959).
353. Eriks, K., and MacGillavry, C. H.: *Acta Cryst.*, **7**, 430 (1953).
354. Errede, L. A., and Hoyt, J. M.: *J. Am. Chem. Soc.*, **82**, 436 (1960).
355. Ewald, A. H.: *Trans. Faraday Soc.*, **55**, 792 (1959).
356. Ewell, R. H., and Eyring, H.: *J. Chem. Phys.*, **5**, 726 (1937).
357. Eyring, H., and Polanyi, M.: *Z. physik. Chem.*, **12B**, 279 (1931).
358. Fairbrother, F., Gee, G., and Merrall, G. T.: *J. Polymer Sci.*, **16**, 459 (1955).
359. Farmer, E. H.: *J. Soc. Chem. Ind. (London)*, **66**, 86 (1947).
360. Farmer, E. H.: *Trans. Faraday Soc.*, **38**, 356 (1942).
361. Farmer, E. H., Ford, J. F., and Lyons, J. A.: *J. Appl. Chem. (London)*, **4, 554** (1954).
362. Farmer, E. H., and Shipley, F. W.: *J. Chem. Soc.*, **1947**, 1519.
363. Farmer, E. H., and Shipley, F. W.: *J. Polymer Sci.*, **1**, 293 (1946).
364. Farr, H. V., and Ruhoff, J. R.: U.S. patent 2,586,459 (Feb. 19, 1952); *Chem. Abstracts*, **46**, 5276i (1952).
365. Fava, A.: *Gazz. chim. ital.*, **83**, 87 (1953); *Chem. Abstracts*, **47**, 12083g (1953).
366. Fava, A., and Bresadola, S.: *J. Am. Chem. Soc.*, **77**, 5792 (1955).
367. Fava, A., and Divo, D.: *Gazz. chim. ital.*, **83**, 98 (1953); *Chem. Abstracts*, **47**, 11914d (1953).

368. Fava, A., and Iliceto, A.: *Ann. chim. (Rome)*, **43,** 509 (1943); *Chem. Abstracts*, **48,** 6181d (1954).
369. Fava, A., and Iliceto, A.: *J. Am. Chem. Soc.*, **80,** 3478 (1958).
370. Fava, A., and Iliceto, A.: *Ricerca sci.*, **23,** 839 (1953); *Chem. Abstracts*, **47,** 9814c (1953).
371. Fava, A., Iliceto, A., and Camera, E.: *J. Am. Chem. Soc.*, **79,** 833 (1957).
372. Fava, A., and Pajaro, G.: *Ann. chim. (Rome)*, **43,** 502 (1953).
373. Fava, A., and Pajaro, G.: *Ann. chim. (Rome)*, **44,** 545 (1954); *Chem. Abstracts*, **49,** 5086c (1955).
374. Fava, A., and Pajaro, G.: *J. Am. Chem. Soc.*, **78,** 5203 (1956).
375. Fava, A., Sogo, P. B., and Calvin, M.: *J. Am. Chem. Soc.*, **79,** 1078 (1957).
375*a*. Fehér, F.: *Chem. Soc. Spec. Publ.*, **12,** 305 (1958).
375*b*. Fehér, F.: *Angew. Chem.*, **67,** 337 (1955).
376. Fehér, F., and Baudler, M.: *Z. anorg. Chem.*, **253,** 170 (1947).
377. Fehér, F., and Baudler, M.: *Z. anorg. u. allgem. Chem.*, **254,** 251 (1947).
378. Fehér, F., and Baudler, M.: *Z. anorg. u. allgem. Chem.*, **254,** 289 (1947).
379. Fehér, F., and Baudler, M.: *Z. anorg. u. allgem. Chem.*, **258,** 132 (1949).
380. Fehér, F., and Berthold, H. J., *Ber.*, **88,** 1634 (1955).
381. Fehér, F., and Berthold, H. J.: *Z. anorg. u. allgem. Chem.*, **267,** 251 (1952).
382. Fehér, F., and Berthold, H. J.: *Z. anorg. u. allgem. Chem.*, **273,** 144 (1953).
383. Fehér, F., and Berthold, H. J.: *Z. anorg. u. allgem. Chem.*, **274,** 223 (1953).
384. Fehér, F., and Berthold, R.: *Z. anorg. u. allgem. Chem.*, **290,** 251 (1957).
385. Fehér, F., and Hellwig, E.: *Z. anorg. u. allgem. Chem.*, **294,** 71 (1958).
386. Fehér, F., and Heuer, E.: *Z. anorg. Chem.*, **255,** 185 (1947).
387. Fehér, F., and Hitzemann, G.: *Z. anorg. u. allgem. Chem.*, **294,** 50 (1958).
388. Fehér, F., Krause, G., and Vogelbruch, K.: *Ber.*, **90,** 1570 (1957).
389. Fehér, F., and Kruse, W.: *Z. anorg. u. allgem. Chem.*, **293,** 302 (1957).
390. Fehér, F., Kruse, W., and Laue, W.: *Z. anorg. u. allgem. Chem.*, **292,** 203 (1957).
391. Fehér, F., Kruse, W., and Laue, W.: *Z. anorg. u. allgem. Chem.*, **294,** 203 (1958).
392. Fehér, F., and Laue, W.: *Z. anorg. u. allgem. Chem.*, **288,** 103 (1956).
393. Fehér, F., Laue, W., and Kraemer, J.: *Z. anorg. u. allgem. Chem.*, **281,** 151 (1955).
394. Fehér, F., Laue, W., and Winkhaus, G.: *Z. anorg. u. allgem. Chem.*, **288,** 113 (1956).
395. Fehér, F., Laue, W., and Winkhaus, G.: *Z. anorg. u. allgem. Chem.*, **288,** 123 (1956).
396. Fehér, F., Laue, W., and Winkhaus, G.: *Z. anorg. u. allgem. Chem.*, **290,** 52 (1957).
397. Fehér, F., and Naused, K.: *Z. anorg. u. allgem. Chem.*, **283,** 79 (1956).
398. Fehér, F., Naused, K., and Weber, H.: *Z. anorg. u. allgem. Chem.*, **290,** 303 (1957).
399. Fehér, F., and Ristić, S.: *Z. anorg. u. allgem. Chem.*, **293,** 307 (1958).
400. Fehér, F., and Ristić, S.: *Z. anorg. u. allgem. Chem.*, **293,** 311 (1958).
401. Fehér, F., and Schulze-Rettmer, R.: *Z. anorg. u. allgem. Chem.*, **295,** 262 (1958).
402. Fehér, F., and Weber, H.: *Ber.*, **91,** 642 (1958).
403. Fehér, F., and Weber, H.: *Z. Elektrochem.*, **61,** 285 (1957).
404. Fehér, F., and Winkhaus, G.: *Z. anorg. u. allgem. Chem.*, **288,** 123 (1956).
405. Fehér, F., and Winkhaus, G.: *Z. anorg. u. allgem. Chem.*, **292,** 210 (1957).
406. Fehnel, E. A.: *J. Am. Chem. Soc.*, **71,** 1063 (1949).
407. Fehnel, E. A.: *J. Am. Chem. Soc.*, **74,** 1569 (1952).
408. Fehnel, E. A., and Carmack, M.: *J. Am. Chem. Soc.*, **71,** 84 (1949).

409. Fehnel, E. A., and Carmack, M.: *J. Am. Chem. Soc.*, **71,** 231 (1949).
410. Fehnel, E. A., and Carmack, M.: *J. Am. Chem. Soc.*, **71,** 2889 (1949).
411. Fehnel, E. A., and Carmack, M.: *J. Am. Chem. Soc.*, **72,** 1292 (1950).
412. Feichtinger, H.: U.S. patent 2,689,246 (Sept. 14, 1954); *Chem. Abstracts,* **49,** 11014d, 14799d (1955).
413. Feichtinger, H., and Tummes, H.: U.S. patent 2,740,815 (Apr. 3, 1956); *Chem. Abstracts,* **51,** 2027d, 8131c (1957).
414. Ferguson, L. N.: *Chem. Revs.*, **43,** 385 (1948).
415. Ferguson, R. C.: *J. Am. Chem. Soc.*, **76,** 850 (1954).
416. Ferington, T. E., and Tobolsky, A. V.: *J. Am. Chem. Soc.*, **77,** 4510 (1955).
417. Ferington, T. E., and Tobolsky, A. V.: *J. Am. Chem. Soc.*, **80,** 3215 (1958).
418. Fields, E. K.: *J. Am. Chem. Soc.*, **77,** 4255 (1955).
419. Fieser, L. F., and Kilmer, G. W.: *J. Am. Chem. Soc.*, **62,** 1354 (1940).
420. Fischer, R., and Jeger, O.: *Helv. Chim. Acta,* **34,** 1084 (1951).
421. Fisher, R. A., and Smith, J. M.: *Ind. Eng. Chem.*, **42,** 704 (1950).
422. Flory, P. J.: "Principles of Polymer Chemistry," Cornell University Press, Ithaca, N.Y. (1953).
423. Fontijn, A., and Spinks, J. W. T.: *Can. J. Chem.*, **35,** 1384 (1957).
424. Fontijn, A., and Spinks, J. W. T.: *Can. J. Chem.*, **35,** 1397 (1957).
425. Föppl, H.: *Angew. Chem.*, **70,** 401 (1958).
426. Ford, J. H., Prescott, G. C., and Colingsworth, D. R.: *J. Am. Chem. Soc.*, **72,** 2109 (1950).
427. Forney, R. C., and Smith, J. M.: *Ind. Eng. Chem.*, **43,** 1841 (1951).
428. Foss, O.: *Acta Chem. Scand.*, **1,** 307 (1947).
429. Foss, O.: *Acta Chem. Scand.*, **4,** 404 (1950).
430. Foss, O.: *Acta Chem. Scand.*, **4,** 866 (1950).
431. Foss, O.: *Acta Chem. Scand.*, **5,** 115 (1951).
432. Foss, O.: *Acta Chem. Scand.*, **6,** 802 (1952).
433. Foss, O.: *Acta Chem. Scand.*, **7,** 1221 (1953).
434. Foss, O.: *Acta Chem. Scand.*, **8,** 469 (1954).
435. Foss, O.: *Acta Chem. Scand.*, **10,** 136 (1956).
436. Foss, O.: *Acta Chem. Scand.*, **10,** 868 (1956).
437. Foss, O.: *Acta Chem. Scand.*, **10,** 871 (1956).
438. Foss, O.: *Acta Chem. Scand.*, **11,** 1442 (1957).
439. Foss, O.: *Acta Chem. Scand.*, **12,** 959 (1958).
440. Foss, O.: Ionic Scission of the Sulfur-Sulfur Bond, in "Organic Sulfur Compounds," vol. I, Pergamon Press, London (1961).
441. Foss, O.: *Kgl. Norske Videnskab. Selskabs, Forh.*, **16,** No. 20, 72 (1943); *Chem. Abstracts,* **41,** 655g (1947).
442. Foss, O.: *Kgl. Norske Videnskab. Selskabs, Forh.*, **19,** No. 20, 72 (1946); *Chem. Abstracts,* **42,** 53d (1948).
443. Foss, O.: *Kgl. Norske Videnskab. Selskabs, Skrifter* 1942–1945, No. 2, pp. 1–132 (1948); *Chem. Abstracts,* **42,** 8154b (1948).
444. Foss, O.: Stereochemistry of Disulfides and Polysulfides, in "Organic Sulfur Compounds," vol. I, Pergamon Press, London (1961).
445. Foss, O.: Structures of Compounds Containing Chains of Sulfur Atoms, pp. 237–278 in "Advances in Inorganic Chemistry and Radiochemistry," vol. 2, edited by H. J. Emeleus and A. G. Sharp, Academic Press, Inc., New York (1960).
446. Foss, O., Furberg, S., and Hadler, E.: *Acta Chem. Scand.*, **5,** 1417 (1951).
447. Foss, O., Furberg, S., and Zachariasen, H.: *Acta Chem. Scand.*, **7,** 230 (1953).

448. Foss, O., Furberg, S., and Zachariasen, H.: *Acta Chem. Scand.*, **8,** 459 (1954).
449. Foss, O., and Hordvik, A.: *Acta Chem. Scand.*, **11,** 1443 (1957).
450. Foss, O., and Hordvik, A.: *Acta Chem. Scand.*, **12,** 1700 (1958).
451. Foss, O., Hordvik, A., and Palmork, K. H.: *Acta Chem. Scand.*, **12,** 1339 (1958).
452. Foss, O., and Jahr, J.: *Acta Chem. Scand.*, **4,** 1560 (1950).
453. Foss, O., and Johnsen, J.: Unpublished work cited by Foss in "Advances in Inorganic and Radiochemistry," vol. 2 (1960) (ref. 445).
454. Foss, O., Johnsen, J., and Tvedten, O.: *Acta Chem. Scand.*, **12,** 1782 (1958).
455. Foss, O., and Larssen, P. A.: *Acta Chem. Scand.*, **8,** 1042 (1954).
456. Foss, O., and Marøy, K.: *Acta Chem. Scand.*, **13,** 201 (1959).
457. Foss, O., and Oyum, P.: *Acta Chem. Scand.*, **9,** 1014 (1955).
458. Foss, O., and Palmork, K. H.: *Acta Chem. Scand.*, **12,** 1337 (1958).
459. Foss, O., and Reistad, T.: *Acta Chem. Scand.*, **11,** 1427 (1957); and data cited in Foss, O., "Advances in Inorganic and Radiochemistry," vol. 2 (1960) (ref. 445).
460. Foss, O., and Schotte, L.: *Acta Chem. Scand.*, **11,** 1424 (1957).
461. Foss, O., and Tjomsland, O.: *Acta Chem. Scand.*, **8,** 1701 (1954).
462. Foss, O., and Tjomsland, O.: *Acta Chem. Scand.*, **9,** 1016 (1955).
463. Foss, O., and Tjomsland, O.: *Acta Chem. Scand.*, **10,** 288 (1956).
464. Foss, O., and Tjomsland, O.: *Acta Chem. Scand.*, **10,** 416 (1956).
465. Foss, O., and Tjomsland, O.: *Acta Chem. Scand.*, **10,** 421 (1956).
466. Foss, O., and Tjomsland, O.: *Acta Chem. Scand.*, **10,** 424 (1956).
467. Foss, O., and Tjomsland, O.: *Acta Chem. Scand.*, **10,** 869 (1956).
468. Foss, O., and Tjomsland, O.: *Acta Chem. Scand.*, **11,** 1426 (1957).
469. Foss, O., and Tjomsland, O.: *Acta Chem. Scand.*, **12,** 44 (1958).
470. Foss, O., and Tjomsland, O.: *Acta Chem. Scand.*, **12,** 52 (1958).
471. Foss, O., and Tjomsland, O.: *Acta Chem. Scand.*, **12,** 1799 (1958).
472. Foss, O., and Tjomsland, O.: *Acta Chem. Scand.*, **12,** 1810 (1958).
473. Foss, O., and Vihovde, E.: *Acta Chem. Scand.*, **8,** 1032 (1954).
474. Foss, O., and Zachariasen, H.: *Acta Chem. Scand.*, **8,** 473 (1954).
475. Foster, R. E., Larchar, A. W., Lipscomb, R. D., and McKusick, B. C.: *J. Am. Chem. Soc.*, **78,** 5606 (1956).
476. Fraenkel-Conrat, H., and Olcott, H. S.: *J. Am. Chem. Soc.*, **66,** 1420 (1944).
477. Franklin, J. L., and Lumpkin, H. E.: *J. Am. Chem. Soc.*, **74,** 1023 (1952).
478. Franzen, V.: *Chem. Ztg.*, **10,** 328 (1959).
479. Fredga, A.: *Acta Chem. Scand.*, **12,** 891 (1958).
480. Friedel, C., and Crafts, J. M.: *Compt. rend.*, **86,** 884 (1878); *J. Chem. Soc. Abstract* **1878,** 670.
481. Friedländer, P., and Lenk, E.: *Ber.*, **45,** 2083 (1912).
482. Friedmann, W.: *J. Inst. Petroleum*, **37,** 40 (1951).
483. Friedmann, W.: *J. Inst. Petroleum*, **37,** 239 (1951).
484. Fristrom, R. M.: *J. Chem. Phys.*, **20,** 1 (1952).
485. Frost, A. A., and Pearson, R. G.: "Kinetics and Mechanism," John Wiley & Sons, Inc., New York (1953).
486. Fuhrman, N., and Mesrobian, R. B.: *J. Am. Chem. Soc.*, **76,** 3281 (1954).
487. Fuson, R. C., Price, C. C., and Burness, D. M.: *J. Org. Chem.*, **11,** 475 (1946).
488. Gannon, J. A., Fettes, E. M., and Tobolsky, A. V.: *J. Am. Chem. Soc.*, **74,** 1854 (1952).
489. Gardner, D. M., and Fraenkel, G. K.: *J. Am. Chem. Soc.*, **78,** 3279 (1956).
490. Gardner, D. M., and Fraenkel, G. K.: *J. Am. Chem. Soc.*, **78,** 6411 (1956).
491. Gaydon, A. G.: "Dissociation Energies," 2d ed., Chapman and Hall, Ltd., London (1953).

492. Geach, C. J., and Habeshaw, J.: British patent 772,443 (Apr. 10, 1957); *Chem. Abstracts*, **51,** 14811g (1957).
493. Gee, G.: *J. Polymer Sci.*, **2,** 451 (1947).
494. Gee, G.: Recent Work on the Inorganic Chemistry of Sulfur, Bristol, 1958, in *Special Publication No.* 12, p. 247, The Chemical Society, London (1958).
495. Gee, G.: *Trans. Faraday Soc.*, **48,** 515 (1952).
496. Gee, G., and Morrell, S. H.: *Rubber Chem. and Technol.*, **25,** 454 (1952).
497. Geigy, J. R., and Co.: D.R.-P. 86,874 (May 11, 1895); *Ber.*, **29,** 530 (1896).
498. Geigy, J. R., and Co.: German patent 87,255; *Chem. Zentr.* **67II,** 613 (1896).
499. George, J., Wechsler, H., and Mark, H.: *J. Am. Chem. Soc.*, **72,** 3891 (1950).
500. Gerischer, H.: *Z. anorg. u. allgem. Chem.*, **259,** 220 (1949).
501. Gerke, G. H.: *Ind. Eng. Chem.*, **31,** 1478 (1939).
502. Gerry, R. T., and Brown, E. V : *J. Am. Chem. Soc.*, **75,** 740 (1953).
503. Ghaisas, V. V., and Tilak, B. D.: *Current Sci. (India)*, **22,** 184 (1953); *Chem. Abstracts*, **48,** 12731i (1954).
504. Gibbons, W. A., and Smith, O. H.: U.S. patent 1,997,967 (Apr. 16, 1935); *Chem. Abstracts*, **29,** 3692[6] (1935).
505. Gilman, H., and Avakian, S.: *J. Am. Chem. Soc.*, **68,** 2104 (1946).
506. Gilman, H., and Jacoby, A. L.: *J. Org. Chem.*, **3,** 108 (1938).
507. Gingrich, N. S.: *J. Chem. Phys.*, **8,** 29 (1940).
508. Glasstone, S.: "Theoretical Chemistry," D. Van Nostrand Company, Inc., Princeton, N. J. (1944).
508*a*. Glasstone, S., Laidler, K. J., and Eyring, H.: "Theory of Rate Processes," McGraw-Hill Book Company, Inc., New York (1941).
509. Glazebrook, R. W., and Saville, R. W.: *J. Chem. Soc.*, **1954,** 2094.
510. Goering, H. L., Abell, P. L., and Aycock, B. F.: *J. Am. Chem. Soc.*, **74,** 3588 (1952).
511. Goering, H. L., Relyea, D. I., and Larsen, D. W.: *J. Am. Chem. Soc.*, **78,** 348 (1956).
512. Golovinski, E.: *Annuaire univ. Sofia, Fac. sci., Chim.*, **50,** pt. 1–2, 169 (1955–1956); *Chem. Abstracts*, **53,** 7967f (1959).
513. Gordon, M.: *J. Polymer Sci.*, **3,** 438 (1948).
514. Gordon, M.: *J. Polymer Sci.*, **7,** 485 (1951).
515. Gordon, M.: *Proc. Roy. Soc. (London)*, **A204,** 569 (1951).
516. Gordy, W.: *J. Chem. Phys.*, **14,** 560 (1946).
517. Gorin, G., Dougherty, G., and Tobolsky, A. V.: *J. Am. Chem. Soc.*, **71,** 3551 (1949).
518. Gould, E. S.: "Mechanism and Structure in Organic Chemistry," Henry Holt and Company, Inc., New York, 1959.
519. Grassie, N.: "The Chemistry of High Polymer Degradation Processes," Butterworth & Co. (Publishers), Ltd., London (1956).
520. Green, A. L., Sainsbury, G. L., Saville, B., and Stansfield, M.: *J. Chem. Soc.*, **1958,** 1583.
521. Greenberg, J., and Sundheim, B. R.: *J. Chem. Phys.*, **29,** 461 (1958).
521*a*. Greene, F. D., Adam, W., and Cantrill, J. E.: *J. Am. Chem. Soc.*, **83,** 3461 (1961).
522. Greensfelder, B. S., and Moore, R. J.: British patent 603,103 (June 9, 1948); *Chem. Abstracts*, **43,** 691g (1949).
523. Gregg, R. A., Alderman, D. M., and Mayo, F. R.: *J. Am. Chem. Soc.*, **70,** 3740 (1948).
524. Gregg, R. A., and Mayo, F. R.: *Discussions Faraday Soc.*, **2,** 328 (1947).

525. Gregg, R. A., and Mayo, F. R.: *J. Am. Chem. Soc.*, **70,** 2373 (1948).
526. Gregg, R. A., and Mayo, F. R.: *J. Am. Chem. Soc.*, **75,** 3530 (1953).
526*a*. Gritter, R. J., and Wallace, T. J.: *J. Org. Chem.*, **26,** 283 (1961).
527. Gur'yanova, E. N.: *Zhur. Fiz. Khim.*, **21,** 411 (1947); *Chem. Abstracts,* **41,** 6786a (1947).
528. Gur'yanova, E. N.: *Zhur. Fiz. Khim.*, **21,** 633 (1947); *Chem. Abstracts,* **42,** 2147h (1948).
529. Gur'yanova, E. N., Syrkin, Ya. K., and Kuzina, L. S.: *Doklady Akad. Nauk S.S.S.R.*, **86,** 107 (1952); *Chem. Abstracts,* **47,** 1475f (1953).
530. Gur'yanova, E. N., and Vasil'eva, V. N.: *Zhur. Fiz. Khim.*, **28,** 60 (1954); *Chem. Abstracts,* **48,** 11,888a (1954).
531. Guthrie, G. B., Scott, D. W., and Waddington, G.: *J. Am. Chem. Soc.*, **76,** 1488 (1954).
532. Haan, Y. M. de: *Physica,* **24,** 855 (1958).
533. Hägg, G.: *Z. physik. Chem.*, **18B,** 327 (1932).
534. Hall, N. F., and Alexander, O. R.: *J. Am. Chem. Soc.*, **62,** 3455 (1940).
535. Hansch, C.: *Chem. Revs.*, **53,** 353 (1953).
536. Hansen, B.: *Acta Chem. Scand.*, **13,** 151 (1959).
537. Hansford, R. C., Rasmussen, H. E., and Sachanen, A. N.: U.S. patent 2,450,659 (Oct. 5, 1948); *Chem. Abstracts,* **43,** 1066e (1949).
538. Hanson, T. K., and Kinnard, L. M.: British patent 696,439 (Sept. 2, 1953); *Chem. Abstracts,* **51,** 15587f (1957).
539. Hara, Y., and Fujise, S.: *J. Chem. Soc. Japan, Pure Chem. Sect.*, **74,** 698 (1953).
540. Haraldson, L., Olander, C. J., Sunner, S., and Varde, E.: *Acta Chem. Scand.*, **14,** 1509 (1960).
541. Harrington, R. E., Rabinovitch, B. S., and Diesen, R. W.: *J. Chem. Phys.*, **32,** 1245 (1960).
542. Harris, E. F. P., and Waters, W. A.: *Nature,* **170,** 212 (1952).
543. Hartman, S., and Robertson, R. E.: *Can. J. Chem.*, **38,** 2033 (1960).
544. Hartmann, M., and Bosshard, W.: *Helv. Chim. Acta,* **24,** 28E (1951).
545. Hartough, H. D.: "Thiophene and Its Derivatives," chap. 3. Interscience Publishers, Inc., New York (1952).
546. Hartshorne, N. H., and Thackray, M.: *J. Chem. Soc.*, **1957,** 2122.
547. Harvey, R. B., and Bauer, S. H.: *J. Am. Chem. Soc.*, **75,** 2840 (1953).
548. Hassel, O., and Viervoll, H.: *Acta Chem. Scand.*, **1,** 149 (1947).
549. Hauser, C. R., and Harris, T. M.: *J. Am. Chem. Soc.*, **81,** 1154 (1959).
550. Havlik, A. J., and Kharasch, N.: *J. Am. Chem. Soc.*, **78,** 1207 (1956).
551. Haynes, W.: "The Stone That Burns," 2d ed., D. Van Nostrand Company, Inc., Princeton, N. J. (1959).
552. Heilmann, R., Gaudemaris, G. de, and Heindl, R.: *Compt. rend.*, **235,** 544 (1952).
552*a*. Henchman, M., and Wolfgang, R.: *J. Am. Chem. Soc.*, **83,** 2991 (1961).
553. Hendrickson, J. G., and Hatch, L. F.: *J. Org. Chem.*, **25,** 1747 (1960).
554. Heppolette, R. L., and Miller, J.: *J. Chem. Soc.*, **1956,** 2329.
555. Hey, D. H.: *J. Chem. Soc.*, **1952,** 1974.
556. Heymann, H.: *J. Am. Chem. Soc.*, **71,** 260 (1949).
557. Hiatt, R. R., and Bartlett, P. D.: *J. Am. Chem. Soc.*, **81,** 1149 (1959).
558. Himel, C. M., and Edwards, L. O.: U.S. patent 2,572,567; *Chem. Abstracts,* **46,** 6149c (1952).
559. Hine, J.: "Physical Organic Chemistry," McGraw-Hill Book Company, Inc., New York (1956).
560. Hirshon, J. M., and Fraenkel, G. K.: *Rev. Sci. Inst.*, **26,** 34 (1955).

561. Hirshon, J. M., Gardner, D. M., and Fraenkel, G. K.: *J. Am. Chem. Soc.*, **75,** 4115 (1953).
562. Hochberg, J., and Bonhoefer, K. F.: *Z. physik. Chem.*, **184A,** 419 (1939).
563. Hodgson, H. H.: *J. Chem. Soc.*, **125,** 1855 (1924).
564. Hojo, M., Takagi, Y., and Ogata, Y.: *J. Am. Chem. Soc.*, **82,** 2459 (1960).
565. Hopff, H.: U.S. patent 2,817,685 (Dec. 24, 1957).
566. Horton, A. W.: *J. Org. Chem.*, **14,** 761 (1949).
567. Horton, A. W.: U.S. patent 2,522,676 (Sept. 19, 1950); *Chem. Abstracts,* **45,** 9556b (1951).
568. Horton, W. J., and Van den Berghe, J.: *J. Am. Chem. Soc.*, **70,** 2425 (1948).
569. Huang, R. L.: *J. Chem. Soc.*, **1956,** 1749.
570. Huang, R. L., and Singh, S.: *J. Chem. Soc.*, **1958,** 891.
571. Hubbard, W. N., Douslin, D. R., McCullough, J. P., Scott, D. W., Todd, S. S., Messerly, J. F., Hossenlopp, I. A., George, A., and Waddington, G.: *J. Am. Chem. Soc.*, **80,** 3547 (1958).
572. Hückel, W.: "Structural Chemistry of Inorganic Compounds," translated by L. H. Long, Elsevier Press, Inc., New York (1950).
573. Hückel, W.: "Theoretical Principles of Organic Chemistry," vol. I, Elsevier Press, Inc., New York (1955).
574. Huggins, M. L.: *J. Am. Chem. Soc.*, **75,** 4126 (1953).
575. Hughes, E. D., Ingold, C. K., Mok, S. F., Patai, S., and Pocker, Y.: *J. Chem. Soc.*, **1957,** 1220.
576. Hull, C M., Olsen, S. R., and France, W. G.: *Ind. Eng. Chem.*, **38,** 1282 (1946).
577. Hull, C. M., Weinland, L. A., Olsen, S. R., and France, W. G.: *Ind. Eng. Chem.*, **40,** 513 (1948).
578. Hurd, C. D., and Gershbein, L. L.: *J. Am. Chem. Soc.*, **69,** 2328 (1947).
578*a*. Huyser, E. S.: *J. Am. Chem. Soc.*, **83,** 394 (1960).
579. Ikenoue, K.: *J. Phys. Soc. Japan*, **8,** 646 (1953).
580. Inaba, T., and Darwent, B. de B.: *J. Phys. Chem.*, **64,** 1431 (1960).
581. Ingold, C. K.: "Structure and Mechanism in Organic Chemistry," Cornell University Press, Ithaca, N. Y. (1953).
582. Ingram, D. J. E., and Symons, M. C. R.: *J. Chem. Soc.*, **1957,** 2437.
583. Ipatieff, V. N., and Friedman, B. S.: *J. Am. Chem. Soc.*, **61,** 71 (1939).
584. Ipatieff, V. N., Pines, H., and Friedman, B. S.: *J. Am. Chem. Soc.*, **60,** 2731 (1938).
585. Jacobsen, H. I., Harvey, R. G., and Jensen, E. V.: *J. Am. Chem. Soc.*, **77,** 6064 (1955).
586. Jaffé, H. H.: *Chem. Revs.*, **53,** 191 (1953).
587. Jaffé, H. H.: *J. Chem. Phys.*, **22,** 1430 (1954).
588. Jarvis, J. A. J.: *Acta Cryst.*, **6,** 327 (1953).
589. Jeffrey, G. A.: *Acta Cryst.*, **4,** 58 (1951).
590. Jeffrey, G. A., and Stadler, H. P.: *J. Chem. Soc.*, **1951,** 1467.
591. Jelinek, C. F.: U.S. patent 2,572,809 (Oct. 23, 1951); *Chem. Abstracts*, **46,** 3557i (1952).
592. Jelinek, C. F.: U.S. patent 2,572,810; *Chem. Abstracts*, **46,** 3558a (1951).
593. Jenne, H., and Becke-Goehring, M.: *Ber.*, **91,** 1950 (1958).
594. Jennen, A.: *Compt. rend.*, **241,** 1581 (1955).
595. Jennen, A., and Hens, M.: *Compt. rend.*, **242,** 786 (1956).
596. Johnson, A. W., and LaCount, R. B.: *J. Am. Chem. Soc.*, **83,** 417 (1961).
597. Johnston, K. M., and Williams, G. H.: *Chem. & Ind. (London)*, **1958,** 328.
598. Jones, R. G., Soper, Q. F., Behrens, O. K., and Corse, J. W.: *J. Am. Chem. Soc.*, **70,** 2843 (1948).

599. Jones, S. O., and Reid, E. E.: *J. Am. Chem. Soc.*, **60,** 2452 (1938).
600. Kaiser, T.: Thesis, Harvard University, Cambridge, Mass. (1959) (F. H. Westheimer, research director).
601. Kaltwasser, H.: *Chem. Tech.* (*Berlin*), **9,** 392 (1957).
602. Kamlet, J.: U.S. patent 2,826,609 (Mar. 11, 1958).
603. Karaulova, E. N., Meĭlanova, D. Sh., and Gal'pern, G. D.: *Khim. Sera-Org. Soedineniĭ,* **1957,** 164; *Chem. Abstracts,* **55,** 1497b (1961).
604. Katz, J. R.: *Trans. Faraday Soc.*, **32,** 77 (1936).
605. Kawaoka, Y.: *J. Soc. Chem. Ind. Japan,* **43,** No. 2, Suppl. binding **53,** 151 (1940); *Chem. Abstracts,* **34,** 6131, 6487 (1940).
606. Kehl, W. L., and Jeffrey, G. A.: *Acta Cryst.*, **11,** 813 (1958).
607. Keil, C., and Plieth, K.: *Z. Krist.*, **106,** 388 (1955).
608. Keller, J. L.: U.S. patent 2,515,233 (July 18, 1950).
609. Kenyon, J., and Young, D. P.: *J. Chem. Soc.*, **1938,** 965.
610. Kern, R. J.: *J. Am. Chem. Soc.*, **77,** 1382 (1955).
611. Kerr, J. A., and Trotman-Dickenson, A. F.: *J. Chem. Soc.*, **1957,** 3322.
612. Kharasch, M. S., and Fuchs, C. F.: *J. Org. Chem.*, **13,** 97 (1948).
613. Kharasch, M. S., Nudenberg, W., and Meltzer, T. H.: *J. Org. Chem.*, **18,** 1233 (1953).
614. Kharasch, M. S., Read, A. T., and Mayo, F. R.: *Chem. & Ind.* (*London*), **57,** 792 (1938).
615. Kharasch, M. S., and Reinmuth, O.: "Grignard Reaction of Nonmetallic Compounds," Prentice-Hall, Inc., Englewood Cliffs, N.J. (1954).
616. Kharasch, N.: *J. Chem. Educ.*, **33,** 585 (1956).
617. Kharasch, N.: Sulfenium Ions, in "Organic Sulfur Compounds," vol. I, Pergamon Press, London (1961).
618. Kharasch, N., and Buess, C. M.: *J. Am. Chem. Soc.*, **71,** 2724 (1949).
619. Kharasch, N., Buess, C. M., and King, W.: *J. Am. Chem. Soc.*, **75,** 6035 (1953).
620. Kharasch, N., Gleason, G., and Buess, C. M.: *J. Am. Chem. Soc.*, **72,** 1796 (1950).
621. Kharasch, N., King, W., and Bruice, T. C.: *J. Am. Chem. Soc.*, **77,** 931 (1955).
622. Kharasch, N., and Havlik, A. J.: *J. Am. Chem. Soc.*, **75,** 3734 (1953).
623. Kharasch, N., Potempa, S. J., and Wehrmeister, H. L.: *Chem. Revs.*, **39,** 269 (1946).
624. Kice, J. L.: *J. Am. Chem. Soc.*, **76,** 6274 (1954).
625. Kice, J. L.: *J. Polymer Sci.*, **19,** 123 (1956).
626. Kimball, G. E.: *J. Chem. Phys.*, **8,** 188 (1940).
627. Kimball, G. E.: Quantum Theory, in "Annual Review of Physical Chemistry," vol. 2, Annual Reviews, Inc., Stanford, Calif. (1951).
628. Kindler, K.: *Ann.*, **431,** 187 (1923).
629. Kindler, K.: German patent 405,675 (Apr. 11, 1924); *Chem. Zentr.*, **96I,** 1529 (1925).
630. Kindler, K., and Körding, P.: *Ann.*, **431,** 222 (1923).
631. Kindler, K., and Li, T.: *Ber.*, **74B,** 321 (1941).
632. King, J. A., and McMillan, F. H.: *J. Am. Chem. Soc.*, **68,** 525 (1946).
633. King, J. A., and McMillan, F. H.: *J. Am. Chem. Soc.*, **68,** 632 (1946).
634. King, J. A., and McMillan, F. H.: *J. Am. Chem. Soc.*, **68,** 1369 (1946).
635. King, J. A., and McMillan, F. H.: *J. Am. Chem. Soc.*, **68,** 2335 (1946).
636. Kipping, F. B.: *J. Chem. Soc.*, **1935,** 18.
637. Kirchhof, F.: *Chem. Zeit.*, **79,** 434 (1955); *Chem. Abstracts,* **49,** 14556e (1955).
638. Klemm, W., and Kilian, H.: *Z. physik. Chem.*, **B49,** 279 (1941).
639. Kloosterziel, H., and Backer, H. J.: *Rec. trav. chim.*, **72,** 185 (1953).
640. Kloosterziel, H., and Backer, H. J.: *Rec. trav. chim.*, **72,** 655 (1953).

641. Koch, H. P.: *J. Chem. Soc.*, **1949,** 387.
642. Koch, H. P.: *J. Chem. Soc.*, **1949,** 394.
643. Koch, H. P.: *J. Chem. Soc.*, **1949,** 401.
644. Koch, H. P.: *J. Chem. Soc.*, **1949,** 408.
645. Koch, H. P., and Moffitt, W. E.: *Trans. Faraday Soc.*, **47,** 7 (1951).
646. Koenig, N. H., and Swern, D.: *J. Am. Chem. Soc.*, **79,** 4235 (1957).
647. Köhler, H., and Michaelis, A.: *Ber.*, **10,** 807 (1877).
648. Kohler, E. P., and Potter, H.: *J. Am. Chem. Soc.*, **57,** 1316 (1935).
649. Kon, G. A. R.: *J. Chem. Soc.*, **1948,** 224.
650. Kooyman, E. C.: *Discussions Faraday Soc.*, **10,** 163 (1951).
651. Kooyman, E. C., Helden, R. van, and Bickel, A. F.: *Koninkl. Ned. Akad. Wetenschap. Proc.*, **56B,** 75 (1953).
652. Kooyman, E. C., and Strang, A.: *Rec. trav. chim.*, **72,** 329 (1953).
653. Kooyman, E. C., and Strang, A.: *Rec. trav. chim.*, **72,** 342 (1953).
654. Kornblum, N., and De La Mare, H. E.: *J. Am. Chem. Soc.*, **74,** 3079 (1952).
655. Kornfeld, E. C.: *J. Org. Chem.*, **16,** 131 (1951).
656. Korshunov, I. A., and Batalov, A. P.: *Zhur. Obshcheĭ Khim.*, **29,** 3135 (1959); *Chem. Abstracts*, **54,** 12981b (1960).
657. Kosak, A. I., and Holbrook, R. L.: *Science*, **117,** 231 (1953).
658. Kosolpoff, G. M.: "Organophosphorous Compounds," John Wiley & Sons, Inc., New York (1950).
659. Kotch, A., Krol, L. H., Verkade, P. E., and Wepster, B. M.: *Rec. trav. chim.*, **71,** 108 (1952).
660. Koutecký, J., Zahradnik, R., and Paldus, J.: *J. chim. phys.*, **56,** 455 (1959).
661. Kratz, G. D., Flower, A. H , and Coolidge, C.: *Ind. Eng. Chem.*, **12,** 317 (1920)
662. Kratz, G. D., Young, H. H., and Katz, I.: *Ind. Eng. Chem.*, **41,** 399 (1949).
663. Krebs, H., and Weber, E. F.: *Z. anorg. u. allgem. Chem.*, **272,** 288 (1953).
664. Kumamoto, J., Cox, J. R., and Westheimer, F. H.: *J. Am. Chem. Soc.*, **78,** 4858 (1956).
665. Kumamoto, J., and Westheimer, F. H.: *J. Am. Chem. Soc.*, **77,** 2515 (1955).
666. Kumler, W. D., and Strait, L. A.: *J. Am. Chem. Soc.*, **65,** 2349 (1943).
667. Kushner, L. M., Gorin, G., and Smyth, C. P.: *J. Am. Chem. Soc.*, **72,** 477 (1950).
668. Kuwaoka, Y.: *J. Soc. Rubber Ind. Japan*, **16,** 322 (1943); *Chem. Abstracts*, **44,** 1740g (1950).
669. Kuwaoka, Y.: *J. Soc. Rubber Ind. Japan*, **16,** 327 (1943); *Chem. Abstracts*, **44,** 1740h (1950).
670. Kuwaoka, Y.: *J. Soc. Rubber Ind. Japan*, **16,** 332 (1943); *Chem. Abstracts*, **44,** 1740i (1950).
671. Kwart, H., and Miller, R. K.: *J. Am. Chem. Soc.*, **78,** 5008 (1956).
672. Kwart, H., and Miller, R. K.: *J. Am. Chem. Soc.*, **78,** 5678 (1956).
673. Laidler, K. J.: "Chemical Kinetics," McGraw-Hill Book Company, Inc., New York (1950).
674. La Mer, V. K., and Read, C. L.: *J. Am. Chem. Soc.*, **52,** 3098 (1930).
675. Landis, P. S., and Hamilton, L. A.: *J. Org. Chem.*, **25,** 1742 (1960).
676. Larson, A. C., and Helmholz, L.: *J. Chem. Phys.*, **22,** 2049 (1954).
677. Lavine, T. F.: *J. Biol. Chem.*, **113,** 583 (1936).
678. Leandri, G., and Tundo, A.: *Ann. chim. (Rome)*, **44,** 63 (1954); *Chem. Abstracts*, **49,** 4563d (1955).
679. Lecher, H. Z.: *Ber.*, **48,** 524 (1915).
680. Lecher, H. Z.: *Ber.*, **48,** 1425 (1915).
681. Lecher, H. Z.: *Ber.*, **53,** 577 (1920).

682. Lecher, H. Z.: *Science,* **120,** 220 (1954).
683. Lecher, H. Z., and Hardy, E. M.: *J. Org. Chem.,* **20,** 475 (1955).
684. Leo, A., and Westheimer, F. H.: *J. Am. Chem. Soc.,* **74,** 4383 (1952).
685. Lerner, M. E., Editor-in-chief: "Bibliography of Rubber Literature, 1949–51," American Chemical Society, Division of Rubber Chemistry, Akron 8, Ohio (1957).
686. Levesque, C. L.: U.S. patent 2,560,296 (July 10, 1951); *Chem. Abstracts,* **46,** 3558b (1952).
687. Levi, T. G.: *Gazz. chim. ital.,* **60,** 975 (1930); *Chem. Abstracts,* **25,** 2421 (1931).
688. Levi, T. G.: *Gazz. chim. ital.,* **61,** 286 (1931); *Chem. Abstracts,* **25,** 4853 (1931).
689. Lewis, G. L., Randall, M., and Bichowsky, F. R. v.: *J. Am. Chem. Soc.,* **40,** 356 (1918).
690. Lien, A. P., McCaulay, D. A., and Proell, W. A.: General Papers, Division of Petroleum Chemistry, American Chemical Society, No. 28, p. 169 (1952).
691. Linstead, R. P.: *Ann. Repts. on Progr. Chem.* (*Chem. Soc. London*), **33,** 294 (1936).
692. Lister, M. W., and Garvie, R. C.: *Can. J. Chem.,* **37,** 1567 (1959).
693. Lister, M. W., and Sutton, L. E.: *Trans. Faraday Soc.,* **35,** 495 (1939).
694. Litvinenko, L. M., Levchenko, N. F., Tsukerman, S. V., and Cheshko, R. S.: *Zhur. Obshcheĭ Khim.,* **29,** 1470 (1959); *Chem. Abstracts,* **54,** 8721d (1960).
695. Long, F. A., and Paul, M. A.: *Chem. Revs.,* **57,** 935 (1957).
696. Longuet-Higgins, H. C.: *Trans. Faraday Soc.,* **45,** 173 (1949).
697. Lorenz, O., and Echte, E.: *Rubber Chem. and Technol.,* **31,** 548 (1958).
698. Lowenbein, A., and Simonis, H.: *Ber.,* **57,** 2040 (1924).
699. Lozac'h, N.: *Bull. soc. chim. France,* 840 (1949).
700. Lozac'h, N.: *Compt. rend.,* **225,** 686 (1947).
701. Lozac'h, N., Denis, M., Mollier, Y., and Teste, J.: *Bull. soc. chim. France,* **1953,** 1016.
702. Lozac'h, N., and Legrand, L.: *Compt. rend.,* **232,** 2330 (1951).
703. Lozac'h, N., and Teste, J.: *Compt. rend.,* **234,** 1891 (1952).
704. Lu, C. S., and Donohue, J.: *J. Am. Chem. Soc.,* **66,** 818 (1944).
705. Lu, C. S., Hughes, E. W., and Giguere, P. A.: *J. Am. Chem. Soc.,* **63,** 1507 (1941).
706. Luft, N. W.: *Monatsh.,* **86,** 474 (1955).
707. Lukashevich, V. O., and Sergeeva, M. M.: *Doklady Akad. Nauk SSSR,* **67,** 1041 (1949); *Chem. Abstracts,* **44,** 1921g (1950).
708. Lukasiewicz, S. J., and Denton, W. I.: U.S. patent 2,515,928 (July 18, 1950); *Chem. Abstracts,* **44,** 9668b (1950).
709. Lunenok-Burmakina, V. A.: *J. Gen. Chem. U.S.S.R.* (Eng. transl.), **27,** 345 (1958).
710. Lüttringhaus, A., and Cleve, W.: *Ann.,* **575,** 112 (1951).
711. Lüttringhaus, A., and Hägele, K.: *Angew. Chem.,* **67,** 304 (1955).
712. Lüttringhaus, A., König, H. B., and Böttcher, B.: *Ann.,* **560,** 201 (1947).
713. Lynton, H., and Cox, E. G.: *J. Chem. Soc.,* **1956,** 4886
714. Lyons, W. E.: *Nature,* **162,** 1004 (1948).
714*a*. Magee, J. L.: *J. Chem. Phys.,* **8,** 677 (1940).
715. Magnusson, B.: *Acta Chem. Scand.,* **13,** 1031 (1959).
716. Malan, R. L., and Dean, P. M.: *J. Am. Chem. Soc.,* **69,** 1797 (1947).
717. Malatesta, L.: *Gazz. chim. ital.,* **77,** 518 (1947).
718. Maloney, J. O., and Teplitz, M.: U.S. patent 2,898,388 (Aug. 4, 1959); *Chem. Abstracts,* **54,** 293d (1960).
719. Mamalis, P., and Rydon, H. N.: *J. Chem. Soc.,* **1955,** 1049.

720. Mangini, A., and Passerini, R.: *Gazz. chim. ital.*, **84,** 606 (1954); *Chem. Abstracts,* **50,** 935c (1956).
721. Mansfield, R. C.: *J. Org. Chem.*, **24,** 1111 (1959).
722. Mansfield, R. C.: *J. Org. Chem.*, **24,** 1375 (1959).
723. Mare, P. B. D. de la: *J. Chem. Soc.*, **1955,** 3180.
724. Maros, L., Koros, E., Fehér, I., and Schulek, E.: *Magyar Kem. Folyóirat*, **65,** 58 (1959); *Chem. Abstracts*, **54,** 13929b (1960).
724*a*. Martin, J. C., and Drew, E. H.: *J. Am. Chem. Soc.*, **83,** 1232 (1961).
725. Martinez, S., Garcia-Blanco, G., and Rivior, L.: *Acta Cryst.*, **9,** 145 (1956).
726. Marvel, C. S., and Weil, E. D.: *J. Am. Chem. Soc.*, **76,** 61 (1954).
727. Maryott, A. A., and Smith, E. R.: Table of Dielectric Constants of Pure Liquids, *Natl. Bur. Standards Circ.* 514 (Aug. 10, 1951).
728. Mathieson, A. M., and Robertson, J. M.: *J. Chem. Soc.*, **1949,** 724.
728*a*. Mayer, R., and Kubasch, U.: *Angew. Chem.*, **73,** 220 (1961).
729. Mayo, F. R.: *J. Am. Chem. Soc.*, **65,** 2324 (1943).
730. Mayo, F. R.: *J. Am. Chem. Soc.*, **80,** 2465 (1958).
731. Mayo, F. R.: Reprints of Papers Presented at the Atlantic City Meeting of the ACS, Division of Paint, Plastics and Printing Ink Chemistry, **19,** 326 (1959).
732. Mayo, F. R., Miller, A. A., and Russell, G. A.: *J. Am. Chem. Soc.*, **80,** 2500 (1958).
733. Mayo, F. R., and Walling, C.: *Chem. Revs.*, **27,** 351 (1940).
734. Mayo, F. R., and Walling, C.: *Chem. Revs.*, **46,** 191 (1950).
735. McAllan, D. T., Cullum, T. V., Dean, R. A., and Fidler, F. A.: *J. Am. Chem. Soc.*, **73,** 3627 (1951).
736. McDaniel, D. H., and Brown, H. C.: *J. Org. Chem.*, **23,** 420 (1958).
737. McEwen, W. K.: *J. Am. Chem. Soc.*, **58,** 1124 (1936).
738. McKay, H. A. C.: *Nature*, **142,** 997 (1938).
739. McKinnis, A. C.: U.S. patent 2,809,204 (Oct. 8, 1957).
740. McMillan, F. H.: *J. Am. Chem. Soc.*, **70,** 868 (1948).
741. McMillan, F. H., and King, J. A.: *J. Am. Chem. Soc.*, **69,** 1207 (1947).
742. McMillan, F. H., and King, J. A.: *J. Am. Chem. Soc.*, **70,** 4143 (1948).
743. McOmie, J. F. M.: *Ann. Repts. on Progr. Chem.* (*Chem. Soc. London*), **45,** 210 (1948).
744. Meehan, E. J., Kolthoff, I. M., and Sinha, P. R.: *J. Polymer Sci.*, **16,** 471 (1955).
745. Meissner, H. P., Conway, E. R., and Mickley, H. S.: *Ind. Eng. Chem.*, **48,** 1347 (1956).
746. Messina, N., and Brown, E. V.: *J. Am. Chem. Soc.*, **74,** 920 (1952).
747. Meyer, B., and Schumacher, E.: *Helv. chim. Acta*, **43,** 1333 (1960).
747*a*. Meyer, B., and Schumacher, E.: *Nature*, **186,** 801 (1960).
748. Meyer, J. A., Stannett, V., and Szwarc, M.: Preprints of General Papers, ACS, Division of Petroleum Chem., p. 11, New York (September, 1960); *J. Am. Chem. Soc.*, **83,** 25 (1961).
749. Meyer, K. H.: "Natural and Synthetic High Polymers," 2d ed., Interscience Publishers, Inc., New York (1950).
750. Mikeska, L. A., and Koenecke, D. F.: U.S. patent 2,806,883 (Sept. 17, 1957); *Chem. Abstracts*, **52,** 5470g (1958).
751. Miller, J. E., Kendrick, N. S., and Crawford, G. W.: *Phys. Rev.*, **99,** 1631 (1955).
752. Miller, P. E., Oliver, G. L., Dann, J. R., and Gates, J. W.: *J. Org. Chem.*, **22,** 664 (1957).
753. Miller, W. S., and King, A. J.: *Z. Krist.*, **94,** 439 (1936).
754. Milligan, B., and Swan, J. M.: *J. Chem. Soc.*, **1959,** 2969.

755. Mills, G. A.: *J. Am. Chem. Soc.*, **62,** 2833 (1940).
756. Mills, G. A., and Urey, H. C.: *J. Am. Chem. Soc.*, **61,** 534 (1939).
757. Mills, G. A., and Urey, H. C.: *J. Am. Chem. Soc.*, **62,** 1019 (1940).
758. Minoura, Y.: *Rubber Chem. and Technol.*, **31,** 612 (1958).
759. Minoura, Y.: *Rubber Chem. and Technol.*, **31,** 615 (1958).
760. Minoura, Y.: *Rubber Chem. and Technol.*, **31,** 808 (1958).
761. Minoura, Y.: *Rubber Chem. and Technol.*, **31,** 815 (1958).
762. Miyoshi, H., and Oda, R.: *J. Chem. Soc. Japan, Ind. Chem. Sect.*, **59,** 224 (1956); *Chem. Abstracts*, **51,** 10413d (1957).
763. Mochulsky, M., and Tobolsky, A. V.: *Ind. Eng. Chem.*, **40,** 2155 (1948).
764. Mockler, R. C., and Bird, G. R.: *Phys. Rev.*, **98,** 1837 (1955).
765. Moeller, T.: "Inorganic Chemistry," John Wiley & Sons, Inc., New York (1952).
766. Moffitt, W. E.: *Proc. Roy. Soc. (London)*, **A200,** 409 (1950).
767. Moore, C. G.: *J. Polymer Sci.*, **32,** 503 (1958).
768. Moore, C. G., and Porter, M.: *J. Chem. Soc.*, **1958,** 2062.
769. Moore, C. G., and Porter, M.: *J. Chem. Soc.*, **1958,** 2890.
770. Moore, C. G., and Porter, M.: *Tetrahedron*, **6,** 10 (1959).
771. Moore, C. G., and Saville, R. W.: *J. Chem. Soc.*, **1954,** 2082.
772. Moore, C. G., and Saville, R. W.: *J. Chem. Soc.*, **1954,** 2089.
773. Moore, M. L., and Johnson, T. B.: *J. Am. Chem. Soc.*, **57,** 1287 (1935).
774. Moreau, R. C.: *Bull. soc. chim. France*, **1955,** 628.
775. Moreau, R. C.: *Bull. soc. chim. France*, **1955,** 918.
776. Moreau, R. C.: *Bull. soc. chim. France*, **1955,** 922.
777. Moreau, R. C.: *Bull. soc. chim. France*, **1955,** 1044.
778. Moreau, R. C.: *Bull. soc. chim. France*, **1955,** 1049.
779. Morningstar, R. E.: *Dissertation Abstr.*, **18,** 1368 (1958).
780. Morrow, R. T., Cristol, S. J., and Van Dolah, R. W.: *J. Am. Chem. Soc.*, **75,** 4259 (1953).
781. Morton, M.: "Introduction to Rubber Technology," Reinhold Publishing Corporation, New York (1959).
782. Mosher, H. S.: The Chemistry of the Pyridines, in "Heterocyclic Compounds," vol. I, edited by R. C. Elderfield, John Wiley & Sons, Inc., New York (1950).
783. Muller, H., and Schmid, E.: *Monatsh.*, **85,** 719 (1954).
784. Mustafa, A., and Kamel, M.: *Science*, **118,** 411 (1953).
785. Muthmann, W.: *Z. Krist.*, **17,** 336 (1890).
786. Najer, H., Chabrier, P., Giudicelli, R., and Joannic-Voisinet, E.: *Compt. rend.*, **224,** 2935 (1957).
787. Nakasaki, M.: *J. Chem. Soc. Japan, Pure Chem. Sect.*, **74,** 403 (1953); *Chem. Abstracts*, **48,** 12017h (1954).
788. Nakasaki, M.: *J. Chem. Soc. Japan, Pure Chem. Sect.*, **74,** 405 (1953); *Chem. Abstracts*, **48,** 12018a (1954).
789. Nakatsuchi, A.: *J. Soc. Chem. Ind. Japan (Suppl. Binding)*, **33,** 408 (1930); *Chem. Abstracts*, **25,** 938 (1931).
790. Nakatsuchi, A.: *J. Soc. Chem. Ind. Japan (Suppl. Binding)*, **35,** 376 (1932); *Chem. Abstracts*, **26,** 5558 (1932).
791. Nakazaki, M.: *J. Inst. Polytech. Osaka City Univ.*, **2C,** No. 1, 19 (1951); *Chem. Abstracts*, **46,** 7067g (1952).
792. Naudé, S. M., and Christy, A.: *Phys. Rev.*, **37,** 490 (1931).
793. Naylor, M. A.: U.S. patent 2,610,980 (Sept. 16, 1952); *Chem. Abstracts*, **48,** 2775g (1954).
794. Naylor, M. A.: U.S. patent 2,640,077 (May 26, 1953).

795. Naylor, M. A.: U.S. patent 2,744,134 (May 1, 1956); *Chem. Abstracts*, **51**, 461b (1957).
796. Naylor, M. A., and Anderson, A. W.: *J. Am. Chem. Soc.*, **75**, 5392 (1953).
797. Naylor, M. A., and Anderson, A. W.: *J. Am. Chem. Soc.*, **75**, 5395 (1953).
798. Naylor, R. F.: *J. Chem. Soc.*, **1947**, 1532.
799. Naylor, R. F.: *J. Polymer Sci.*, **1**, 305 (1946).
800. Neureiter, N. P., and Bordwell, F. G.: *J. Am. Chem. Soc.*, **81**, 578 (1959).
801. Neureiter, N. P., and Bordwell, F. G.: *J. Am. Chem. Soc.*, **82**, 5354 (1960).
802. Newman, M. S.: *J. Org. Chem.*, **9**, 518 (1944).
803. Newman, M. S., and Lowrie, H. S.: *J. Am. Chem. Soc.*, **76**, 6196 (1954).
804. Nightingale, D., and Carpenter, R. A.: *J. Am. Chem. Soc.*, **71**, 3560 (1949).
805. Nozaki, K., and Bartlett, P. D.: *J. Am. Chem. Soc.*, **68**, 1686 (1946).
806. Oae, S., and Price, C. C.: *J. Am. Chem. Soc.*, **80**, 3425 (1958).
807. Oae, S., and Price, C. C.: *J. Am. Chem. Soc.*, **80**, 4938 (1958).
808. Oae, S., and Zalut, C.: *J. Am. Chem. Soc.*, **82**, 5359 (1960).
809. Oberhauser, F. B., Herrera, F. A., Muñoz, M. S., Torres, H. F., Wiehr, G., and Bertrand, J. T.: *Rev. quím. farm.*, **8**, 12 (1951); *Chem. Abstracts*, **46**, 4183i (1952).
810. O'Brien, J. L., and Gornick, F.: *J. Am. Chem. Soc.*, **77**, 4757 (1955).
811. Odioso, R. C., Parker, D. H., and Zabor, R. C.: *Ind. Eng. Chem.*, **51**, 921 (1959).
812. Ogg, R. A., and Polanyi, M.: *Trans. Faraday Soc.*, **31**, 482 (1935).
813. Oldham, K. G.: work cited by C. A. Vernon in *The Chemical Soc. Spec. Publ. No.* 8, p. 19 (1957).
814. Olsen, C. M., Hull, C. M., and France, W. G.: *Ind. Eng. Chem.*, **38**, 1273 (1946).
815. Olson, A. R., and Youle, P. V.: *J. Am. Chem. Soc.*, **62**, 1027 (1940).
816. Onyszchuk, M., and Sivertz, C.: *Can. J. Chem.*, **33**, 1034 (1955).
817. Orchin, M., and Woolfolk, E. O.: *J. Am. Chem. Soc.*, **67**, 122 (1945).
818. Orchin, M., Woolfolk, E. O., and Reggel, L.: *J. Am. Chem. Soc.*, **71**, 1126 (1949).
819. Otsu, T.: *J. Polymer Sci.*, **21**, 559 (1956).
820. Otsu, T., Nayatani, K., Muto, I., and Imai, M.: *Makromol. Chem.*, **27**, 142 (1958).
821. Ott, A. C., Mattano, L. A., and Coleman, G. H.: *J. Am. Chem. Soc.*, **68**, 2633, (1946).
822. Oughton, B. M., and Harrison, P. M.: *Acta Cryst.*, **10**, 479 (1957).
823. Overberger, C. G., Baldwin, D. E., and Gregor, H. P.: *J. Am. Chem. Soc.*, **72**, 4864 (1950).
824. Overberger, C. G., and Godfrey, J. J.: *J. Polymer Sci.*, **40**, 179 (1959).
825. Oyum, P., and Foss, O.: *Acta Chem. Scand.*, **9**, 1012 (1955).
826. Pallen, R. H., and Sivertz, C.: *Can. J. Chem.*, **35**, 723 (1957).
827. Palmer, K. J.: *J. Am. Chem. Soc.*, **60**, 2360 (1938).
828. Parham, W. E., and Gadsby, B.: *J. Org. Chem.*, **25**, 234 (1960).
829. Parham, W. E., and Harper, E. T.: *J. Am. Chem. Soc.*, **82**, 4936 (1960).
830. Parker, A. J., and Kharasch, N.: *Chem. Revs.*, **59**, 583 (1959).
831. Parker, A. J., and Kharasch, N.: *J. Am. Chem. Soc.*, **82**, 3071 (1960).
832. Parker, L. F. C.: *India Rubber J.*, **108**, 387 (1945).
833. Pascual Teresa, J. de, and Sánchez Bellido, H.: *Anales real soc. españ. fís. y quím. (Madrid)*, **52B**, 557 (1956); *Chem. Abstracts*, **51**, 6537b (1957).
834. Pascual Teresa, J. de, and Sánchez Bellido, H.: *Anales real soc. españ. fís. y quím. (Madrid)*, **52B**, 563 (1956); *Chem. Abstracts*, **51**, 6537f (1957).
835. Patrick, J. C.: *Trans. Faraday Soc.*, **32**, 347 (1936).
836. Patrick, T. M.: *J. Org. Chem.*, **17**, 1009 (1952).
837. Pattison, D. B., and Carmack, M.: *J. Am. Chem. Soc.*, **68**, 2033 (1946).
838. Pauling, L.: "The Nature of the Chemical Bond," 1st ed., Cornell University Press, Ithaca, N.Y. (1945).

839. Pauling, L.: "The Nature of the Chemical Bond," 3d ed., Cornell University Press, Ithaca, N.Y. (1960).
840. Pauling, L.: *Proc. Natl. Acad. Sci. U.S.*, **35,** 495 (1949).
841. Pauling, L., and Brockway, L. O.: *J. Am. Chem. Soc.*, **59,** 13 (1937).
842. Peachey, S. J., and Skipsey, A.: *J. Soc. Chem. Ind. (London)*, **40,** 5T (1921).
843. Pearson, R. G., and Dillon, R. L.: *J. Am. Chem. Soc.*, **75,** 2439 (1953).
844. Pearson, T. G., and Robinson, P. L.: *J. Chem. Soc.*, **1930,** 1473.
845. Penney, W. G., and Sutherland, G. B. B. M.: *J. Chem. Phys.*, **2,** 492 (1934).
846. Penney, W. G., and Sutherland, G. B. B. M.: *Trans. Faraday Soc.*, **30,** 898 (1934).
847. Pepper, D. C.: *Nature,* **158,** 789 (1946).
848. Perdock, W. G., and Terpstra, P.: *Rec. trav. chim.*, **62,** 687 (1943).
849. Peschanski, D.: *Compt. rend.*, **227,** 770 (1948).
850. Peters, E. M., and Smith, W. T.: *Proc. Iowa Acad. Sci.*, **57,** 211 (1950); *Chem. Abstracts,* **46,** 993g (1952).
850*a*. Peters, G.: *J. Am. Chem. Soc.*, **82,** 4751 (1960).
851. Phillips, G. M., Hunter, J. S., and Sutton, L. E.: *J. Chem. Soc.*, **1945,** 146.
852. Piechulek, W., and Suszko, J.: *Bull. intern. acad. polon., Class sci. math. nat.*, **1934A,** 455; *Chem. Abstracts,* **29,** 2933 (1935).
853. Pierson, R. M., Costanza, A. J., and Weinstein, A. H.: *J. Polymer Sci.*, **17,** 221 (1955).
854. Pines, H., Kvetinskas, B., and Ipatieff, V. N.: *J. Am. Chem. Soc.*, **77,** 343 (1955).
855. Pinkus, A. G., Kim, J. S., McAtee, J. L., and Concilio, C. B.: *J. Am. Chem. Soc.*, **79,** 4566 (1957).
856. Pinkus, A. G., Kim, J. S., McAtee, J. L., and Concilio, C. B.: *J. Am. Chem. Soc.*, **81,** 2652 (1959).
857. Pinkus, A. G., Kim, J. S., McAtee, J. L., and Concilio, C. B.: *J. Polymer Sci.*, **40,** 581 (1959).
857*a*. Pinkus, A. G., and McAtee, J. L.: *Chem. Eng. News,* **38,** 44 (Sept. 5, 1960).
858. Pinkus, A. G., and Piette, L. H.: *J. Phys. Chem.*, **63,** 2086 (1959).
859. Pitts, J. N., Thompson, D. D., and Woolfolk, R. W.: *J. Am. Chem. Soc.*, **80,** 66 (1958).
860. Pitzer, K. S.: "Quantum Chemistry," Prentice-Hall, Inc., Englewood Cliffs, N.J. (1953).
860*a*. Pitzer, K. S.: *J. Am. Chem. Soc.*, **79,** 1804 (1957).
861. Plattner, P. A.: Dehydrogenation with Sulfur, Selenium, and Platinum Metals, in "Newer Methods of Preparative Organic Chemistry," p. 21, first American edition, translated and revised by E. C. Armstrong, Interscience Publishers, Inc., New York (1948).
862. Pollard, C. B., and Braun, J. C.: *J. Am. Chem. Soc.*, **77,** 6685 (1955).
863. Pollard, F. H., and Jones, D. J.: Symposium on Recent Work on the Inorganic Chemistry of Sulfur, Bristol, 1958, in *Special Publication No.* 12, The Chemical Society, London (1958).
864. Porter, H. D.: *J. Am. Chem. Soc.*, **76,** 127 (1954).
865. Potter, E. B. V.: British patent 709,293 (May 19, 1954); *Chem. Abstracts,* **49,** 10374d (1955).
866. Powell, R. E., and Eyring, H.: *J. Am. Chem. Soc.*, **65,** 648 (1943).
867. Price, C. C.: *J. Polymer Sci.*, **1,** 83 (1946).
868. Price, C. C., and Hydock, J. J.: *J. Am. Chem. Soc.*, **74,** 1943 (1952).
869. Price, C. C., and Oae, S.: "Sulfur Bonding," The Ronald Press Company, New York (in press).
870. Price, C. C., and Schwarcz, M.: *J. Am. Chem. Soc.*, **62,** 2891 (1940).
871. Price, C. C., and Zomlefer, J.: *J. Am. Chem. Soc.*, **72,** 14 (1950).

872. Prins, J. A.: *Physica,* **20,** 124 (1954).
873. Prins, J. A., Schenk, J., and Hospel, P. A. M.: *Physica,* **22,** 770 (1956).
874. Prins, J. A., Schenk, J., and Wachters, L. H. J.: *Physica,* **23,** 746 (1957).
875. Pryor, W. A.: *J. Am. Chem. Soc.,* **80,** 6481 (1958).
876. Pryor, W. A.: *J. Am. Chem. Soc.,* **82,** 2715 (1960).
877. Pryor, W. A.: *J. Am. Chem. Soc.,* **82,** 4794 (1960).
877*a*. Pryor, W. A.: Abs. of Papers, Am. Chem. Soc. Meeting, Chicago, September, 1961, page 72Q.
877*b*. Pryor, W. A.: Unpublished data.
878. Pryor, W. A., and Ferstandig, L. L.: *J. Am. Chem. Soc.,* **82,** 283 (1960).
878*a*. Pryor, W. A., and Pickering, T. L.: To be published.
878*b*. Pryor, W. A., and Pultinas, E. P.: To be published.
879. Putnam, G. L., and Kobe, K. A.: *Trans. Electrochem. Soc.,* **74,** 1 (1938); *Chem. Abstracts,* **32,** 5707[2] (1938).
880. Radford, H. E., and Rice, F. O.: *J. Chem. Phys.,* **33,** 774 (1960).
880*a*. Raley, J. H., and Collamer, D. O.: *J. Am. Chem. Soc.,* **74,** 1606 (1952).
881. Raley, J. H., Rust, F. F., and Vaughan, W. E.: *J. Am. Chem. Soc.,* **70,** 1336 (1948).
882. Rankov, G., and Papov, A.: *Annuaire univ. Sofia, Fac. sci.,* **45,** 127 (1948–1949); *Chem. Abstracts,* **45,** 1995b (1951).
883. Rashevskaya, S.: *J. Gen. Chem. U.S.S.R.,* **10,** 1089 (1940); *Chem. Abstracts,* **35,** 3985[4] (1941).
884. Rasmussen, H. E., Hansford, R. C., and Sachanen, A. N.: *Ind. Eng. Chem.,* **38,** 376 (1946).
885. Rasmussen, H. E., and Ray, F. E.: *Chem. & Ind. (London),* **60,** 593 (1947).
886. Rasmussen, H. E., and Ray, F. E.: *Chem. & Ind. (London),* **60,** 620 (1947).
886*a*. Reid, E. E.: "Organic Chemistry of Sulfur" (in three volumes), Chemical Publishing Company, Inc. (1958–1961).
887. Reutov, O. A., Karpov, T. P., Uglova, E. V., and Malyanov, V. A.: *Izvest. Akad. Nauk S.S.S.R., Otdel. Khim. Nauk,* **1960,** 1311; *Chem. Abstracts,* **54,** 23637e (1960).
888. Rice, F. O., and Ditter, J.: *J. Am. Chem. Soc.,* **75,** 6066 (1953).
889. Rice, F. O., and Sparrow, C.: *J. Am. Chem. Soc.,* **75,** 848 (1953).
890. Rinehart, K. L., Curby, R. J., and Sokol, P. E.: *J. Am. Chem. Soc.,* **79,** 3420 (1957).
891. Rinker, R. G., Gordon, T. P., Mason, D. M., and Corcoran, W. H.: *J. Phys. Chem.,* **63,** 302 (1959).
892. Ripamonti, A., and Vacca, C.: *Ricerca Sci.,* **28,** 1880 (1958); *Chem. Abstracts,* **53,** 7711e (1959).
893. Ritter, J. J., and Sharpe, E. D.: *J. Am. Chem. Soc.,* **59,** 2351 (1937).
894. Roberts, J. D., McElhill, E. A., and Armstrong, R.: *J. Am. Chem. Soc.,* **71,** 2923 (1949).
895. Roberts, J. D., Streitwieser, A., and Regan, C. M.: *J. Am. Chem. Soc.,* **74,** 4579 (1952).
896. Roberts, R. M., and Cheng, C.: *J. Org. Chem.,* **23,** 983 (1958).
897. Rogers, M. T., Barrow, G. M., and Bordwell, F. G.: *J. Am. Chem. Soc.,* **78,** 1790 (1956).
898. Roncari, H.: *Ing. chim.,* **17,** 229 (1933); *Chem. Abstracts,* **28,** 3723[7] (1934).
899. Ross, G. W.: *J. Chem. Soc.,* **1958,** 2856.
900. Rothstein, E.: *J. Chem. Soc.,* **1937,** 309.
901. Rothstein, E.: *J. Chem. Soc.,* **1940,** 1550.

902. Rothstein, E.: *J. Chem. Soc.*, **1940,** 1553.
903. Rothstein, E.: *J. Chem. Soc.*, **1940,** 1558.
904. Rueggeberg, W. H. C., Chernack, J., Rose, I. M., and Reid, E. E.: *J. Am. Chem. Soc.*, **70,** 2292 (1948).
905. Rueggeberg, W. H. C., Cook, J., and Reid, E. E.: *J. Org. Chem.*, **13,** 110 (1948).
906. Ruhrchemie, A. G.: British patent 709,573 (May 26, 1954); *Chem. Abstracts*, **49,** 11003h (1955).
907. Runge, F., Jumar, A., and Held, P.: *J. prakt. Chem.*, **8,** 44 (1959).
908. Russell, G. A.: *J. Am. Chem. Soc.*, **78,** 1047 (1956).
909. Russell, G. A.: *J. Am. Chem. Soc.*, **79,** 3781 (1957).
910. Russell, G. A.: *J. Org. Chem.*, **23,** 1407 (1958).
911. Russell, G. A., and Brown, H. C.: *J. Am. Chem. Soc.*, **77,** 4578 (1955).
912. Russell, K. E.: *J. Phys. Chem.*, **58,** 437 (1954).
913. Ruzicka, L.: Constitution and Relationships in the Sesquiterpene Series, in *Fortschr. Chem.*, **19A,** No. 5, p. 1 (1928).
914. Ruzicka, L., Meyer, J., and Mingazzini, M.: *Helv. Chim. Acta*, **5,** 345 (1922).
915. Ruzicka, L., and Rudolph, E. A.: *Helv. Chim. Acta*, **10,** 915 (1927).
916. Ruzicka, L., and Seidel, C. F.: *Helv. Chim. Acta*, **5,** 369 (1922).
917. Ruzicka, L., and van Veen, A. G.: *Ann.*, **468,** 133 (1929).
918. Ruzicka, L., and van Veen, A. G.: *Ann.*, **468,** 143 (1929).
919. Ryle, A. P., and Sanger, F.: *Biochem. J.*, **60,** 535 (1955).
920. Samén, E.: *Arkiv Kemi, Mineral., Geol.*, **24B,** No. 6 (1947); *Chem. Abstracts*, **42,** 6313f (1948).
921. Samén, E.: *Arkiv Kemi*, **1,** 231 (1949); *Chem. Abstracts*, **44,** 1400d (1950).
922. Samuel, D., and Westheimer, F. H.: *Chem. & Ind. (London)*, **1959,** 51.
923. Sanger, F.: *Nature*, **171,** 1025 (1953).
924. Saville, R. W.: *J. Chem. Soc.*, **1958,** 2880.
925. Schaafsma, Y., Bickel, A. F., and Kooyman, E. C.: *Rec. trav. chim.*, **76,** 180 (1957).
926. Schaafsma, Y., Bickel, A. F., and Kooyman, E. C.: *Tetrahedron*, **10,** 76 (1960).
927. Schaefer, H. F.: *Proc. Indiana Acad. Sci.*, **59,** 153 (1950); *Chem. Abstracts*, **45,** 8485f (1951).
928. Schaeffer, H. F., and Palmer, G. D.: *J. Chem. Educ.*, **17,** 473 (1940).
929. Scheele, W., and Birgham, K.: *Kautschuk u. Gummi*, **10,** WT 214 (1957); *Chem. Abstracts*, **52,** 775e (1958).
930. Scheele, W., Birgham, K., and Schlüter, G.: *Kolloid-Z.*, **160,** 173 (1958); *Chem. Abstracts*, **53,** 3754f (1959).
931. Scheele, W., and Franck, A.: *Kautschuk u. Gummi*, **11,** WT 51 (1958); *Chem. Abstracts*, **52,** 9641b (1958).
932. Schenk, J.: *Physica*, **23,** 325 (1957).
933. Schenk, P. W., and Thümmler, U.: *Z. Elektrochem.*, **63,** 1002 (1959).
934. Schmidt, M., and Talsky, G.: *Ber.*, **90,** 1673 (1957).
935. Schmidt, U., Lüttringhaus, A., and Trefzger, H.: *Ann.*, **631,** 129 (1960).
936. Schmitt, J., and Lespagnol, A.: *Compt. rend.*, **230,** 551 (1950).
937. Schmitt, J., and Suquet, M.: *Bull. soc. chim. France*, **1955,** 84.
938. Schmitt, J., and Suquet, M.: *Bull. soc. chim. France*, **1956,** 755.
939. Schöberl, A., Tausent, H., and Gräfje, H.: *Naturwissenschaften*, **43,** 445 (1956).
940. Schomaker, V., and Pauling, L.: *J. Am. Chem. Soc.*, **61,** 1769 (1939).
941. Schomaker, V., and Stevenson, D. P.: *J. Am. Chem. Soc.*, **63,** 37 (1941).
942. Schönberg, A., and Amiz, G.: *J. Org. Chem.*, **22,** 1677 (1957).
943. Schönberg, A., and Barakat, M. Z.: *J. Chem. Soc.*, **1949,** 892.

944. Schönberg, A., and Mustafa, A.: *J. Chem. Soc.*, **1949,** 889.
945. Schönberg, A., Mustafa, A., and Askar, W.: *Science,* **109,** 522 (1949).
946. Schönberg, A., Rupp, E., and Gumlich, W.: *Ber.*, **66,** 1932 (1933).
947. Schönberg, A., Stephenson, A., Kaltschmitt, H., Pettersen, E., and Schulten, H.: *Ber.*, **B66,** 237 (1933); *Chem. Abstracts,* **27,** 2149 (1933).
948. Schotte, L.: *Arkiv Kemi,* **8,** 579 (1955).
949. Schotte, L.: *Arkiv Kemi,* **9,** 361 (1956).
950. Schulek, E., and Koros, E.: *Acta Chim. Acad. Sci. Hung.*, **3,** 125 (1953); *Chem. Abstracts,* **47,** 10390e (1953).
951. Schulek, E., and Koros, E.: *Magyar Kém Folyóirat,* **56,** 426 (1950); *Chem. Abstracts,* **46,** 1380f (1952).
952. Schulek, E., Koros, E., and Maros, L.: *Acta Chim. Acad. Sci. Hung.*, **10,** 291 (1956); *Chem. Abstracts,* **51,** 5611g (1957).
952*a*. Schwarzenbach, G., and Egli, H. A.: *Helv. Chim. Acta,* **17,** 1176 (1934).
953. Schwarzenbach, G., and Fischer, A.: *Helv. Chim. Acta,* **43,** 1365 (1960).
954. Schwenk, E., and Papa, D.: *J. Org. Chem.*, **11,** 798 (1946).
955. Scott, A. B.: *J. Am. Chem. Soc.*, **71,** 3145 (1949).
956. Scott, C. E., and Price, C. C.: *J. Am. Chem. Soc.*, **81,** 2670 (1959).
957. Scott, C. E., and Price, C. C.: *J. Am. Chem. Soc.*, **81,** 2672 (1959).
958. Scott, D. W., Finke, H. L., Gross, M. E., Guthrie, G. B., and Huffman, H. M.: *J. Am. Chem. Soc.*, **72,** 2424 (1950).
959. Scott, D. W., Finke, H. L., McCullough, J. P., Gross, M. E., Pennington, R. E., and Waddington, G.: *J. Am. Chem. Soc.*, **74,** 2478 (1952).
960. Scott, W., and Bedford, C. W.: *Ind. Eng. Chem.*, **13,** 126 (1921).
961. Scott, W., and Watt, G. W.: *J. Org. Chem.*, **2,** 148 (1937).
962. Selker, M. L., and Kemp, A. R.: *Ind. Eng. Chem.*, **36,** 20 (1944).
963. Selker, M. L., and Kemp, A. R.: *Ind. Eng. Chem.*, **39,** 895 (1947).
964. Selwood, P. W.: "Magnetochemistry," 2d ed., Interscience Publishers, Inc., New York (1956).
965. Sexton, A. R., and Britton, E. C.: *J. Am. Chem. Soc.*, **70,** 3606 (1948).
966. Shantz, E. M., and Rittenberg, D.: *J. Am. Chem. Soc.*, **68,** 2109 (1946).
967. Sharada, K., and Vasudeva Murthy, A. R.: *Z. anorg. u. allgem. Chem.*, **306,** 196 (1960).
967*a*. Shavitt, I.: *J. Chem. Phys.*, **31,** 1359 (1959).
968. Shaw, E. J., and Phipps, T. E.: *Phys. Rev.*, **38,** 174 (1931).
969. Shchukina, M. N., and Predvoditeleva, G. S.: *Proc. Acad. Sci. U.S.S.R. Chem. Sect.* (Eng. transl.), **110,** 565 (1956); *Chem. Abstracts,* **51,** 4996b (1957).
970. Shelton, J. R., and McDonel, E. T.: *Rubber Chem. and Technol.*, **33,** 342 (1960).
971. Sheppard, N., and Sutherland, G. B. B. M.: *J. Chem. Soc.*, **1947,** 1540.
972. Shioda, H., and Kato, S.: *J. Soc. Org. Synthet. Chem. Japan,* **15,** 361 (1957); *Chem. Abstracts,* **51,** 16393e (1957).
973. Shirley, D. A., and Roussel, P. A.: *Science,* **113,** 208 (1951).
974. Short, W. F., Stromberg, H., and Wiles, A. E.: *J. Chem. Soc.*, **1936,** 319.
975. Shostakovskiĭ, M. F., Prilezhaeva, E. N., and Shapiro, E. S.: *Izvest. Akad. Nauk, S.S.S.R., Otdel. Khim. Nauk,* **1955,** 734; *Chem. Abstracts,* **50,** 7080f (1956).
976. Shriner, R. L., Struck, H. C., and Jorison, W. J.: *J. Am. Chem. Soc.*, **52,** 2060 (1930).
977. Sice, J.: *J. Phys. Chem.*, **64,** 1573 (1960).
978. Siebert, H.: *Z. anorg. Chem.*, **271,** 65 (1952).
979. Siebert, H.: *Z. anorg. u. allgem. Chem.*, **275,** 210 (1954).

980. Sime, J. G., and Abrahams, S. C.: *Acta Cryst.*, **13,** 1 (1960).
981. Simonsen, J., and Barton, D. H. R.: "The Terpenes," vol. 3, pp. 2–3, Cambridge University Press, New York, 1952.
982. Sivertz, C.: *J. Phys. Chem.*, **63,** 34 (1959) and private communications.
983. Sivertz, S., Andrews, W., Elsdon, W., and Graham, K.: *J. Polymer Sci.*, **19,** 587 (1956).
984. Skell, P. E.: Private communication.
985. Skell, P. S., and Allen, R. G.: *J. Am. Chem. Soc.*, **82,** 1511 (1960).
986. Skell, P. S., and Woodworth, R. C.: *J. Am. Chem. Soc.*, **77,** 4638 (1955).
987. Skell, P. S., Woodworth, R. C., and McNamara, J. H.: *J. Am. Chem. Soc.*, **79,** 1253 (1957).
988. Skjerven, O.: *Kolloid Z.*, **152,** 75 (1957); *Chem. Abstracts,* **51,** 14354e (1957).
989. Slaugh, L. H.: *J. Am. Chem. Soc.*, **81,** 2262 (1959).
990. Slaugh, L. H., and Raley, J. H.: *J. Am. Chem. Soc.*, **82,** 1259 (1960).
991. Slobodkin, N. R., and Kharasch, N.: *J. Am. Chem. Soc.*, **82,** 5837 (1960).
992. Slobodkin, N. R., and Kharasch, N.: *J. Org. Chem.*, **25,** 866 (1960).
993. Smiles, S., and Hutchinson, A. M.: *J. Chem. Soc.*, **101,** 570 (1912).
994. Smith, W. V.: *J. Am. Chem. Soc.*, **68,** 2059 (1946).
995. Société pour l'industrie chimique à Bâle (CIBA Ltd.): British patent 558,774 (Jan. 20, 1944); *Chem. Abstracts,* **41,** 488g (1947).
996. Solimene, N., and Dailey, B. P.: *Phys. Rev.*, **91,** 464 (1953).
997. Sørum, H.: *Acta Chem. Scand.*, **7,** 1 (1953).
998. Sørum, H., and Foss, O.: *Acta Chem. Scand.*, **3,** 987 (1949).
999. Specker, H.: *Z. anorg. Chem.*, **261,** 116 (1950).
1000. Spindt, R. S., and Stevens, D. R.: U.S. patent 2,470,876 (May 24, 1949); *Chem. Abstracts,* **43,** 7501c (1949).
1001. Spindt, R. S., Stevens, D. R., and Baldwin, W. E.: *J. Am. Chem. Soc.*, **73,** 3693 (1951).
1002. Staněk, J.: *Collection Czechoslov. Chem. Communs.*, **12,** 671 (1947); *Chem. Abstracts,* **42,** 5876i (1948).
1003. Staněk, J.: *Chem. Listy,* **41,** 159 (1947); *Chem. Abstracts,* **45,** 583a (1951).
1004. Staněk, J.: *Chem. Listy,* **45,** 224 (1951); *Chem. Abstracts,* **46,** 2528d (1952).
1005. Staněk, J.: *Collection Czechoslov. Chem. Communs.*, **15,** 392 (1950); *Chem. Listy.* **44,** 253 (1950); *Chem. Abstracts,* **45,** 5136g, 10224c (1951).
1006. Stanley, E.: *Acta Cryst.*, **6,** 187 (1953).
1007. Staudinger, H., and Freudenberger, H.: *Ber.*, **61,** 1576 (1928).
1008. Steinrauf, L. K., Peterson, J., and Jensen, L. H.: *J. Am. Chem. Soc.*, **80,** 3835 (1958).
1009. Stepukhovich, A. D.: *Zhur. Priklad. Khim.*, **22,** 605 (1949); *Chem. Abstracts,* **45,** 2703d (1951).
1010. Stevenson, D. P., and Beach, J. Y.: *J. Am. Chem. Soc.*, **60,** 2872 (1938).
1011. Stevenson, D. P., and Cooley, R. A.: *J. Am. Chem. Soc.*, **62,** 2477 (1940).
1012. Stevenson, D. P., and Russell, H.: *J. Am. Chem. Soc.*, **61,** 3264 (1939).
1013. Stewart, J. M., and Cordts, H. P.: *J. Am. Chem. Soc.*, **74,** 5880 (1952).
1014. Stirling, C. J. M.: *Chem. & Ind. (London),* **1960,** 933.
1015. Stockmayer, W. H., Howard, R. O., and Clarke, J. T.: *J. Am. Chem. Soc.*, **75,** 1756 (1953).
1016. Strandberg, M. W. P., Wentink, T., and Kyhl, R. L.: *Phys. Rev.*, **75,** 270 (1949).
1017. Straw, H. A.: U.S. patent 2,640,078 (May 26, 1953); *Chem. Abstracts,* **48,** 3995h (1954).

1018. Strecker, W., and Spitaler, R.: *Ber.*, **59,** 1754 (1926).
1019. Streitwieser, A.: *Chem. Revs.*, **56,** 571 (1958).
1020. Streitwieser, A.: *Tetrahedron Letters*, **6,** 23 (1960).
1021. Streitwieser, A., and van Sickle, D. E.: Abstracts of Papers, Organic Chemistry Symposium of the ACS, p. 74, Seattle, Wash., June 15, 1959.
1022. Strickland, T. H., and Bell, A.: Abstracts of Papers, p. 23-P, ACS Meeting, Atlantic City, N.J., Sept., 1959.
1023. Strickland, T. H., and Bell, A.: U.S. patent 2,821,552 (Jan. 28, 1958).
1024. Studebaker, M. L., and Nabors, L. G.: *Rubber Chem. and Technol.*, **32,** 941 (1959).
1025. Suter, C. M., and Maxwell, C. E.: *Org. Syntheses*, **18,** 64 (1938).
1026. Sutton, L. E., and Hampson, G. C.: *Trans. Faraday Soc.*, **31,** 945 (1935).
1027. Swain, C. G., and Scott, C. B.: *J. Am. Chem. Soc.*, **75,** 141 (1953).
1028. Swain, C. G., Stockmayer, W. H., and Clarke, J. T.: *J. Am. Chem. Soc.*, **72,** 5426 (1950).
1029. Symons, M. C. R.: *J. Chem. Soc.*, **1954,** 3676.
1030. Symons, M. C. R.: *J. Chem. Soc.*, **1957,** 2440.
1031. Symons, M. C. R.: *Quart. Revs.*, **13,** 99 (1959).
1032. Szmant, H. H., and Brost, G. A.: *J. Am. Chem. Soc.*, **73,** 4175 (1951).
1033. Szmant, H. H., and Lapinski, R. L.: *J. Am. Chem. Soc.*, **74,** 4395 (1952).
1034. Szmant, H. H., and Suld, G.: *J. Am. Chem. Soc.*, **78,** 3400 (1956).
1035. Szperl, L.: *Roczniki Chem.*, **ii,** 291 (1923); *Chem. Abstracts*, **18,** 1290 (1924).
1036. Szperl, L.: *Roczniki Chem.*, **6,** 728 (1926); *Chem. Abstracts*, **21,** 3603 (1927).
1037. Szwarc, M., Leight, C. H., and Sehon, A. H.: *J. Chem. Phys.*, **19,** 657 (1951).
1038. Tanasescu, I., and Nanu, I.: *Ber.*, **72B,** 1083 (1939); *Chem. Abstracts*, **33,** 5825[9] (1939).
1039. Tarbell, D. S., and Lovett, W. E.: *J. Am. Chem. Soc.*, **78,** 2259 (1956).
1040. Tarbell, D. S., and McCall, M. A.: *J. Am. Chem. Soc.*, **74,** 48 (1952).
1041. Tartar, H. V., and Draves, C. Z.: *J. Am. Chem. Soc.*, **46,** 574 (1924).
1042. Taylor, P. G., and Beevers, C. A.: *Acta Cryst.*, **5,** 341 (1952).
1043. Thain, E. M.: Private communication to C. A. Vernon cited in *Chem. Soc. Spec. Publ. No.* 8, p. 30 (1957).
1044. Thayer, H. I.: U.S. patent 2,496,319 (Feb. 7, 1950).
1045. Thayer, H. I., and Corson, B. B.: *J. Am. Chem. Soc.*, **70,** 2330 (1948).
1046. Thiel, M., and Asinger, F.: *Ann.*, **610,** 17 (1957).
1047. Thiel, M., Asinger, F., and Schmiedel, K.: *Ann.*, **611,** 121 (1958).
1048. Thiel, M., Asinger, F., and Trümpler, G.: *Ann.*, **619,** 137 (1958).
1049. Thomas, W. J., and Strickland-Constable, R. F.: *Trans. Faraday Soc.*, **53,** 972 (1957).
1050. Tillett, J. G.: *J. Chem. Soc.*, **1960,** 37.
1051. Tinyakova, E. I., Dolgoplosk, B. A., and Tikhomolova, M. P.: *J. Gen. Chem. U.S.S.R.* (Eng. transl.), **25,** 1333 (1955); *Chem. Abstracts*, **50,** 4810c (1956).
1052. Tinyakova, E. I., Khrennikova, E. K., and Dolgoplosk, B. A.: *J. Gen. Chem. U.S.S.R.* (Eng. transl.), **28,** 1682 (1958); *Chem. Abstracts*, **53,** 1177c (1959).
1053. Tinyakova, E. I., Khrennikova, E. K., Dolgoplosk, B. A., Reich, V. N., and Zhuravleva, T. G.: *J. Gen. Chem. U.S.S.R.* (Eng. transl.), **26,** 2767 (1956).
1054. Tobolsky, A. V., and Baysal, B.: *J. Am. Chem. Soc.*, **75,** 1757 (1953).
1055. Tobolsky, A. V., and Eisenberg, A.: *J. Am. Chem. Soc.*, **81,** 780 (1959).
1056. Tobolsky, A. V., and Eisenberg, A.: *J. Am. Chem. Soc.*, **82,** 289 (1960).
1057. Tobolsky, A. V., and Mesrobian, R. B.: "Organic Peroxides," Interscience Publishers, Inc., New York (1954).
1058. Toennies, G., and Lavine, T. F.: *J. Biol. Chem.*, **113,** 571 (1936).

1059. Toland, W. G.: *J. Am. Chem. Soc.*, **82,** 1911 (1960).
1060. Toland, W. G.: Preprints, ACS., Division of Petroleum Chemistry, **5,** C-15 (1960).
1061. Toland, W. G.: U.S. patent 2,531,172 (Nov. 21, 1950).
1062. Toland, W. G.: U.S. patent 2,587,666 (Mar. 4, 1952).
1063. Toland, W. G.: U.S. patent 2,670,370 (Feb. 23, 1954).
1064. Toland, W. G.: U.S. patent 2,695,313 (Nov. 23, 1954).
1065. Toland, W. G.: U.S. patent 2,722,473 (Nov. 1, 1955).
1066. Toland, W. G.: U.S. patent 2,722,546 (Nov. 1, 1955).
1067. Toland, W. G.: U.S. patent 2,722,547 (Nov. 1, 1955).
1068. Toland, W. G.: U.S. patent 2,722,549 (Nov. 1, 1955).
1069. Toland, W. G.: U.S. patent 2,783,266 (Feb. 26, 1957).
1070. Toland, W. G.: U.S. patent 2,845,449 (July 29, 1958).
1071. Toland, W. G.: U.S. patent 2,856,424 (Oct. 14, 1958).
1072. Toland, W. G.: U.S. patent 2,900,412 (Aug. 18, 1959).
1073. Toland, W. G., Hagmann, D. L., Wilkes, J. B., and Brutschy, F. J.: *J. Am. Chem. Soc.*, **80,** 5423 (1958).
1074. Toland, W. G., and Wilkes, J. B.: *J. Am. Chem. Soc.*, **76,** 307 (1954).
1075. Toland, W. G., Wilkes, J. B., and Brutschy, F. J.: *J. Am. Chem. Soc.*, **75,** 2263 (1953).
1076. Tolberg, R. S., and Pitts, J. N.: *J. Am. Chem. Soc.*, **80,** 1304 (1958).
1077. Tompson, C. W., and Gingrich, N. S.: *J. Chem. Phys.*, **31,** 1598 (1959).
1078. Toussaint, J.: *Bull. soc. chim. Belg.*, **54,** 319 (1945).
1079. Townes, C. H., and Dailey, B. P.: *J. Chem. Phys.*, **17,** 782 (1949).
1080. Truce, W. E., and Boudakian, M. M.: *J. Am. Chem. Soc.*, **78,** 2748 (1956).
1081. Truce, W. E., and Boudakian, M. M., Heine, R. F., and McManimie, R. J.: *J. Am. Chem. Soc.*, **78,** 2743 (1956).
1082. Truce, W. E., and Goldhamer, D. L.: *J. Am. Chem. Soc.*, **81,** 5795 (1959).
1083. Truce, W. E., and Goldhamer, D. L.: *J. Am. Chem. Soc.*, **81,** 5798 (1959).
1084. Truce, W. E., Goldhamer, D. L., and Kruse, R. B.: *J. Am. Chem. Soc.*, **81,** 4931 (1959).
1085. Truce, W. E., and Knospe, R. H.: *J. Am. Chem. Soc.*, **77,** 5063 (1955).
1086. Truce, W. E., and Kruse, R. B.: *J. Am. Chem. Soc.*, **81,** 5372 (1959).
1087. Tsurugi, J.: *J. Chem. Soc. Japan, Pure Chem. Sect.*, **76,** 190 (1955) and private communication.
1088. Tsurugi, J.: *Nippon Kagaku Zasshi*, **77,** 1716 (1956); *Chem. Abstracts*, **53,** 3856e (1959).
1089. Tsurugi, J.: *Rubber Chem. and Technol.*, **31,** 762 (1958); *Bull. Univ. Osaka Pref.*, **A5,** 161 (1957); *Chem. Abstracts*, **51,** 15987c, 17846g (1957).
1090. Tsurugi, J.: *Rubber Chem. and Technol.*, **31,** 769 (1958); *Bull. Univ. Osaka Pref.*, **A5,** 169 (1957); *Chem. Abstracts*, **51,** 17846i, 15987d (1957).
1091. Tsurugi, J.: *Rubber Chem. and Technol.*, **31,** 773 (1958); *Bull. Univ. Osaka Pref.*, **A5,** 173 (1957); *Chem. Abstracts*, **51,** 17847b (1957).
1092. Tsurugi, J., and Fukuda, H.: *Rubber Chem. and Technol.*, **31,** 788 (1958); *Bull. Univ. Osaka Pref.*, **A6,** 145 (1958).
1093. Tsurugi, J., and Fukuda, H.: *Rubber Chem. and Technol.*, **31,** 800 (1958); *J. Soc. Chem. Ind. Japan*, **60,** 362 (1957); *Chem. Abstracts*, **53,** 8070b (1959).
1094. Tsurugi, J., and Nakabayashi, T.: *J. Org. Chem.*, **24,** 807 (1959).
1095. Tsurugi, J., and Nakabayashi, T.: *J. Org. Chem.*, **25,** 1744 (1960).
1096. Tsurugi, J., and Nakabayashi, T.: *Rubber Chem. and Technol.*, **31,** 779 (1958); *Bull. Univ. Osaka Pref.*, **A5,** 135 (1958); *Chem. Abstracts*, **51,** 17847d (1957), **53,** 2670 (1959).

1097. Tsurugi, J., Nakabayashi, T., and Yamanaka, T.: *J. Chem. Soc. Japan,* **77,** 578 (1956); *Chem. Abstracts,* **52,** 9047i (1958).
1098. Tuller, W. N.: "The Sulfur Data Book," McGraw-Hill Book Company, Inc., New York (1954).
1099. Turner, D. L.: *J. Am. Chem. Soc.,* **70,** 3961 (1948).
1100. Turner, D. L.: *J. Am. Chem. Soc.,* **72,** 3823 (1950).
1101. VanderWerf, C. A., McEwen, W. E., and Zanger, M.: *J. Am. Chem. Soc.,* **81,** 3806 (1959).
1102. Varga, J., and Benedek, P.: *Magyar Kém. Folyóirat,* **56,** 36 (1950); *Chem. Abstracts,* **45,** 1947h (1951).
1103. Vaughan, W. E., and Rust, F. F.: *J. Org. Chem.,* **7,** 472 (1942).
1104. Vernon, C. A.: *Chem. Soc. Spec. Publ. No.* 8, 17 (1957).
1105. Vesterberg, A.: *Ber.,* **36,** 1903 (1903).
1106. Vigide, F. G., and Hermida, A. L.: *Inform. quím anal.* (*Madrid*), **13,** 61 (1959); *Chem. Abstracts,* **54,** 5314c (1960).
1107. Voge, H. H.: *J. Am. Chem. Soc.,* **61,** 1032 (1939).
1108. Voge, H. H., and Libby, W. F.: *J. Am. Chem. Soc.,* **59,** 2474 (1937).
1109. Vogel, A. I.: *J. Chem. Soc.,* **1948,** 1833.
1110. Vogel, A. I., Cresswell, W. T., Jeffery, G. H., and Leicester, J.: *J. Chem. Soc.,* **1952,** 514.
1111. Voronkov, M. G., and Broun, A. S.: *J. Gen. Chem. U.S.S.R.* (Eng. transl.), **19,** 395a (1949); *Chem. Abstracts,* **44,** 1955g, 6413i (1950).
1112. Voronkov, M. G., and Broun, A. S.: *Zhur. Obshcheĭ Khim.,* **18,** 70 (1948); *Chem. Abstracts,* **42,** 5007h (1948).
1113. Voronkov, M. G., Broun, A. S., Karpenko, G. B., and Gol'shteĭn, B. L.: *J. Gen. Chem. U.S.S.R.* (Eng. transl.), **19,** 1357 (1949); *Chem. Abstracts,* **44,** 1955b (1950).
1114. Voronkov, M. G., and Gol'shteĭn, B. L.: *Zhur. Obshcheĭ Khim.,* **20,** 1218 (1950); *J. Gen. Chem. U.S.S.R.* (Eng. transl.), **20,** 1263 (1950); *Chem. Abstracts,* **45,** 1577c (1951), **46,** 3531d (1952).
1115. Wall, L. A., and Brown, D. W.: *J. Polymer Sci.,* **14,** 513 (1954).
1116. Walling, C.: "Free Radicals in Solution," John Wiley & Sons, Inc., New York (1957).
1117. Walling, C.: Abstracts of Papers, Organic Chemistry Symposium of the ACS, p. 83, Seattle, Wash., June 19, 1959.
1118. Walling, C.: *J. Am. Chem. Soc.,* **70,** 2561 (1948).
1119. Walling, C., Basedow, O. H., and Savas, E. S.: *J. Am. Chem. Soc.,* **82,** 2181 (1960).
1120. Walling, C., Briggs, E. R., Wolfstirn, K. B., and Mayo, F. R.: *J. Am. Chem. Soc.,* **70,** 1537 (1948).
1121. Walling, C., and Helmreich, W.: *J. Am. Chem. Soc.,* **81,** 1144 (1959).
1122. Walling, C., and Jacknow, B. B.: *J. Am. Chem. Soc.,* **82,** 6108 (1960).
1123. Walling, C., Jacknow, B. B., and Thaler, W.: Abstracts of Papers, ACS Meeting, p. 59-P, Atlantic City, N. J., Sept., 1959.
1124. Walling, C., and McElhill, E. A.: *J. Am. Chem. Soc.,* **73,** 2927 (1951).
1125. Walling, C., and Miller, B.: *J. Am. Chem. Soc.,* **79,** 4181 (1957).
1126. Walling, C., and Rabinowitz, R.: *J. Am. Chem. Soc.,* **81,** 1137 (1959).
1127. Walling, C., Seymour, D., and Wolfstirn, K. B.: *J. Am. Chem. Soc.,* **70,** 1544 (1948).
1128. Walling, C., Seymour, D., and Wolfstirn, K. B.: *J. Am. Chem. Soc.,* **70,** 2559 (1948).

1128*a*. Walsh, A. D.: *Trans. Faraday Soc.*, **43,** 60 (1947).
1129. Walton, J. H., and Parsons, L. B.: *J. Am. Chem. Soc.*, **43,** 2539 (1921).
1130. Walton, J. H., and Witford, E. L.: *J. Am. Chem. Soc.*, **45,** 601 (1923).
1131. Wang, C. H., and Cohen, S. G.: *J. Am. Chem. Soc.*, **79,** 1924 (1957).
1132. Wang, C. H., and Cohen, S. G.: *J. Am. Chem. Soc.*, **81,** 3005 (1959).
1133. Warren, B. E., and Burwell, J. T.: *J. Chem. Phys.*, **3,** 6 (1935).
1134. Wegler, R., Kuehle, E., and Schaefer, W.: *Angew. Chem.*, **70,** 351 (1958).
1135. Weitkamp, A. W.: *J. Am. Chem. Soc.*, **81,** 3430 (1959).
1136. Weitkamp, A. W.: *J. Am. Chem. Soc.*, **81,** 3434 (1959).
1137. Weitkamp, A. W.: *J. Am. Chem. Soc.*, **81,** 3437 (1959).
1138. Wells, A. F.: *J. Chem. Soc.*, **1949,** 55.
1139. Wells, A. F.: "Structural Inorganic Chemistry," Oxford University Press, New York (1950).
1140. Wertz, J. E., and Vivo, J. L.: *J. Chem. Phys.*, **23,** 2193 (1955).
1141. Wessely, F., and Grill, F.: *Monatsh.*, **77,** 282 (1947).
1142. Wessely, F., and Siegel, A.: *Monatsh.*, **82,** 607 (1951).
1143. Westheimer, F. H.: *Chem. Soc. Spec. Publ. No.* 8, 1 (1957).
1144. Westlake, H. E.: *Chem. Revs.*, **39,** 219 (1946).
1145. Westlake, H. E., and Dougherty, G.: *J. Am. Chem. Soc.*, **63,** 658 (1941).
1146. Westlake, H. E., Laquer, H. L., and Smyth, C. P.: *J. Am. Chem. Soc.*, **72,** 436 (1950).
1147. Wheatley, P. J.: *Acta Cryst.*, **6,** 369 (1953).
1148. Wheeler, T. S., and Francis, W.: U.S. patent 1,907,274; *Chem. Abstracts,* **26,** 3342 (1932), **27,** 3487 (1933).
1149. Wheland, G. W.: "Resonance in Organic Chemistry," John Wiley & Sons, Inc., New York (1955).
1150. Whitney, R. B., and Calvin, M.: *J. Chem. Phys.*, **23,** 1750 (1955).
1151. Willgerodt, C.: *Ber.*, **20,** 2467 (1887).
1152. Willgerodt, C.: *Ber.*, **21,** 534 (1888).
1153. Willgerodt, C., and Merk, F. H.: *J. prakt. Chem.* [2], **80,** 192 (1909).
1154. Williams, A. L., Oberright, E. A., and Brooks, J. W.: *J. Am. Chem. Soc.*, **78,** 1190 (1956).
1155. Wilson, I. R., and Harris, G. M.: *J. Am. Chem. Soc.*, **82,** 4515 (1960).
1156. Wilson, K. B.: British patent 796,726; *Chem. Abstracts,* **53,** 261a (1959).
1157. Wilson, M. K., and Badger, R. M.: *J. Chem. Phys.*, **17,** 1232 (1949).
1158. Winstein, S., Grunwald, E., Buckles, R. E., and Hanson, C.: *J. Am. Chem. Soc.*, **70,** 828 (1948).
1159. Winstein, S., Heck, R., Lapporte, S., and Baird, R.: *Experientia,* **12,** 138 (1956).
1160. Winter, E. R. S., and Briscoe, H. V. A.: *J. Chem. Soc.*, **1942,** 631.
1161. Woodrow, C. C., Carmack, M., and Miller, J. G.: *J. Chem. Phys.*, **19,** 951 (1951).
1162. Wuyts, H.: *Bull. soc. chim.*, **35,** 166 (1906).
1163. Wyckoff, R. W. G.: "Crystal Structures," vol. 1, chap. 5, p. 24, Interscience Publishers, Inc., New York (1948).
1164. Wynberg, H.: *J. Am. Chem. Soc.*, **80,** 364 (1958).
1165. Yakel, H. L., and Hughes, E. W.: *Acta Cryst.*, **7,** 291 (1954).
1166. Yukawa, Y., and Kishi, Y.: *Mem. Inst. Sci. and Ind. Research, Osaka Univ.*, **8,** 163 (1951); *J. Chem. Soc. Japan, Pure Chem. Sect.*, **72,** 371 (1951); *Chem. Abstracts,* **46,** 7061b (1952).
1167. Yukawa, Y., Tokuda, F., and Amono, S.: *J. Chem. Soc. Japan, Pure Chem. Sect.*, **73,** 498 (1952); *Chem. Abstracts,* **48,** 2000e (1954).
1168. Zachariasen, W. H.: *J. Chem. Phys.*, **2,** 109 (1934).

1169. Zaugg, H. E., Rapala, R. T., and Leffler, M. T.: *J. Am. Chem. Soc.*, **70,** 3224 (1948).
1170. Zeiss, H. H., and Matthews, C. N.: *J. Am. Chem. Soc.*, **78,** 1694 (1956).
1171. Zelinsky, R. P., Turnquest, B. W., and Martin, E. C.: *J. Am. Chem. Soc.*, **73,** 5521 (1951).
1172. Ziegler, K., Orth, Ph., and Weber, K.: *Ann.*, **504,** 131 (1933).
1173. Zimmerman, H. E., and Thyagarajan, B. S.: *J. Am. Chem. Soc.*, **80,** 3060 (1958).
1174. Zimmerman, H. E., and Thyagarajan, B. S.: *J. Am. Chem. Soc.*, **82,** 2505 (1960).

NAME INDEX

SUBJECT INDEX